# THE VISUAL DOMINANT IN
## Eighteenth-Century Russia

# THE VISUAL DOMINANT

## IN *Eighteenth-Century Russia*

Marcus C. Levitt

NIU PRESS

*DeKalb*

Published by the Northern Illinois University Press, DeKalb, Illinois   60115

Manufactured in the United States using acid-free paper.

Design by Shaun Allshouse

Library of Congress Cataloging-in-Publication Data

Levitt, Marcus C., 1954–

The visual dominant in eighteenth-century Russia / Marcus C. Levitt.

p. cm.

Includes bibliographical references and index.

ISBN 978-0-87580-442-2 (clothbound : acid-free paper)

1. Russian literature—18th century—History and criticism.

2. Visual perception in literature. 3. Vision in literature.  I. Title.

PG3007.L486 2011

891.709'002—dc23

2011016778

Etching by Giacomo Zatta after Pietro Novelli, "Tsar Peter the Great Founds the City of St. Petersburg in Ingria, at the mouth of the Neva on the Baltic, in the Spring of the Year 1703" (1797), published by Antonio Zatta e Figli, Venice.  36.6 x 40.8 cm.  Ashmolean Museum, University of Oxford.

*To Betsy and Jesse—you light up my life!*

# CONTENTS

# ILLUSTRATIONS

# ACKNOWLEDGMENTS

A book that has taken this long to produce accumulates debts too numerous to repay but which at moments like this deserve to be made visible. My profound gratitude goes to the many friends and colleagues who have provided advice, encouragement, criticism, and stimulating dialogue over the years. These include: Victor Zhivov, Irina Reyfman, Alexander Levitsky, Gitta Hammarberg, Gary Marker, Ronald Vroon, Joachim Klein, Elise Wirtschafter, Olga Tsapina, Lev Berdnikov, Roger Bartlett, W. Garreth Jones, Petr Bukharkin, Lidiia Sazonova, Tatiana Artem'eva, William Todd, Amanda Ewington, Wendy Salmond, Sarah Pratt, Tatiana Smoliarova, Hilde Hoggenboom, Luba Golburt, Kelly Herold, Maria Shcherbakova, and the late Stephen Baehr and Anna Lisa Crone. Thanks, too, to my colleagues at the Institute of Russian Literature (Pushkin House) of the Russian Academy of Sciences: Natal'ia Kochetkova, Nadezhda Alekseeva, Sergei Nikolaev, Vladimir Stepanov, and the late Galina Moiseeva, Elena Mozgovaia, and Iurii Stennik. My fond gratitude also goes to my colleagues at the University of Southern California, including John Bowlt, Tom Seifrid, Lada Panova, Alik Zholkovsky, Brad Damaré, and Susan Kechekian for their continued help, advice, and support.

Thanks also go to the publishers for permission (or confirmation of my right) to incorporate sections of previous published works into this one: "Dialektika videniia v Puteshestvii Radishcheva," in *A. N. Radshchev: Russkoe i evropeiskoe prosveshchenie: materialy mezhdunarodnogo simposiuma, 24 iiulia, 2002 g.*, ed. N. D. Kochetkova (St. Petersburg: Sankt-Peterburgskii tsentr Rossiiskoi akademii nauk, 2003), 36–47; "The 'Obviousness' of the Truth in Eighteenth-Century Russian Thought," in *Filosofskii vek, 24: Istoriia filosofii kak filosofii*, eds. T. V. Artem'eva and M. I. Mikeshin (St. Petersburg: Sankt-Peterburgskii tsentr istorii idei, 2003), 1:236–45; "Oda kak otkrovenie: O pravoslavnom bogoslovskom kontekste lomonosovskikh od," in *Slavianskii almanakh 2003* (Moscow: Indrik, 2004), 368–84; "'Vechernee' i 'Utrennee razmyshleniia o Bozhiem velichestve' Lomonosova kak fiziko-teologicheskie proizvedeniia," *XVIII vek* 24 (2006), 57–70; "Virtue Must Advertise: Dashkova's 'Mon histoire' and the Problem of Self-Representation," in *The Princess and the Patriot: Ekaterina Dashkova, Benjamin Franklin, and the Age of Enlightenment*, ed.

Sue Ann Prince (Philadelphia: American Philosophical Society, 2006), 39–56. All but the first of these articles were also reprinted (and the Russian articles translated) in my *Early Modern Russian Letters: Selected Articles*, Studies in Russian and Slavic Literatures, Cultures, and History (Boston: Academic Studies Press, 2009).

Lastly, there is an indebtedness that can never be adequately expressed—to my wife and life companion Alice Taylor, who encouraged me to take up the subject of this book in the first place and who served as my best reader and editor. The book is improved immeasurably due to her help.

**Note on Translations**

Except where indicated, translations are my own. In translating poetry my first concern was to convey the meaning. In translating passages from Lomonosov's odes, for example, I have eliminated many of the syntactical inversions, which makes these works difficult even in the original. I have employed the Library of Congress transliteration system, although I have changed names in "-skii" to "-sky" in the text (e.g., Trediakovsky rather than Trediakovskii), and simplified or anglicized spellings of names (e.g., Ksenia, not Kseniia, Catherine not Ekaterina, Paul not Pavel). In the notes and transliterated Russian quotations I have kept more strictly to the LC system. I have also used standard or simplified English spellings for character names in plays (e.g., Hieronima, Hamlet, Ilmena, Stalverkh, Mohammed, Darius, Cyrus, instead of Ieronima, Gamlet, Il'mena, Stal'verkh, Mogamet, Darii, Kir), giving the original in parenthesis on first mention in cases where there might be confusion. I also use the Germanized forms of names like Küchelbecker and Staehlin (Stählin), although the Russianized forms (Kiukhel'beler, Shtelin) are also given at first mention.

# THE VISUAL DOMINANT IN
*Eighteenth-Century Russia*

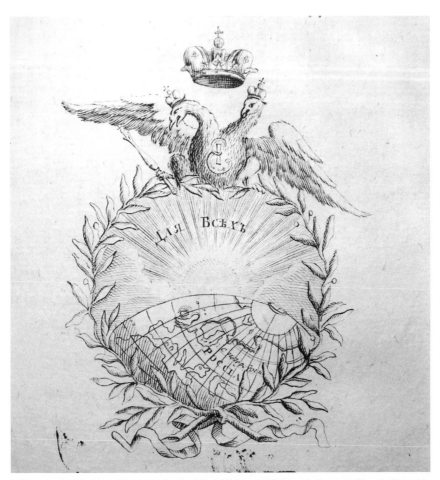

This engraving, the cover illustration for the July 1758 issue of *Ezhemesiachnyia sochineniia* (*Monthly Compositions*), the journal of the Academy of Sciences, depicts the sun coming up over the globe, which is neatly laid out in a longitudinal-latitudinal grid. More specifically, the sun is rising over RUSSIA—clearly mapped as part of Europe—and over the city of St. Petersburg, and its beneficial rays make Russia and its accomplishments, as broadcast by the journal, visible to the world—"FOR EVERYONE." The celestial vignette is encircled by a laurel garland, suggesting peace and prosperity, as well as imperial political hegemony. It is capped by the traditional double-headed eagle bearing the monogram and crown of Empress Elizabeth. The imperial eagles' motherly perch and cosmic wingspan seem to both protect and support the earth.

# Introduction

## *An Archaeology of Vision*

"The forming of the five senses is a labor of the entire history of the world down to the present."
—Karl Marx, *Economic and Philosophical Manuscripts*

"Could a greater miracle take place than for us to look through each other's eyes for an instant?"
—Henry David Thoreau, *Walden*

The Enlightenment emphasis on vision as the privileged means of understanding the world played a particularly important role in the development of modern Russian culture, for which the imperative *to become visible, to be seen* was a central motivation and goal. This, in short, is the central proposition of this book. The French philosopher Bruno Latour has written that "a new visual culture redefines both what it is to see, and what there is to see,"[1] and the goal of this book is to demonstrate the new Russian eighteenth-century mode of vision—how Russians saw the world, the special power they accorded sight—and, correspondingly, to reconstruct what they saw. The trauma of the French revolutionary and Napoleonic period, which had a profound intellectual impact on Russia, led to the discrediting of Russia's quintessential Enlightenment "ocularcentrism."[2] This occasioned the remarkable inability of later generations to see what had earlier seemed so self-evident and undeniable. By the 1830s, eighteenth-century Russian culture had become irrelevant, unworthy of consideration, and invisible, as if it had never existed. The goal of this work is to clear away some of the anachronistic barriers to sight and to begin to reconstruct that era—to try, as far as possible, paraphrasing Thoreau, "to look through their eyes for an instant." This archaeological project aims to reconstruct the eighteenth-century Russian paradigm of sight as a unique formation, to explore this era's mode of vision and to recover a cultural tradition heretofore largely unseen.

Since ancient Greece at least, and in the Judeo-Christian tradition in general, sight has been a privileged means of cognition, pervading our language and thought patterns. The words for truth and vision, sight and knowledge, are connected throughout the Indo-European tongues.[3] In ancient Greek, knowledge (*eidenai*) is "the state of having seen," and in various Germanic and Slavic languages, the verbs for "to see" and "to know" are related (in Russian, *videt'*/*vedat'*).[4] In Russian as in English, our everyday language and intellectual discourse are saturated with sight metaphors such as "speculating," "clarifying," "reflecting," and "illuminating." These terms are so omnipresent as to have themselves become unseen, felt as culturally neutral, and taken for granted. In order to adequately understand the past, the cultural historian must discern the dynamic modulations and shifts within the hierarchy of the senses over time and appreciate their changing cultural valences. For sight is neither neutral, biologically determined, automatic, nor natural, but a complex, culturally conditioned phenomenon, historically specific and hence in need of decoding.[5]

While the connection of sight and knowledge is deeply embedded in the classical and Judeo-Christian tradition, it has often been taken as a key to the "century of light," the "Enlightenment" (as these labels themselves suggest). Broadly speaking, Enlightenment culture was inspired in this regard by Cartesian philosophy and in the political and artistic realms by the brilliant court of Louis XIV, the "Sun King."[6] The problem of vision in the Enlightenment is central, for example, to the works of the distinguished French critic Jean Starobinski, who saw in Rousseau's "quest for transparency" a starting point for modern self-consciousness.[7] The "ocularcentric" eighteenth century has also served as a starting point for the critique of the Western philosophical and cultural tradition, as traced most notably by Martin Jay in *Downcast Eyes: The Denigration of Vision in Twentieth-Century French Thought*.[8] The issue of sight and its problematic status has come to be seen as a central thread in modern Western philosophy, from Descartes, Kant, and Hegel, through Nietzsche, Heidegger, Sartre, and Merleau-Ponty, as well as Benjamin, Foucault, and Derrida.[9] The American philosopher R. J. Snell traces the roots of the modern disillusionment with philosophy even further back to Plato, and attributes the erosion of the classical Platonic-Cartesian-Kantian philosophical tradition precisely to the presumed link between seeing and knowing, which he describes as based on "intuitionism," the assumption of a "God's-eye view." Snell sees the challenge to modern philosophy as establishing the possibility of knowing on some alternative basis.[10] It is precisely this core intuitionist belief in the transcendent power of vision, reinforced by central tenets of Eastern Orthodox theology, that offers a key to eighteenth-century Russian thought and self-image.

In contrast to the sizeable and sophisticated recent body of literature on Western paradigms of vision, however, the visual in Russian culture has attracted scant attention, and the works that have considered the intersections of Russian literature and the visual in recent years have dealt almost exclusively with the modern period (the nineteenth and especially early twentieth centuries), or with icons.[11] The few scholars who have attempted broad comparisons of Russian and Western paradigms of sight generally concur that Russian culture thoroughly rejected the Cartesian Enlightenment paradigm as alien. I. A. Esaulov, for example, trying to define Russia's "visual dominant," contrasts Russia's traditional, medieval "iconic type of visuality" (*ikonichnost'*), which he considers central to Russian culture, to a Western (i.e., non-Russian) illusionistic paradigm deriving from the Renaissance.[12] Esaulov's opposition derives from the work of the theologian Pavel Florensky (1882–1937), who made a pathbreaking case for both the religious and aesthetic nature of the icon as a visual artifact.[13] Russia's "visual dominant"—its culturally privileged mode of seeing and representation—is thus defined in neo-Slavophile terms as a reversal of modern, Western, Renaissance visual values that are founded on "the rationalization of sight."[14]

Esaulov's term "visual dominant" suggests a conception of seeing that defines an epoch's cultural consciousness; it differs in emphasis from the related notion of a "scopic regime," used to define the visual distinctiveness of a particular medium, gender, or culturally specific mode of vision.[15] While Esaulov's concept is valuable, the received wisdom that defines Russian culture as exclusively anti-ocularcentric is inaccurate. This view suggests that "the path of secularizing the invisible, its domestication or justification by means of the visible, in a word, the path that was considered Western in Russia, was unacceptable for Russian thought."[16] To classify Russian culture in this way is understandable insofar as "Russian thought" is defined as the Russian philosophical school that formed in the later nineteenth century, a tradition that as a rule rejected the eighteenth century out of hand as un-Russian and Western (a neo-Slavophile position represented by such thinkers as Florensky,

Semen Frank, and Lev Shestov).[17] In fact, however, the visual was uniquely privileged in eighteenth-century Russian culture, and as such provides a vital key to that culture's hierarchy of values. The visual—with an emphasis on visibility, the need to be seen and appreciated—played a crucial role in the formation of early modern Russian identity. The challenge posed by Peter the Great's opening a "window to Europe" was to see, to make others see, and to be seen.[18] Furthermore, eighteenth-century Russia's visual dominant was not merely a Western import or a passing infatuation, but had deep indigenous roots in Orthodox culture and theology; one cannot fully appreciate the later nineteenth-century anti-ocularcentric, logocentric tradition without taking into account the fact that it represents a profound dialectical negation of the preceding cultural configuration. While the notion of such a dialectical scheme is more or less a commonplace in cultural history, in this case the negation was so remarkably profound as to have practically erased (made invisible) its originary traces. Nineteenth-century Russia fiercely turned away from sight in favor of the word, retreating from grandiose imperial façades into the dark and mysterious (and newly devised) world of the "Russian soul."

## "Russia" and "the West": Deceptive Dichotomies

The generally held opinion that Russian thought rejected Western visual paradigms suggests not only the novelty of the argument being presented in this book, but also the deeply ingrained historiographical problem of defining what is "Russian" or "Western." These terms are heavily loaded and often directly impinge on evaluations of eighteenth-century Russia. The cultural biases often inherent in the terms are strikingly illustrated in an episode Princess Dashkova describes in her memoirs in which she pointedly overturns received wisdom on the subject. She describes a discussion in which she bested the illustrious Austrian state chancellor Prince von Kaunitz, who expressed the notion that Peter the Great was the "Creator of Russia." Dashkova countered that this fallacious idea was due to the "sheer vanity" of "foreign writers," and she held forth on the richness of pre-Mongol Russia, the conquest of Siberia, Russia's centuries' old treasures of religious art, as well as the "historians [i.e., medieval chroniclers] who left more manuscripts that all the rest of Europe put together."

> "Do you count for nothing," replied Prince Kaunitz, "the fact that he [Peter the Great] drew Russia nearer to Europe and that it is only since his day that she has become known?"

"A great Empire, Prince, [Daskova objected] with all the resources of wealth and power, such as Russia possesses, has no need to be drawn nearer to anything."[19]

Dashkova undoubtedly relished the shock value of challenging a widespread opinion, yet the evaluation of Peter the Great's legacy, both in Russian cultural consciousness and in that of historians, is a problem that reflects a larger tension. The use of the terms "Russia" and "the West" suggest either/or dichotomies and contain a lot of value-laden historiographical baggage. The terms presume entities that pretend to discrete geographical, sociological reality, yet clearly serve mythological and ideological ends.

James Billington illustrates the tendency to oppose Russia and the West as a dichotomy in a recent book meant for popular consumption. He describes the pattern of artistic and cultural assimilation as moving from West to East, a confrontation between advanced "civilization" and backwardness:

First, and without much warning, this seemingly proud and self-centered people [the Russians] suddenly takes over some new type of enterprise lock, stock, and barrel from precisely that more advanced foreign civilization which they had previously reviled. Second, having taken over in finished form someone else's exemplary model of a new art medium, they suddenly produce a stunningly original and even better version of their own. This is often accomplished at precisely the time that people elsewhere have concluded that the new medium had exhausted its creative possibilities. Finally, having lifted the new art form to a higher level, Russians themselves tend to cast it down and break it apart—leaving behind only fragments of their best creations for future generations.[20]

Despite the obvious limitations of such a sweeping generalization and its specific terms, this basic scheme has often been applied to the Russian version of Enlightenment culture.[21] Many have argued that Russia assimilated the ideas of the Age of Reason from the West not so much as an imperative to scrutinize its values in light of reason, but as a new dogma.[22] The Russian Enlightenment in these terms was a kind of uncritical "romanticizing of Reason."[23] According to this interpretation, Russia uncritically, and somewhat naïvely (as may be expected from a less "advanced" nation) accepted the new Western ideal—a faith in the power of reason—precisely as a faith, something self-evidently and obviously true. Billington's notion of Russia's having borrowed a Western paradigm and taken it "to a new level" may also be applied to the rise of

Russian ocularcentrism as related in this book, insofar as ocularcentrism may be taken as a kind of encapsulation of the Enlightenment faith in self-evident reason.

In Billington's scheme, Russian classicism as a literary style took hold in mid-eighteenth-century Russia, when it was already on the wane in Western Europe, and produced a remarkable version of its own, whose legacy was subsequently renounced, much as the political and cultural legacy of the USSR is now being systematically discredited. Billington's formulation exemplifies the kind of dualistic scheme that evaluates "Russia" against the criterion of the "West," whether from a Slavophile, pro-Russian position, or, as in Billington's specific case, from a Westernizing and Eurocentric perspective that stigmatizes indigenous culture as lacking—as backward, provincial, and immature.

In contrast, Iuri Lotman and Boris Uspensky have analyzed the functioning of this kind of zero-sum, binary scheme as itself an ideological construct, and explored the Russia-West dichotomy not as objective reality but as an axiological system. In such a system, self-image is sharply polarized, projected as a diametrically opposed ideal and its negation, Self and Other, with one or the other hypostasis taken as privileged. Thus "Russia" and "the West" do not stand for objective entities but represent inverted aspects of self-projection that are mutually dependent and that hence must be seen in terms of the larger dynamic functioning of the whole.[24] In either case, as projection of an ideal or its negation (a demonized, unacceptable self), the signifiers "Russia" and "the West" hardly represent an objective description of actual phenomena. Furthermore, within this construct, historical change can only be envisaged as total change, insofar as the field of possibilities is sharply divided into divine and demonic spheres and any modification, however minor, necessitates the overthrow of the entire structure. The alternative to total change is total stasis, in which the perfection of the given system is asserted as a utopian heaven on earth. Russian culture thus offers the paradox of a "discontinuous" culture that continually rejects itself, caught in cycles of revolutionary upheaval and totalitarian stagnation.[25]

Lotman and Uspensky isolate two specific mechanisms for change in such a sharply polarized system, both of which assume the appearance of total upheaval, but which at a deeper level preserve the system's remarkable stability: either the name is kept but the value is reversed (e.g., a formerly demonized West becomes the ideal) or the name is changed but the basic value remains (e.g., the "emperor" assumes the place of the "tsar," Leningrad reverts to St. Petersburg, and so on). In either case, despite the appearance of total change and dislocation, the underlying system of values retains a fundamental continuity, as older, ostensibly discarded values are actually reasserted and even regenerated. Taking Feofan Prokopovich's play *Vladimir* (1705) as an example, Lotman and Uspensky build upon the clear parallel between the grand prince who converted Russia to Christianity in 988 and Peter the Great, who "converted" Russia to the new Enlightenment faith.[26] While Peter's modernization suggests a total break with the past and with "Russian" principles in favor of "the West," it in fact reverts to or reanimates (in renamed or inverted form) older, even archaic cultural values. In Prokopovich's play, characters associated with traditional "Russian" values are denigrated, while "Europeanized" manners become the new norm, so that Orthodox traditionalists who oppose Peter's reforms are paralleled to the nasty and farcical pagan sorcerers who oppose Vladimir's conversion. According to Lotman and Uspensky, Peter's revolution actually revived certain archaic pre-Christian pagan ideas and practices—former "anti-behavior" was legitimized. (Similarly, after the fall of Communism, the former bogey of Western cutthroat capitalism was accepted as a behavioral norm.) From this perspective, Russia's assimilation of Enlightenment values appears as a "change of faith rather than a rejection of faith . . . , a change from one faith to another rather than a transition from a religious outlook to a philosophical view. . . . Of course there was a real process of Europeanization of eighteenth-century culture. However, it rarely coincided with what the bearers of the culture themselves considered as Europeanization."[27]

Lotman and Uspensky's scheme thus provides a useful way of conceptualizing the reflexive and contingent nature of Russian identity formation, and suggests, despite external appearances, that "the eighteenth century was deeply and organically a part of Russian culture itself."[28] Thus while Russian ocularcentrism—from the point of view of Billington's scheme—might be seen as an example of borrowing and breathing new life into an already fading European paradigm, Lotman and Uspensky's model would suggest that it was by no means merely an alien Western import but was (to borrow Lotman's phrase) one of the "deeply rooted constructive ideas of the culture." The very term for "Enlightenment," for example, as Lotman and Uspensky point out, was not only a calque of the European term, but also "simultaneously coincided with the Church Slavonic homonym [*prosveshchenie*], which signified the Christian importance of apostolic activity in enlightening (baptizing) the pagans."[29] The Lotman-Uspensky model points to two interconnected issues explored in this book: eighteenth-century Russian culture's bipolar self-image (the terms in which it defined itself), and basic Orthodox ideas about vision that were operative at a deep level, whether explicitly stated or not.

On its own, neither Billington's quasi-"sociological" view of cultural adaptation nor Lotman and Uspensky's functional and "mythological" analysis offers a fully satisfactory or comprehensive explanatory model. While both of these schemes offer compelling ways to describe the discontinuous model of Russian cultural development, they may also underplay conscious elements of continuity. Billington's scheme denies indigenous impetus altogether, while Lotman and Uspensky's model emphasizes the hidden, unacknowledged connections with older cultural paradigms. Like Billington's, it may overlook areas in which basic elements of the earlier culture are consciously upheld and defended. Like other national Enlightenments, the Russian eighteenth century may be seen as an attempt to modernize, not deny, national culture.[30] Furthermore, the violence of the later tradition's rejection of the eighteenth century caused a profound rupture in national self-image, encoded in the opposition between Russia and the West, that has both distorted the historical record and bedeviled the formation of modern Russian national identity.

The challenge is to accommodate the notions of otherness suggested both by Billington and by Lotman and Uspensky, to find a balance between an idealized self-image (a fiction, a myth) and the complex negotiation of a self-in-the-process-of-becoming. The past is always to some extent a retrospective fiction; that in the present case the dialogue of modern Russian identity was disrupted does not mean that it did not exist or that under less apocalyptic circumstances the values it promoted could not have taken other more productive paths. "The law of retrospection" (as Tolstoy calls it in *War and Peace*) can be a trap. According to this idea, in Gary Saul Morson's words, "knowing the outcome of events, one may ignore the alternative futures that were available in the past."[31] This has been the fate of many phenomena and entire periods of Russian history, but it applies especially to the eighteenth century.

## Several Methodological Caveats

In the well-known preface to his translation-adaptation of Paul de Tallement's *Voyage to the Island of Love* of 1730, Trediakovsky argued that "a translator is different from a creator in name only." As many scholars have also argued, in the conditions of eighteenth-century Russian culture, the process of assimilating West European forms was creatively active and selective rather than "slavishly imitative." Translation entailed "transplantation" from one soil to another, in which the new creation changed character in assimilating itself to the new linguistic and cultural environment.[32] Furthermore, as a conscious cultural practice, "borrowing did not imply inferiority or ignorance; borrowing belonged to the 'continuity' and 'echo' [Joseph Brodsky] that was high culture. The Enlightenment culture of eighteenth-century Europe, at least as received in Russia, was an open-ended and cosmopolitan affair."[33] For these reasons, Russian literary production (marked by the selective choice and reworking of sources) is taken here to represent Russian values.

This analysis makes little attempt to contextualize eighteenth-century Russian culture in terms of Western Europe, although in general terms it provided not only a principal audience for Russian self-display (if only an imagined one), but also the immediate cultural forms for emulation. The French legacy and that of Louis XIV was surely a major inspiration for the Russian court and model of many of the arts introduced during the eighteenth century, although its status as a cultural exemplar for Russia has yet to be analyzed. To cite one example, Amanda Ewington has recently described the complex nature of Sumarokov's "vision of the Catherinean age as analogue to the *grand siècle* of Louis XIV."[34] While the quest for glory and for the recognition of virtue reflected in Sumarokov's tragedies owe a basic debt to Corneille, as filtered through other playwrights, especially Racine and Voltaire, the sources of Sumarokov's views of aristocratic honor are debated.[35] This, like so many other areas of eighteenth-century Russian culture, awaits further study, and it is hoped that this work will help frame some of the issues for such investigation.[36]

Another important piece of the cultural equation—how Western Europeans perceived Russia—also mostly takes a secondary place to the problem of Russia's quest for visibility and the process of appropriating "the West" into Russian culture. Western views of Russia tended to follow a similar binary logic as that described by Lotman and Uspensky, either idealizing or demonizing the new Russia, and foreign opinion certainly was (and remains) a major factor in Russian politics and self-image.[37] The great drama of Russian self-image in the eighteenth century was played out in the "universal theater" of "the society of political peoples," and it was these peoples—i.e., Western Europe—that made up the main part of the projected audience, however fictitious. Nevertheless, for the practical purposes of this analysis, the Western perception of Russia in the eighteenth century is a factor that while crucial for the argument shall, of necessity, mostly be taken for granted.[38]

## The Visual and the Visible

As Edward Young noted in his *Night Thoughts*, a very popular text in later eighteenth-century Russia, when one opens one's eyes it feels as if one can grasp the infinite:

> Unbroken, then, illustrious, and entire,
> Its ample Sphere, its universal Frame,
> In full Dimensions, swells to the Survey;
> And enters, at one Glance, the ravisht Sight. [. . .]
> Take in, at once, the Landscape of the world.[39]

Writing a book, however, demands limiting the field of vision, and the chapters in this book focus primarily on particular literary genres and texts as illustrations, verbalizations—landmarks, as it were—describing the larger dynamic process of projecting a modern Russian identity. It may seem paradoxical to make an argument about ocularcentrism based on literary sources, which in some sense are always inevitably logocentric, and so before describing the more delimited landscape of this narrative, a few words of explanation are in order concerning the notion of visual culture.

This investigation does not deal with what things look like or with formal visual analysis of material culture, although it is hoped that it will help stimulate such exploration. It would have been tempting, for example, to describe the creation of St. Petersburg as the supreme monument to Enlightenment visual culture and to include such dramatic manifestations of the Russian concern with the visual as urban planning, architecture, landscape architecture and gardening, ceremonial and theatrical arts (from fireworks to grand opera), painting, sculpture, engraving, art collecting and display, haberdashery, jewelry, hair styling, porcelain and mirror-making, as well as other arts, many of which first appeared and in many cases reached their pinnacle during this epoch.[40] The task set here is in a sense more primary, insofar as (to return to Latour's distinction) defining what it is to see precedes and defines what is seen. The concern here is not so much the visual per se as the quest for visibility, the cultural and psychological pursuit of self-validation. The discourse of vision and verbal constructs of sight (in poetry, drama, philosophy, moralistic essays, theology, memoirs, etc.) are examined to provide primary evidence for understanding the special privileged character of vision of the epoch, its "visual dominant." This book is meant both as a rereading of various central (and some not so well-known) texts and an attempt at a broader revisualization of Russian eighteenth-century culture "through its own eyes."

To state this issue in a different way, a picture may "speak a thousand words," but only to those that understand the language. The very phrasing of this proverbial truth—that pictures *speak words*—suggests the need to verbalize the visual in order to construct meaning. While vision may be the most intellectual of the senses, the most analyzed and most central in the classical and Judeo-Christian traditions, it may also be argued on a strictly methodological level that visual evidence can never stand alone. The need to verbalize the visual is not merely profoundly ingrained in our tradition, a master metaphor of our discourse—the very notion of "theory" stems etymologically from the Greek word for seeing—it necessarily arises in making sense of any visual artifact.[41] There is simply no such thing as "visual evidence" anterior to cultural context and to language, either that of the target culture or of its interpreter, and no way to have any specific sense of why things look the way they do and what they are meant to communicate without understanding their historical context and production. To deny this fact means to run the risk of interpreting the evidence in our own contemporary (that is, anachronistic) terms, however "natural" or transparent it may seem. In other words, the evidence of vision does not stand alone, but is always, to a greater or lesser extent, culturally mediated and historically contingent, and language is the primary and necessary vehicle of this mediation.[42] That is not to say that visual evidence may not be unique and uniquely valuable, but that before such evidence can be appreciated, the basic cultural and psychological codes that give it meaning must be comprehended. Only once that is done will visual sources reveal themselves to be the hugely rich, semiotically saturated sources of information that they are, revealing the "thousand words" and more.

## The Rise and Fall of Russian Ocularcentrism

Given the impossibility of words to "take in, at once, the Landscape of the world," the topography of this narrative sketches several key moments that trace the changing relations between visuality and identity in eighteenth-century Russian culture. It traces the trajectory of early modern Russian self-image from jubilant self-discovery to serious reflection, anxiety, and crisis—the rise and fall, as it were, of Russian Enlightenment ocularcentrism. The first chapter is offered as "Prolegomena," considering both the historiographical tradition that refused to see the eighteenth century, and introducing some of the basic tools used to chart the argument. The cultural and visual revolution wrought by Peter the Great are here described (using Richard Wortman's term, as "the Petrine scenario"), as well as the various discursive traditions that came into play.[43] Subsequent chapters examine representative or problem works and traditions, some well known, some obscure. Lomonosov's odes as an exercise in visual self-discovery are the subject of chapter 2, and the focus of chapter 3 is the jubilation that the odes project, understood in terms of the centuries' old Orthodox mystical theology of light. The genre of tragedy (historical drama) is considered in chapter 4, in terms of retrospective self-imaging and as a response to some of the problems posed by the Petrine scenario. Enlightenment moral discourse associated with the transparency of virtue is discussed in chapter 5, taking autobiography as an example of the classicist view of the virtuous self. The next chapter explores the extraordinary optimism of Russian Enlightenment ocularcentrism that held the truths of sight to be self-evident in the material universe. The "physicotheological" tradition (in particular, Trediakovsky's *Feoptiia*) asserted that divine reason was obvious (or at least easily accessible) through material, sensible, ocular means. Also considered in this chapter is the "vanity of vanities" theme that cast doubt on such optimistic, ocularcentric presumptions. Chapter 7 represents somewhat of an exception to the others, in that the focus shifts to a particular historical episode—the riot that occurred in Moscow in September 1771, during an outbreak of the plague. The fact that the flash point for the disturbance concerned the proper veneration of an icon provides a point of reference for examining the clash of conflicting "scopic regimes" and cultural narratives. The anxiety that had been mostly latent in Russian Enlightenment ocularcentrism dramatically came to the fore in Radishchev's controversial *Journey from St. Petersburg to Moscow*, which is the subject of chapter 8. The "dialectic of vision" that informs the *Journey* offers a key to its seemingly contradictory messages that alternate between the steadfastly virtuous, optimistic ocularcentrism of the previous generation, and the anxiety-ridden interiority and negation to come. This violent rejection of the eighteenth-century faith in the visual is described in the concluding chapter, as are several of the anti-ocularcentric labels, including the metaphors of Russian culture as a "Potemkin village" and as a "mirage," that were products of the dismantling of Enlightenment notions of vision, and which have become ingrained in modern discourse on Russia. Many more chapters on the topic of Russian visibility in the eighteenth century remain to be written and will surely modify and amend this work—chapters on other literary genres, such as comedy and satire; on Catherine the Great's extremely influential role; on urban planning; the growth of tourism; as well as on the various arts and aspects of material culture mentioned above. It is hoped that this book will begin to bring this rich and crucial epoch in Russian culture and its way of seeing out of the shadows.

# CHAPTER ONE

# Prolegomena
## *Making Russia Visible*

"In infinite space many civilizations are bound to exist, among them
societies that may be wiser and more "successful" than ours. I support
the cosmological hypothesis which states that the development of the
universe is repeated in its basic characteristics an infinite number of times.
Further, other civilizations, including more "successful" ones, should exist
an infinite number of times on the "preceding" and "following" pages of
the Book of the Universe. Yet we should not minimize our [own] sacred
endeavors in the world, where, like faint glimmers in the dark, we have
emerged for a moment from the nothingness of dark unconsciousness into
material existence. We must make good the demands of reason and create a
life worthy of ourselves and of the goals we only dimly perceive."
—Andrei Sakharov, Nobel Prize Lecture (1975)[1]


"Here everything has been created for visual perception."
—Madame de Staël on St. Petersburg[2]

For many people, including many Russians, modern Russian
culture begins with the nineteenth century. Before that, there is nothing, a great
blank or but a faint glimmer in the dark. The central role of Peter the Great in
"turning Russia to the West" in the early eighteenth century is acknowledged,
but the subsequent hundred years is more or less of a blind spot, an interim
or at best a preparatory phase, a lacuna to be triumphantly filled by the grand
tradition of Russian literature beginning with the golden age of Pushkin. As

a Russian scholar sums up the general consensus: "Pushkin as the *start* of our cultural and historical road—this idea seems to us today to be irrefutable, the point of departure for all further judgments concerning [Russia's] cultural development."[3] Before turning to examine that epoch, it is important first to recognize how the later Russian tradition has often turned a blind eye toward it, ignored, downplayed, or utterly rejected it. Certainly, the glories of Russian literature of the nineteenth century, the magnificent achievements of Pushkin, Gogol, Turgenev, Dostoevsky, Tolstoy, and others, canonized as Russia's major contribution to world civilization, have helped to outshine and overshadow all that came before. Yet it is important to realize the extent to which the canonized tradition—and the very language generally used to speak of the eighteenth century in Russia—itself represents a reflection (however in a glass darkly) or mirrored inversion of the eighteenth century's own self-image and discourse.

As noted in the preface, the historiography of eighteenth-century Russian culture follows a typical pattern, what the historian Georges Florovsky described as a "discontinuous" model of Russian culture: while in the Russian political realm the more or less continuous growth of the centralized state from the sixteenth century through the modern period may be observed, Russian cultural self-consciousness has been marked by a series of sudden, cataclysmic shifts and sharp new starts.[4] At the other end of the historical cycle, there is a chronic erosion and then collapse of the former value system; Soviet Russia has been subjected to devaluation analogous to that suffered by eighteenth-century culture. This parallels the common wisdom that, as in the eighteenth century, an artificial state-sponsored propaganda culture, imposed from the top down, self-destructed due to its own inner bankruptcy. Many post-Soviet Russians want to turn back the clock to the prerevolutionary period, to find the sources of "true culture" in the past (the inverse of the revolutionary desire to seek them in the future). In retrospect, each value system appears as a failed experiment, a gap in Russian development to be forgotten or overturned as quickly as possible. The Russian eighteenth century, like the Soviet phase, began and ended with radical cultural reorientations, at the beginning a violent, top-down turnaround, and at the end a slower erosion of values leading to a no less devastating self-negation.[5]

It is hard to overestimate the importance of both ends of this process as defining moments for Russian cultural self-image. Peter the Great's "turn to the West" represents the archetypal moment of modern Russian cultural transformation, and serves as a foundation myth for eighteenth-century Russian self-image, and for modern Russian self-image in general; this book is an additional commentary on its influence and ramifications. Yet it is also necessary to consider the many elements of objective continuity that make Peter's transformation seem less of a revolution, and that play a major role—conscious or unconscious—in the tradition. Many recent historians have excavated and explored basic elements of continuity—linguistic, political, and religious—that the Petrine foundation myth has served to obscure.[6] As Dashkova's retort to von Kaunitz cited in the preface—"A great Empire, Prince, . . . has no need to be drawn nearer to anything"—suggests, the Petrine myth was subject to revision, and the cultural legacy of pre-Petrine Russia could also serve as a source of conscious pride and value.

## From Oblivion to Glory

The Petrine foundation myth played out as a parable of vision—a Promethean Peter the Great bringing the light of European culture to his country. This was expressed in a dramatic way in the oft-quoted speech by State Chancellor Count G. I. Golovkin on October 22, 1721, in which he bestowed upon Peter in the name of the Senate and Synod the triple titles of "all-Russian Emperor," "the Great," and "Father of the Fatherland."[7] This was a very significant moment in Peter's reign, politically and symbolically, and arguably also for European history. The speech commemorated the victorious conclusion of the Great Northern War, Russia's more than two-decade-long conflict with Sweden. It triumphantly acknowledged Russia as an empire, with Peter elevated from tsar to emperor. The Treaty of Nystadt cemented Russia's hold on the Baltic and hence the security of the new capital St. Petersburg, opened up northern trade routes, and confirmed Russia's place as a major power both on land and sea. From the European perspective, this treaty marked Russia's new role in the modern state system as an arbiter of the European balance of power.

Golovkin stated:

> By means of Your Royal Majesty's glorious and courageous military and political deeds, [achieved] through Your own unceasing labors and leadership alone, we, Your loyal subjects, have been brought out of the darkness of ignorance and into the universal theater of fame, and, so to speak, brought forth from nonexistence into being and incorporated into the society of political peoples, as is known not only to us but to the whole world.[8]

This is a very rich passage, describing an archetypal moment the echoes of which may be heard in a variety of other texts and media throughout the century, from odes and sermons to statuary and painting. To begin with, the proclamation expresses some of the basic binary oppositions associated with the Petrine myth: *darkness* versus *light* and *ignorance* versus *knowledge*, here inscribed in a dramatic scenario. The phrase "onto the universal theater of fame"—literally, "into the theater of glory of the entire world" (*na featr slavy vsego sveta*)—contains a possible wordplay on the two meanings of "svet," which may signify "the world" or "light"—or, in the present case, perhaps both. Coming into the light is described as a moment of creation ex nihilo, a radical ontological shift, marking Russia's movement from "nonexistence" into "being" (*iz nebytiia v bytie*). This notion echoed Leibniz's phrase, echoing Locke (who in turn quoted Aristotle), that likened Peter's reform of Russia to writing upon a "sheet of white paper," a tabula rasa.[9] To be brought into the light, to be seen, to make oneself seen by others means not only to join "the society of political peoples" and to gain recognition in the "universal theater of fame," but also to attain metaphysical realty, to have content, to achieve existence itself. By contrast, to be satisfied with one's situation and to remain in the dark, unobserved, would be tantamount to oblivion.[10] Sight here is "new" in two senses—not merely a new way of seeing, but the acquisition of sight itself after total sensory deprivation, which was equivalent to lacking existential being. I see and am seen, therefore I am. In chronological terms, this is a shift so radical that there is no "before," and as with Peter's newly adopted calendar, starting with January 1, 1700, which was another way of putting Russia into a European frame of reference, a change in measuring time was equated with entering "real" time, a state of self-conscious existence.

Golovkin's speech presents Russia's emergence or creation—her stepping out and being seen "by the whole world"—as a grandly theatrical moment. Peter appears as the Great Man or demiurge who single-handedly opens the curtain and calls forth a dazzling light show, inscribing Russia into the European Enlightenment script. Russia now enters "the society of political [*politicheskikh*] peoples," itself a phrase replete with associations. It indicates Russia's new social role, joining a larger community (Aristotle's "political animal" [*Politics* 1.2.9], an animal intended to live in a city, a social creature). As Aristotle's definition suggests, "politics" (Gr. *politikos*) derives from *polis* (city), and the stage for Peter's dramatic transformation was centered on the new city of St. Petersburg. "Politics" also carried over the Greek meaning of "courteousness, politeness," which was a crucial element in the Enlightenment notion of "civilizing" by means of ameliorating manners; "civility," like "politics" (in some contexts interchangeable) suggested both political and behavioral or cultural norms. "Politics" was also often associated (and etymologically confused) with "politeness," from the Latin *politus* (the root here is *polire*, to polish), and also with "police," which like "politics" also derives from *polis* (city).[11] In the eighteenth century, and in Russia particularly, the main job of the ruler was seen as creating a "well-ordered police state," in the positive sense of "the development of civilized conditions as a result of actions by the state," from the top down.[12]

## The Orthodox Background

Golovkin's paean to Peter unites three larger discourses that feed into eighteenth-century Russian culture: Orthodox, Enlightenment, and Imperial Roman. Vision plays a central role within each of these paradigms. To begin with the first, as Victor Zhivov notes of Golovkin's speech, "The formula 'from nonexistence into being,' subsequently repeated constantly in eighteenth-century panegyric literature, refers to the most important prayer of the [Orthodox] liturgy (Praefatio, *Agios o Theos*): 'Holy God . . . who hast brought all things into being from non-being.' The new order Peter had created was not only a new political construction, but also a new religious reality into which mankind was entering."[13] The phrase also connects the Petrine revolution to the act of creation in the first lines of Genesis (translation from the Slavonic text): "In the beginning God made heaven and earth. The earth was not visible [*nevidima*] and not formed, and darkness [*tma*] was above the abyss, and the divine spirit carried above the water. And God said: let there be light. And there was light." Cosmos proceeded out of chaos, the seen out of the unseen, the netherworld into Peter the Great's "paradise."[14] In Nicholas Boileau's famous translation of Pseudo-Longinus's "On the Sublime" (1672), this revelatory moment—the so-called *fiat lux* (let there be light)—was described as the archetypal sublime experience and a touchstone for high-style poetry, and this moment from Genesis was often explicitly invoked in descriptions of Peter. Among these is the image of Peter as creator of St. Petersburg, as seen, for example, in Falconet's monument, in which a godlike Peter holds out his hand over the waters as if commanding the city to rise.[15] In general, echoes of biblical and specifically Orthodox cosmology, with its vision-oriented theology and imagery, reverberate throughout Russian eighteenth-century culture.[16]

Light and light-discourse, of course, is fundamental in the Christian tradition, but the "theology of light" holds a particularly magisterial place in Russian Orthodoxy. To discuss the problem of vision in Orthodoxy means practically to recapitulate the entire Orthodox tradition.[17] The special, potentially divine status of vision dominates two of the richest areas of Russian Orthodox spirituality, the defense of icons and the Hesychast mystical tradition. Russia's conversion to Christianity in the late ninth century took place within the context of the defeat of Byzantine iconoclasm, a moment that came to be known in the Eastern church as "the Triumph of Orthodoxy." The name was given to a yearly feast day, the first Sunday of Lent and the sixth before Easter, and icon veneration continued (and continues) to mark the special nature of Russian Orthodox devotion.[18] What Jaroslav Pelikan has termed Eastern Orthodoxy's "rehabilitation of the visual," the affirmation of the potentially divine nature of matter—and hence also of the physical senses—was based on the miracle of Incarnation.[19] The Hesychast tradition, discussed in the third chapter, made use of many of the same arguments, and, like defenses of icon veneration, described and upheld a doctrine centering upon divine vision.[20]

A second trend in the Orthodox tradition that played a major role in eighteenth-century Russian ocularcentrism was more obviously amenable to a specifically "Enlightenment" brand of Orthodoxy.[21] This was what has been called Orthodoxy's "moderate rationalist theology" represented by Basil the Great, Gregory Nazianus, and John of Damascus, which defended the place of reason in theology, and which was cited by Lomonosov in his justification of modern science.[22] It was this trend that also fed into "physicotheology," analyzed in chapter 5. Both trends in Orthodox theology—the Hesychast and moderate rationalist—concurred in their defense of icon veneration and also advocated what we may call "optical optimism," or a faith in theophany (God's manifestation to men, or epiphany [bogoiavlenie]), albeit in different ways.

One famous example of the exalted status of sight in the Orthodox tradition is the paean to Boris and Gleb, the first Russian saints, taken from the *Russian Primary Chronicle* under the year 1015. The assassination and apotheosis of these brother-saints occupies a special position in the Russian tradition, insofar as their passion-suffering, in imitation of Christ, was held to have consecrated the Russian land.[23] This conversion-consecration, like the Petrine narrative, is described in terms of bringing sight—both the manifestation of divine light and the ability to perceive it—from heaven to earth:

> Ye have appeared amid bright rays, enlightening like beacons the whole land of Rus'. Appearing in faith immutable, ye have ever driven away the darkness. Rejoice, ye who have won an unslumbering eye, ye blessed ones who have received in your hearts the zeal to fulfill God's holy commandments.

Rejoice, brethren united in the realms of golden light, in the heavenly abodes, in glory unfading, which ye through your merits have attained. Rejoice, ye who are brightly radiant with the luminance of God, and travel throughout the world expelling devils and healing diseases. Like beacons supernal and zealous guardians, ye dwell with God, illumined forever with light divine, and in your courageous martyrdom ye enlighten the souls of the faithful. The light-bringing heavenly love has exalted you, wherefore ye have inherited all fair things in the heavenly life: glory, celestial sustenance, the light of wisdom, and beauteous joys.[24]

Light embodies the trinity of truth, beauty, and the good, and allows the Russian people, "united in the realms of golden light," to "dwell with God." On a broad cultural level, there was a fundamental parallel, and at times direct genetic connections, between Orthodox and Enlightenment paradigms of vision. As noted in the preface, the very term for "Enlightenment" in Russian could accommodate both traditional Orthodox and modern European notions, and this was more than just a coincidence of terms.[25] It may be argued that central Enlightenment philosophical concerns, in particular, the exploration of the limits of the senses and of human cognition, represented a secularized recapitulation of centuries-long theological disputes that remained part of collective cultural memory. Orthodox underpinnings offer one explanation for the remarkable optimism and utopian (theophanic) faith manifested in eighteenth-century Russian ocularcentrism. In the chapters that follow, this general proposition will be explored in regard to various specific literary and cultural contexts, as both sides of the equation—"Orthodox" and "Enlightenment"—are far from monolithic and require more specific characterization.

## The Roman Connection

The second discursive tradition echoed in Golovkin's speech is that of Imperial Rome. Rome provided the discourse and political ideology of empire; the title "Father of the Fatherland" that Golovkin's speech celebrated was the one the Roman Senate had accorded Augustus in 2 BC, and it was no coincidence that Peter brought Russia "into the society of political peoples," not merely by enlightened domestic policies, but by making Russia into a continental military power. As it had elsewhere in Europe, Rome also provided the prototype of successful assimilation of the Greek cultural legacy. Early nineteenth-century critics like Küchelbecker (Kiukhel'beker), Venevitinov, and Chaadaev rejected this "imitative" aspect of the Roman legacy in favor of the ideal of ancient Greece, which for them represented originality and philosophical independence. For Venevitinov, this was manifested in his philosophical preference for Plato over Aristotle; as a political model, Küchelbecker and his Decembrist cohort favored Republican over Imperial Rome.[26] But for eighteenth-century Russia, as for other early modern states, Imperial Rome was the ideal, and demonstrated that cultural emulation was a venerable and respected path to greatness. Much of the trappings and image-making of Peter's revolution referred to Imperial Rome, from his new titles, to court ceremonial, to the building of triumphal arches, to the introduction of sculpture as an art, to the coining of medals and modeling of the new civil script.[27] Furthermore, Peter's cult of glory—his "glorious and courageous military and political deeds," which Golovkin asserted had brought Russia out into "the universal theater of fame"—owed much to the cult of Imperial Rome, both as filtered through the later Western tradition and as assimilated through contemporary readings and translations of the classics, which now became a fundamental part of every educated Russian's cultural heritage. Like the Roman, eighteenth-century Russian culture was city-centered, focused on the new capital of St. Petersburg, both as a central geographical locus of Europeanization—the famous "window on the West" (Francesco Algarroti's phrase, made famous by Pushkin's *The Bronze Horseman*[28])— and also the center of imperial imagery and discourse. St. Petersburg, built as a showplace, also played a major role in exemplifying and enacting Roman paradigms of sight. The Roman model contributed significantly to public political spectacle in Russia, and also to the cult of civic virtue and the cultural imperative that insisted "*Contemtu famae, contemni virtutes*" ("Condemn fame, condemn virtue").[29] Virtue must be seen, paraded onto the world stage and be appreciated, for it to be considered genuinely virtuous. The very word "virtue," which in Latin implies "manliness," as it stems from "*vir*" (man), also suggests the gendered nature of this discourse, which was nevertheless adapted to the series of female rulers who followed Peter on the Russian throne.[30] Further, the trope of the world stage not only suggests the theatricalism of the era, but also a geographical metaphor, describing Russia's new and grandiose place in the world and her imperial pretensions. The Roman discourse of Stoic virtue, as described in chapter 5, also provided some of the terms to describe the ideal self.

## Russian Enlightenment

The third discursive strand present in Golovkin's speech is that of the Enlightenment. Scholars have long debated the appropriateness of speaking about "the Enlightenment" in Russia, but it seems more fitting to speak of a Russian variant of the Enlightenment, or, as J. G. A. Pocock has put it, to speak not of "the Enlightenment" (most commonly defined in terms of France and the philosophes) but of a plurality of "Enlightenments." Pocock puts forward two criteria for defining the latter pluralized category, "first, as the emergence of a system of states, founded in civil and commercial society and culture, which might enable Europe to escape from the wars of religion without falling under the hegemony of a single monarchy"; and second, "as a series of programmes for reducing the power of either churches or congregations to disturb the peace of civil society by challenging its authority. Enlightenment in the latter sense was a programme in which ecclesiastics of many confessions might and did join."[31] Russia after Peter easily fits these criteria, with allowance for its relatively underdeveloped "civil and commercial society and culture."[32] As Martin Malia has shown, Russia entered into the European balance of power with remarkable ease, and occupied one end of a broad but unified political spectrum of eighteenth-century states.[33] Creating a new model of civil society in which the role of the church was strictly circumscribed was one of the salient features of the Petrine reforms; as is well known, Peter let the Russian patriarchate lapse, and in its place extended the cameralist system to the church, creating the Holy Synod. The church administration was thus incorporated into the state apparatus, a process that led to the nationalization of church property in the 1760s.[34] Furthermore, the Enlightenment as a program in which clerics actively participated was certainly true of Russia, both insofar as the traditions of Latin humanism and Renaissance culture in general had first come to Russia through the church in the later seventeenth century, and also in light of the fact that many of the architects of Peter's reforms, including those relating to the church, were ecclesiastics (the foremost among them, Feofan Prokopovich). Orthodox discourse formed a basic component of eighteenth-century Russian culture, and by mid-century, the vernacular literary language itself, whose creation Peter had prompted as a replacement for Slavonic (then downgraded to "Old Church Slavonic"), had come to be known as *slaveno-rossiiskii* (Slaveno-Russian), thus advertising a harmonious amalgamation of religious and secular culture.[35]

The mythical narrative pictured in Golovkin's speech manifests a new Enlightenment understanding of illumination. Hans Blumenberg describes the way it may be distinguished from the earlier, medieval, attitude: "The truth does not reveal itself; it must *be revealed*."[36] It requires action, assistance, and the acquisition of a new special perspective. In the given passage, this heroic role is supplied, of course, by Peter. This also suggests several ongoing tensions within the Russian Enlightenment model of vision. While one must see to reach understanding, one may also see and be dazzled, or even blinded; one cannot see the face of God and survive. "Baroque" vision that aims to impress and astound may come into conflict with the "classicist" demand for precise rational understanding; vision may evoke wonder and it may provoke analysis and criticism.[37] This may be considered an aspect of the tension between Platonic and Aristotelian vision. There is a further potential dissonance in Golovkin's scenario of revelation between the automatic, "obvious" nature of the truth—as something that is spontaneously absorbed, immediate, and self-evident—and the fact that it requires an initial jolt or action from without, that "acquisition of new perspective" provided by Peter. The automatic acceptance or assertion of something as natural or obvious may involve its own brand of blindness, covering up or repressing anxiety or doubt. A third tension lies in the issue of audience for Peter's spectacle. On the one hand, there is the relationship between all-powerful ruler and "loyal subjects"; mutual seeing may encourage sociability and open up an implicit public sphere, but as part of a "police state" sight may also imply supervision, surveillance, and panoptic control as described by Foucault. On the other hand, there is the problem of staging selfhood for the benefit of the Other, for "the whole world," with an eye to foreign public or political opinion. There is an imperative to be seen and to be recognized, to reap glory, but there is also the danger of disgrace, of *prezrenie*, literally, "being looked through, over, or down upon," being scorned or disdained. The assertion of self as a visual construct, which is an ongoing work in progress, thus leaves open the possibility of failure, with the as-yet-not-fully-constructed self-image open to the charge of remaining a mere "mirage" or "Potemkin village."

## The Mirror Stage

The narrative of Russian cultural self-image described so far—of a triumphant entrance into the world/light, and of self-definition described in terms of vision, all edged with an anxiety of failure—dovetails in striking ways the model of human identity formation that Jacques Lacan popularized as "the mirror stage."[38] Even if we do not accept the mirror stage as an accurate model of human psychology, this notion offers a useful metaphor for conceptualizing early human self-consciousness in terms of the visual that may fruitfully be applied to cultural history.[39] The mirror stage is named for "the startling spectacle of the infant in front of the mirror," when a child between the ages of six and eighteen months, still unable to hold itself up fully, fixes upon an external vision of itself and internally constructs a totalizing self-image. Vision is central to this psychic process insofar as, in Elizabeth Grosz's words, "the sense of sight is the only one of the senses that directs the child to a *totalized* self-image. Other senses can, at best, lead to a body-image conceived as an aggregate—precisely the body-in-bits-and-pieces. Only the simultaneity afforded by sight confirms the integrity of a cohesive self and body. None of the other senses have this ability to perceive 'synchronically,' in a non-linear and non-temporal fashion."[40] This image of a cohesive self is a fiction, a projection of what it hopes to become; the new image of self is an anticipation of power and control, and because of that the mirror self is a "mirage." The word "mirage" itself comes from "*miroir*," to mirror, and means precisely mirroring as illusion. The mirror (mirage) self thus establishes a dynamic relation (in Lacan's words) "between the organism and its reality—or, as they say, between the *Innenwelt* and the *Umwelt*," an ever-shifting dialectic that defines a person's psychic life.[41] The child's anticipatory, future-oriented self-imaging, which "decisively projects the formation of the individual into history," as Jane Gallop has noted, also makes "the past" into an ever-evolving retroactive self-projection, that is, it defines the past in terms of an (equally subjective) fiction of self in the future, a temporality she labels "future perfect."[42]

In relating the Petrine entry into history to the mirror stage, of special importance is the extraordinary sense of exaltation ("jouissance" in Lacan's terms) that accompanies the new imaging of self, an "ecstasy based on the hope of gigantic possibilities."[43] While Lacan and, in general, Western commentators on vision as far back as the eighteenth century, often focus on the dangers involved in seeing, in Russia it is hard to overestimate the positive moxie of this initial moment of self-discovery as expressed in the Petrine scenario. The confidence it expressed in Russia's gigantic possibilities was central to the era's self-image. Russia tended to take ocularcentric positions to their extreme, accepting a highly unproblematized and optimistic version of the European discourse on sight. This optimism may be accounted for in various ways. The very fact that Russia was attempting to achieve in mere decades what had taken Europe centuries made the thrill of establishing selfhood all the greater. The light of knowledge was entering Russia faster, more suddenly, and more triumphantly, ushered in, as it was, by Peter himself. As Voltaire asked in his concluding sentence of the *History of Russia Under Peter the Great*: "The sovereigns of nations long civilized will say to themselves: 'If, in the frozen regions of ancient Scythia, one man, by his own unaided genius, has accomplished such great things, what should we not achieve, in kingdoms where the accumulated labors of several centuries have made everything easy for us?'"[44] The extravagant rhetoric testifies not only to the fact that this reading was pointedly addressed to the insufficiently enlightened Louis XV, but also to the great allure of the Russian experiment to the Enlightenment imagination, which both reflected and affected Russian self-image.

Another explanation for this exultation may be sought in Russia's older patterns of cultural reception—whether interpreted in a positive or negative light. As scholars have suggested, Russian assimilation of foreign value systems, from Byzantine Christianity through Marxism, has gravitated toward the extreme, totalizing, and utopian. In Lotman and Uspensky's semiotic terms, Russian culture is oriented not toward "culture" in the sense of a gradual accumulation of hard-fought experience or institution-building, but toward ultimate, eschatological truths. The periodic revolution in value systems reflects a desire for total and immediate truth, the acceptance of a new absolute rather than the deployment of some new critical principle. On the one hand, this is, we might say, an "anti-cultural" model of culture, and offers the paradox of a tradition that periodically negates itself. On the other, the glories of Russian culture—from the splendors of Russian Orthodox art to the novels of Dostoevsky and Tolstoy—have often centered on the glorification and defense of faith, as something necessary for salvation, however extreme or unpalatable the implications. As noted in the preface, James Billington characterizes this paradoxical originality of the Russian genius as specifically the capacity to adopt a foreign cultural or artistic pattern and take it to its sublime, extreme limits, milk it for all it is worth, lay bare its glories and its limitations, and then discard it.

Golovkin's scenario describes the first jubilant step of this process. Lotman and Uspensky characterize Russia's acceptance of Enlightenment culture as a "change of faith," and Marc Raeff has likewise noted how Russians "came to inject into the critical and analytical ideas of eighteenth-century Enlightenment an almost romantic passion, a moral concern."[45] While one of the central cultural myths of the Enlightenment had to do with establishing the truth on the bedrock of science and reason, all but the most radical thinkers of the second half of the eighteenth century acknowledged that reason itself was necessarily predicated on faith; for Descartes this was the divine light of truth needed to escape the solipsism of a world in which the senses may deceive.[46] In this sense Russia's "romantic" embrace of the Enlightenment underscores an essential aspect of that cultural movement as a new faith. In the cultural sphere this allowed the reformulation of traditional values in modern rationalist terms. It also gave divine sanction to the new political order, which aimed to overcome the violence and turmoil of the previous century of religious and political violence. The new faith was proclaimed under the banner of reason and science, whose most basic postulates followed from "the rationalization of sight" that may be seen as the crucial act of the Renaissance that paved the way to modernity. The new cognitive role of sight is arguably central to this faith, as it remains for modern scientific-technological culture.[47]

The ocularcentrism described in this book reflects this early modern "romantic" faith in enlightened reason, and suggests some of the special conclusions and tensions to which this gives rise.[48] For most of the century, Russian culture proceeded under the banner of jubilant optimism, and a generally uncontested conviction of the efficacy of sight. Lomonosov's triumphal odes examined in the next chapter offer a dramatic, pathbreaking example of this.

# CHAPTER TWO

# The Moment of the Muses

*Lomonosov's Odes*

"For Anna is a unique wonder of today's world.

In the presence of her glory all that exists becomes most glorious,

In the presence of the great one everything becomes manifestly magnificent;

Everything assumes its best aspect. What is bad or malicious

Becomes good and amenable to love."

—Trediakovsky, "Epistle from Russian Poetry to Apollo"

The desire for visibility undoubtedly plays an important part in all human activity, and especially in political culture, in which ostentatious display may bolster and legitimize an individual's—or a regime's—hold on power. Such self-presentation figured centrally in Russia's early modern stage of national development. Displaying Russia "on the stage of universal fame," as pictured in the Petrine scenario, involved an anticipatory vision of future greatness, of maturity and completeness, accompanied by a jubilant sense of self-affirming achievement. This exhilarating vision is nowhere more evident than in the triumphal ode, which expresses in most eloquent terms faith in the perfectly mirrored self, a theophanic or utopian faith in vision that also reflected Eastern Orthodoxy's theology of sight. This analysis of the odes occupies two chapters. In the current one, Lomonsov's odes are examined from the point of view of coming into selfhood, considering the imperative to be seen, the interplay between self and audience, the special role of the tsar, and the way in which the odes respond to the anxieties that threaten this image. In the following chapter, the revelatory power of the odes is accounted for by reference to the Eastern Orthodox mystical view of sight.

## Lomonosov and the "Second Revelation" of the Self

The triumphal ode has long been acknowledged as eighteenth-century Russia's most well-known and characteristic literary artifact. It played a key role in the literary process, leading the way to a new definition of the literary language and to the definition of a classicist system of genres. It also established poetry as the voice of imperial court culture, which itself sponsored and shaped high cultural activity for much of the century.[1] The function of the ode as the voice of praise also accorded with Russian Orthodox religious culture, whose most basic imperative was "true glorification" (the etymological meaning of *Pravoslavie*—as opposed to that of the English term, "Orthodoxy," which derives from "correct doctrine"). As Stephen Baehr, Boris Uspensky, and Victor Zhivov have argued, the ode was at the center of a new "religion of state" and "political theology" that accorded the tsar attributes formerly reserved for God (Russia's version of "divine right" monarchy).[2] Perhaps in no other sphere was the self-affirming jubilation of emergent Russian self-consciousness as eloquent and unabashed as in the triumphal ode. The ode celebrated Russia's political might and new-found civilization—her entrance into "the universal theater of fame"—and her victory over gloomy oblivion, to which it relegated her enemies and naysayers.

L. V. Pumpiansky, examining the establishment of classicism in Russian literature, pondered the central place that the triumphal ode acquired in eighteenth-century Russian culture. In particular, he noted Lomonosov's famous "Ode on the Taking of Khotin" of 1739, prototype for the new syllabo-tonic versification system, as a basic turning point, asking what it was that gave it such extraordinary impact. He differentiated between the Petrine revelatory moment (what we have referred to as the Petrine scenario) and this one, another moment of self-realization, an "ecstatic confession of faith in the self":

> To understand the genesis of this feat of genius in 1739, we need to imagine that first moment when rapture with the West suddenly—like an explosion—turned into rapture with Russia as a western country. This was the second revelation in the history of the Russian people: first Europe's grandeur is revealed, as something overwhelming, like the sun; then it is revealed that Russian grandeur also exists, and moreover, it is of the very same quality! This rapture thus avows *a single* faith, in both Russia and Europe [odnim vostorgom mozhno ispovedat' i Evropu i Rossiiu]! We call this the "post-Petrine" revelation—the second revelation—of the Russian people. It was precisely this moment of ecstatic

confession of faith in *the self* that Russian linguistic consciousness associated
with the awakening of rhythm [i.e, the birth of poetry]. The Russian people
never experienced a more powerful discovery.[3]

While the modern European ode had reflected a passion (*vostorg*, also: rapture,
ecstasy) for classical times, similar to that which Russia now felt for Europe, in
comparison to Russia, Pumpiansky continues, the European odic impulse was
"insignificant." The European ode may have "preserved in its depths a cinder
[*ugolek*] of this passion," but when

> it fell into Russia it suddenly burst into a conflagration. What was illumined
> here, the ode as Russia's fate, or Russia as the ode's? Such phenomena occur
> simultaneously and are inseparable. The Russians suddenly understood
> themselves: they had already known for forty years that they were striving for
> greatness, but suddenly, on the path to greatness, they realized that greatness.
> This was a decisive moment in cultural history because the moment when the
> self achieves greatness is the moment of the Muses. And the first sign of the
> Muse's presence is style. For the first time, in the Khotin ode, there was style,
> and this is more important than everything we have discussed above.[4]

Pumpiansky sees the importance of Lomonosov's achievement as the crucial
moment of articulation, when Peter's revelatory vision was embodied in
a literary style. The articulation of the vision in art represents, in some
basic sense, its fundamental achievement, because "style is the feature
separating art from reality, a moat around art's walls, making it unreachable;
in other words, style is derealization [*derealizatsiia*]. Verses without style
are doggerel [*virshi*] . . . . [I]t is only with style that distinctions can be
made; the stage is flooded with light, and everything comes alive, and
things are distinguished from one another." According to Pumpiansky, the
"derealization" of art, its "unreachable" quality, is, paradoxically, what
allows it to testify to reality, raising a mere "account" (*otchet*) to the level of
art, a state of ontological fixedness.[5] He thus explains the central importance
of Lomonosov's odes to eighteenth-century Russian consciousness as a
moment of cultural articulation.

The "second revelation" as described by Pumpiansky remarkably restages
the first. Lomonosov's verse, like Peter's opening of the curtain, reveals
a "stage flooded with light" upon which "everything comes alive" and
achieves individuality—the initial vision is now embodied in words, given
new permanence. Peter, it will be recalled, had demanded an entirely new

language, calling for a literary language in the "simple" vulgar tongue to replace Slavonic, and he had created a new "civil" script for it. But devising a new alphabet was far simpler than fabricating a language, and the next generation faced (in Victor Zhivov's words) the truly "titanic task" of codifying a new Russian literary tongue; crucial normative aspects of the language "had to arise practically in a vacuum, insofar as linguistic practice as it had developed here was almost completely without order."[6] The "form" of the new language—its visual and symbolic representation—thus also graphically suggested the anticipated grand content, which the odes now tried to describe. As Pumpiansky explains it, Lomonosov's ode not merely fixed the Petrine myth in writing, as had others before him, but achieved the special literary status of art. "Having a style" means not only speaking intelligibly (that is, using a culturally recognized linguistic medium, i.e., poetry, in a successful manner) but also doing so for the first time (in essence, the creation of speech itself). To some extent, Pumpiansky's apologia for Russian classicism may partake in that idealization of the logos observable in later Russian criticism, which put a phenomenological premium on "having a literature." Yet the magical sense of jubilant self-discovery that Pumpiansky describes was a defining moment in eighteenth-century Russian cultural self-consciousness, one that was felt in particularly visual terms. His account builds upon a long tradition that took Lomonosov's first ode as a major milestone of cultural self-definition.[7] Alexander Radishchev, for example, described Lomonosov's achievement in the Khotin ode as a birth that validated Russia's value, a step on her path to glory: "Its unusual style, power of expression, and imagination, which almost made it come alive, amazed the readers of this new work. And this first-born child [*chado*] of an imagination striving forward along an untrodden path served as proof, together with other things, that once a people directs itself toward perfection, then it moves toward glory not by one small path alone, but simultaneously via many routes."[8]

## Jubilatory Display: The Imperative to Be Seen

The nature of sight as an expression of this vision is the overwhelming preoccupation of Lomonosov's odes. To start with, the discourse of the triumphal ode is often in the imperative mode, and the summons to look, to see, to heed is the most incessant of its commands. Seeing oneself as a separate entity also implies being seen by others and having one's independence validated; to have others see is the externalized confirmation of inner self-discovery. The various ways in which the odes perform this visual validation are complex, and take up much of the following discussion. To begin with, here is a sampling of the dozens of passages in Lomonosov's odes that begin with visual imperatives:

Воззри на света шар пространный
Воззри на понт, Тебе подстланный
Воззри в безмерный круг небес;
Он зыблется и помавает
И славу зреть Твою желает
Светящих тьмами в нем очес. (8:108–109)[9]
[Look at the broad sphere of the world / Look at the Pontus, stretched out below You / Look at the measureless circle of the heavens; / It surges and beckons / And wants to see your glory / In its abysses of shining eyes.]

Внемлите все пределы света (8:772)
[Behold all the bounds of the earth]

Взирай на нивы изобильны,
Взирай в полки велики, сильны
И на размноженный народ (8:638)
[Look upon the abundant fields, / Look at the regiments, great and strong / And at the burgeoning people]

Бодрись, мой дух, смотри, внимай:
Сквозь дым небесный луч блистает! (8:748)
[Be bold, my spirit, look, behold: / A heavenly ray shines through the smoke!]

Воздвигнися в сей день, Россия,
И очи окрест возведи (8:655)
[Rise up on this day, Russia, / Raise your eyes and look around]

Воззри к нам с высоты святыя,
Воззри, коль широка Россия,
Которой дал Ты власть и цвет. (8:565)
[Look to us from the holy height, / Look, how wide is Russia / To which You gave power and blossom.]

Смотрите в солнцевы пределы
На ранней и вечерней дом;
Смотрите на сердца веселы,
Внемлите общих плесков гром. (8:633)
[Look at the extremes of the sun / At its early and evening abode; / Look at the joyous hearts / Heed the thunder of general adulation.]

Воззрите с высоты святыя,
Коль светло в наши дни Россия
Петровой Дщерью процвела! (8:503)
[Look from the holy height / How brightly Russia in our days / Has bloomed thanks to Peter's daughter!]

Воззри на венценосну Внуку (8:505)
[Look upon the crowned grandson]

Взирайте на Петрову Дщерь (8:637)
[Look upon Peter's daughter]

Воззри на горы превысоки,
Воззри в поля Свои широки,
Где Волга, Днепр, где Обь течет:
Богатство, в оных потаенно,
Наукой будет откровенно,
Что щедростью Твоей цветет. (8:202–3)
[Look at the mountains most high, / Look at your broad fields, / Where the Volga, Dniepr, Ob flow: / The riches hidden in them / Will be revealed by science / That, thanks to your generosity, blossoms.]

Воззрите, смертны, в высоту!-
И правда тишину лобзает,
Я вижу вечну красоту. (8:750)
[Look, mortals, to the heights! / And truth kisses tranquility, / I see eternal beauty.]

The wide variety of parties to whom the odes are addressed will be considered in a moment. What is common to these summonses to look are the expression and evocation of triumphal jubilation, emphasized among other things by repetition and exclamation.[10] Jubilation is the basic emotional register of the odes, as the effect of odic vision:

Какие представляет виды
Отрадой восхищенный ум? (8:796)
[What sights does my mind, / Ecstatic with joy, present before me?]

О Муза, усугубь твой дар,
Гласи со мной в концы земныя,
Коль ныне радостна Россия! [. . .]
Веселый взор свой обращает
И вкруг довольства исчисляет (8:221–22)
[Oh Muse, intensify your gift / And voice with me to the ends of the earth /
How joyful Russia is today! ( . . .) / She turns her joyful gaze, / And counts her
blessings all around]

А ты, возлюбленная Лира,
Правдивым щастьем веселись (8:402)
[And you, beloved lyre, / Be joyful with righteous happiness]

As these lines suggest, many of the commands to look and be joyful are
demands to appreciate Russia's greatness—her physical size and expanse,
her rulers, her victories, her spreading power and fame. The breadth and
scope of what is being seen corresponds to the breathtaking power of sight
to instantaneously encompass what seems like limitless space. As eloquently
expressed in Edward Young's *Night Thoughts*, the world

Unbroken, then, illustrious, and entire,
Its ample Sphere, its universal Frame,
In full Dimensions, swells to the Survey;
And enters, at one Glance, the ravisht Sight. [. . .]
Take in, at once, the Landscape of the world,
At a small Inlet, which a grain might close,
And half create the wondrous World, they see.
Our *Senses*, as our *Reason*, are Divine.[11]

Landscapes, which are the subject of so much attention in the odes, both serve
as concrete illustration of Russia's greatness and, as this passage suggests, also
serve to characterize the remarkable "divine" nature of vision itself. According
to Lacan, the infant's perception of the mirrored image of the self "appears
to him above all in a contrasting [greater] size,"[12] and this well describes the
world as seen in the ode, which is envisioned in global and cosmic perspective.

The bigness of the world, the universe, and especially of the Russian Empire, make for perhaps the most fitting object for the grandiose, all-seeing gaze, and also reflects the imperial dimension of Russian self-image.[13] If the focus of traditional Muscovite identity had been spiritual or religious (as suggested by the closeness of the words for peasant—*krest'ianin* [from *krest*, "cross"]—and Christian—*khristianin*—or by the identification of those who live in Russia as *pravoslavnye* [orthodox] rather than as Russians), the odes dramatically suggest a new emerging self-consciousness of Russia—more correctly, the Russian Empire[14]—as a geographical and political entity, and they celebrate the empire's wealth and diversity, its natural potential, ethnic and military might.[15] Odes, as well as many other aspects of court and imperial culture, from fireworks and masquerades to triumphal arches and landscape gardening, celebrated the consciousness of Russia's dramatically expanding imperial borders, marking as they often did the successful conclusion of various military and diplomatic ventures.[16] New interest in the nature of the planet—from astronomy and still-debated heliocentrism to Russian participation in scientific and colonial expeditions—also informed the odes' global perspective (especially for Lomonosov, a leading Russian scientist).

This global perspective is presented from a privileged—at times supernaturally advantaged—point of view: that of an eagle soaring above the clouds (an image of the odic poet going back to Pindar and Horace that in Lomonosov's odes is usually connected with war), the view from the top of a mountain, or from the sky. Those who are privy to such sight (from whose perspective the reader experiences it) include Apollo on his chariot; the sun; various rulers or their spirits, including that of Peter; eagles; the poet; and God Himself. Such landscapes display the "contrasting size" (magnification) of the Russian Empire, emphasizing its military might; its tremendous natural resources and potential (especially those that science can uncover); the nation's glory and reputation; and also reflect the nature of the poet's own inspiration. Typically, they emphasize Russia's spectacular breadth and spaciousness (e.g., words related to *shirota* and *prostrannost'*), often referring to the four points of the compass, the world's oceans, a listing of Russia's rivers or other geographical markers, and so on. On the one hand, vision is instantaneous and revelatory, able to "take in, at once, the Landscape of the world." On the other, Russia's immensity is emphasized by reference to its lack of boundaries and the impossibility of vision to encompass the infinite (e.g., "*predelov net*," "*ne viden krai*," "*kontsa ne zrit*" ) and by the cosmic scope of the odes, addressed to "the ends of the earth" (*kontsy zemnyia*) and even to "the ends of the universe" (*kontsy vselenny*). The revelatory power of sight is also repeatedly contrasted to the limited capacity of words, what L. I. Sazonova refers to as "the motif of the inexpressible."[17]

According to Lacan, a sense of "primordial discord" is inherent in mirror-stage consciousness, as there exists a necessary gap between the jubilant anticipatory self and the self as it actually exists, still in an infantile, only partially mobile condition. The gap is made more or less obvious by the presence of a third party or "other" in the world outside. Mirror-stage coming-to-consciousness also necessarily entails alienation, insofar as for someone "to identify themselves as an autonomous coherent self they must first distinguish themselves from others and their social environment."[18] Thus the mirror stage signals a new jubilant articulation of autonomy, yet simultaneously demonstrates dependence on external reality, as self-recognition is also a self-differentiation.[19] Because of this division (the clash between desired autonomy and inevitable dependence) the mirror stage also generates another basic element of human psychology: aggression. As Sean Homer puts it, "the relationship between self and other" manifested in the mirror stage is "fundamentally conflictual. . . . We are caught in a reciprocal and irreducible dialectic of alienation" and aggressivity.[20]

The basic strategy the odes may be said to employ in dealing with this problem is to envision various images of the other within the text itself. The odes thus create their own fictionalized audience(s) as a part of the ideally mirrored world. The audiences portrayed in the odes function as a positive if solipsistic self-reinforcement. They easily divide into those who bolster the jubilant assertion of Russia's greatness—which constitute the great majority—and those who are distinctly Other, Russia's enemies, a small minority whose challenges are inevitably crushed. The enemy (both as Russia's military foes and as a psychological mirror inversion, the imaging of an "anti-self") offers a convenient outlet for aggression, although the enemy-other of the odes is demonized to the point that it offers no real resistance and functions as still another support for the ideal self-image.

Just as elements of landscape and geography serve as an illustration of the cosmic sense of self, so too the various audiences envisioned in the odes may be seen in psychological terms as self-projection. In an ode of 1754, an old man is impressed by the celebrations for the birth of Pavel Petrovich:

> Там слышны разны разговоры.
> Иной, взводя на небо взоры:

Велик Господь мой,—говорит,—
Мне видеть в старости судилось
И прежде смерти приключилось,
Что в радости Россия зрит! (8:558–59)
[Various conversations may be heard there. / One person, raising his sights to heaven, / Says, "Great is My Lord: / In old age, and before death arrives, / It has been ordained for me / To see that Russia sees (herself) in gladness!"]

That is, this old man blesses God because he has lived to see Russia see gladly! This moment, in a real sense, restates the substance of Lomonosov's odes as jubilant display, recording the joy of sight. The joy of the odes is experienced by all of Russia, and indeed Lomonosov's second ode, of 1741, is according to the title itself "pronounced by Russia rejoicing" (*veseliashchaiasia rossiia proiznosit*). Beyond the jubilation itself, this moment of *seeing Russia see gladly* also offers a microcosm of the odes' mirroring function: both describing their anticipated effect on others and also as a kind of mirrored, almost solipsistic, visual self-confirmation.[21] Seeing "Russia see herself" may substitute for what is actually seen ("Russia") that remains unexpressed or unexpressable, but may also suggest a glorious vision.[22]

"Russia rejoicing" may thus be considered both the subject matter as well as the basic audience for the odes. Within the universe of the ode, however, the manifold summonses to jubilant display like those sampled above are directed to a variety of specific audiences, not only the royal personages named in the odes' titles, those to whom the poems are most obviously directed. The odes' addressees span a surprisingly heterogeneous gamut of individuals living and dead, places, supernatural and natural phenomena. A partial list includes: Russia, Russians, Turks, Swedes; peoples of the world or of the Russian Empire; Russia's enemies; Stockholm, Petersburg (*Petropol'*); Pindar; Frederick the Great; nature and various specific natural elements (waters, winds, hills, fields, mountains, trees, rivers, whirlwinds); the sun; sciences (mechanics, chemistry, geography, meteorology); the universe; "the ends of the earth"; heroes; Russian heroines; rulers and judges of the world; "bloody battle"; the pyramids; God; mythological gods (Apollo, Bellona, Mars, Athena); nymphs; heaven (*nebo* and *nebesa*); glory; the Muse, Muses, or the lyre; and the poet himself. (Occasionally, some of these characters—e.g., God or Peter the Great—answer back.) The very proliferation of addressees suggests their collective rhetorical character. In line with their cosmic scope, the odes' vision is presented to "the universe," to "all of creation" and "the entire world"—which also number among the named audiences:

Дивится ныне вся вселенна (8:59)
[Today the entire universe marvels]

И громкую повсюду славу
Едва вместить вселенной всей! (8:61)
[The entire universe can hardly accommodate / (This) loud, all-pervasive glory!]

Внушай свои вселенной речи;
[. . .] ею весь пространный свет
Наполненный, страшась, чудится (8:83)
[Inspire the universe with your speeches. (. . .) / The whole wide world, / Filled with it (Elizabeth's glory), marvels in awe]

Вся тварь со многим страхом внемлет,
Великих зря Монархов Дщерь (8:84)
[All of creation heeds with great terror / Beholding the daughter of great monarchs]

Ея великолепной славой
Вселенной преисполнен слух (8:656)
[The universe overflows with the sound / Of her magnificent glory.]

Европа и весь мир свидетель,
Народов разных милион,
Колика ныне добродетель
Российский украшает трон.
О как сие нас услаждает,
Что вся вселенна возвышает,
Монархиня, Твои дела!
Народов Твоея державы
Различна речь, одежда, нравы,
Но всех согласна похвала. (8:219–20)
[Europe and the whole world, / A million other nations, are witness / Of how great the virtue is / That today adorns the Russian throne. / O how delighted we are / That the whole universe praises / Your deeds, Monarch! / The peoples of your domain / Are of different speech, clothes, mores, / But all as one in your praise.]

Europe, the whole world, a million other nations, all of creation, the whole universe, the peoples of the empire—the ever-proliferating imagined audiences seem to merge into one super all-inclusive *all* that is unanimous in its jubilation. (The minority voice—Russia's enemies—will be considered below.)

These audiences also transcend time and space. Another of the odes' addressees is posterity—the anticipated future self—which marks one of the poet's main goals for writing: to make Russia's glory visible to future generations, for whom what is present (it is anticipated) will have already gloriously come to pass. This is the mirror-stage temporal thinking Gallop describes as "future perfect."[23] Poetry assumes the nature of a heroic trophy or monument, and suggests the sculptural and ekphrastic function of odic verse—poetry meant to commemorate great events as well as to accompany or illustrate triumphal ceremonies. In the following case, the ode explicitly functions as a kind of a triumphal monument:

> Хотя твои махины грозны,
> Но сплавлю их в зваянный вид,
> Чтоб знали впредь потомки позны,
> Что ныне свет в России зрит. (8:99)
> [Though your instruments strike fear, / I will fuse them into sculptured form, / So that later generations will know / What the world sees today in Russia.]

Happy imaginings of an anticipated audience extend not only to picturing the amazement of future generations, but also to consoling thoughts about what people of the past would have thought had they been able to see the new Russia:

> Когда бы древни веки знали
> Твою щедроту с красотой,
> Тогда бы жертвой почитали
> Прекрасный в храме образ Твой.
> Что ж будущие скажут роды?
> [. . .] Возвысят глас свой до небес:
> Великий Петр нам дал блаженство,
> Елисавета совершенство. (8:101)
> [If ancient ages had known / Your generosity and beauty / They would have honored your / Beautiful image in a temple with a sacrifice. / What will future generations say? / (. . .) They will raise their voices to the heavens: / Great Peter gave us happiness, / Elizabeth—perfection.]

The vision of perfection described by the ode thus transcends time as well as specific audience.

If the fundamental subject of the odes may be said to be Russia's newly arisen greatness, the basic action they depict is its sudden and miraculous appearance, of which jubilation is the by-product. This action constitutes a movement from sorrow to happiness, gloom to radiance, sorrowful past to blissful present—a movement between those various bipolar oppositions that make up the invariant motifs of Lomonosov's poetic world. Not only are the fundamental oppositions (of light and dark, joy and gloom) themselves important, but also the stress on the process of opening up, revelation, discovery, and the concomitant transition from gloomy despair to almost uncontrollable delight, from loss or absence to exaltation. Hence the key time of day in the odes is usually not simply daytime but sunrise or daybreak, the moment of awakening, when visual acuity is heightened, and the light seems "brighter than day." (Midday—the sun's "zenith"—also figures occasionally.) Analogously, summer plays a supporting role to spring, when the earth suddenly comes alive, as the sun brings warmth and life. Both mark the advent of vision. Significantly, the agent of this miraculous transformation and source of new vision (or rather, the making possible of vision itself) is the tsar, who is consistently likened to the sun as a divine force.

The basic odic action may also be seen as an iteration of the Petrine scenario; the triumphal revelatory moment is repeated many times and often with direct or metaphorical connection to Peter himself. Peter, primarily as founder of modern, Imperial Russia, is ever-present in Lomonosov's odes, and appears directly or indirectly in approximately one out of every four stanzas.[24] Of course, the triumphal ode as practiced in Europe and in Russia was a distinctly court genre, and one fundamental purpose of these references was support for dynastic legitimacy and to enhance the glory of the reigning house, celebrating its military and political successes as well as coronations, marriages, births, and anniversaries. Thus the odes are full of references to "Peter's house," "Peter's seed" or "seeds," his tribe, blood, descendants, throne, branch, roots, and so on, as well as to his spirit (*dukh*), deeds, and to "Peter's city" (St. Petersburg, often referred to in the odes as "Petropolis" [*Petropol'*, i.e., Peter's City]).[25] One of the main odic tags for Elizabeth is "Peter's daughter" (*dshcher' Petrova*), reflecting what was arguably her strongest claim to the throne. (She came to power via a court revolution.) Lomonosov's final two odes, dedicated to Catherine II, also sound the Petrine theme strongly, proclaiming her (who had no blood claim to the throne at all) also "Peter's daughter" and a new Elizabeth.[26]

Yet clearly the odes' incessant references to Peter reflect something deeper than the dynastic issue, and promote the new imperial ideology Peter introduced, as well as Russia's commitment to enlightened modern ideals. Furthermore, Peter and his successors stand not merely as light-bringers but as light-creators. As noted, the Petrine scenario likened the tsar to the God of Genesis summoning Russia forth from oblivion to being, and the *fiat lux* is recalled several times in the odes. For example, it is recalled in Elizabeth's ascent to the throne, in which the unhappy Russia of "before" is related not to the oblivion of pre-Petrine times as in Golovkin's speech, but to the darkness of the previous reign:

> Уже народ наш оскорбленный
> В печальнейшей нощи сидел.
> Но Бог смотря в концы вселенны,
> В полночный край свой взор возвел,
> Взглянул в Россию кротким оком
> И, видя в мраке ту глубоком,
> Со властью рек: Да будет свет.
> И бысть! О твари Обладатель!
> Ты паки света нам Создатель,
> Что взвел на трон Елисавет. (8:140)
> [Our people, humiliated, was trapped / In the saddest night. / But God looked to the ends of the universe, / Raised His gaze to the midnight land, / Looked at Russia with gentle eye / And, seeing her in profound darkness / Spake, powerfully: Let there be light. / And there was! O Master of Creation! / You again are Creator of light for us / In raising Elizabeth to the throne.]

Elizabeth's ascension to the throne is thus explicitly likened to the Creation—of light, of the world—ex nihilo (a "profound darkness" that could be related to "oblivion" and "lack of civilization").[27] As in Golovkin's speech, the word *svet* has a possible dual valence, signifying both "light" and "world," thus emphasizing the equation of seeing and being.

Here and elsewhere in the odes, the moment of entrance or arrival often occurs through doors or gates that suddenly open, or from behind a curtain that is suddenly raised, and is marked by lifting up eyes to a sudden or panoramic sight. The motif of opening appears in various contexts, usually associated with sight. The word for "open" in Russian (*otkryt'* and *otverzti* and variants) also has a visual component, and may also mean "reveal," "discover," and even "to found (a city)" (e.g., *"Otverzsia v slave bozhii grad"* [8:649]). In the odes doors are also often opened to Enlightenment and the sciences (e.g., 8:564, 8:796–97).[28] The special nature of vision is often signaled by the gesture of stretching forth (*prostirat'*, *prostert'*, etc.) of the eyes or spirit, which also suggests a hand gesture, and which sometimes explicitly accompanies the sight-gesture—for example:

> О вы, щастливыя науки!
> Прилежны простирайте руки
> И взор до самых дальних мест. (8:400)
> [Oh you, fortunate sciences! / Assiduously stretch out your arms / And vision to the very farthest places.]

Phrases of the type "Let me stretch forth my spirit's gaze" ("*Pozvol' mne dukha vzor prostert'*") (8:649) also recall Genesis, and the motion of stretching out an arm also became specifically associated with Peter, as most famously illustrated in Falconet's *Bronze Horseman*.

In the ninth stanza of the Khotin ode, dedicated to a military victory, Peter descends from the clouds through a heavenly door to frighten off Russia's foes. It is a cosmic moment full of thunder and lightning, when all of aroused nature—reflected in the poet's own state of emotional turmoil—reacts:

> Что так теснит боязнь мой дух?
> Хладнеют жилы, сердце ноет!
> Что бьет за странной шум в мой слух?
> Пустыня, лес и воздух воет!
> В пещеру скрыл свирепство зверь;
> Небесная отверзлась дверь;
> Над войском облак вдруг развился,
> Блеснул горящим вдруг лицем,
> Умытым кровию мечем
> Гоня врагов, Герой открылся. (8:21–22)
> [What is it that so constricts my spirit? / My veins grow cold, my heart aches! / What strange noise beats upon my ear? / The desert, forest, and air are wailing! / The beast has hidden its ferociousness in a cave, / The heavenly door swung open / Above the troops a cloud suddenly split apart, / Suddenly with a burning face flashing forth, / Sword bathed in blood, / In pursuit of the foe, the Hero was revealed.]

Among the contrasts here are those between wild beast and noble human being; hiding or closing (*skryl*) and opening (*otkrylsia, otverzlas', razvilsia*); the darkness of the cave and the burning brightness of the sky; down and up; cold and hot; concealment and uncovering. The moment of visual revelation is brought to a crescendo by the stimulation of the other senses—especially hearing and touch, as images of heroic actions of the past transport the poet in his present. The theatricality of this and similar moments that take place as if on stage suggest the ode's connection to court ceremonial.[29]

The "Ode on the Arrival of Her Majesty the Great Sovereign Empress Elizabeth Petrovna from Moscow to St. Petersburg in 1742 Following Her Coronation" depicts Elizabeth as having delivered Russia by making a grand entrance from a door in the sky:

> Священный ужас мысль объемлет!
> Отверз Олимп всесильный дверь.
> Вся тварь со многим страхом внемлет,
> Великих зря Монархов Дщерь,
> От верных всех сердец избранну,
> Рукою Вышняго венчанну,
> Стоящу пред Его лицем,
> Котору в свете Он Своем
> Прославив щедро к Ней взирает,
> Завет крепит и утешает. (8:84)
>
> [Holy terror overtakes my mind! / Olympus opened the all-powerful door. / All creation with great awe attends, / Seeing the Daughter of Great Monarchs, / Chosen by all faithful hearts, / Crowned by the hand of the Most High, / Standing before His face; / Generously glorifying her, He gazes / At her in His light / Confirming His covenant and giving comfort.]

Judeo-Christian imagery blends here with the classical in order to emphasize the divine legitimacy of Elizabeth's rule, as God himself is depicted as an adoring spectator (or perhaps stage manager?) of the empress's entrance as well as the agent of her elevation.

The stanzas cited above incorporate two very rich and central aspects of vision in Lomonosov's odes—one is the image of the sun, and the other the special power of God's sight, both in being seen and in actively looking at others. Divine vision combines an ontological function (Elizabeth stands "in His light") with that of witness (together with "all of creation"), and serves as an active force—a gaze that bestows terror or comfort. This active power of vision may be taken to be a function of divine power that influences external reality (like thunderbolts) or something that produces an inner effect, or both. These aspects of sight are also associated with Russian rulers, who are depicted as having special visual powers, and who act as "icons" of the divine—God's representatives on earth.[30]

In the odes the sun is not only presented as a metaphor, a powerful image of the godlike emperor or empress, but also glorified in exalted, quasi-religious terms. The sun is not only the source of light, which makes vision possible, but also the source of life itself; the sun is "tsar" of the physical universe. The sun is the "eye and soul of the planets" (possibly a reference to heliocentrism), an eye that both sees all and emanates warmth, joy, power, life.[31] It both creates paradise and makes its visible:

> Но о небес пресветло око,
> Веселых дней прекрасный Царь!
> Как наша радость, встань высоко,
> Пролей чистейший луч на тварь (8:104)
> [But O most bright eye of the heavens, / Beautiful tsar of joyous days! / Stand high, like our happiness, / Pour forth your purest rays on creation]

> О Ты, пресветлый предводитель
> От вечности текущих лет,
> Цветущих, дышущих живитель,
> Ты око и душа планет,
> Позволь ко твоему мне дому,
> Ко храму твоему златому,
> Позволь, приближившись, воззреть.
> Уже из светлых врат Сафирных
> Направил коней ты Ефирных:
> Ржут, топчут твердь, спешат лететь. (8:790)
> [Oh you, most bright leader / Of years flowing from eternity, / Giver of life, of that which blossoms and breathes, / You, oh eye and soul of the planets, / Allow me to gaze at you, as you / Draw nearer your home / Your golden temple![32]/ Already from the bright sapphire gates / You have directed your ethereal steeds, / They neigh, stamp the ground, hurry to fly.]

The sun makes many grand entrances in the odes, as in the ascension ode of 1746, which is practically a hymn to the sun in its sight- and joy-giving salvific aspect:

И се уже рукой багряной

Врата отверзла в мир заря,

От ризы сыплет свет румяной

В поля, в леса, во град, в моря,

Велит ночным лучам склониться

Пред светлым днем и в тверьди скрыться,

И тем почтить его приход.

Он блеск и радость изливает

И в красны лики созывает

Спасенный днесь Российский род. [. . .]


О утра час благословенный,

Дражайший нам златых веков!

О вестник щастья вожделенный

Для нас и будущих родов!

Ты коль велику дал отраду,

Когда открыл Петрову граду

Избавльшия Богини зрак!

Мы в скорбной темноте заснули,

Но в радости от сна вспрянули,

Как ты нощный рассыпал мрак. (8:138–40)

[And with a scarlet hand / The sunrise opened the gates into the world, / From out of its frame[33] scatters reddish light / Onto fields, forest, city, sea, / Orders the nocturnal rays to yield / Before the bright day, and to hide away in the earth, / And thus to honor its arrival. / It pours forth splendor and gladness / And summons forth the beautiful faces / Of the Russian people, today saved. (. . .) // Oh blessed morning hour, / Dearer to us than the golden ages! / Oh longed-for messenger of happiness / For us and for future generations! / You gave such great joy / When you revealed to Peter's city / A vision of the saved goddess! / We fell asleep in bitter darkness, / But sprung awake from sleep in joy / When you dispersed the nocturnal gloom.]


The mixing of present and past tenses here, characteristic in the odes, blurs the boundaries between the celebration of a salvational moment achieved in the past and the sense of jubilation in the present that is based on anticipatory, future happiness ("longed-for messenger of happiness / For us and for future generations!"). The odes then deliver a sign or message concerning the visionary revelation of something on the cusp of coming into being. Compare also the words placed in the mouth of the legendary Russian Prince Gostomysl in the ode celebrating the birth of Ioann III:[34]

Твое коль, Рурик, племя славно!

Коль мне твоя полезна кровь!

Оттудуж нынь взошло Светило,

Откуду прежне щастье было.

Спешите скоро те лета,

Когда увижу, что желаю.

О младом Свете больше чаю,

Неж предков слава мне дала. (8:39–40)

[How glorious is your tribe, Riurik! / How do I value your blood! / From this today has risen a Luminary / From which former happiness came. / Come quickly, those years / When I will see what I desire. / I have more hope for the young World / Than the glory given me by predecessors.]

Here in a somewhat awkward blurring of temporalities, a figure from the past anticipates future glory (i.e., that which is realized in the present). History may be glorious, but it serves as the foundation for the even greater anticipated glory of a greater future, the "young World" (or "young Light") represented by the newborn tsar, likened to a rising sun.[35]

Sun-worship thus segues into ruler-worship, as descriptions of the sun's many gifts become elaborate metaphors for the monarch's glorious deeds and features, as well as for the rapture inspired in the poet. For example:

Но, о прекрасная планета,

Любезное светило дней!

Ты нынѣ, чрез пределы света

Простерши блеск твоих лучей,

Спасенный север освещаешь

И к нам веселый вид склоняешь,

Взирая на Елисавет

И купно на Ея доброты:

От Ней текут на всех щедроты,

Как твой повсюду ясный свет. (8:141–42)

[But O, wonderful planet, / Kind luminary of the days! / Today, spreading forth the shine of your rays / Across the bounds of the earth, / You illuminate the north that has been delivered / And incline your joyous sight to us, / Gazing on Elizabeth / And on her goodness: / From Her flow generosities onto everyone / Like your everywhere clear light.]

Such extended comparisons of royal figures to the sun are varied and abundant.

In some, the empress, like the sun, represents the resurrecting power of nature and control over it:

Когда в Отеческой короне
Блеснула на Российском троне
Яснее дня Елисавет;
Как ночь на полдень пременилась,
Как осень нам с весной сравнилась,
И тьма произвела нам свет. (8:217)
[When wearing the Fatherland's crown / Elizabeth, clearer than day, / Shone on the Russian throne; / It was as if night turned into noon, / Autumn equaled Spring / And darkness brought forth light.]

Как лютый мраз она [весна] прогнавши
Замерзлым жизнь дает водам,
Туманы, бури, снег поправши,
Являет ясны дни странам,
Вселенну паки воскрешает,
Натуру нам возобновляет,
Поля цветами красит вновь:
Так ныне милость и любовь
И светлый Дщери взор Петровой
Нас жизнью оживляет новой. (8:96)
[Just as she (Spring), having banished the cruel frost, / Gives life to frozen waters; / Having taken care of fogs, storms and snow, / Reveals bright days to countries, / Again resurrects the universe, / Renews nature for us, / Adorns the fields with flowers once more; / So today mercy and love / And the bright gaze of Peter's daughter / Enlivens us with new life.]

In one of his later odes, of 1752, Lomonosov justifies (and lays bare) his extensive use of the empress-as-sun metaphor:

Что часто солнечным сравняем
Тебя, Монархиня, лучам,
От нужды дел не прибегаем
К однем толь много крат речам:
Когда ни начинаем слово,
Сияние в тебе зрим ново
И нову красоту доброт;

Лишь только ум к тебе возводим,

Мы ясность солнечну находим

И многих теплоту щедрот. (8:498–99)

[That we often compare You, Monarch, / To the sun's rays, / It's not that we
return so many times / To the same themes for lack of material, / But whenever
we begin to write, / We see new brilliance shining in you / And new beauty in
your goodness. / We only need lift our spirit to you / And we find the clarity of
the sun / And the warmth of your many generosities.]

Looking at the empress is like looking at the sun, as a kind of light of truth,
a realization of the perfect union of the good, the true, and the beautiful.
Significantly, the solar light of the odes does not cause blindness, a threat one
might expect of such ultimate vision. Instead, in the optimistic world of the
odes, the sun only magnifies the jubilatory effect of sight, which is always
revealing and empowering (except for Russia's enemies). "We only need lift
our spirit to you / And we find the clarity of the sun." This is one of many
moments when sight and spirit, inner (spiritual) and outer (physical) vision,
are one, a basic feature of "theophanic vision" that will be examined in the
following chapter. The monarch of the odes represents not only the ideal object
of the poet's vision, an objective correlative to the soul's ecstasy, but—like the
sun—a power that makes sight itself possible.

The main purpose of the triumphal ode is joyful display, and one of its
main thrills comes from experiencing, and having others appreciate, the sight
of members of the royal family. Vision by nature is dual, and involves both an
outward thrust—active looking or gazing—and the relatively passive act of
being seen and acted upon, perceived by others. The action of the monarch's
gaze is especially powerful, as in the following instances of joyful vision:

Коль сладко путник почивает

В густой траве, где ключь течет,

Свое так сердце утешает,

Смотря на вас, Елисавет. (8:135)

[Just as a traveler sweetly reposes / In thick grass, by a stream, / One's heart
finds consolation / Looking at you, Elizabeth.]

Какую радость ощущаю?

Куда я ныне восхищен?

Небесну пищу я вкушаю,

На верьх Олимпа вознесен!

Божественно лице сияет
Ко мне и сердце озаряет
Блистающим лучем щедрот! (8:394)
[What joy am I experiencing? / Why am I now in such ecstasy? / I savor heavenly food, / I am raised to the top of Olympus! / Her face shines like a god / And lights up my heart / With a shining ray of generosity!]

Екатеринин взор любезный,
Подобие и дух Петров,
Отрада наша и покров (8:745)
[Catherine's lovely sight, / The likeness and spirit of Peter, / Is our joy and protection]

И се Богиня несравненна,
Возлюбленна и просвещенна
Сияет радостным лицем,
Обитель нашу посвящает
И дверь ученьям отверзает
Во всем владычестве Своем. (8:796–97)
[And this incomparable Goddess / Beloved and enlightened / Shines with a joyous face, / Consecrates our abode / And opens the door to knowledge / In all of Her domains.]

The description of sight as a force acting upon others is described in the last two examples in terms of the empress's "shining face" (*litse*, elsewhere also as *lik*), and recalls the divine face (*lik*) of an icon, which—to extend the traditional image of an icon as a window to the divine—both draws our vision into the sacred realm of the spirit and radiates power outwards (e.g., the power to cure disease). Trediakovsky's "Epistle from Russian Poetry to Apollo" offers a striking description of this kind of imperial sight that magically transforms everything that gazes upon it:

Полно сердце всяких благ, тем щедролюбиво;
Что величества на всей блещет луч небесный,
Всяк народ, весь мир о том славою известный; [. . .]
Ей! величеством на ней большим украсится,
Коль бы ни сияла где оным вся порфира,
Ибо Анна ныне есть токмо чудо мира.
Менится при славной всё, что ни есть, в преславно,

При великой всё растет в величайше явно;
Лучший всё приемлет вид. Худо что и злобно,
Пременяется в добро и в любовь удобно.[36]

[Her heart is full of all goodness, and hence loving generosity; / Due to her fame every nation, the entire world knows / That her divine ray of greatness shines on everything (. . .) / Hey! Great majesty would adorn her all the more / Even if the porphyry (beautifying) her did not shine, / For Anna is today simply a wonder of the world. / In her glory, everything, whatever it may be, becomes most glorious, / In her greatness, everything grows into what is manifestly the greatest; / Everything assumes its best aspect. What is bad or malicious / Becomes good and amenable to love.]

This light of glory makes the glory of the world all the more manifest; the transcendent immanence of the divine is no longer simply imminent—it has already arrived, at least to some degree. Like sunlight, royal sight is revelatory and acts "simply" and automatically on the world ("For Anna is today simply a wonder of the world"). Sight is not merely a function of the one who looks but a kind of divine emanation from the empress, like solar rays.

## The Enemy, or Odic Aggression

The ruler's gaze can offer happiness and mercy or sorrow and punishment, which corresponds to the basic division in the odes between friendly and hostile looking. The enemy in the odes represents an inversion of the ideal self, and the jubilant visual glorification of Russian selfhood increases in inverse proportion to the enemies' humiliation and annihilation. The anger and aggression that according to the Lacanian model stems from inner insecurity due to a recognition of the fictional nature of the jubilantly mirrored self is directed outward at the enemy of that ideal self, deflecting the threat and serving to bolster faith in the validity of mirrored sight. Thus if jubilation is the first, then arguably the second predominant emotional register of the odes is anger addressed at Russia's enemies, who are doomed to sink into the oblivion analogous to that from which Peter had rescued Russia:

Мы славу Дщери зрим Петровой,
Зарей торжеств светящу новой.
Чем ближе та сияет к нам,
Мрачнее ночь грозит врагам. (8:82)

[We see the glory of Peter's daughter, / Lighting up our celebrations like a new dawn. / The closer it shines for us / The more gloomily does night threaten our enemies.]

In the same ode of 1742, which refers to the Swedish military threat, Lomonosov describes Russia as a cosmic ideal that can withstand any challenge, even that offered by the rest of the world:

> Хотя бы вы на нас воздвигли
> Союзны ваши все страны,
> Но тщетны былиб все походы:
> Незнаемые вам народы,
> Что дале севера живут,
> Того по вся минуты ждут,
> Что им велит Елисавета,
> Готовы стать противу света. (8:94)

[Even if you raised against us / A coalition of all of your countries, / Your campaigns would all be in vain: / Peoples unknown to you / Who live beyond the north[37] / Are ready any minute / For what Elizabeth may order, / Ready to stand against the world.]

This stanza describes a basic "us versus them" dichotomy, creating and then countering an almost nightmarish image of all those who might not recognize Russia banded together to attack. This it juxtaposes to the reassuring power of those (still to be enlightened) peoples of the empire unknown to the West, which Russia is bringing out of the darkness of oblivion. These peoples thus suggest another double for Russia, as well as the pledge of anticipated invincibility.

While expressions of hostility certainly befit a genre that often celebrates military achievements, they also suggest the deeply laden dialectical relationship between the ideal self-image and its inverted projection onto the other. The harshly defensive aggressivity of the odes thus functions to justify and buttress the ideal mirrored self, as threats envisioned and overcome offer another source of jubilation. In the odes, hostility feeds righteous jubilation, as the very defensiveness of the emotion signals the aggression that is an inevitable (inverted) by-product of mirrored self-imaging:

> Целуйте ногу ту в слезах,
> Что вас, Агаряне, попрала,

Целуйте руку, что вам страх
Мечем кровавым показала.
Великой Анны грозной взор
Отраду дать просящим скор;
По страшной туче воссияет,
К себе повинность вашу зря.
К своим любовию горя,
Вам казнь и милость обещает. (8:25–26)

[Tearfully kiss the foot / That trampled you down, people of Hagar, / Kiss the arm that struck fear in you / With bloody sword. / Great Anna's threatening gaze / Can fast give joy to a supplicant; / If she sees your obedience to her, / It will shine through a terrible thundercloud. / Burning with love for her own / It promises you punishment and mercy.]

Joy and terror, love and hate, mercy and revenge, promise and threat, brightness and gloom—these are constantly linked and contrasted in the odes, and are commonly dispensed, as in this passage, by the gaze of the monarch. This intense emotional pairing does not merely characterize the enemy, but also the inner "lyric disorder" that characterizes the odic persona. The poet describes the link between joy and terror both in terms of his inner experience and in terms of the monarch's image (in the following passage apparently figuring as part of a military triumph). He addresses his own joyful emotion:

Красуйся в сей блаженный час,
Как вдруг триумфы воссияли,
Тем вящше озарили нас,
Чем были мрачнее печали.
О радость, дай воспомянуть!
О радость, дай на них взглянуть!
Мы больше чувствуем отрады,
Как скорби видим за тобой:
Злочастья ненавистны взгляды
Любезный красят образ твой. (8:743)

[Show your beauty at that blessed hour, / When suddenly triumphs shone forth; / The more they illumined us / The gloomier seemed our woes. / O joy, let us remember! / O joy, let us look upon them! / We feel the more delight / The more sorrows we see behind you: / The hated looks of evil fate / Adorn your benevolent image.]

Characteristically, external reality, including the enemy, seems to be subsumed into the poet's inner world, and become part of his emotional drama.

The enemy is described with marked hostility, as evil, rapacious, malicious, prideful, arrogant, and, especially, jealous—jealousy (*zavist'*) being another type of flawed vision. This is not only a morally reprehensible kind of looking, as these emotionally laden attributes suggest. Culturally and linguistically the clash between good and evil may be conceptualized even more starkly as an opposition between looking and not looking. Vision itself is equated with goodness, mercy, and love, while the Russian word for "hatred" (*nenavist'*) etymologically suggests the failure or refusal to look (*ne-na-videt'*—not to look upon).[38] Perhaps this derives from some cultural taboo against, or danger of looking at extremes—at that which is either too bright or too dark—but it might also suggest a different opposition: that by definition, seeing is a positive good, and not seeing represents an existential lack or absence, as does evil in the Eastern Orthodox theological tradition. As noted, looking at the sun in the odes does not result in blindness, but rather magnifies the joyful experience of truth. "Evil seeing" is then an oxymoron: seeing is by definition good, and evil manifested as incorrect, insufficient, or purposefully distorted vision.

The enemy is associated with darkness, night, gloom, blindness, and the inability to see clearly due to pride (e.g., prevented by a "proud" or "brazen eye" [*gordoe oko, derzkoe oko*]). The enemy is

> Кто гордостью своей дерзнет,
>
> Завидя нашему покою,
>
> Против Тебя восстать войною (8:207)
>
> [The one who dares, in pride, / Envious of our peace, / To rise up in war against you]

The enemy-other are described in biblical terms as non-believers (in the case of Turks, "people of Hagar," Muslims), and in Enlightenment terms as "barbarians," or "Goths" (*goty, gotfskie strany*, in the case of the Swedish foe). Enemies call forth the desire for bloody punishment and revenge on the part of the Russians because they are the ones who violate peace, and their defeat is consistently described as shameful (*styd* and *sram*); in sharp and obvious contrast, Russian troops are consistently brave, and are compared to Roman heroes.[39] Furthermore, the enemies' sorry fate is often couched in terms of correcting or punishing their fallacious and self-aggrandizing vision, for example:

Мы дерский взор врагов потупим,

На горды выи их наступим,

На грозных станем мы валах. (8:143)

[We will blunt the arrogant gaze of our enemies, / We will step on their proud necks, / We will stand on their dread ramparts.]

The sight of a battlefield after the enemy has been ravished offers a graphic lesson, an inversion of the jubilant "ravisht Sight" of landscape that was earlier glorified:

Но естьли хочешь видеть ясно,

Коль росско воинство ужасно,

Взойди на брег крутой высоко,

Где кончится землею понт;

Простри свое чрез воды око,

Коль много обнял Горизонт;

Внимай, [. . .]

Народы, ныне научитесь,

Смотря на страшну гордых казнь (8:90–91)

[But if you want to see clearly / How terrifying are Russian troops, // Go high up the steep shore / Where land and sea meet; / Direct your eye across the waters, / The horizon embraced so much; / Take heed (of the bloody scene of devastation) (. . .) // Peoples, learn a lesson today, / Seeing the terrible punishment of the proud]

As noted, the divine vision of the monarch also has a double function, active and passive, and both of these in turn have a positive and negative (inverted) aspect. The glorious, divine emanation may quietly turn the "bad or malicious" into the "good and amenable to love," or it may actively drive away evil, for example, when it strikes terror into the enemy.

Таков Екатеринин лик

Был щедр, и кроток, и прекрасен;

Таков был Петр - врагам ужасен (8:143)

[Just as Catherine (I)'s face was / Generous and meek and beautiful, / So was Peter's terrifying to his foes]

Similarly, while the sunrise brings glory (light, daytime, clarity, life, etc.) to

Russia, it betokens gloom (darkness, night, eclipse, death) to her enemies. Sight that is "generous," "meek," "merciful," "joyous" to the good is "terrifying" and "horrifying" to the evil. This light renders truth—good or evil—visible. The ruler's sight, like that of God, has the power to protect and preserve, but also to actively destroy (see 8:26, cited above, on "Great Anna's threatening gaze" that "promises punishment and mercy"). The empress's gaze can bring happiness or woe, protect or threaten, be generous or punishing. She shares this power with God. As God Himself describes it in an ode of 1757:

> Я кротким оком к вам воззрю;
> Жених как идет из чертога,
> Так взойдет с солнцем радость многа;
> Врагов советы разорю. (8:637)
> [I will look to you with gentle eye; / As a bridegroom comes forth from the hall, / So much joy will arise with the sun; / (But) I will bring ruin to the enemies' councils.]

Notably, the verb for "bringing ruin" (*razorit'*) that rhymes here with "looking upon" (*vozzriu/razoriu*) also comes from the root for sight (*zor*), which is also related etymologically to *pozor* (shame) and *ozornik* (one who misbehaves). Sight can bring either blessing or curse. Evil characters in the odes are, by definition, those whose vision is "poisoned by envy" or by pride, so that when the light of truth appears they can only try to hide away in the dark so as not to be exposed (later other villains will be investigated—like Sumarokov's famous tragedic villain Dimitrii the Pretender—who do not scruple to flaunt their evil). This situation reverses the solar paradise described above. Hence, as an evil Turkish soldier perishes,

> Иной в последни видя зорю,
> Закрой, - кричит, - багряной вид,
> И купно с ним Магметов стыд;
> Спустись поспешно с солнцем к морю. (8:21)
> [Another, seeing the sunset for the last time, / Cries out, cover up this crimson sight / And with it also the Mohammedan's shame; / Hurry, lower yourself with the sun into the sea.]

Sunrise is replaced by sunset, light surrenders to darkness, what is open closes, what had arisen now declines, what was alive dies, and joyful display is replaced by shameful covering. Similarly:

Шумит с ручьями бор и дол:

Победа, Россская победа!

Но враг, что от меча ушол,

Боится собственного следа.

Тогда, увидев бег своих,

Луна стыдилась сраму их

И в мрак лице зардевшись скрыла.

Летает слава в тьме ночной,

Звучит во всех землях трубой,

Коль Россская ужасна сила. (8:24)

[Forest and vale make noise with the streams: / Victory, Russian victory! / But the enemy, who ran from our sword / Fears his own trace. / Then, seeing their retreat, / The moon was shamed by their disgrace / And hid its face in gloom, having fallen asleep. / Fame flies through the nocturnal darkness / Sounding its trumpet through all the lands: / How terrible is Russian might.]

Here we see the ekphrastic image of fame flying through the sky with its trumpet, an allegorical emblem transferred from the baroque visual register into the verbal. Glory can penetrate the dark of night and justice can see through a storm cloud, just as shame seeks the dark but can be exposed by the light of day and trumpeted to all the lands. Light and sight in the world of the triumphal ode exist in a utopia where what is good or bad is extremely well (hyperbolically) marked, whatever time of day.

Neither the potential errors involved in seeing nor the ethics of praise become a major stumbling block. The all-seeing force of visibility renders all attempts at deception vain, as in the case below in which Western diplomacy tries to mask approaching Swedish aggression:

Но что за ветр с вечерних стран

Пронырства вас закрыл в туман?

Не зрила чтоб того Россия,

Что ваших войск приход значит?

Зачем ваш збор у нас стоит?

В закрытье видны мысли злыя.

В шерсти овечьей знатен волк.

Хоть Аннин зрак от нас высоко,

Вторая есть, Которой око

Зрит, твой к чему намерен полк. (8:45)

[But what wind of intrigue is this from western lands / That has covered you in fog? / Was it so that Russia would not see / What the approach of your troops means? / Why do you amass and stand so close? / Evil hidden thoughts are visible. / A wolf is recognizable in sheep's clothing. / Though Anna's vision is high above us / There is yet another Whose eye / Sees what your regiments intend.]

The "other" here refers to Anna Leopol'dovna, regent for the infant Ioann III, who would become Emperor Ivan VI in 1740–1741, following the death of Empress Anna (Ioannovna), described here as looking from on high.[40] In the case of Anna's unpopular favorite Biron (Ernst Johann von Biron), whose brief regency had preceded that of Anna Leopol'dovna, he might have given himself over to "blind" self-aggrandizement, as described below, but his high station could not hide his evil or prevent his inevitable fall:

Проклята гордость, злоба, дерзость
В чюдовище одно срослись;
Высоко имя скрыло мерзость,
Слепой талант пустил взнестись! (8:38)
[Accursed pride, malice, impudence / Grew together into one monster, / A lofty name hid the abomination / A blind (i.e., empty) talent tried to exalt itself!]

As explored later, deceptive evil may pose far more of a problem in tragedies, though still not an intractable one.

Throughout the odes, evil usually appears in full retreat. As is clear from the passages cited above, nature takes active sides in the cosmic drama, and may be allied either with the jubilant forces of life (springtime, sunrise, birth) or with their enemy, the uncontrollable "anger of the elements" (*gnev stikhii*) (8:102 and 155, both quoted below). One powerful recurring image for the principle of negative nature, an "unnatural nature" that might be taken as a nightmarish image of the alienating forces striving against the mirrored self, is that of the giants of Greek mythology, who, angered by Zeus's victory over their brothers the Titans, staged their own unsuccessful cosmic assault on heaven.[41] The giants' revolt is described as a threat not only to humankind, but also to "the natural order" itself:

Я духом зрю минувше время:
Там грозный злится исполин
Рассыпать земнородных племя

И разрушить натуры чин!

Он ревом бездну возмущает,

Лесисты с мест бугры хватает

И в твердь сквозь облака разит.

Как Этна в ярости дымится,

Так мгла из челюстей курится

И помрачает солнца вид. (8:141)

[I see the past age with my spirit, / There an awesome giant rages / To disperse the tribe of the earth-born / And to destroy the order of nature! / He incites the abyss with his roar, / Grabs icy knolls from their places / And smites the firmament through the clouds. / As Aetna billows smoke in fury / So vapor rises from his jaws / And obscures the sight of the sun.]

The suppression of the revolt, then, may be seen both as an image of what preceded the Petrine scenario, and also of the seething, primordial forces that would seem to continue to threaten the ideal, mirrored self.[42] The image of the giants' extreme elemental violence thus also serves to characterize an ongoing threat to Russia and Russian selfhood, in the passage below specifically referring to the hellishness of Turkish military tactics (8:19 and 876n). Biblical imagery ("the chosen people" in conflict with Hagar's race) combines with the image of hell wanting to burst its bounds and boil over:

Не медь ли в чреве Этны ржет

И, с серою кипя, клокочет?

Не ад ли тяжки узы рвет

И челюсти разинуть хочет?

То род отверженной рабы,

В горах огнем наполнив рвы,

Металл и пламень в дол бросает,

Где в труд избранный наш народ

Среди врагов, среди болот

Чрез быстрой ток на огнь дерзает. (8:19)

[Is it not copper in the womb of Aetna hissing / And gurgling with boiling brimstone? / Is it not hell tearing at its heavy bonds / And wanting to spread its jaws? / It is the race of the spurned slave-woman, / Having filled the mountain troughs with fire / (That) throws down metal and flame / Where our chosen people, at labor / Among the enemies, among the swamps / Through the fast flow challenges the fire.]

Elsewhere, the giants' revolt is used to characterize Elizabeth's battle against the forces of ignorance and their vain attempts to overthrow enlightened civilization:

Что, дым и пепел отрыгая,
Мрачил вселенну, Энцелад
Ревет под Этною рыдая,
И телом наполняет ад;
Зевесовым пронзен ударом,
В отчаяньи трясется яром,
Не может тяготу поднять,
Великою покрыт горою,
Без пользы движется под тою
И тщетно силится восстать, -

Так варварство Твоим Перуном
Уже повержено лежит (8:400)
[Belching smoke and ash / Enceladus[43] shrouded the universe, / Bellows, wailing, under Aetna / And fills hell with his body; / Transfixed by Zeus's blow / In despair he shakes with fury, / He cannot lift the weight, / Covered with a great mountain, / He moves uselessly under it / And vainly strives to rise up. // Thus barbarism already lies prone / Laid low by Your thunderbolt]

The revolt of the giants serves as a dramatic example of the monarch-hero's function to subdue and control the natural elements, to assert natural law and hierarchy, and to turn nature itself—as in the following passage—into a "happy sign":

Однако если враг оставит
Коварну зависть сам собой,
То нас желанный мир прославит,
И тем возвысит нас Герой.
Стихии, ярость укрочайте,
Туманы, в ясны дни растайте,
Являй веселый, небо, зрак,
Целуйтесь, громы, с тишиною,
Упейся, молния, росою,
Стань, ряд планет, в щастливый знак. (8:108)
[However, if an enemy abandons / His perfidious jealousy all by himself, / The peace we desire will glorify us, / And the hero will thus raise us up. / Elements,

subdue your fury, / Mists, melt away into clear days, / Show your joyful aspect, sky, / Thunder, kiss tranquility, / Lightning, get drunk on dew, / Align yourself, planets, into a happy sign.]

The giants' failed revolt thus serves as one of Lomonosov's more powerful images for the enemy/other/inverted self, a personification of the forces threatening the integrity of Russia and the ideal self. This dark side of the mirror suggests an elemental chaos that had to be subdued in the primordial past but that also continues to threaten even in the present. Nevertheless, in the odes these forces are consistently "laid low," "trampled down," triumphantly destroyed, or sent back to the nether regions from which they came, although their very recurrence in different contexts suggests a continuing threat.

## Odic Anxiety: Future Not So Perfect?

As opposed to the attacks mounted by enemies, so triumphantly parried, there are moments when more perplexing doubts do seem to surface. Here, for example, the poet directly addresses his "troubled spirit":

Престань сомненьем колебаться,
Смятенный дух мой, и поверь:
Неложны то мечтанья зрятся,
Но истинно Петрова Дщерь
К наукам матерски снисходит,
Щедротою в восторг приводит.
Ты, Муза, лиру приими
И чтоб услышала вселенна,
Коль жизнь наукам здесь блаженна,
Возникни, вознесись, греми. (8:395)
[Cease wavering with doubts / My troubled spirit, and have faith: / Those are not false dreams you see, / But Peter's daughter in truth / Is maternally deferential to the sciences, / And her generosity enraptures us. / You, Muse, take up the lyre, / And so that the universe will hear / How blessed it is here for the sciences. / Arise, get up, ring out.]

These are rhetorical doubts, recalling the "lyric disorder" that is a hallmark of odic poetics, and they are met with rhetorical answers meant to revive faith and inspiration. The doubts themselves over "false dreams"—cracks in the jubilant mirror?—seem to feed an almost desperate impulse to triumphal display. At stake here is the entire odic enterprise: can the vision be believed or maintained? Put differently, can the poet genuinely and completely believe in the impossibly perfect, utopian, anticipated self he has described?

It has already been suggested that one of the audiences envisioned in the odes is an anticipated future self, and this is an area that sparks the odic bard's most serious self-reflection. If the goal of the odes is to make Russian glory visible to future generations—which, in the following stanza, seems to be compared to the construction of a triumphal arch— what will future generations think, the poet asks, when they see an image of Elizabeth's heroism?

Что вы, о позные потомки,
Помыслите о наших днях?
Дела Петровой Дщери громки
Представив в мысленных очах
И видя зрак изображенный,
Среди Героев вознесенный,
Что молвите между собой?
Не всяк ли скажет быть чудесно,
Увидев мужество совмесно
С толикой купно красотой? (8:143–44)

[What will you, O later descendants, / Think about our days? / Imagining with your inner (mental) eyes / The loud deeds of Peter's daughter / And seeing her image depicted, / Exalted among heroes, / What will you say among yourselves? / Will not everyone say that it is miraculous / To see bravery combined / With such beauty?]

Just as the ode advertises a perfect match between Elizabeth's bravery and beauty, and between inner and outer, physical and spiritual sight, so too does it envision an ideal imagined reader who will consider it miraculous but not unbelievable, and who will accept the world of the ode, so to speak, at face value. That this might not actually come to pass does occur to the poet— witness the rhetorical questions that conclude the passage, which allow for at least some measure of doubt.

The ultimate focus of the poet's fear, and measure for his inner doubts, is—not accidentally—the opinion of other poets. On the one hand, he fears oblivion—the possibility that he will not be able to measure up to the poets of old whom he emulates:

Красуйся, дух мой восхищенный,
И не завидуй тем творцам,
Что носят лавр похвал зеленый;
Доволен будь собою сам.
Твою усерднейшую ревность
Ни гнев стихий, ни мрачна древность
В забвении не могут скрыть,
Котору будут век хранить
Дела Петровой Дщери громки,
Что станут позны честь потомки. (8:102)
[Wax beautiful, my ecstatic spirit, / And do not envy those creators / Who wear
the green laurels of praise; / Be satisfied with yourself. / Neither the anger of
the elements, / Nor gloomy age can hide / Your most heartfelt zeal in oblivion, /
The resounding deeds of Peter's Daughter / Will be preserved for an age. / And
become the honor of far descendants.]

The poet feels the need to exhort himself, to command his ecstasy to even
greater bliss. On the other hand, and more curiously, it is not so much his
own envy of other poets that disconcerts the bard—he is satisfied that he will
preserve the glorious Petrine legacy from oblivion—but rather the *envy of
future poets for him* that seems to offer the more serious threat. It is not that
he has proven incapable of singing loud and zealous panegyrics, but that—he
fears—later poets will begrudge him his "righteous praises":

Завистно на меня взирая
И с жалостию воздыхая,
Ко мне возносят скорбный глас:
О коль ты счастливее нас!
Наш слог исполнен басней лживых.
Твой - сложен из похвал правдивых. (8:100)
[Gazing on me enviously / And piteously sighing, / They will raise to me their
bitter voice: / Oh, how much happier you (were) than we (are)! / Our language
is full of lying fables. / Yours is composed of righteous praises.]

The poet imagines that bards of the future will not so much envy him his
talent but the fact that he lived in such a glorious ("poetic") age that gave him
material he could praise in all righteousness, whereas all they can come up
with in the impoverished future, whatever their talent, will be "lying fables."[44]
Thus he turns the tables on his potential future critics: it is not that his odes

offer flattery and hypocrisy (which was indeed the judgment of some critics of the next generation, most notably, Radishchev), but that if later poets are unable to keep pace with his level of righteous praise, it means that they no longer inhabit the Golden Age.[45] Their reality is inferior, and it is this that turns odic discourse into "lying fables." Lomonosov thus describes, and perhaps attempts to defuse, the course of his own later reception.

Characteristically, Lomonosov resolves the problem of incipient anxiety and doubt by returning to the image of the ideal ruler, Elizabeth. Later, when Derzhavin, Dashkova, Kapnist, and others held a mirror up to Catherine, the image was not always so flattering, but for Lomonosov the ruler is an ultimate locus and source of true vision:

> На чтобы вымышлять нам ложно
> Без вещи имена одне,
> Когдабы было нам возможно
> Рожденным в Росской быть стране,
> В сие благословенно время,
> В которое Петрово семя,
> Всех жен хвала Елисавет
> Сладчайший Музам век дает.
> В ней зрятся истинны доброты,
> Геройство, красота, щедроты. (8:100)
> [Why should we bother to falsely invent / Mere names with no content, / When it is possible for us / Born in the Russian land / At this blessed time / In which Peter's seed / Pride of all women, Elizabeth, / Gives the Muses their sweetest age? / One sees in her genuine virtues, / Heroism, beauty, generosity.]

Name and thing are one, inner and outer vision correspond, internal and external reality match, truth, beauty, and goodness coincide. The sign, or icon, preserves its signifying power. (As with a holy icon, the act of faith is central.) This was a set of correlations that was to be intensely scrutinized and explored, as Lomonosov's odes and their highly optimistic discourse on sight became a touchstone for subsequent considerations of Russian self-image.

# CHAPTER THREE

# Bogovidenie
## Orthodox Vision and the Odes

$A$ fundamental structural problem of monotheism concerns the knowability of God. If God is by definition a perfect and absolute being, existing on a transcendent level that is inaccessible to human beings, how can He be known or communicate with us? On the one hand, there are the various miraculous forms of revelation, either through special intermediaries (angels, messengers, prophets, or, like Jesus, an incarnation into human flesh) or via more or less direct encounters, through natural or supernatural phenomena (floods, pillars of fire, burning bushes, dreams, visions, special signs) and God's direct speech. However, apart from miraculous revelations of transcendent truth, how may this truth be known in a world that in the eighteenth century came increasingly to be seen as ruled by fixed, impersonal laws of nature that, by definition, exclude the very possibility of the miraculous? The focus of the chapters that follow is an exploration of the various Eastern Orthodox approaches to this problem that underlay Russian attitudes toward sight. Often in Orthodoxy, the divine is revealed or described in terms of vision. The very word for theology—*bogoslovie*, literally, "words about God"—may sometimes be replaced by *bogovidenie*, "vision of God" or "divine sight."[1] In various trends in Orthodoxy as well as in their reflections in secular literature, the character of God-vision may differ significantly; these are not necessarily exclusive types of seeing, but often imply different levels of knowing, and in literary terms are connected to different genres and their attendant philosophical positions.

One of the most striking aspects of Lomonosov's odes, something that led the way for eighteenth-century Russian culture as a whole, is their overriding optimism, an overpowering image of Russia's new and anticipated greatness, which, as explored in the previous chapter, was expressed in terms of looking and being seen. The odes' jubilation embraced not only Russia's visible entry "onto the stage of political peoples," but also its acquisition of a "style," a voice, a literature, and even of existence itself. Odes replayed and amplified the revelatory core of the Petrine scenario, which recalled Russia's conversion to Christianity and the creation of mankind "from nonexistence" in Genesis. This ocularcentric faith stemmed from the odes' profound roots in the Orthodox tradition, which was active on deep levels of cultural memory and value-producing cultural mechanisms. In theological terms, the odes reiterate the bliss of divine revelation. Lomonosov's odes are not only full of references to the Bible and other sacred Christian texts, but also are arguably deeply indebted to mystical Orthodox thought concerning the nature of revelation and divine vision.[2] This discussion of mystical Orthodox thought is based on the works of St. Gregory Palamas (1296–1359) and the tradition elaborated by his twentieth-century interpreters, the so-called "neo-Palamite" theologians, who have elaborated on the special Orthodox view of divine vision.[3] Writing in Greek, Palamas offered an explanation and justification of the mystical experience of seeing God, one whose full acceptance in the Orthodox East marked a doctrinal divide with the Latin West.[4] Although probably unacquainted with Palamas's writings, Lomonosov had graduated from the Moscow Slaviano-Greco-Latin Academy and had a solid grounding in Orthodox theological heritage as perceived in the eighteenth century.[5] The argument here is not that Lomonosov knew of Palamas, or even that he was necessarily consciously aware of the Orthodox theology of light, but that it nevertheless pervades his poetic vision.

"The threefold division of the spiritual life" in Orthodoxy commonly distinguishes between the practice of virtue; the knowledge or contemplation of created things (both material and immaterial); and the knowledge or contemplation of God.[6] These may also be seen as steps in spiritual ascent. The second stage, the contemplation of created things, will be examined in chapter 5, in the context of the Enlightenment tradition of "physicotheology." Palamas was concerned with the third and highest kind of sight, what Kallistos Ware (after Evagrius Ponticus, student of Origen) calls "theology in the strict sense . . . the unmediated knowledge of God."[7] Knowing God involves overcoming the seeming contradiction between God's necessarily "absolute incomprehensibility" and the possibility of direct, unmediated understanding that Palamas insisted was experienced on a daily basis by saints—what Vladimir Lossky refers to as "the accessibility of the inaccessible nature."[8] Because God is fundamentally unknowable, attempts to approach the divine characteristically begin with a radical negation of all that is not-God. This is the starting point for apophatic theology, the realm of the double negative: the more completely the things of this world are relinquished, the closer one can hope to approach divine otherness, as an experience beyond sensory or rational knowledge. The apophatic approach is thus not merely a negation (that might merely be taken as a verbal or philosophical exercise) but an attempt "to surpass words and concepts, to reach out toward the transcendent, and so to attain an unmeditated, supra-rational experience of the Divine. . . . [Thus] the way of negation is in reality the way of super-affirmation . . . so overwhelmingly positive that its true character can only be conveyed through negations."[9] Words are insufficient for expressing divine truths, which can neither be deduced by reason nor described by language. Theology itself must be conceived as based on experience rather than ideas or knowledge per se.[10]

Russian Orthodox writers traditionally expressed mistrust of philosophical systems, decried as "external wisdom," "(false) philosophizing" (*mudstrovanie*) and "wordifying" (*razglagol'stvovanie*); similar labels were often applied to classical philosophy and to philosophy in general. As opposed to "empty words," i.e., constructing abstract logical systems, the task of the theologian was sometimes likened to a singer who makes music, often by analogy to the psalmist playing on a many-stringed lyre (see Lomonosov's description of "the divine singer, David" in 8:636, quoted in the last chapter, who is clearly a stand-in for the odic poet).[11] Like the singer, the theologian's main task is not to analyze God's character but to evoke the experience of His glory and to give praise.

This experience is beyond words. To some extent this issue may be related to the kind of visual extravagance seen above in the odes, as well as their repeated suggestion of the limits of verbal expression.[12] For example, Lomonosov complains of the impossibility of giving adequate expression to his feelings:

> Но ею [славой] весь пространный свет
> Наполненный, страшась, чудится:
> Как в стих возможно ей вместиться? (8:83)[13]
> [But the entire vast world / Overflowing with (Empress Elizabeth's glory), marvels, awestruck: / How can it be contained in verse?]

> Кому возможно описать
> Твои доброты все подробну?

Как разве только указать
В Петре природу в том подобну? (8:65)
[Who is able to describe / In detail all of your beneficent acts? / How, other than
just to point / To your nature, similar to Peter's?]

In some sense passages like these might be taken as a modernized version
of the medieval topos of the inexpressibility of feelings in words that defines
the author's humble attitude toward divine truths to which he would give
expression, thus emphasizing the sacred nature of the text. In the odes this topos
may also suggest the lyric persona's humility and political subordination, as he
defines himself as "all-subservient slave" (*vsepoddanneishii rab*) in relation to
the monarch's greatness (8:59, 127, 394, 498, 557, 648, 742, 751, 772, 788).[14]
But the motif of the "inexpressible" in the context of Russian panegyrics and
odes points to something more than merely literary or political etiquette.[15] It
emphasizes the problem of the limitations of communicability (especially, that
of words), but at the same time contrasts with the central, potentially limitless
power of vision that reference to the Orthodox tradition may help explain.

## Divine Vision and "Uncreated Light"

Palamas believed that divine vision and unmediated, positive knowledge of
God had been proved by the experience of the saints, and hence was possible
for all human beings; he was a leading defender of the monastic Hesychast
tradition that espoused ascetic techniques for achieving such a special state
of divine vision and inner calm (*hesychia*).[16] Just what was the nature of this
vision? Palamas, and the Orthodox tradition following him, distinguished three
types of light and visual faculty that may also be associated with the threefold
stages of spiritual ascent. The first is sensual light, perceived physically by
the eyes. The second is mental, the "mind's eye," the light of imagination
(image-making) and understanding.[17] The third combines and transcends the
preceding two. Palamas describes them this way:

> The light of the intelligence is different from that which is perceived by the
> senses; in effect, the sensible light reveals to us objects proper to our senses,
> whereas the intellectual light serves to manifest the truth that is in our thoughts.
> Consequently, sight and intelligence do not perceive one and the same light, but
> it is proper to each of these two faculties to act according to their natures and
> within their limits. However, when those who are worthy of it receive grace and

spiritual and supernatural strength, they perceive by their senses as well as by their intelligence that which is above all sense and all intellect.[18]

This third and highest type of light is divine, what Lossky describes as the "uncreated, eternal, divine and deifying light"; it is "above all sense and all intellect" but also subsumes them.[19]

The notion of this "uncreated light" is based on a distinction between knowing God "in His essence" (*v sushchnosti*)—something that is by definition impossible—and comprehending God through His emanations, His "energy" or "energies." (The essence/energies distinction and the extent to which it may be accommodated by Catholic theology remains a matter of debate.[20]) The two categories, essence and energies, Palamas argued, correspond to the differences between God as Creator, as an active force whose motives and hence essential nature are unknowable, a God who acts at particular moments in time, and God as an inactive or passive force that simply is, something eternal and omnipresent that pervades the universe (including physical nature). "Created light" is part of the physical universe and is perceived sensually and mentally; "uncreated light"—the Orthodox term used in preference to "supernatural," to distinguish it from the Catholic notion—is an emanation of divine energy. According to the Catholic (and generally, the Western Christian) view, both "the supernatural" and "grace" originate from God as Creator, and depend completely on divine agency. In contrast, for Orthodoxy, God's energies— the "uncreated light"—also grace—is a divine presence accessible within the world. As Ware puts it, "The whole cosmos is a vast burning bush, permeated but not consumed by the uncreated fire of the divine energies"; the fire is omnipresent but only perceived by those spiritually able to see.[21] Another metaphor Palamas uses to describe the essence/energy distinction is that of someone looking in a mirror. One can see one's image, a function of light as an emanation or energy, and it is a true image of what is reflected, but one can get no inkling of one's essential being. Similarly, "God, who is inaccessible in His essence, is present in His energies 'as in a mirror,' remaining invisible in that which He is."[22] Depending on one's own spiritual state, one can experience God to a greater or lesser extent via such imaging, but one cannot know His essence.

The distinction between the various kinds of vision is somewhat blurred in the odes, but it is possible to discern the existence of divine, spiritual sight that is more than the purely physical and intellectual, the equivalent of "uncreated light." In eighteenth-century Russian poetry in general, two kinds of sight are commonly contrasted, the sensual and the spiritual, inner and outer. This is made explicit in Kheraskov's ode "Mir" ("The World"), which describes "two lights," playing on the homonym "*svet*," meaning both "world" and "light":

> Во свете вижу скрытый свет;
> Един из тел совокупленный,
> Другой безплотный и нетленный,
> И в мире мир другой живет.[23]
> [I see a hidden light in the world; / One is made up of matter, / The other bodiless and imperishable, / And in this world another world lives.]

The description of "hidden light," "bodiless [lit., without flesh] and imperishable," suggests "uncreated light." While "hidden" and "bodiless" could possibly also refer to intellectual sight, "imperishable" seems to support a Palamite reading.

An analogous interpretive problem—distinguishing between "spiritual" vision that is a product of mental activity and that which partakes of the divine spirit—also arises in Lomonosov's odes. Vision proceeds almost interchangeably from *um* (mind), *dukh* (spirit), and *mysl'* (thought), as well as from the eyes, at least implicitly. The following are characteristic formulations:

> Мой дух красу любови зрит (8:131)
> [My spirit sees love's beauty]

> Я духом зрю минувше время (8:141)
> [I see past ages with my spirit]

> Я вижу умными очами (8:502)
> [I see with mental (spiritual) eyes]

> Позволь мне духа взор простерть (8:649)
> [Permit me to extend my spirit's vision]

> Бодрись, мой дух, смотри, внимай (8:748)
> [Take courage, my spirit, look, attend]

> И мысленно тогда взирал (8:92)
> [And then looked mentally]

Представив в мысленных очах (8:143)
[Imagining in mental eyes]

Представь теперь в уме своем;
Воззри на Дон и край Понтинской (8:87)
[Imagine now in your mind; / Look upon the Don and Pontic land]

На верьх Парнасских гор прекрасный
Стремится мысленный мой взор (8:147)
[To the beautiful top of the Parnassus Mountains / Strains my mental gaze]

Но спешно толь куда восходит
Внезапно мой плененный взор?
Видение мой дух возводит
Превыше Тессалийских гор! (8:66)
[But to where so hurriedly / Is my captive gaze suddenly raised? / My vision leads my spirit up / Much higher than the Thessalian Mountains!]

In a few cases, the poet's special vision is also equated with "vision of the heart," which is also associated with divine vision in Orthodoxy (and in Palamas in particular). For example, in the 1746 ode: "serdtse, prosveshchenno / Velichestvom Bogini Sei / Na budushchie dni vziraet" (the heart enlightened / By means of this goddess's greatness / Gazes on future days) (8:217; cf. also 8:22 and 8:394).[24] The odes' sources of vision, as in the quotes above, blur the distinctions between the two meanings of "spirit" and "spiritual," which in Russian as in English may be taken either as a function of human cognition (thought, imagination, mind) or as divine and transcendent.[25] To some extent, this blurring of categories is a question of semantics; while in some contexts, for example, "*um*" refers to mind or intellect (as in the modern usage), in eighteenth-century Russian it may also signify "spirit" (as in the French, "esprit," from which it is perhaps a calque).[26] This may also be seen as characteristically baroque polysemanticism and decentering of language, as in the following examples that blur or confuse the rational and the emotional ("thoughts" that are charged with irrational passions):

Годину ту воспоминая,
Среди утех мятется ум! (8:217)
[Recalling that time / My spirit (mind) quakes amid delights!]

О коль мечтания противны
Объемлют совокупно ум! (8:649)
[O how these horrid reveries / Together absorb my mind!]

Так мысль в веселье утопает (8:129)
[Thus my thought drowns in joy]

С надеждой смешенны отрады
В объяты страстью мысли льют. (8:132)
[Joyful thoughts mixed with hope / Passionately join in (lit., pour into) an embrace.]

Блаженство мыслям непонятно! (8:395)
[Bliss incomprehensible to thought!]

К Тебе горяща мысль открылась (8:65)
[To You a burning idea was revealed]

Еще плененна мысль мутится! (8:100)
[My captive thought is still baffled!]

Какие представляет виды
Отрадой восхищенный ум? (8:796)
[What sights are presented / To my spirit (mind) ecstatic with joy?]

Каким молниевидным блеском
Восхитился внезапно ум? (8:501)
[What brilliance, like lightning, / Has suddenly enraptured my spirit (mind)?]

These examples also reiterate the heightened emotionalism of Lomonosov's odes.

Lomonosov's images suggest the progress from physical to spiritual, from the second to third stage of vision, that is, to the level of Palamas's uncreated light, although this remains a matter of interpretation. However, the very blurring of categories seems to mark vision's ascent to divine vision, insofar as the third-stage unmediated knowledge of God, as in Palamas's uncreated light, not only transcends the physical and intellectual but also informs and fulfills these other species of vision.[27] As described in the passage from Palamas cited earlier, "when those who are worthy of it receive grace and spiritual and supernatural strength, they perceive by their senses as well as by their intelligence that which is above all sense and all intellect," that is, the senses and intelligence continue to function, perhaps even at a heightened level.[28] The two (or three) kinds of vision, sensual and spiritual, coexist and mutually illuminate each other; the body (and human sight) is not transcended or "overcome" but is filled with divine spirit, "deified."[29] While divine transparency is possible via a perfect balance between the inner and outer light, inner light is nevertheless primary, the ontological (gnoseological) foundation for "the human capacity to see." Palamas explains that just as "sensational vision cannot act without light shining from without, so too the mind as possessor of mental feeling could not see and act by itself if Divine light had not illuminated it."[30] Such knowledge is the most reliable: "The essence of all this is comprehended by properly mental feeling. I say 'feeling' because of the clarity, obviousness, perfect reliability and the non-fanciful nature of understanding, and besides this because the body also somehow communes with the mental action of grace, reorients itself in accord with it, and itself becomes filled with a kind of sympathy for the innermost secrets of the soul";[31] "in truth a person sees only through the spirit, and not by mind or body; by some kind of supernatural knowledge he knows precisely that he sees the light that is higher than light."[32]

This is more than merely negative (apophatic) knowledge: "Vision is higher than negation"; such knowledge is "inexpressible and inevitable."[33] It is unmediated, based on experience, and derives from "double" vision; on the one hand sensual, physical, and mental (to some extent rational), and on the other, spiritual. "To some extent" because Palamas specifically rejects the conclusions of pure reason as "fantasy," as empty abstract mentation. Moreover, imagination is included among the features characterizing the earthly mind. The result is a paradoxical "lack of knowledge that is higher than knowledge, and knowledge that is higher than understanding, inner unity with the innermost and an inexpressible vision, a mysterious and unexpressed contemplation and taste of the eternal light."[34] It is "inexpressible and unexpressed," yet true. It is "higher than understanding" in the sense that "by means of some supernatural knowledge he [a person] knows precisely that he is seeing light that is higher than light, but how he sees, he does not know at that time, indeed he cannot penetrate the nature of his vision due to the unanalyzable character of the spirit by which he sees."[35] While a person may prepare him or herself for such an experience, practice ascetic acts, say special prayers, and so on, ultimately such vision is an inexplicable miracle, a mystery, an expression of divine grace.

In Western European Enlightenment thought the philosophical contrast between mind and spirit derived in part from the way Descartes posed the problem, according to which (as for medieval ascetics in the Platonic tradition) the human mind could be cleansed of everything contingent and earthbound and be raised up to the contemplation of God as pure reason. This view, transmitted by European literature, may also have been a source for Lomonosov's usage; it is not necessary to be sure that Lomonosov knew of Palamas and the Orthodox theology of light to appreciate that its emphasis on the efficacy of divine vision informed his poetic vision.[36] From the neo-Palamist Orthodox point of view, however, the Platonic position falls short because of its failure to accept the essence/energies dichotomy that informed the notion of "uncreated light." It also fails because it prioritizes a rational notion of transcendence that does not recognize the divine element within creation that is universally accessible via experience. While both traditions acknowledge the special nature of miraculous, ecstatic experience, for Palamas and Orthodox theologians this is not an isolated, "created," or "supernatural" phenomenon, occurring in exceptional cases, but the goal of all Christian experience—"to partake in the divine nature" (2 Peter 1:4).

In Orthodox thought, the state of this partaking in the divine nature is ecstasy—a state of wonder, astonishment, a "ravishing of the spirit," accompanied by a sense of the loss of freedom.[37] This special mode of experiential knowledge involves both the "loss of self" and the attainment of a higher, reflexive consciousness gained by "standing outside" oneself (suggested by the literal Greek meaning of *ecstasis*, "putting out of place," hence: "withdrawal of the soul from the body, mystic or prophetic trance").[38] Flesh and spirit take part in the miracle of transfiguration (*preobrazhenie*, also: *priobshchenie* or union, communion) so that human beings can be "deified" (*obozhestvit'sia*). According to Palamas, "tasting the eternal light" and the "fusion" with the divine are accompanied by fever, joyousness, ecstasy, rapture, and pleasure. Spiritual shock also has physical consequences. According to Palamas, "in prayer we sense divine pleasure untouched by sorrow from mental feeling. . . . [I]n this pleasure the body also miraculously transforms, filled with God's love."[39]

Ecstasy, of course, is the principle emotional register of Lomonosov's odes, and on some basic level the experience conveyed in them may be equated to the ecstatic "divine vision" of mystical Orthodoxy. The odes offer a miraculous vision of Peter's new Russia, the incarnation of paradise on earth.[40] This vision reflects the ecstatic personal state of the poet and his vision, constantly drawn upward. The poet plays the role of the psalmist, or prophet, and the world is presented through his inspired eyes. G. A. Gukovsky describes the state of the lyric "I" in words that could easily be taken in the Orthodox religious sense:

"The emotional basis of Lomonosov's entire system serves him as the theme of each of his works as a whole; and this is lyrical ascent, ecstasy; this is the exclusive theme of his poetry, which merely receives different coloration in the various odes (and also in his speeches). For Lomonosov, the carrier of the ecstasy, that is, the single vehicle for the lyrical theme, is the soul that resides in a state of the strongest affect, being carried up to the heavens [*voznesennaia k nebesam*], to Parnassus; earthly objects do not meet his gaze that is carried off [*voskhishchennyi*] to the Habitation of the Muses; everything appears amplified to it, raised to the status of the divine."[41] The world described in Lomonosov's odes, expressed by a "soul that resides in a state of the strongest affect," may simply represent a metaphor for the poet's intensely subjective, ecstatic state, although it is a subjectivity that in mystical terms rises to the supremely objective. Gukovsky continues: "Indeed the ecstatic poet is guided in his singing not by reason but rapture; his imagination soars, flying through space in a moment, through time, destroying logical connections like lightning, simultaneously illuminating diverse places."[42] Referring to the unusual use of language in these odes, Gukovsky asserts that "The word, limited by its concrete, so to speak earthly meaning, inhibits his upward flight. . . . There results a confusion between thinking about objects and abstractions, and the destruction of borders between them."[43] Thus the common motif of the Russian Empire's great size and the impossibility of taking it all in (its "lack of bounds," whose "end cannot be seen") is not primarily the registration of a fact but a characterization of the poet's spiritual state. If he "sees no end" (*kontsa ne zrit*) it does not mean that his sight is weak (analogous to the insufficient power of language), but that Russia's greatness is without bounds, like the poet's rapture.[44]

Characteristic generic markers of the ode like poetic "ecstasy" (*vostorg*), "ardor" (*zhar*), and "rapture" (*voskhishchenie*) correspond to Orthodox eschatological discourse describing the special state of the soul's initiation into the divine. In more precise theological terms, ecstasy especially marks "the early stages of the mystical life," the moments in which "the hidden treasures of divine wisdom" are newly revealed.[45] The word "rapture" (*voskhishchenie*) literally means a physical ascent to God, an involuntary rising up, a kind of spiritual abduction, as in the case of St. Paul, who "was caught up [*voskhishchen*] into Paradise and heard inexpressible words, which a person is not permitted to speak [or: which is impossible for a person to retell]" (2 Corinthians 12:4). Here, as in the odes, the experience of rapture is inexpressible.[46] According to Symeon the New Theologian as paraphrased by Lossky, Paul on the road to Damascus "was blinded and struck down by the apparition of the divine light" because, "not yet having faith in Christ" the experience was unexpected and alien. Ecstasy may thus be contrasted to lesser degrees of contemplating divine wisdom, to initiation, as well as to the soul which "progresses in the spiritual life [and] no longer knows ecstasies," but instead "has the constant experience of the divine reality in which it lives."[47] Symeon the New Theologian likens ecstasy (again, in Lossky's words) "to the condition of a man born in a dark prison feebly lit by a single lamp, who can thus have no conception of the light of the sun or of the beauty of the outside world, who suddenly catches a glimpse of a landscape bathed in sunlight through a crack in the wall of his prison. Such a man would be carried away, and would be 'in ecstasy.'"[48] Palamas describes the "most joyful reality, which ravished St. Paul" and the divine vision that turned him into "all eye."[49] The ecstatic vision of the odes clearly belongs to this revelatory type.

Light's aesthetic role is no less important than its ontological and gnoseological functions. The issue here is the way in which beauty is made manifest by divine vision, "aesthetics" in the etymological sense of the word as "sensual perception or sensation" (from the Greek *aisthesis*) that is divinized like the body during the process of theosis or "deification."[50] "So when the saints contemplate this divine light in themselves, seeing it by the divinizing communion of the Spirit, through the mysterious visitation of perfecting illuminations—then they behold the garment of their deification, their mind being glorified and filled by the grace of the Word, beautiful beyond measure in His splendor, just as the Divinity of the Word on the mountain glorified with divine light the body conjoined to it."[51]

That Palamas resorts to a biblical, literary trope ("they behold the garment of their deification") in order to describe the "communion of the Spirit" returns us to the problem of expressing the inexpressible in words. Although according to Palamas, miraculous vision is characterized by "clarity, obviousness, perfect reliability, and the non-fanciful nature of understanding" it is still inexpressible and beyond logical explanation. How can this be? On the one hand, for Palamas this is ultimately a question of faith in what "God-seers" have experienced: "The monks know that the essence of God transcends the fact of being inaccessible to the senses, since God is not only above all created things, but is even beyond Godhead. . . . This hypostatic light, seen spiritually by the saints, they know by experience to exist, as they tell us, and to exist not symbolically only, as do manifestations produced by fortuitous events; but it is an illumination immaterial and divine, a grace invisibly seen and ignorantly known."[52] The saints' vision is perfectly transparent. But on the other hand, how can what is "invisibly seen and ignorantly known" be conveyed to others? The problem here is not so much one of faith (whether or not mystical experience is taken seriously), but of the limits of communication. What is seen cannot be expressed in words; in the world of dark glass (1 Corinthians 13:12) one requires symbols, imagination, and "manifestations produced by fortuitous events." "Not for nothing," writes Palamas, "do they speak of them [God's "inexpressible gifts"] only by means of using examples and metaphorically, not because they also see them in examples and metaphors, but because one cannot show what has been seen in any other way."[53]

Lomonosov employs complex poetics and baroque means to express rapture that defies description in these terms. Given the disequilibrium between material and spiritual sight, understanding and expression, which words themselves confuse, "examples and metaphors" are inevitable. This applies not only to the rich rhetorical arsenal used in panegyric writing, but also to the function of classical and pagan imagery. In the ode of 1742, for example, the poet's vision of the "Maiden in the sun" from Revelation includes the image of the mountains of Thessaly, and the Maiden (Mary) casts "thunderbolts" (*razit perunom*) down at her enemies.[54] On the one hand, baroque discourse has a "fundamentally metaphorical nature," in which (as Zhivov and Uspensky write) "religious occasions may make reference both to the Christian and to the classical pagan traditions, which are freely combined here, subordinate to the laws of semantic multidimensionality that is intrinsic to baroque culture."[55] According to these authors, the combination of Christian and classical imagery "neutralizes" or does away with the potential conflict that arose in Orthodox consciousness during the process of sacralizing the monarch. For Zhivov and Uspensky, these elements of the classical, pagan heritage became part of the new religious consciousness of the later seventeenth century. On the other hand, for Palamas himself, the "fundamentally metaphorical nature" of language is inevitable since any attempt to express the inexpressible cannot help but resort to "examples and metaphors."

The corporeal world becomes a metaphor through which the poet describes the indescribable state of his soul, as vision (revelation) in the odes transcends the physical bounds of time and space. As Palamas tries to approximate the experience:

> Beyond the purity of mind in prayer the light of the Holy Trinity blazes up and the mind is then raised up higher than prayer, [so that] this should be called not [mere] prayer but the birth of pure prayer, sent by the Spirit, when the mind prays not a prayer, but is carried away in ecstasy to an incomprehensible [*nepostizhimaia*] reality, where ignorance is higher than knowledge. The saint

experiences this delightful spectacle that has enraptured the spirit [*um*], forced it to retreat from everything [*isstupit' iz vsego*; possibly: become possessed] and become wholly concentrated in itself as light conveying revelation, but not the revelation of bodies experienced by the senses, not limited in height, depth, or breadth; he himself in general cannot see any limit to the light that he sees and that illumines him, which is something like a sun, infinitely brighter and larger than anything in the world; and he stands there in the middle of it, having wholly become vision [*ves' sdelavshis' zreniem*]—that is what it is like.[56]

As noted above, he further describes the "most joyful reality, which ravished St. Paul," and his absolute vision that turned him into "all eye." The light of revelation, in Palamas as in the odes, is "not limited in height, depth, or breadth," and the God-seer, like the poet, "in general cannot see any limit to the light that he sees and that illumines him." In this sense, the ode may be compared to prayer, understood not as a verbal form but as a visual experience of theophany. Because of the impossibility of expressing the divine experience, Palamas's own attempt to describe it in words, as he himself was well aware, could in the last analysis only be metaphorical, approximate, and taken on faith, based on personal experience of the divine (one's own or that of others) rather than on philosophical debate. The same is true, perhaps, for the mystical reading of Lomonosov's odes proposed here.

# CHAPTER FOUR

# The Staging of the Self

"Let us look to ancient times
The Russian past is full of themes.
Already a legion of Great Men
Is coming forth from darkness into light,
Led up into an all-illumined theater,
Clothed in the sunny dawn."
—Lomonosov, "Ode to Empress Elizaveta Petrovna . . . On the Most
Radiant Gala Holiday of Her Highness's Ascension to the All-Russian
Throne, November 25, 1761"

"I see everything . . . but want to see nothing."
—Mstislav, in Nikolev's *Sorena and Zamir*

Russian classicist tragedy, which dealt predominantly with historical subject matter, represents a further stage in the dynamic of Russian self-consciousness. The mirror-stage model again offers a compelling framework, insofar as this development is experienced as "a temporal dialectic that decisively projects the formation of the individual into history."[1] History emerges as a crucial arena, a laboratory in which the inner world of the self can test itself against the outer world of objective reality. However, breaking out from the inner world into the outer is not a simple, instant, unambiguous progression. Picturing the self as whole and independent also implies separation, alienation, and as in Jane Gallop's description, this movement into history carries tragic implications, likened to the expulsion from Eden. Thus in eighteenth-century Russia, realizing a national history assumed an ambiguous role. On the one hand, it promised to ground national identity in something real; on the other, it exposed a potentially fatal lack—a tragic fall from grace. Bridging this gap constituted the task of Russian classicist tragedy. As the Lacanian model emphasizes, the historical self is always largely a retroactive fiction, projected backwards and shaped by one's currently anticipated future. The child's image in the mirror represents the anticipated, future self, but also projects backwards (onto the "void") to create an idealized retroactive image of the self "as it was before."[2] At the start of the process there is much less history against which the self may be tested, and the retrospectively mirrored self more clearly manifests its fictional roots, and is still close to that initial, ecstatic sense of national greatness that is so eloquently expressed in Lomonosov's odes.[3] The past appears not so much an objective confrontation with Otherness as another facet of self-mirroring.

Early modern Russian consciousness posed the question of what came before as a serious challenge to national identity. The potential exposure of the emptiness of the past, and hence the nullity of the present, was inherent in the Petrine scenario, which after all posited Russia before Peter as a blank slate, as a state of oblivion or non-being. Foreign commentators, who, as noted, spoke to both extremes of the self-other polarity, quickly spotted this potential weak spot in the Petrine myth of origins. Where, for example, Voltaire supported the positive vision of a new, childlike nation, the "glory of the young World" that exposed the corruption of the old (i.e., old regime Europe), Russia-bashers like Rousseau could give an opposite interpretation. The same biological metaphors that stressed Russia's youth and anticipated its grand future could be marshaled to describe a state of infantilism or even premature senility. Russia's birth onto the European stage could thus be described as fatally overdue or prematurely forced, depriving the nation of the necessary time for natural development. Probably the most inflammatory of such statements was by Rousseau in *The Social Contract* of 1762. He began with what was perhaps the most sensitive point, damning Russia to eternal infancy for failing to reach genuine youth:

> Youth is not infancy. There is for nations, as for men, a period of youth, or, shall we say, maturity, before which they should not be made subject to laws; but the maturity of a people is not always easily recognizable, and, if it is anticipated, the work is spoilt. One people is amenable to discipline from the beginning; another, not after ten centuries. Russia will never be really civilized, because it was civilized too soon. Peter [the Great] had a genius for imitation; but he lacked true genius, which is creative and makes all from nothing. He did some good things, but most of what he did was out of place. He saw that his

people was barbarous, but did not see that it was not ripe for civilization: he wanted to civilize it when it needed only hardening. His first wish was to make Germans or Englishmen, when he ought to have been making Russians; and he prevented his subjects from ever becoming what they might have been by persuading them that they were what they are not. In this fashion too a French teacher turns out a pupil to be an infant prodigy, and for the rest of his life to be nothing whatsoever. The empire of Russia will aspire to conquer Europe, and will itself be conquered. The Tartars, its subjects or neighbours, will become its masters and ours, by a revolution which I regard as inevitable. Indeed, all the kings of Europe are working in concert to hasten its coming.[4]

From a Russian point of view, Rousseau's depiction suggests a worst-case realization of mirror-stage anxieties, an almost satirical inversion of the Petrine scenario. Gallop notes apropos of Lacan's infant that "what appears to precede the mirror stage is simply a projection or a reflection. There is nothing on the other side of the mirror,"[5] and Rousseau asserts Russia's shameful lack of historical substance, of genuine selfhood. The very metaphor of Russia's newness could be taken to imply that Russians prior to Peter were nothing but ignoble, uncivilized barbarians, bumbling in the dark and totally beholden to the West for whatever civilization they may have managed to assimilate.[6]

This, however, was a worst-case scenario, notable in that it was only much later that Russians began to take this challenge to their national identity seriously.[7] In the Russian psycho-historical scenario, the full tragic consequences of this alienating consciousness—and the horrifying specter of having no "usable past"—did not come to a head until the post-Napoleonic era, a period that signaled the almost total eclipse of the eighteenth-century cultural paradigm. In eighteenth-century Russian consciousness, however, history still took the part of the jubilant self, and served as a happy extension of faith in Russia's edenic present and anticipated glorious future. If the fundamental imperative of the Petrine scenario, in Golovkin's words, was to bring Russia "out of the darkness of ignorance and into the universal theater of fame . . . , from nonexistence into being and incorporated into the society of political peoples," theater itself was a powerful instrument as well as a metaphor for the display of Russia's new glory. The basic narrative it sought to present validated the ideal self in the face of all external challenges. This powerful boost to self-image was one reason that Russian classicist tragedy took a close second place to the ode as the genre of highest prestige, and while it was still in many ways a court-oriented genre, it helped the theater as an institution create, enhance, and shape a new public sphere.[8]

Lomonosov's ode of 1741, cited earlier, suggests the way in which anxiety could be overcome in the face of eager anticipation:

Оттудуж нынь взошло Светило,
Откуду прежне щастье было.
Спешите скоро те лета,
Когда увижу, что желаю.
О младом Свете больше чаю,
Неж предков слава мне дала. (8:39–40)[9]
[From this today has risen a Luminary / From which former happiness came. / Come quickly, those years / when I will see what I desire. / I have even more hope for the young World (also: Light) / Than the glory of our ancestors has given me.]

While some passing anxiety over the opinion of future generations might occasionally crop up in the odes, the overriding faith in the future envisioned here generally reigned. In this passage history dawns like a triumphant sunrise. Yet how could "former happiness" have come from a luminary risen only today? There is a tension if not a contradiction between the transcendental time characteristic of odic vision (in these lines, the blurring of past, present, and future, as indicated by the mixing of tenses) and the "before and after" of the Petrine scenario that draws a sharp line between darkness and light, oblivion and existence. Nevertheless, the glory so eagerly awaited (the time "When I will see what I desire") sheds its retrospective light not only on the present but also on the past.

## Poetry and History: Making Glory Visible

The late Renaissance literary theory that had taken root in Russia in the later seventeenth century defined the principal task of poetry as fundamentally historical. The poet's primary function (to quote Feofan Prokopovich's *De arte poetica* of 1705, published 1786) was to "compose praises of great men and pass on the memory of their glorious deeds to posterity."[10] In broad terms, the function of art was to offer proper praise, to make famous, to render visible. More narrowly, this definition helps explain the preeminence of the triumphal ode in eighteenth-century Russia, for its purpose was explicitly panegyrical; in this sense it was the most "poetic" of all genres. The ode's purpose was to commemorate historically significant events and to preserve their memory, making this a historical genre. Many odes also contain historical material of the more obvious kind: references to heroes and heroic episodes of the national past. This reservoir of material for jubilation is thematized in Lomonosov's ode of 1761:

> Воззрим на древни времена!
> Российска повесть тем полна.
> Уже из тьмы на свет выходит,
> За ней великих полк Мужей,
> Что на театр всесветный взводит
> Одетых солнечной зарей. (8:746–47)
> [Let us look to ancient times! / The Russian past is full of themes. / Already a legion of Great Men / Is coming forth from darkness into light, / Led up into an all-illumined theater, / Clothed in the sunny dawn.]

Lomonosov then produces a parade of Russian leaders including Sviatoslav, Vladimir, Vladimir Monomakh, Alexander Nevsky, Dmitrii Donskoi, the Ivans, Aleksei Mikhailovich, and Peter. These lines offer a dramatic re-visioning of the Petrine scenario, as the poet leads the Great Men out onto the bright stage of universal history, and the moment of sunrise seems to recede ever further into the past. History is there for the looking and describing, a treasure house of heroic events from which to choose. The ambiguity of the word *povest'*—even more than the term "history"—suggests the blurring of boundaries between the past as objective reality and as a possibly fictional narrative: "*Rossiiska* povest' *tem polna*" may mean either "the Russian *past* [what happened] is full of themes" or "the Russian *telling of the past* [the narrative of the past] is full of themes."[11] Significantly, both notions—of telling and seeing, history and vision—stem from the ancient Indo-European root for *povest'* (*\*weid-*, "to see,"), which in English produced such words as wisdom, story, and history, again indicating the equation of sight and truth. History is a canvas upon which one can project one's present glory. This ambiguity is significant insofar as it may suggest that the "coming forth from darkness into light" refers not to a specific historical moment (e.g., Peter's appearance) that would suggest "nothing on the other side of the mirror," but to the insufficient telling of the past, something that Lomonosov was "already" in the process of remedying. The mechanism of self-imaging represented in historical writing—as well as in tragedy—is here laid bare, conceptualized not as a kind of retroactive fictionalization (in harsher terms, falsification), but as making something immanent manifest to vision.[12]

Lomonosov explains this point explicitly in several of his own historical writings, where in countering anti-Russian foreign writers he suggests that the crucial issue is not whether or not Russia has a past worthy of glorifying (it has), but the necessity of making it visible, bringing the past into the light with the requisite artistry. He reiterated this argument in the well-known "Foreword on the Utility of Church Books in the Russian Language," which introduced his two-volume collected works of 1758.[13] Lomonosov here expresses the belief that the basic function of literature, as of history, is to illuminate the nation's glory. He paraphrases Horace, whose words were to have such a profound influence in shaping the image of the poet in later Russian literature:

> This short reminder should be sufficient to inspire those who strive to glorify the Fatherland in their natural [native] language, in the knowledge that if there are no skillful writers using it and if it declines all of the nation's glory will be greatly eclipsed. Where is the ancient Spanish language, the Gallic, the British and others, together with the deeds of these nations? Not to mention the languages of illiterate peoples in other parts of the world, which after centuries of war and migration have been obliterated. They too had their heroes, they too had their outstanding deeds in society [*v obshchestvakh*], they too experienced marvelous natural phenomena; but all were plunged into profound oblivion [*vse v glubokom nevedenii pogruzilis'*].[14] Horace says:

> There were heroes before Atrides
> But time has hidden them from us.
> The immortal voice of poets
> Left us no view of their deeds.[15]

> . . . Just such happiness has fallen to the lot of our Fatherland through Peter's enlightenment and has indeed been established through the generousity of his great daughter. Supported by her the verbal arts will never fall into decline in Russia. The most distant ages will read of the great deeds of Peter's and Elizabeth's century and, just like us, feel the same heartfelt emotion. How can there not appear modern Virgils and Horaces? Elizabeth-Augustus now reigns. (8:591–92)

Lomonosov's treatise thus also touches on the crucial connection between language and national identity. As opposed to the later Russian tradition, which saw this connection in essentializing Romantic terms as an issue of uniqueness and original genius, and as something which either exists or does not, Lomonosov expresses a sense of optimistic Enlightenment universalism. Glory is a shared human commodity, there for the finding and depiction; therefore there is no stigma attached to being a latecomer, as barriers of time and space may be overcome. The Greeks were simply "lucky" to have come first, and those who follow—the Romans and other nations—are not condemned to inferior status; indeed the Romans—as in this passage—represent the model of creating a successful national literary tradition via emulation. The oblivion of the past resides not in its ontological nullity but in the viewer's epistemological limitations; it is our ignorance (*nevedenie*) of the past that marks its oblivion, and that—hence—poets may rectify.

One of the striking features of the Russian tragedic repertoire as established by Alexander Sumarokov,[16] founder of the first national theater company in 1756, was the fact that, with some exceptions, it took its subject matter from the national past, especially from the earliest period, Kievan Rus'.[17] Thus tragedy turned to the period of Russia's origins, where the scarcity of factual information available allowed or even demanded significant poetic license. This contrasts strongly with French classicist tragedy as established by Corneille and Racine, which did not commonly look to French history for subject matter, but took its plots mainly from Greek mythology or ancient Roman legend that were in turn mostly absent from the Russian tragedic repertoire.[18] Voltaire was the exception and innovator; in *Zaire* he imitated what he considered English practice, especially that of Shakespeare, in "using real names and real historical events as a background for national tragedy."[19] For French theater, this was not much more than a footnote, while as Iu. V. Stennik has suggested, for Russian eighteenth-century drama the national past took the place of classical mythology. Stennik also noted the strong influence of history as depicted in tragedy on what we may call the era's visual imagination: "[In making historical subjects the plots for tragedy] Sumarokov was the innovator, and it must be said that he was able to cope with this challenge brilliantly, insofar as his practice defined for many decades to come the decisive significance of national history as a basic theme for the art of Russian classicism, not only theater but also painting and sculpture. . . . This reflected the growth of national self-consciousness in this period, and at the same time gave the subject matter of eighteenth-century dramaturgy a special, heightened charge of historiosophical power—which one cannot say, for example, about French classicist drama."[20] Russian classicist tragedy was "historiosophical," that is, the image of history it projected carried powerful cultural and philosophical weight.[21] On the other hand, from a modern perspective, eighteenth-century Russian tragedy manifests a striking lack of concern for historical verisimilitude and makes free use of the past to represent present concerns.[22] This includes the use of outlandish fabricated names (e.g., Ramida, Semira, Sorena, Zanida, Zenida, Zaneta, Astrada, Osnelda, Ilmena, Aspafin, Idarn, Nadir, Zamir, Stalverkh, Premysl, Gikarn, Otan, Vitozar, Vozved, Korans, Liubochest, and so on), the absence of historical realia in the plays, and the anachronistic inclusion of inappropriate terms like "tsar," "grandee," and "rifle," not to mention "Russia" and "Russian." Furthermore, the basic substance of these plays relates far more to contemporary problems of Russian self-image—political, moral, and theological—than to any actual historical issues. Most commentators since the early nineteenth century have noted this ahistorical (or non-historicist) nature of Russian tragedy, and indeed this was a major factor limiting its appeal in later periods.[23]

Stennik discusses why, with the possible exception of Sumarokov's last tragedy, *Dimitrii the Pretender* (*Dimitrii Samozvanets* [1771]),[24] his other historical plays do not concern themselves with Russia's "special fate," an issue that so preoccupied nineteenth-century writers. Sumarokov had, Stennik summarizes, an

> ahistorical approach to understanding the past, that is, [he approached history] as a man of his own epoch. The idea of Russia attaining a new political status in Europe, and the new notions connected with this—concerning (aristocratic) ethical norms, the responsibilities of the monarch (the concept of enlightened monarchy), and so on—are all present in his tragedies, despite the old Russian coloration. Given such an approach, collisions that derived from the consciousness of Russia's own peculiar historical development simply could not have arisen. The main thing was to see Russia—retrospectively addressed to her ancient past—as in no way inferior to other European countries.[25]

## Picturing Calamity

Like the odes, classicist tragedy highlights elements of display and heightens emotionalism. However, in tragedies the jubilant display that follows from the paradisiacal world in the odes is mostly replaced by the extreme distress of life-or-death situations. If the odes describe a utopian vision of anticipated happiness, tragedy responds to an anti-utopian crisis, presented in equally vivid visual terms. The function of the tragic in classicist tragedy is strikingly non- or even anti-tragic in the traditional sense, insofar as the psychological and historiographical thrust of these plays is to overcome all obstacles and to validate the heroic, virtuous self against all odds. In this sense classicist tragedy shares with panegyric odes the didactic function of celebrating virtue. As in the odes, display is essential, in this case as the means to exorcise or eliminate error or evil by its exposure and to publicly validate the countervailing power of virtue.

Typically, these plays place their protagonists in worst-case situations. For example, in the following passage from Nikolev's *Sorena and Zamir*, the heroine Sorena describes her predicament while asking her confidante Zenida to bolster her resolve to undertake violent heroic action:

> Не ужас представляй к наменью Сорены.
> От робости твоей не будет в ней премены.
> Но ах! представь ты ей несчастие ее:
> Представь растерзано отечество свое,
> Градов развалины, домов опустошенье,
> Родни, друзей, граждан всеобщее лишенье;
> Представь на мысль ее текущую их кровь,
> Их трупы, члены их,—представь те бедства вновь,
> Которы были нам тираном причиненны,
> И после ты представь, к чему мы осужденны,
> Что впредь для бедствия готовит нам тиран. (Trag. 484)[26]
> [Don't picture the horror of Sorena's intention. / Your timidity will not cause her to change her mind. / But oh! Picture rather her misfortune to her: / Picture her devastated fatherland, / Cities in ruin, homes deserted, / The universal deprivation of family, friends, citizens; / Picture in your mind their blood flowing, / Their corpses, dismembered—picture those troubles again / That the tyrant has caused for us, / And then picture what we are condemned to, / And what further tribulations the tyrant is preparing for us.]

What is pictured here so insistently, an image of the "devastated fatherland," inverts the typically ideal world of the ode, and suggests the larger context of classicist tragedic drama. This passage is also typical of the tragedies' insistent emphasis on sight. This is a visual, pictorial canvas, describing that which the audience is repeatedly urged to contemplate (the command here translated "to picture"—*predstav'*, also means "imagine," literally, "put [images] before" oneself, and occurs in more than half of the lines). The fact that Sorena refers to herself in the third person underscores her noble, somewhat distanced and abstract call to virtue, and also serves to externalize her inner world for the audience. She calls upon Zenida not simply to imagine all of these horrible sights, but, even more specifically, to "picture her misfortune to her (*predstav' ty ei neschastie ee*)," to imagine or place before her her misfortune, to mirror Sorena's troubles back to Sorena, to see the way she sees and to allow her to contemplate herself at a distance, as if she were standing outside and watching herself. This simultaneously makes her inner conflict visible—a visual externalization of her emotional state—and also objectifies it, lending it a sense of independent validity. The setting of the "devastated fatherland" thus reiterates the rupture between inner and outer worlds—the fall from wholeness that marks the challenge to break out into the world of history. Yet it also externalizes or projects the crisis, as it were, onto the world, ascribing the evil exclusively to that world while the pure and virtuous heroine retains her inner integrity inviolate. The image of history thus remains largely subjective, a mirroring-back.

The fundamental dramatic innovation of eighteenth-century Russian tragedy was to put this kind of intense inner human conflict out onto the stage, to make it visible, to give it eloquent voice. It was a laboratory in which the ideal self could be imagined and tested, could be put into situations that strained the outer limits of virtue, thereby revealing its resilient magnificence.[27] This is a utopian staging of ideals, which defines the tragedy's aesthetic power as well as the nature of its engagement with history. Tragedy's claim for transparency— the externalizing and display of moral conflict—determined its fundamental nature as drama.

This theater was little concerned with aspects of performance that we might associate with "theatricalism," although it would be more accurate to distinguish between varieties of theatricalism and spectacle. As opposed to baroque traditions of school drama, for example, classicist dramaturgy employed a minimal cast; a pared-down, clearly ordered dramatic structure (usually five acts); "classical" Alexandrine verse (iambic hexameter with regular caesura); only the most essential props (e.g., a sword or dagger, to be used at the prescribed moments); and, as far as we know, a relatively restrained use of costume and set design.[28] More baroque traditions remained active in court spectacle and lived on in other theatrical genres like opera and ballet, and in the last quarter of the century also made a partial comeback in more serious genres. For example, Catherine the Great's historical works for the stage were theatrical extravaganzas that explicitly broke with classicist rules of genre.[29]

While classicist tragedy did away with many things that made up baroque spectacle, it was no less concerned with the specular. But the baroque theatrical aesthetic (speaking in broad terms) aimed to overwhelm the audience's sight, pointing to the limits of the visible and thus to the need for otherworldly, spiritual understanding. In sharp contrast, classicism strove to eliminate everything that distracted from true and correct seeing. Its goal was to make the essential truth visible, to harmonize inner and outer understanding. Classicist vision put stress on the sight of things of this world—the validity of sensual vision—and on the harmony between inner and outer sight. In terms of language and poetics, this translated into classicism's general insistence on grammatical, lexical, and metrical precision, a minimum of metaphor, the avoidance of hyperbole and oxymoron (characteristic figures of baroque poetics), and the closest possible correlation between sign and signifier.[30] This is apparent in characters' insistence on the validity of sight, the external expression of inner truth, and the importance of correct naming.

The world of classicist tragedy, like that of the odes, is utopian, binary, and thoroughly ocularcentric. The tragedies both reflect and invert the odic vision of anticipated happiness. As in Sorena's picturing of the "devastated fatherland," tragedy presented an anti-utopian, fallen world, the world to which the ode consigned Russia's enemies, which in the discourse of tragedy is commonly described as "inverted," "perverse," or "perverted" (the *prevratnyi*, *prevrashchennyi*, or *razvratnyi mir*). The paradise of light and unhindered vision is obscured by darkness and evil, as the action is played out between the opposing extremes of light and dark (*svet—t'ma*), revelation and concealment (*otkrytie—sokrytie*), deception and manifestation (*obman—iavlenie*), liberation and imprisonment (often from a dungeon—a "*temnitsa*," or place of darkness), as well as between the extremes of seeing and hating (*videt'—nenavidet'*), a pair that both connects sight, knowledge, and love, and that also associates hatred with blindness and ignorance. To see correctly is to understand and to love.

In both the amorous and the political realms, the problem in tragedy manifests itself as a question of true vision, and the need to make the truth (virtue, honor, love) visible despite all obstacles. Sumarokov's *Khorev* (1747), the first Russian classicist tragedy and prototype for the entire tradition, is a useful point of departure. *Khorev* presented the two basic elements of most tragic plots: the political conflict, usually over a ruler's right to the throne, and a concomitant amorous intrigue in which public and filial duty clashed with the private claims of the heart. In the third act, the heroine Osnelda, caught between love for her enemy's brother Khorev and loyalty to her defeated father, describes her situation dramatically as she raises a dagger above her head and considers suicide:

Хотя душа чиста, но погибает слава.

И, может быть, уж я действительно грешу,

Что я в девичестве сим пламенем дышу.

А свет, превратный свет того не рассуждает,

Не праведным судом, но злобой осуждает.

О нравы грубые! О дни! О времена!

Щедрота, истина суть праздны имена.

Злодейство в жизни сей беспрестанно жаждет,

А бедная душа, живуща в теле, страждет.

О чем жалеем мы,—что наша жизнь кратка?

И чем нам кажется она быть толь сладка?

Приди, желанна смерть! Закрой слезящи очи

И раствори врата Оснельде вечной ночи!

Но что сие есть смерть? Порог из света вон,

Живот—мечтание и преходящий сон.

А ты, о счастливых дражайшая утеха,

Любовь! Прости! Мне нет, мне нет в тебе успеха.

Возлюбленнейший зрак! Престань мечтаться мне;

Не пригвождай меня к мучительной стране!

Не пригвождай моих смущенных мыслей к свету

И тщетно не давай приятного обету!

Подите от меня вы, нежны мысли, прочь,

Не представляйте мне бедою тиху ночь,

Не рушьте моего желанного покою,

Да нетрепещущей скончаю жизнь рукою. (DS 56)

[Although my soul is pure, my reputation (glory) is perishing. / And perhaps I am indeed sinning, / Because in my maidenhood I am burning with passion. / But the world, the perverse world, does not consider this, / And condemns with malice rather than judge righteously. / Oh coarse manners! Oh, days! Oh, times! / Mercy, truth are idle names. / Evildoing thirsts incessantly in this life, / While the poor soul, living in the body, suffers. / Why do we complain that our life is short? / Why do we consider it to be so sweet? / Come, death that I desire! / Close my tearful eyes / And open the gates to eternal night for Osnelda! / But what is this death? / Threshold out of this world, / Life—dreaming, a transient sleep. / And you, oh most precious consolation of the happy, / Love! Farewell! I have had no success with you. / Beloved image! Cease appearing in my dreams; / Do not nail me to this land of torments! / Do not nail my troubled thoughts to this world / Nor give pleasant promises in vain! / Be gone from me, gentle thoughts, away, / Do not present the quiet night to me as a misfortune, / Do not destroy my hoped-for peace. / I will end my life with an untrembling hand.]

Osnelda describes what may be seen as the main challenge to all positive heroes of Russian classicist tragedy: "Though my soul is pure, my reputation [also: "fame" or "glory"] is perishing" (*Khotia dusha chista, no pogibaet slava*). They must, at any cost, make their virtue visible.[31] Osnelda sees herself overwhelmed by evil. Given the fact that she finds herself in such a negative context, to "close tearful eyes" means to reject evil, and to die—to "open the gates to eternal night"—corresponds to seeing the truth, being with God, and being reunited with true love. Opening the gates to death and to eternal night is thus equated to closing tearful eyes; to remain alive "nailed to this land of torments" seems itself a kind of living death, akin to crucifixion.

Much of the action of tragedy occurs in this realm of the double negative, the anti-utopian context. The mostly paradisial context of the odes becomes the "devastated fatherland," as in Osnelda's speech or the Byzantium that Femist describes to Mohammed in Maikov's *Femist and Hieronima*:

Византия, дотоль цветущий в свете град,

Под властью твоей преобратился в ад (Trag. 311)

[Byzantium, until now a city blossoming in the world (or: in light), / Under your rule has been transformed into hell]

In the hellish context, inherently bad actions (such as suicide) undertaken by tragic protagonists are positive, and mark their heroism and nobility. Similarly, from the anti-utopian perspective, death, not life, may be sweet, and life bitter, as in Osnelda's rejection of life's sweetness cited earlier, or as Femida puts it in Sumarokov's *Artistona*:

Когда толико часть мне данная развратна,

Мне жизнь моя мерзка и смерть уже приятна.

Я больше не могу бесчестия нести. (DS 171)

[Because the portion given me is so perverse, / My life is revolting to me and death pleasant. / I can no longer bear dishonor.]

In *Sorena and Zamir*, Sorena uses similar logic—here in terms of sight—to justify murder:

Вот злейший плод любви; но средств иных не видя,
Пойдем злодейство вслед, злодейство ненавидя; [. . .]
Но средство есть. Отмщу, хоть мщенья ненавижу.
Близ пропасти Замир, и в мщеньи зла не вижу. (Trag. 465 and 474)
[Here is the most evil fruit of love; but, not seeing any other means, / Let us
follow in the tracks of evildoing, (even though) hating evil. (. . .) / But there is a
means. I will avenge, although I hate vengeance. / Zamir is near the abyss, and
I see no evil in reprisal.]

She declares, "Ubiistvo podvig moi, venets moi otomshchenie!" ("Murder is
my achievement, vengeance is my crown!") (Trag. 483) and we seem to hear
an echo of later revolutionary terrorists when she declares that

Тирана истребить есть долг, не злодеянье,
И если б оному внимали завсегда,
Тиранов не было б на свете никогда;
Имел бы на земли закон единый царство. (Trag. 483–84)
[To exterminate a tyrant is a duty, not a crime. / And if this were always observed,
/ There would never be any tyrants in the world, / There would be the rule [of]
one single law on earth.]

Similarly, if in a positive context suicide is inherently a bad action,[32] as Zamir
argues,

Коль гонят вольность, честь, а мужество без действа,
В самоубийстве нет тогда уже злодейства;
Оно есть долг тогда; а жизнь беречь позор.
Умрем и пресечем несносный к нам презор (Trag. 472)
[If freedom and honor are driven out, and manliness is foiled, / Suicide is no
longer an act of evil; / It is then a duty, and preserving life a disgrace. / Let us die
and end this unbearable contempt]

As one of the characters in Radishchev's *The Journey from St. Petersburg
to Moscow* puts this moral paradox in a parting testament to his son, "if you
are able to die in virtue [i.e, in a good context], be also able to die in vice
and be, so to speak, virtuous in vice itself." He continues, "If outrageous
fortune hurl upon you all its slings and arrows, if there is no refuge left on
earth for your virtue, if, driven to extremes, you find no sanctuary from

oppression, then remember that you are a man [*chelovek*], call to mind your greatness [*velichestvo*], and seize the crown of bliss which they are trying to take from you. Die. As a legacy I leave to you the words of the dying Cato."[33] Suicide is a double negative that equals a positive, here depicted as an act of supreme virtue, no less heroic than giving one's life in battle or in struggle against a tyrant.

Correct vision (understanding) is crucial in all of these cases. Sorena's lines once again equate "not seeing" with "hating," and Zamir also describes the opposition of life and death in terms of sight. Death offers a way of escaping disgrace and contempt, both varieties of bad sight (*pozor, prezor*—"shame, disdain"—both based on *zor*, sight). Bad sight (here, being seen covered with shame) is thus associated with living in the "perverse world." Bad sight can involve seeing as well as being seen; bad sight is tainted, a kind of blindness, a death-in-life.

Good sight, on the other hand, must often be purchased, or paradoxically maintained, through death. From the perspective of the fallen world, death—the other world—represents truer reality (the true utopia), while it is the things of this world seen through a glass darkly that may appear as phantoms or a dream. If in the fallen world the good suffer and the evil flourish, in its opposite, the ideal world, virtue is revealed and love rewarded. In Sumarokov's *Sinav and Truvor*, Ilmena, like most tragic protagonists, is prepared to meet her maker at any moment, and meditates upon the realm of death (here, a double negative, a life-in-death; note that the play is set in pre-Christian times). The terms of her speech explicitly equate love, sight, and life:

> Пускай разрушится и жизнь и существо:
> Мя в нову изведет природу Божество,
>     И преселюсь из мест, которых ненавижу,
> Туда, где-либо я и Трувора увижу.[34]
> Мне боги подадут иное бытие
> И человечество возобновят мое.
>     Они всесильны, им в природе все возможно,
> И упование Ильменино не ложно. [. . .]
>     Там воля разуму престанет быть преслушна,
> Сердца там твердые и мысль великодушна. (DS 128–29)

[Let my life and essence be destroyed: / Divinity will lead me into a new nature / And I will leave these places which I despise, / For the place where I will possibly see Truvor again. / The gods will give me another being / And will renew my humanity. / They are all powerful, everything is possible for them in nature, / And Ilmena's hope is not false. (. . .) / There the will ceases to disobey reason, / There hearts are firm and thought is magnanimous.]

Even while Ilmena seems to suggest that the laws of nature extend into the afterlife, she wonders whether the passions will continue to exist there or not. In any case, the positive aspects of the negated anti-utopian world (the utopian afterlife) are here remarkably elaborated. This is a fundamentally different, other kind of existence, the *there* that offers a "new nature" and a renewed humanity, and where will and reason, heart and mind harmonize. It is also a place, notably, where sight is restored (whereas this world— *these* places—are, in the absence of truth and love, something illusory and deceptive, evil, to be hated, despised, rejected, not to be seen).

For Sumarokov's tragic protagonists, facing death is generally preferable to taking action that might throw a shadow upon their honor. This may help account for his plays' somewhat static quality, whose structure Gukovsky describes in terms of the "device of repetition-gradation of the very same situation" as the protagonists repeatedly contemplate incompatible ethical alternatives.[35] This also contributes to what may be described as the protagonists' Stoic stance, insofar as passive virtue is advocated over heroic action. The plays' intense emotionalism is distant from the Stoic calm advocated by Russian philosophical poetry on the theme from Ecclesiastes of *vanitas vanitatum*, examined in chapter 8. But as in Ecclesiastes, consciousness of the world's vanity and evil offers protection against despair, and is connected with the perception of "bad sight" (or more properly, its negation, the refusal to accept the sight of evil).

The above discussion might seem to suggest that "good seeing" is only possible in some other, ideal world, or the afterlife, but what we are calling utopian vision—as in the odes—is also immanent, possible to realize on earth. As Gostomysl in *Sinav and Truvor* puts the issue,

> Нет счастья на земли, на небесах оно:
> Оставлено богам и смертным не дано.
> Дано, но мы его страстями разрушаем,
> Друг друга общего спокойствия лишаем.
> Где только человек печется о себе,
> Жилища тамо нет, о истина! тебе. (DS 125)
>
> [There is no happiness on earth, it is in heaven: / It is reserved for the gods and not given to mortals. / (No,) it is given, but we destroy it with passions, / And deprive each other of tranquility. / Where a person's only concern is for himself / There is no place for you, O truth!]

That is, tragedy subscribes to the odes' faith in the establishment of true vision on earth, not merely in heaven. Nevertheless, the very terms of their absolutizing axiological system emphasize the fact that the world of the tragedies—like eighteenth-century Russian culture in general—operates within a metaphysical and idealist philosophical framework.

Thus, to sum up, the challenge for tragic protagonists is to preserve good sight or make the switch from bad sight to good, even if it means rejecting evil by accepting death. Much of the substance of tragedy consists of contemplating these either/or alternatives, as the protagonists swing between good and evil fortune.[36]

## Khorev: The Vindication of Vision

*Khorev*, Sumarokov's first and in many ways paradigmatic tragedy, offers a clear example of this. The action of the play hinges on bad seeing, a deception (*obman*), or to be more specific, a misperception: Prince Kii comes to distrust his younger brother Khorev after Stalverkh, a Kievan noble and his main advisor, overhears a conversation between Khorev and Osnelda and concludes that they are plotting treason. Osnelda is the daughter of Zavlokh, who has been forcibly overthrown by Kii; he now stands outside the city with an army that he has gathered to try and reclaim it. For their part, Khorev and Osnelda are torn between love for each other and their fraternal and filial duties, respectively. Nevertheless they are committed to fulfill their responsibilities—Khorev to lead Kii's army against Zavlokh, and Osnelda to spurn the suit of her father's enemy; this is the point at which Osnelda makes her despairing speech cited above. They still have some hope to reconcile Kii and Zavlokh, indeed the union of Khorev and Osnelda would seem to resolve the conflict between the two houses. However, word of letters secretly exchanged between Osnelda and Zavlokh in which he rejects the idea of his daughter's marriage to Khorev, and the lovers' conversation, misconstrued as treason by Stalverkh and conveyed to Kii, are enough to convince him to order Osnelda put to death. The main action of the play devolves into two sub-plots. One concerns Osnelda and her struggle to maintain her honor, first under the pressure of Khorev's love and subsequently against Kii's accusations. The second revolves around Kii's growing suspicions and fatal error.

As Osnelda complained about her loss of reputation, "Mercy, truth—are idle names." The mission of the noble characters in classicist tragedy is to give meaning back to these concepts, to reconcile inner and outer truth, to restore the correspondence of signs with their signifiers—to reestablish the truth both of language and divine sight. As for Khorev, the larger challenge that his brother's suspicion poses is to ensure that "his deeds will be vindicated [appear correct] before the whole world" ("Dela pred svetom vsem ego iavliatsia pravy" [DS 72]). Khorev experiences a poignant moment when he finds himself straddling diametrically opposed semiotic perspectives, as he wonders whether his love for Osnelda should be considered the height of happiness (from the perspective of the immanent, divine context) or as cruel misfortune (considering its practical consequences in the perverse world). Tragic characters suffer existential ambiguity as the context in which they act changes, altering the signification of words and actions. For example, a dream (*son*, in Russian also, "sleep") may be either a positive marker, a paradisiacal vision of love "seen as if in a dream" (*zritsia, kak vo sne*), as in the passage below, or a signal of death, darkness, and oblivion, as in Osnelda's speech quoted earlier. After hearing a declaration of love from his beloved, Khorev is still left in a quandary, insofar as he knows the great obstacles that remain before he and his lover can be united:

Чего желается и что нам толь приятно,
То кажется всегда нам быть невероятно
И зрится, как во сне. Но, о престрашный сон!
Какое множество в сем счастии препон!
Приятные часы! Вы щедры мне и люты.
Какими я могу назвать сии минуты?
Несчастными почесть? Мне много счастья в них!
За счастливы приять? Что зляй минут мне сих?! (DS 43)
[What is desired and what is so pleasant for us / Always seems to be so improbable, / Seen as if in a dream. But oh, what a most horrible dream! / How many obstacles to this happiness! / Pleasant hours! You are generous to me, and cruel. / How should I refer to these minutes? / Consider them unhappy? How much happiness they contain! / Regard them as happy? How could they be more hurtful (evil) to me?!]

Is their love a dream or a nightmare? Whereas this rhetorical problem underscores the fragility of Khorev's position, for Kii the problem of seeing and understanding is central to the well-being of the state and of the other characters. In *Khorev* and many Russian tragedies of the era, seeing correctly or being blinded by appearances—whether intentionally or not—emerges as one of the fundamental problems of being a good ruler. Kii himself acknowledges this challenge early on and vows to avoid deception, pledging to verify the truth with his own eyes. When Stalverkh comes to him with his suspicions, Kii responds:

Сталверх! Ты верен мне, но дело таково
Восходит выше сил понятья моего.
Кому на свете сем вдруг верити возможно?
Хочу равно и ложь и истину внимать
И слепо никого не буду осуждать.
Мятусь, и лютого злодея видя в горе.
Князь—кормщик корабля, власть княжеская—море,
Где ветры, камни, мель препятствуют судам,
Желающим пристать к покойным берегам.
Но часто кажутся и облаки горами,
Летая вдалеке по небу над водами,
Которых кормщику не должно обегать;
Но горы ль то иль нет, искусством разбирать.
Хоть все б вещали мне, там горы, мели тамо,
Когда не вижу сам, плыву без страха прямо. (DS 48)

[Stalverkh! You are loyal to me, but this matter / Exceeds my power of understanding. / Who on this earth can believe something so unexpected? / I want to be equally aware of both truth and falsehood / And I will not condemn anyone blindly. / I am disturbed, and in my grief see [myself] a fierce evildoer. / A prince is the pilot of a ship, and princely power—the sea, / On which winds, rocks, shoals all offer obstacles to those / Who wish to reach peaceful shores. / But clouds flying across the sky far off above the waters / Often only appear to be mountains / Which the pilot does not have to avoid; / But it takes skill to figure out what they are. / Even if I have been told to beware of mountains and shoals, / If I do not see them for myself, I will sail fearlessly ahead.]

The tragedy for Kii is that despite his best efforts to avoid error, including interviews with eyewitnesses, so as to be assured that "the course of events [be] completely visible" (*tok deistva viden ves'*), his passions still gain the upper hand. The importance of this problem is underscored by the fact that the traditional image of the "ship of state" is one of the few metaphors Sumarokov employs.[37]

Kii only comes to see truly when it is already too late, and the final catastrophe of the play is charted in terms of vision, blindness, and revelation. Each of the three main male protagonists—Kii, the now twice-defeated

Zavlokh, and Khorev—successively confront the sight of the dead Osnelda. "What do I see?!" asks Kii, upset at "such a spectacle" (*zrelishche takoe*) of his mistake; "Hide the horrible world from my eyes!" ("Sokroisia ot ochei moikh protivnyi svet!"), he declares, describing himself as now left "in darkness" (*vo t'me*). Like defeated armies in the odes, those who have done evil try and hide their shame from the light of day. Similarly, Stalverkh goes off and drowns himself—a clearly unheroic end, like that which Kii pictures for himself at the mere thought of the shame Khorev's alleged treason would bring:

> Хорев! Когда таков в очах моих ты зрелся?! [. . .]
> Где скрыть бесчестие? О град! О княжеск дом!
> Пустите убежать мне вас, умрети ныне,
> В лесах скончати жизнь и смерть приять в пустыне! (DS 66)
> [Khorev! When have you appeared like this to my eyes? (. . .) / Where can I hide the dishonor? Oh, city! O princely house! / Let me run away from you now to die, / To end my life in the forest or accept death in the desert!]

Zavlokh too is shocked by the sight of Osnelda's body, and asks the rather strange question: "In what condition [also: sight, appearance] will you, Osnelda, now begin to look at me?!" ("V kakom ty stanesh' mia, Osnel'da, vide zreti?!" [DS 78]). He seems concerned not so much with the radical change that has taken place in *her*, as with how his daughter's death reflects on him, how it will affect the way he is seen. Similarly, in Kheraskov's *Venetian Nun (Venetsianskaia monakhina)*, Mirozi has (he thinks) had his son Korans put to a shameful death, but is more concerned with displaying the exculpatory evidence and clearing Korans's (and hence his own) honor:

> Благодарю Творца, что стал о всем известен.
> Мой сын был слаб в любви, но умер не бесчестен.
> Пойду, сие письмо народу покажу
> И, что мой сын Коранс невинен, докажу. (Trag. 351)
> [I thank the Creator that everything has become known. / My son was weak in love, but died without dishonor. / I will go and show this letter to the people, / And prove that my son Korans was innocent.]

In the finale of *Khorev*, the title character finally arrives on the scene to lament that he "will never gaze upon Osnelda again." He spurns Kii's offer that he assume the throne in his place, and compares his distress to a dream and to the "dark night," because when Osnelda "is hidden from my eyes" ("*skryvaetsia ona ot glaz moikh*"), "my light has already gone out completely" ("*sovsem pomerk uzhe moi svet*"). He imagines "Osnelda in tears before my eyes" ("*Osnel'da v slezakh pred ochi*") and pictures "all of the joys / Which I sought in love and in beauty" ("I predstavliaiutsia mne vse utekhi te, / Iskal kotorykh ia v liubvi i krasote!" [DS 81]). The play ends as he turns his blade on himself in order to join his beloved, "even in hell."[38] Thus the moment of Aristotelian "reversal and recognition" plays out in expressly visual terms, as the various characters' virtues and deceptions are successively revealed and displayed.

## The Great Soul

The problem of revelation and deception, good and bad sight, is thus woven into the fabric of Russian classicist tragedy, often serving as the engine of the plot, placing heroes and heroines in situations where they must struggle to make the truth manifest. This raises ethical and psychological problems for them concerning the limits of their own willingness to conceal, and hence defines their heroic qualities and their greatness of soul (*velikodushie*). As the above analysis has already clearly shown, the protagonists of classicist tragedy are of a special breed. Like everything else in this bipolar world, characters in these plays are divided into hero(in)es and villains, and the closer to power, the sharper the divide. As we have also seen, this differentiation also applies to good and bad seeing (and to good and bad *not* seeing). There are a series of special qualities that mark the hero(in)e, and that also reflect the broader moral discourse of the era. One fundamental such opposition is between "humanity" (*chelovechestvo*) and "brutishness" (*zverstvo*, from *zver'*, wild animal, beast; or, alternatively, as *skotstvo*, from *skot*, cattle or livestock). In *Artistona*, for example, the eponymous heroine describes a good ruler:

> Ты правосудие и милость наблюдал
> И подданным своим в себе пример являл,
> Что человечество от зверства отделяет
> И в чем нас естество над скотством возвышает. (DS 161)
> [You observed justice and mercy / And showed your subjects an example in yourself / Of what distinguishes humanity from beasts / And how nature elevates us above brutishness.]

To be a human—in Russian, a *chelovek*, more properly, "a person"—had strong connotations in the eighteenth century. Some of its associations, as in the above passage, relate to the special qualities of the ruler, as the highest incarnation of humanity and its universal ideals (here connected with dispensing justice and mercy in an unselfish way). The ruler of the triumphal ode, characterized by miraculous powers of vision, often appears in tragedies in an anti-utopian context in which the limits of this vision are interrogated.

The ruler's sight is often crucial to a tragedy's outcome, and is a problem that touches virtually all of the major characters, for whom seeing correctly may present a major moral challenge. Those fully "human" characters who manifest true vision in the tragedies are described as possessing a "great" or "pure soul" (*velikaia, chistaia dusha*), something closely associated, though perhaps not always completely synonymous, with *velikodushie* (magnanimity, literally, "great-souledness") as a moral quality; those who do not (e.g., villains and tyrants) are inversely marked by *malodushie*, faint-heartedness (literally, "small-soul-edness," a lack of soul). Thus in Ilmena's meditation on the nature of the ideal world after death cited above, one aspect of her "resurrected humanity" (*chelovechestvo*) consists of a "firm heart" plus "manganimous thought" (*mysl' velikodushna*). Greatness of soul (also: *velichestvo* or *velikost' dushi*) is also synonymous with nobility (*blagorodstvo*) and the upholding of honor (*chest'*).[39] Honor also implied honesty (*chestnost'*, as in English, etymologically connected to honor), and indicates the fundamental connection between magnanimity and the demand for the complete externalization—making visible—of virtue.

The tragic hero's magnitude of soul (as of any hero perhaps) is measured in terms of the willingness to preserve the noble idea at all costs, even the loss of life. Like a Stoic philosopher, the truly great soul was immune to misfortune and disdained the evils of this world, including death. In Zamir's speech justifying suicide quoted above, he refuses to be seen in a shameful or despicable way, and notes that

> Нам руки скованы, но души в нас свободны.
> Великости души что может нас лишить? (Trag. 473)
> [Our hands are tied, but the souls in us are free. / What can deprive us of greatness of soul?]

Similarly, Sorena taunts her tormentor, Mstislav:

Без страха смерть вкусить—дар свыше всех искусств;

Неведом он тому, в ком царствует пороки (Trag. 477)

[To taste death without fear is a gift higher than all the arts; / It is unknown to those in whom vices reign]

Virtue trumps life itself. In other cases, accepting death is a reaction to frustration in the face of great evil, a desire not to acknowledge its sway:

На что мне в свете жить и лучше умереть,

Как нежели всегда перед глазами зреть

Несносные беды и лютые напасти

И силу чувствовать в крови бесплодной страсти. (Trag. 249)

[Why live? It's better for me to die / Than to always see before my eyes / Intolerable evils and cruel disasters / And to feel the power of fruitless passion in my blood.]

Facing death boldly is one of the clearest markers of the great soul and of the highest qualities of the *chelovek*. One dramatic instance, again from *Khorev*, also offers a curious twist on patterns of sight established in the play. Osnelda has an almost transcendent moment of vision, in which she is able to open her eyes and look death in the face. Elsewhere in the play, looking at, or "opening one's eyes to evil," is marked as negative, for example, when Osnelda sarcastically challenges her evil tormentors to look upon her sufferings and enjoy them (DS 52), or when the virtuous find looking at evil intolerable and morally repugnant. In contrast, in her last moments Osnelda refuses to shut her eyes, as if challenging death itself to a duel. She tells Kii:

Не мни, чтоб я свирепств твоих боялась

Или бы с жизнию скорбяща расставалась.

Я в бедности, в плену, я в узах в сей стране,

Но смерть трепещуща приближится ко мне

И робко разлучит мое с душою тело,

Увидючи меня на гроб мой зрящу смело.

Стремися жизнь отнять, стремися, погубляй

И все свирепости свои на мне являй! (DS 69)

[Don't think I am afraid of your savageries / Or that I will lament in parting from life. / I (have lived) in poverty, captivity, bondage in this country, / But it is death that will tremble when it approaches me, / And it can only separate soul from my body timidly, / Seeing me staring boldly at my grave. / Take away my life, go ahead, destroy me, / Manifest all of your savageries upon me!]

As Osnelda looks directly at death, she imagines that it will flinch, not her. Osnelda is obviously challenging Kii, but she is also defying death itself, in a manner that seems—in terms of the system of oppositions set up in the play— almost superhuman. Osnelda's vision seems to transcend a simple dichotomy of life and death, asserting the eternal integrity of her undefeated soul. Here death turns out to be prey to faintheartedness (*malodushie*) and to Osnelda, the brave, heroic, masculine one who exemplifies *muzhestvo* (courage, which like "virtue" in English is etymologically marked as male). Her bold vision resembles that of a Russian soldier described earlier in the play who "Though death is in his eyes, sees with fearless eye" ("Khot' smert' v ochakh ego, on zrit besstrashnym okom" [DS 63]), or that of Oskold bravely facing death in *Semira* (DS 209).[40] Osnelda's prophetic words of challenge to Kii—"You harm yourself in harming an innocent" ("Ty sam sebia branish', nevinnogo brania" [DS 70])—also suggest her martial valor (*bran'* means warfare). For although Osnelda now has to drink the poison, it is Kii who is vanquished.

Great souls are self-contained, marked by unswerving constancy and unity of self and purpose. To some extent, this ideal of wholeness may be connected to the ideal ruler of the odes, although what exists unproblematically in the odes is continually challenged in the tragedies. Recall Lomonosov's recasting of the Petrine scenario, presenting Peter as the archetypal "Great Man" or simply *the* Man (*Chelovek*):

Ужасный чудными делами
Зиждитель мира искони
Своими положил судьбами
Себя прославить в наши дни;
Послал в Россию Человека,
Каков неслыхан был от века. (8:199–200)
[Awesome in marvelous deeds, / The founder of the world, from time immemorial / Laid it down as inevitable / That He would glorify Himself in our days; / He sent to Russia a Man / Unheard of in the ages.]

As opposed to those who are in a state of inner turmoil and who "wage war against themselves" ("*sam s soboiu voinu vedet*") (8:221)—characteristic of people in the tragic context—or even those who shine for one particular excellence, Elizabeth is praised for her miraculous completeness, wholeness, and unity, qualities that connect her back to Peter the Great:

Весьма не обычайно дело,
Чтоб всеми кто дарами цвел: [. . .]

Тебя, богиня, возвышают

Души и тела красоты,

Что в многих разделясь блистают;

Едина все имеешь Ты.

Мы видим, что в Тебе единой

Великий Петр с Екатериной

К блаженству нашему живет. (8:220–21; cf. 8:151–52)

[It is extremely unusual / That one person bloom with all gifts (. . .) / The beauty of your soul and body / Elevate you, goddess. / That which in others shines separately, / You have united. / We see that in you alone / Great Peter and Catherine (I) / Are alive, to our happiness.]

This ideal unity is also political, as the ruler is also "of one soul" (*edinodushnyi*) with her subjects, as in Lomonosov's 1764 ode to Catherine the Great:

Блаженны мы, что Ей послушны:

Покорность наша—к счастью путь!

О вы, страны единодушны,

Согласием едина грудь,

Обыкши жить в Монаршей воле,

Ликуйте: Правда на престоле,

И Ей премудрость приседит,

Небесными блеснув очами,

Богини Нашея устами

Законы вечные гласит (8:794)

[Blessed are we, that we are obedient to her: / Submission is our path to salvation! / Oh you, unanimous country, / A single breast in harmony, / Accustomed to live by the monarch's will, / Rejoice! Truth is on the throne, / And Wisdom sits with her, / Her divine eyes sparkling, / And speaks divine laws / Through the lips of our goddess]

The tragedies interrogate the limitations of this ideal, although in them the "great soul" combines the odic ruler's unity of self with political virtues, and the challenges to it serve to demonstrate its inflexibility. As Zamir explains in *Sorena and Zamir*:

Великая душа сей крайности не знает.

Она всегда равна как в счастьи, так в бедах.

Не власть тиранская ее приводит в страх;

В себе имея всё, она не знает плена,

Приводит в страх ее свободе лишь измена. (Trag. 476)

[The great soul does not know this extreme (of giving in to necessity). / It is always the same, in happiness as in misfortune. / It is not a tyrant's power that can inspire terror in it; / Having everything within, it knows no restriction; / It is only terrified of betraying its freedom.]

Here, the suggestion of a tyrant that the hero "give in to necessity" is itself spurned as "an extreme," and the great soul's total adherence to virtue—to the point of welcoming death—is, in contrast, presented as the behavioral norm. Similarly, Artistona declares the great soul to be independent of the external world:

Пускай в злодействии вся плавает вселенна,

Оркантова душа чиста и непременна. (DS 140)

[Let the entire universe swim in evildoing, / Orkantov's soul is pure and undeviating.]

Or as Malmira advises the betrayed Fedima in the same play:

Оставь в лукавстве мир, ты с инстиной живи.

Когда угодна жизнь по радостям катится,

Великия души тогда еще не зрится. [. . .]

Пусть счастье зверствует, ты бедствы презирай. (DS 137)

[Leave the world to its deceptions, you live with truth. / If life were content to roll along with gratifications, / No great soul would be seen. (. . .) / Let happiness brutalize, you should disdain misfortunes.]

Or, to go even farther, as we have noted in cases of the double negative, persecution of the great soul merely serves to highlight its greatness, a badge of honor. As Gostomysl puts it in *Sinav and Truvor*:

Коль чистая душа не хочет быть превратна,

За добродетели и мука ей приятна. (DS 106)

[If a pure soul does not want to be sullied (false, transformed, inverted), / Even torment is pleasant in the name of virtue.]

At moments like these, tragic heroes may gravitate toward a quasi-Stoic self-containment, which might also suggest a retreat from the political arena.[41] In

Lomonosov's *Tamira and Selim*, virtue stands alone as the ultimate arbiter and witness of correct vision, whatever external calamities may come:

> Едина видит то с презорством добродетель;
> Среди громов и бурь недвижимо стоит -
> Сама себе хвала, сама себе свидетель;
> Хоть мир обрушится, бесстрашну поразит. (8:344)
> [Virtue alone sees with perspicacity; / Amid thunder and storms it stands unmovable, / Praise unto itself, witness unto itself; / Even if the world crumbled, it would remain fearless.]

While it might seem from this that virtue stands alone, as will be argued at greater length in the next chapter, in eighteenth-century Russia, virtue was not its own reward—it still had to be seen, staged, and appreciated. Still, the divine perspective remained the ultimate criterion of value, because God's vision is by definition perfect and uniform:

> Свет можно обмануть, но Бога никогда.
> Злодейство перед ним злодейство есть всегда. (Trag. 481)
> [The world may be deceived, but God—never. / Evildoing to him is always evildoing.]

Nevertheless, virtue demands to be seen in classicist tragedy, whose fundamental mission—however isolationist the sentiments it may have at times expressed—is to reveal the retrospectively mirrored self in a very public way, to put its innermost values out on stage so that they could be seen and their nobility appreciated.

## Psychology and Physiognomy

Greatness of soul is revealed in situations of psychological stress, although the use of the word "psychology" with reference to classicist tragedy—and to the eighteenth-century Russian conception of the self in general—requires qualification. There was no notion yet of the "psyche" as unconscious arbiter of action, and questions of motivation that arose referred rather to the qualities and status of the soul (*dusha*), so-called "pneumatology," and thus fell into a category of philosophy and metaphysics.[42] In theater and beyond, the driving forces behind human behavior were all to be seen on the surface, and the motives that contemporary thinkers might discuss in terms of deep or hidden psychological conflicts were conceptualized, rather, as moral ones, choices that defined different categories of "soul"—*velikodushie* versus *malodushie*—a clash between passion and reason, good and bad sight. The hidden or unseen was connected to things that were shameful and dishonorable.

Furthermore, inner qualities of soul were held to manifest themselves externally, through the eyes, the traditional "windows to the soul," and also through the face (*litso, litse, lik*), which in the Orthodox tradition had the additional connotation of reflecting one's divine image (like the face—*lik*—on an icon, an image of the divine). The ancient idea that inner qualities of character could be read in a person's looks made a dramatic comeback in the eighteenth century in the newly popular "science" of Lavater's physiognomy, which enjoyed some popularity in Russia.[43] The problem of externalized essence (and perceived disjunctions between the inner and outer self) is a common one in Russian tragedy, in which the characters typically expect physiognomy to reveal the inner truth. When Gostomysl confronts the unhappy lovers Ilmena and Truvor in Sumarokov's *Sinav and Truvor*, for example, he can quickly read the truth in their eyes:

> Написано уже на ваших мне очах;
> Сокрыто таинство во обоих сердцах. (DS 93)
> [The secret hidden in both of your hearts / Is already written for me in your eyes.]

On the other hand, in Rzhevsky's *The False Smerdius*, Otan does not realize that Smerdius [Smerdii]—who looks just like the real one—is a fake, and he cannot reconcile the man's face and soul. Someone with Smerdius's good face should act like Smerdius, in a good way:

> От самых детских лет я зрел и знал его,
> Но ныне уж не зрю в нем Смердия того.
> Вся Персия тому, весь двор и я свидетель,
> Сколь он отечество любил и добродетель,
> Сколь сердце тихое и душу он имел,
> И в свете никого он огорчать не смел,
> Написано всегда в очах его то было,
> Что сердце кроткое ему ни говорило. [. . .]
> Но днесь уж он не тот, окроме лишь лица.

Почто в нем не лице вы, боги, пременили
И лучше бы его вы душу сохранили. (Trag. 228)
[I knew and saw him from our childhood years, / But today I do not see that
Smerdius in him. / All of Persia, the entire court and I are witness / How he
loved virtue and the fatherland, / What a gentle heart and spirit he had, / And
that he never gave offense to anyone. / Whatever his humble heart dictated / Was
always written in his eyes. / (. . .) But now he is not the same, apart from his face.
/ Would it not have been better, gods, if you had made changes in his face / And
preserved his (quality of) soul?]

Similarly, in Kheraskov's *The Venetian Nun*, Zaneta comes to a judge to
plead for the life of Korans, who, it turns out, is the judge's own son. Their
resemblance suggests to her (wrongly) that the judge will have mercy on the
poor boy:

Когда имеешь ты лице с Корансом сходно,
И сердце можешь ты иметь ему подобно. [. . .]
Я, может быть, прошу гонителя его,
Обманута твоим наружным постоянством. (Trag. 346–47)
[If you have a face resembling Korans's / You may have a heart like his. (. . .)
/ Perhaps I will be able to forgive his persecutor, / Deceived as I was by your
external likeness (literally, "constancy")]

Deception poses a direct challenge to true judgment. As suggested in
the analysis of *Khorev*, the problem of seeing correctly and making the
truth manifest is central to tragedy's overall mission, as the probity of the
great soul is continually tested. This extends to the integrity of its sight, the
harmony of inner and outer, physical and spiritual vision. Many tragic plots
hinge on purposeful deceptions, as when trickery is used to usurp thrones
or conspiracy is used to overthrow them.[44] Tyrannical rule is associated
not only with bad seeing but also with attempts to mislead others's sight.
In Lomonosov's *Tamira and Selim*, for example, the evil Mamai attempts
to disguise the fact that he has been defeated by the Russians, hoping to
recoup his losses by means of an advantageous marriage. In Rzhevsky's
*The False Smerdius* and Sumarokov's *Dimitrii the Pretender*, the villains
are bogus tsars, usurpers concerned with maintaining their deception, and
the tyrannical conqueror Mstislav in *Sorena and Zamir* tries to use an evil
ruse to entrap the virtuous Polovetsian princess Sorena. In other tragedies,
plot turns often involve positive characters who are forced to use deception

and disguise for noble ends. For example, in Maikov's *Femist and Hieronima* (*Femist i Ieronima*), royal survivors of the Ottoman conquest of Constantinople pretend to be Turks in order to restore the Paleologues to power. In plays like Kheraskov's *Venetian Nun* and Sumarokov's *Artistona*, positive characters also use ruses, this time to deceive other good characters, but for altruistic motives.

Plots of deception and revelation bring the problem of seeing and being to center stage, as both great souls and evil ones debate the merits of openness and transparency. The use of deception poses a direct moral challenge for those of great soul, who in general spurn all subterfuge. In *Femist and Hieronima*, the evil Mohammed (Mogamet Vtorii, i.e., Sultan Mohammed II) has ordered his trusted servitor Soliman—who is actually Femist, of the Byzantine Comnenus (Komnin) clan in disguise—to kill Hieronima, daughter of the overthrown Paleologue emperor, for her refusal to give in to his amorous overtures. However, Hieronima is also Femist's long-lost love, and Soliman-Femist sends her away to try and save her. He wonders what he will say to Mohammed:

> Пути к спасению у нас отъяты всюду,
> И нет спасения нам больше ниоткуду! [ . . . ]
> Коль придет он сюда узреть увядший зрак,
> Скажу, что предпочла княжна сей казни брак.
> [All paths to salvation have been taken away from us, / And there is nowhere from which salvation might come! (. . .) / If he comes here to see the sight of her, lifeless, / I will say that the princess preferred marriage to execution.]

That is, that she changed her mind. But then he catches himself:

> Ах нет! такое ли твое, несчастный, свойство,
> Чтоб ты употребил обман, а не геройство?
> Такая ли, Фемист, душа тебе дана? (Trag. 295)
> [Oh, no! Is this your character, miserable one, / To use deception instead of (taking) heroic action? / Is this the sort of soul you have been given, Femist?]

A noble soul, in other words, cannot deceive. Lying, dissembling, cunning, hypocrisy, deception, flattery, betrayal (*pritvorstvo, lukavstvo, litsemerie, obman, lest', izmena*) on the outside contradict great-soul-edness (*velikodushie*) on the inside.

This is the dilemma that various other tragic protagonists also struggle with when faced with crises. Many take categorical stands, like Semira:

Тебе мой нрав знаком, притворства я гнушаюсь
И в лести никогда ни с кем не упряжняюсь. (DS 202)
[You know my ways, I abhor dissembling / And flattery is never my way
with anyone.]

Also in *Semira*, when the hero Oskold is betrayed by his kinsman
Vozved, the recipient of the intelligence, Oleg, has no sympathy for
this "abominable betrayal" (*merzkaia izmena*) and takes no note of his
repentence:

Возвед:
Став винен, государь, раскаянье творю
И заблуждение свое я ясно зрю.

Олег:
Не заблуждение, свое бездельство видишь.
Ты гнусен предо мной, коль чести ненавидишь.
(Витозару).
Отдай его на смерть. (DS 205–6)
[*Vozved*: Having been faulted, sire, I repent. / I see my delusion clearly. / *Oleg*:
No delusion—it is your worthlessness you see. / If you hate honor, I consider
you vile. / (*To Vitozar*:) / Take him away to death.]

Vozved's clear vision comes too late, while to those like Oleg and Semira
the light of truth is immediate and unmistakable. There are many similar
moments in classicist tragedy where the great soul is disgusted and
indignant at the sight of evil. Aspafin, for example, gives eloquent vent to
the Persians' noble anger at being ruled over by the counterfeit Smerdius,
the sight of whom they find intolerable:

Возможно ль вобразить,—о солнце, ты свидетель,—
Чтоб под являющим сим видом добродетель
Толь гнусная душа, скрываяся, жила.
[Can one imagine—oh sun, you are my witness— / That in the guise of virtue /
Such a foul soul was living in concealment?]

He accuses Otan—wrongly—of participating in the deception:

На старость лет своих, на сан свой невзирая,

И стыд, и долг, и честь, и совесть презирая,

Отечество в обман старался уловлять;

Чтоб похищенной власть державы разделять.

Как сыном Персии назваться можешь боле,

Коль терпишь хищника на здешнем ты престоле?

И как ты допустил, в украденном венце

Чтоб Персию тягчил он, Смердия в лице? (Trag. 230)

[In your older years, despising your rank, / Disdaining shame, duty, and honor, and conscience / You tried to enmesh the fatherland in deception, / To divide up the power of a pilfered kingdom. / How can you still be called a son of Persia / If you can tolerate a predator on our throne? / And how could you let him, in the person of Smerdius, / Oppress Persia in a stolen crown?]

And later:

Друзья, какой позор, что днесь на Киров трон

Взошел мидянин-волхв и нами правит он.

О персы храбрые! Какое поношенье!

Мы терпим стыд, позор и ото всех презренье.

И тот ли здесь народ толико робок стал,

Которым прежде Кир вселенну устрашал? (Trag. 233)

[Friends, what a disgrace, that a Midian sorcerer / Would ascend to Cyrus (Kir)'s throne and rule us. / O brave Persians! What an abomination! / We tolerate shame, disgrace, and disdain from everyone. / Has that people with whom Cyrus terrified the universe / Now become so timid?]

Again, the problem is conceptualized in terms of sight (imagining, witnessing, guise, hiding, disgrace, disdain) centering on how one is seen by others, the dishonor of having a "foul soul" on the throne that is witnessed by the world.

In the case of frustrated love, Truvor suggests a fairly benign type of deception: he suggests that he and Ilmena avoid the world's scrutiny and run away to live "in the desert" (i.e., uninhabited places, in the Russian context, usually, in the forest).[45] Ilmena, however, takes an uncompromising stand against what she sees as hypocrisy:

Колико тщится днесь Ильмена лицемерить!

Хотя бы я клялась, никто не будет верить.

Как я тебя люблю, не можно вобразить,

Нельзя никак любви сильнее заразить,

Что скоро действие, мой князь, тебе покажет,

И кто-нибудь когда о том тебе расскажет.

Правители небес, которых так мы чтим,

Хотят того, чтоб мы уподоблялись им.

Явлюся дочерью геройскою в народе

И, победив себя, дам действовать природе.

Хоть мя в порочну жизнь она не вовлечет,

Но злополучие конечно пресечет. (DS 110)

[However much Ilmena would now dissemble (it would fail)! / Even if I would swear, no one would believe it. / How much I love you, you cannot imagine, / It is totally impossible to be more infected by love, / As soon my actions, prince, will show, / And as someday someone will relate to you. / The rulers of the heavens whom we so revere / Want us to emulate them. / I am (or: I appear to be) a heroic daughter among the people / And, conquering myself, allow nature to act. / Although it will not entice me to a life of vice, / Misfortune may well make mine a short one.]

Ilmena is unable to *litsemerit'* (dissemble, be hypocritical—literally, "to measure [i.e., adjust] her face"). Her heroic, reasoning self—here aligned with "nature"—overcomes her "infected," passionate self that would "entice her to a life of vice" by ignoring duty to family, state, and people. Furthermore, she suggests, her noble ways are so obvious that no one would accept such a change in character. An ignominious escape, or hiding oneself away, would be a shameful act of *malodushie*, and from the point of view of the divine, all-seeing light of virtue, impossible. Ilmena explicitly emulates the gods in her resolution to reveal rather than conceal, to be honorable, open, and honest, and the conception of her position offers a microcosm of the tragic stage as a "universal theater of fame." Ilmena presumes that she is acting within a divine, transparent context, one in which good and evil acts preserve their face value.

Many other great souls also resolutely refuse to compromise on this, and staunchly maintain their consistency of character and unity of purpose, at times even unto death. Otan in *The False Smerdius* takes this stance:

Не должно говорить неправды и врагу,

Я сделать никогда притворства не могу. (Trag. 234)

[One should not speak untruth even to an enemy. / I can never dissemble.]

However, this does not keep him from engaging in political conspiracy. Others, like Femist, who questioned the heroism of deception, accede to the double negative argument that justifies the use of evil against evil, deception against deception. Femist's earlier compunction against pretense, by the way, might have seemed somewhat misplaced, considering that he had spent the past five years since the fall of Constantinople masquerading as Soliman in order to overthrow those whom he served! Femist, who had rejected deception even though he had seen no quarter "from which salvation might come," subsequently agreed to the idea to entrap Mohammed by using guile. His justification is that two wrongs can make a right when the context is one of universal evil and deception, and the motive so fair:

Сим можем мы одним прервать народно бедство.

Не должно ль, чтоб тому я лестию отмщал,

Кто лестию своей других владык прельщал

И клятвой Греции падение составил?

Чрез хитрости его нас целый свет оставил;

Он пропасть нам сию лукавством ископал,

Так должно, чтоб в сию он пропасть сам ниспал.

Теперь все способы к отмщению имея,

Восстанем и пойдем на лютого злодея!

Прельстим прельстившего обманами весь свет,

Пойдем и свободим народ от лютых бед.

Коль будет моея свет хитрости свидетель,

Он хитрость такову почтет за добродетель,

Которой варвара я области лишу. (Trag. 299)

[By this means alone can we end the people's misfortune. / Is it not proper that the one upon whom I took revenge by means of flattery / Was the one who enticed other sovereigns with flattery / And oaths, and caused Greece's fall? / Due to his cunning the whole world abandoned us; / He dug a pit for us with craftiness / So is it not appropriate that he himself fall down into it? / Let us rise up and attack this cruel villain! / Let us entice the one who enticed the whole world with deceptions, / Let us go and free the people from cruel misfortune. / If the world will be witness to my cunning, / It will consider such cunning to be virtue / By which I deprive the barbarian of his domain.]

While deception is plotted, and sight thus thwarted, "the whole world," which had been deceived, will nevertheless bear witness that this deception/ counter-deception is actually virtue—that from a superior, objective, or external standpoint, the context of the action makes all of the difference in evaluating it.

One of the strongest justifications for the use of deception is made by Shuisky in *Dimitrii the Pretender*. He needs to convince his daughter Ksenia to go along with his plan to humor the tyrant while secretly plotting his overthrow. He asserts that

> Когда имеем мы с тираном сильным дело,
> Противоречити ему не можем смело.
> Обман усилился на трон его венчать;
> Так истина должна до времени молчать,
> Доколь низвержется сие с России бремя. [. . .]
> Кто силе уступать при нужде не умеет,
> В развратном мире жить понятья не имеет. (DS 257 and 267)
> [When we are dealing with a powerful tyrant / We cannot boldly contradict him. / Deception became strong enough to place him on the throne, / So truth must be silent until such time / As this burden falls from Russia. (. . .) / A person who is unable to yield to necessity / Has no idea of how to live in the perverse world.]

"In the perverse world" where deception reigns, one must not contradict a tyrant, like the world of betrayed love that Malmira imagines in *Artistona*, in which "the world is full of deceit, and fidelity has entirely vanished!" ("svet obmanom poln, i vernost' vsia propala!" [DS 136]). Like Ilmena, Semira, and others quoted above, Georgii and Ksenia of *Dimitrii the Pretender* have "no inkling of how to live" in such a world. This is what makes them heroic; deception—hiding their love and feigning indifference—goes against their characters:

**Георгий:**
> Скрывайся в сердце ты, горячая любовь,
> Престань воспламенять мою кипящу кровь
> И нежным перестань ея прельщаться взглядом,
> Дабы не стал тебе взгляд сей смертельным ядом!
> Умолкни, страсть моя, и нужде покорись,
> Жар, пламень мой, во хлад и в стужу претворись!
> Скрывайтесь, нежности, колико станет мочи!

**Ксения:**

> Взирайте на него без нежности вы, очи,—
> Не прежние текут минуты сладких дней,—
> И соглашайтеся с притворностью моей! [. . .]
> И верностью к нему не востревожьте мысли! (DS 269–70)
> [*Georgii*: Hide yourself away in my heart, fiery love, / Cease inflaming my boiling blood / And stop being tempted by her tender glance, / So that this glance does not turn into fatal poison for you! / Be silent, my passion, and submit to necessity. / Fever, flame of mine, turn to cold and frost! / Hide away, endearments, as strength allows! / *Ksenia*: Look upon him without tenderness, you eyes— / These are not the former minutes of our sweet days— / And comply with my simulation! (. . .) / Do not trouble me with thoughts of loyalty to him!]

Both reluctantly agree to try their best, because as Georgii has noted:

> Язык мой должен я притворству покорить,
> Иное чувствовать, иное говорить
> И быти мерзостным лукавцам я подобен.
> Вот поступь, если царь неправеден и злобен. (DS 258)
> [I must make my tongue submit to pretense, / To feel differently, to speak differently, / And be like a despicable swindler. / This is how to behave if the tsar is unjust and malicious.]

Georgii, like many other such reluctant deceivers, proves unable to keep up the charade for long. Simulation is especially hard for the great soul when it involves deceiving a lover. For instance, when Artistona explains why she used a letter to reject Otan in order to save him rather than going in person:

> Могла ль бы я сокрыть,
> Отказ ему сказав, презрение притворно,
> И зря его, начать с ним речь вдруг толь упорно?
> Притворство таково толь тяжче всех наук,
> Коль тяжче всех мое мученье лютых мук.
> Искусство лютое сердец окамененных
> И человечества бесстудием лишенных! [. . .]
> Хотя, природа, ты дала мне чистый дух,
> Но по всему о мне пройдет народу слух,
> Что я тому, кого как душу я любила,

Для славолюбия бесстыдно изменила. (DS 149)

[Telling him of my rejection, / Could I have pretended, feigned disdain, / And, seeing him, had the strength to keep it up? / Such deception is hardest of all the arts, / Just as my suffering is the worst of cruel torments. / [This is] the cruelest art, that of hearts turned to stone / And, lacking shame, divested of humanity! / (. . .) / Although you, nature, gave me a pure spirit / The rumor will go out among the people / That for the love of fame I shamelessly betrayed / The one I loved like my own soul.]

Words—in Artistona's case, notably, dictated by an evil third party—are more malleable and less trustworthy than sight, and as in the present instance can quickly translate into false rumor (*slukh*, literally, hearing). The loss of face is almost unbearable for the pure spirit, as Artistona appears to join the company of dishonorable tyrants, inhuman beasts, and evil barbarians. Yet from the higher perspective, "Izmenu mnimuiu liubov' proizvela" ("Love produced sham betrayal") (DS 148)—this is only a deceptive deception, a pretended pretence, a negated negation. As another character justifies her actions at the end of the play, "Ona prinuzhdena byla nevernoi byt'" (DS 183)—she was forced to be untrue.

Furthermore, the more one appreciates its necessity, the more such pretended pretence may appear an attribute of the great soul. As Gikarn urges Artistona,

Спасай любовника, кажися быть спокойна
И буди своего родителя достойна.
Великодушие такое возыметь,
Чтоб горесть крайнюю подать спокойствам зреть,
В которой рвется дух, ослабевает тело,
Не дев и не мужей—одних героев дело. (DS 151)

[Save your beloved, appear to be tranquil, / And be worthy of your parent. / Assume such magnanimity / That you will be able to make extreme grief— / That which rends the spirit, and saps the body— / Be seen by others as serenity. / This is a deed for heroes alone, not mere men and women.]

Here, to deceive others' sight is *velikodushie*, heroism, fidelity to family. The use of deception is necessary, rational, and noble, and the choice that Gikarn presents Artistona is analogous to many others in which reason must overcome passion for love to function according to a higher logic.[46]

## Tyrannical Delights

Deception poses a different set of concerns for "foul souls," in particular, for bad rulers, for whom seeing and being is not so much a problem of ethics or self-image as one of tactics, and in this context touches on some of the central political issues of the period. The binary context is in full force. On the one hand, Pantiziv reminds the false Smerdius, even while he advises him how best to deceive, that tsars cannot have secrets; the sight of truth will eventually be revealed:

> Не мни, чтоб тайность мог иметь ты в жизни сей.
> Нет сокровенного в чертогах у царей. (Trag. 246)
> [Do not think that you can keep a secret in this life. / Nothing can be hidden in a tsar's chambers.]

On the other hand, in the anti-world of the tyrant, deception is everywhere, and the truth universally persecuted. Otan describes the situation in the same play:

> Все здесь отечество, любезный друг мой, страждет
> И тщетно помощи себе в напастях жаждет;
> Кого оно себе считает за отца,
> В том видит своего мучения творца.
> Везде лазутчики рассыпаны по граду,
> Как волки хищные, скитаются по стаду,
> И ищут, чтоб кого поймать и уязвить
> И чтоб какий донос сыскать и объявить. (Trag. 228)
> [The entire fatherland is suffering, my dear friend, / And thirsts in vain for help in its misfortunes; / The one it considers as its father / Is seen as the cause of its torment. / Spies are scattered all about the city / Like predatory wolves wandering through the flock, / Searching for someone to catch and attack, / And for denunciations to find and publish.]

In this anti-utopian setting, what makes the good cry makes the evil laugh, and if love is a consolation or delight (*utekh, uteshenie*) for lovers, for bad rulers it is evil that consoles:

> Мук зрение и слух мучителям есть смех,
> И всех приятнее тиранских им утех.
> [. . .] мучителям скорбящих житие

Приятно зрелище, и слезы, питие. (DS 146 and 155)
[The sight and sound of torments is a laugh for tormentors, / And for them the more tyrannical, the more pleasant. / (. . .) for tormentors the life of those who sorrow / Is a pleasant spectacle, and their tears, nectar.]

Similarly, as Sorena says to Mstislav, "Your joy is to inspire terror among the people" ("Tvoe veselie—rozhdat' v narode strakh" [Trag. 477]), and Osnelda challenges her beloved Khorev to come to her rescue, bitterly telling him to "Look and be joyful at my sufferings" ("Smotri i veselis' stradaniiami moimi" [DS 52]).

As evil predators seek to root out the good, and see evil everywhere, they can never feel secure in this anti-world of deceptions. Hieronima taunts Mohammed, who seeks his hidden enemy Femist, with the idea that the sight of tyrants will always be untrustworthy:

Коль хочешь ты сего героя познавати,
Так должен ты, тиран, здесь всех подозревати,
Подозревати ты весь должен будешь свет,
Сыскать тебе его иного средства нет;
Живуши греки внутрь и вне престольна града—
Все мстители и все суть Комниновы чада. (Trag. 308)
[If you want to recognize who this hero is / Then you, tyrant, must suspect everyone here, / You must suspect the entire world, / There is no other means left to you to find him; / Greeks living within and outside the capital city / All seek revenge and are all progeny of the Comneni.]

In a perverse context great souls may use false appearances righteously (to be seen wrongly), tyrants have no choice but to see badly, to see evil wherever they look (*podozrevat'*, to suspect, literally suggesting "to see from under," in an underhanded way).

Deceptive (and defective) sight, then, is a fundamental feature of tyranny:

Сие являет нам тиранское правленье,
Что он готов всегда на казни и мученье.
Коль царь сомнителен о подданных своих,
Знать, судит по себе, имея зло на них. (Trag. 228)
[This displays tyrannical rule to us, / That is always ready to use repression and torment. / If the tsar is unsure of his subjects, / It means he judges by himself, and has evil intentions for them.]

In contrast, for the good ruler:

> Политика царей не есть закон коварства,
> Но добродетели и целость государства. (Trag. 481)
> [The policy of (good) tsars is not the law of cunning, / But the virtue and safety of the state.]

While deception and bad seeing are thus fundamental features of tyrants, they do not extend to self-deception, at least not in the usual modern sense of the term. While a ruler may be in error (as Kii was in *Khorev*), or even be a creature of deception—a false tsar and usurper, as in the case of the False Smerdius and Dimitrii the Pretender—this is self-comprehended evil, in a way that may jar or even seem contradictory to the modern reader.[47] Dimitrii represents the culmination of this kind of foul soul and the epitome of the self-defeating logic of illogic. Although a "pretender," he does not pretend; the Russian here is *samozvanets*, literally, "self-called" or "self-proclaimed," and he—like other evil rulers in Russian tragedy—openly declares and justifies his evil. When Ksenia challenges his statement that all people are evil and worthy of punishment, and asks if he includes himself in their number, he responds that

> Когда бы менее самолюбив я был,
> Давно б Димитрия Димитрий погубил,
> И если б было льзя с собою разделиться,
> Я стал бы мукою своею веселиться,
> Готовый сам себе в мученьи сострадать
> И на отчаянье отчаян соглядать. (DS 277)[48]
> [If I loved myself less (or: If I were less prideful), / Dimitrii would long ago have destroyed Dimitrii, / And were it possible for me to split myself, / I would enjoy torturing myself, / Ready to pity myself in my torment / And despairing to spy on despair.]

Here is a kind of inverted mirroring, a glorying not in jubilation but in despair, and an embrace not of self-display and triumphant existence but of negation and self-oblivion. In theological terms, evil is depicted here—to borrow the Grand Inquisitor's description of the devil from *The Brothers Karamazov*—as "the spirit of self-destruction and nonexistence [*nebytie*, oblivion]."[49] In Dimitrii the logical contradiction of evil is laid bare as the principle of deception in its paradoxically self-comprehended, "non-deceived" essence. If for a noble soul, suicide may represent a positive assertion of virtue, a negation of the world's evil, in Dimitrii's case it represents the inverse: the self-destructive nature of evil made manifest.[50] Just as sight and the good (or love) are linked, so are their opposites: evil, hatred, and not-seeing.

## Conclusion: The Case of *Vadim of Novgorod*

The analysis so far has centered on the retrospectively idealized synchronic image of selfhood in classicist tragedy. The question remains to what extent Russian theater was able to go beyond mirror-stage subjectivism to become more genuinely "historical" and self-reflexive. This question is not easily answered. Among the central issues that come up here are the plays' relation to politics and the nature of the conflicts with authority that they dramatize.[51] Russian classicist tragedies are generally set within an autocratic context, whether described in terms of monarchy, despotism, or tyranny—labels that echoed eighteenth-century European debates over the nature of the Russian political system, starting with Montesquieu.[52] This contrasts with Western European classicist drama whose political focus was often on Republican Rome, for example, Corneille's *Horace* and *Cinna*, Addison's *Cato*, Voltaire's *Brutus, Cataline, The Death of Caesar*, and so on.[53] Soviet attempts to read Russian classicist tragedy as politically oppositionist are misdirected; autocracy generally serves as the political context and not the target of Russian classicist tragedy.[54] Clearly, one important issue here has to do with the radically changed political and cultural climate that resulted from the French Revolution and the Napoleonic invasion; after this era no more classicist tragedies were written, and the subsequent Russian theatrical tradition repudiated their legacy.[55] A well-known episode highlights this interpretive shift: the striking about-face on the part of the plays' main reader, Catherine the Great. Her changing responses to historical drama suggest both the crucial role of the cultural context in gauging a play's intentions, and how sharply that context could change.

In 1785 the Moscow Governor-General Count Ia. A. Bruce (Brius) came to Catherine advising her to ban Nikolev's *Sorena and Zamir* from the stage due to its harsh criticism of the despotic Tsar Mstislav, which, as seen above, included the justification of tyrannicide. The empress replied, "I am surprised, Count Iakov Aleksandrovich, that you want to halt the presentation of a tragedy, evidently received with pleasure by the entire public. The idea of the verses that you pointed out has no relationship to your Sovereign. The author attacks the willfulness (*samovlastie*) of tyrants, while you call Catherine your mother."[56] Catherine's response—clearly meant for public consumption—

is remarkable in several respects. First of all, it acknowledges the authority of public opinion and of the theater, as Catherine even aligns herself with its values (as "mother" and protector rather than as autocrat and tyrant).[57] Secondly, she accepts the "social contract" or interpretive community implied in, and created by, Russian theater, subscribing to both the expectation of its rights and its demands on her as a good tsar. Catherine acknowledges the validity and autonomy of the public, but at the same time insists that its interests are identical to hers (or rather, that they fully acknowledge her as their well-meaning mother). Catherine's own discourse aligns her with the utopian image of the ideal tsar and, more pointedly, the ideal mother, allowing her children their innocent entertainments but denying any alienating hostility or political conflict of interest. She allies herself with the value system of tragic drama, associating herself with the Great Man and viewing the fallen world of tragedy as an alien zone that "has no relationship to your Sovereign." Her response represents the height of *velikodushie*.

The potentially harsh political message inherent in many of these plays depicting evil tyrants could thus be deflected by the plays' own presumption that the "perverse world" they depicted was precisely that, an inversion of existing reality. This allowed Catherine to deny allegorical readings and any direct relevance to existing political conditions. But while she implicitly accepts the right of the public sphere to render judgment, there is also a presumption—marked by Catherine's expression of surprise at Bruce's suspicions—that criticisms of her rule are implausible, both because of the acknowledgement of her maternal status and perhaps also her subjects' not fully mature development—that psychologically the theater functioned, to use Wirtschafter's phrase, "like children's play."[58]

Politics, of course, colors our own judgment, and this is perhaps the larger point: what one sees depends on how one sees. Over time readers' assumptions and cultural context—and hence the meanings gleaned from a work of literature—significantly change. With the onset of the French Revolution, the interpretive context was radically transformed, and Catherine executed a political volte-face, marked by her well-known acts of repression and censorship, including the arrest and exile of Novikov and Radishchev and the public burning of Ia. B. Kniazhnin's posthumously published tragedy *Vadim of Novgorod* (*Vadim Novgorodskii*) in 1793. The change of direction and repressive acts signaled (and indeed encouraged) a new perspective from which the old moral and political certainties were subject to radical reinterpretation, so that the plays could now be read as attacks on the empress's tyranny. It became all too easy to spot covert allegorical connections between Catherine and literary villains. Lines from Rzhevsky's *The False Smerdius* of 1769 cited earlier could now sound quite different than at the time they were written:

> Сие являет нам тиранское правленье,
> Что он готов всегда на казни и мученье.
> Коль царь сомнителен о подданных своих,
> Знать, судит по себе, имея зло на них. (Trag. 228)
> [Here we have a display of tyrannical rule, / That he (the tyrant) is always ready to kill and torture. / If a tsar is unsure of his subjects, / It means he judges by himself, and has evil intentions for them.]

The case of Kniazhnin's *Vadim of Novgorod* is particularly indicative of this problem insofar as its intention—or "message"—seems inseparable from how one perceives the cultural and interpretive context. As opposed to Novikov, who was not arrested for any palpable treasonous activity, and to Radishchev, whose *Journey from St. Petersburg to Moscow* did more or less directly challenge Catherine's legitimacy, Kniazhnin's position in *Vadim of Novgorod* is much harder to pin down and remains the subject of disagreement. The play juxtaposes Vadim to Riurik, a Varangian outsider who has taken over monarchial power in Novgorod to quell civil disturbance, having done away with the city's traditional republican rule at its citizens' own bidding. Vadim returns after a military campaign and vehemently rejects Riurik's legitimacy as well as his daughter Ramida's desire to become his queen. He refuses to accept Riurik's magnanimity even after military defeat at his hands and instead chooses suicide. As Andrew Wachtel has argued, the issue was complicated by the fact that Catherine herself had used the subject allegorically in her own plays that were labeled "imitations of Shakespeare" and that had explicitly broken with classicist dramatic conventions.[59] Wachtel argues that in Catherine's plays "we are meant to see Riurik as an ideal despot of the type Catherine fancied herself . . . Catherine's play illustrates, allegorically if you like, . . . that a foreigner is perfectly fit to rule Russia, assuming that this foreigner is an enlightened ruler. . . . The play then is, in great measure, about the legitimacy of autocracy and particularly of a foreign-born autocrat."[60] Furthermore, Wachtel stresses that the empress was fashioning what he calls an "intergeneric dialogue" between her plays and her more strictly historical *Notes on Russian History* that had covered the same material. That is, Catherine was taking greater liberties in her plays than the historical record itself would allow, and by this repetition she was calling attention to what she was doing. I. N. Boltin's preface that accompanied the 1791 and 1793 editions of Catherine's play *From the Life of Riurik* and the German translation stated that the play "is not composed of fabricated events but of real and true events," and Catherine herself asserted in the introduction to *The Start of Oleg's Reign* that "there is more historical truth than invention" in it.[61] Yet as Wachtel argues, invention was still clearly evident, and Catherine was consciously basing the play on conjectures that were out of place in her history.[62]

Scholars have traditionally assumed that Catherine's harsh reaction to *Vadim of Novgorod* was due to its political content. Wachtel, however, sides with those who have judged the play politically inoffensive, and suggests that Catherine "was more angered by the literary and historical polemic [around Riurik—that is, that Kniazhnin disputed her interpretation of the episode] . . . than she was by the work's ambiguous political content."[63] This seems at best an exaggeration, as it is hard to gainsay Catherine's own references to *Vadim* as "the second work of a dangerous kind that had been published [i.e., after Radishchev's *Journey*]."[64] But it is possible to frame the issue differently: Catherine had herself opened the door to criticism both by underscoring the allegorical nature of her plays and—even more so—by allegorizing her own rule; Catherine's own plays and the allegorical reading she encouraged publicly highlighted the question of her own legitimacy.[65] In this context any deviation from her self-glorifying historical image (whether intentional or not) would likely be headed for trouble, especially in the retrospective light of the French Revolution and Radishchev's *Journey*.

The grounds for Catherine's displeasure remain problematic insofar as ever since its banning, critics of *Vadim* have disagreed on its political message, whether (in the words of its first publisher, Princess Dashkova), the play "was less dangerous to sovereigns than many a French tragedy acted at the Hermitage"[66] or whether, as many later readers including the Decembrists have felt, the play was outspokenly anti-autocratic. William Edgerton has taken this dispute one step further, arguing that *Vadim*'s divided reception as either innocuous and pro-autocratic or revolutionary and pro-democratic reflects the fact that "the presentation of the conflict between Riurik and Vadim may [itself] have been deliberately and artistically ambivalent."[67] In *Vadim*, he argues,

> both Riurik and Vadim are portrayed in very positive terms. His tragedy is a dramatization of the conflict between two political principles [enlightened monarchy and republicanism]. . . . In the whole tragedy there are no negative characters, no villains. . . . As Kniazhnin's formulation of the problem shows, each argument is incomplete and one-sided. Vadim rightly maintains that

autocracy is bad because power corrupts, but he fails to explain how the
Novgorodians could have prevented the abuse of their liberties that led to the
collapse of the Republic. Riurik, for his part, demonstrates in word and deed
that he has proved himself an enlightened, just, and virtuous ruler, uncorrupted
so far by his power and beloved by his subjects; but he fails to explain how an
autocratic system can provide protection to the people against less virtuous, less
incorruptible rulers.[68]

Such ambiguity—the clash of irreconcilable truths—is on some level
inherent in the zero-sum confrontations that make up the substance of
classicist tragedy. As in the case of the parental versus political allegiances
with which so many classicist protagonists struggle, binary oppositions
easily segue from opposing values marked as good and bad to the opposition
of two truths. In Kniazhnin's play, Vadim's daughter Ramida is torn between
obedience to her father and love for his enemy Riurik, and Edgerton argues
that this love conflict sheds light (probably unintentional) on the political
one, since Vadim the advocate of democracy acts quite despotically toward
his daughter.[69] One might add that Vadim's republicanism is less radical
than it may have sounded after 1793, insofar as Kniazhnin's play frames the
conflict in the usual terms of Russian tragedy as a clash between the power
of the monarch and that of oligarchs ("grandees" [*vel'mozhi*]), both of whom
allege to represent the people (*narod*) (see Trag. 573 and 587).[70] In *Vadim
of Novgorod*, Riurik claims election to single rule by the people, which he
restages at the end, removing his crown but being called back by popular
acclaim (a version of the so-called "calling of the Varangians," which had
been subject of great controversy for nationalist reasons).[71] In Kniazhnin's
play there is, arguably, still room for doubt, insofar as (as Edgerton asserts)
Vadim's argument that absolute power is inherently flawed and subject to
abuse is not answered (and is probably not answerable). It is only answered
in the context of the play by Riurik's noble behavior and rhetoric, which
are irreproachable.[72]

Unlike other tragedies in which the defeated father (villain) capitulates or
commits suicide and thus allows the lovers to reunite, in *Vadim* the heroine
Ramida both proves her fidelity to her father Vadim and her inability to live
without Riurik. Proclaiming "See if I am worthy of being your daughter!"
("Smotri—dostoina l' ia byt' docher'iu tvoeiu"), she stabs herself. Vadim,
who had condemned Ramida for loving Riurik, now praises Ramida as
his beloved daughter, "with truly heroic blood," and kills himself after
addressing Riurik:

В средине твоего победоносна войска,

В венце, могущий все у ног твоих ты зреть,—

Что ты против того, кто смеет умереть? (Trag. 591)

[In the midst of your victorious troops, / Crowned, and able to see everyone at your feet— / How can you defeat one who dares to die?]

Like a great soul, Vadim manifests his unconquered virtue. Riurik is left to suffer alone in his virtue, and to uphold duty and social responsibility:

Страдая, жертвой я быть должен сей стране

И, должности моей стенающий блюститель,

Чтоб быть невольником, быть должен я властитель! (Trag. 592)

[Suffering, I must sacrifice myself to the state / And, sorrowful guardian of my office, / I must be the ruler, and hence be a slave!]

Vadim and Riurik's nobility are both characterized in terms of light and dark, seeing and being seen, of the kind explored so many times in this chapter; both are characterized by *velikodushie*, by their desire to manifest virtue, and their readiness to self-sacrifice.

Edgerton's ambivalence hypothesis suggests that Kniazhnin raised the interpretive problem to a higher level, questioning the basis of political authority, and that the answers that are offered leave room for doubt. Even if Riurik (representing Catherine) has maintained the highest level of virtue, for which he claims divine and human sanction as well as political transparency (in explicitly visual terms, e.g., Trag. 575), Vadim argues that single-person rule leaves the door open to abuse. From this perspective, the play does not offer easy answers to the political dilemma, but demands of the audience a measure of deliberation and mature judgment. Significantly, the allegorical substance of the political problem centers not only on Catherine's legitimacy, but also on the people's capacity for self-governance. Riurik defends his legitimacy as the choice of the people, who demanded that he accept the throne, as well as on the basis of his own dedicated observance of the laws, while Vadim denounces the people's servility and lack of civic awareness.[73] As Edgerton suggests, the choice is offered between autocracy that is potentially but not yet despotic, and republicanism that is unready to assume the burden of self-rule. In this sense, *Vadim of Novgorod* suggests that classicist tragedy was on the cusp of realizing something truly *tragic* (in the ancient sense of the loss of certainties), going beyond the solipsistic mirror stage to start to face up to harsh social-political realities and to engage the world in more complex, self-reflexive, mature ways. If this is a correct reading, the tradition of classicist tragedy breaks off just at a moment at which the threshold was ready to be crossed.[74]

# CHAPTER FIVE

# Virtue Must Advertise

## *The Ethics of Vision*

"Many consider virtue to be harsh and intolerant to human weaknesses. True, for people suffering from vice, virtue is insupportable, and they can therefore never be happy; but for those who are able to think and feel, nothing is as pleasant as virtue."
—Daskhkova, "On True Well-Being" (1783)[1]

The focus of previous chapters has been the images of the jubilant self in triumphal odes and the heroic self retrospectively projected back into history in tragedy, which offered a validation of an ideal self exalted by tragic circumstances. In this chapter the analysis is extended to apply the values expressed in tragedy to the sphere of ethics and self-representation. In this sphere as well, eighteenth-century Russian ocularcentrism brought together strands of Orthodox, classical Roman, and contemporary Enlightenment thought. Russian self-image of the age was profoundly marked by a substantively new requirement that was central to early modern sociability: the need to be seen and approved.[2]

Self-display—so central to the theatricalism that was examined in the previous chapter, which celebrated virtue on stage—was a prominent feature of eighteenth-century culture in general, from lavish court ceremonial, to architecture, urban planning, landscape gardening, clothing, and the fine arts. These gave visible proof of Russia's imperial grandeur, demanding recognition of national greatness to vie with that of the rest of Europe. Beyond a simple marker of power and viability, visual display also played a key role on the level of psychology and ethics, according to the conviction that (to put it baldly) *virtue must advertise*. Moral philosophy helped to ground the self and the desire for visibility in ethical terms, as it translated the ideal of the tragic stage into universal values and justified the ideal self projected by the mirror stage. Autobiography, on the other hand, represented an arena in which these ethical imperatives were put to the test, describing the struggle for virtue in everyday life. They provided a forum in which virtue insufficiently rewarded in the present could look to the validation of posterity.

## Classicist Autobiography

Autobiography by its very nature starkly forefronts the writer's self, and the two major Russian eighteenth-century examples of this genre examined here, Derzhavin's *Zapiski* (*Notes*) and Dashkova's *Mon histoire*, are both notorious for their outspoken self-promotion and apologetics. These works dramatically highlight one of the key problems to which all life writing is subject. As H. M. Hyde has described Dashkova's memoirs, they "possess all the faults of the mass of autobiographical writings. They are incomplete, partial, and inaccurate; they exaggerate the significance of many incidents, while minimizing that of many others; they lack proportion; and many most important statements of fact which they contain require to be tested by reference to external authorities. They must therefore be read with caution."[3] Of all types of self-representation, life writing, which offers up the writer to the judgment of the public and posterity, is arguably most prone to, and perhaps inevitably tainted with, personal bias and self-serving distortions. But for that very reason, memoirs like those of Dashkova and Derzhavin offer a remarkable projection of the authors' ideal self-image. It is the very "faults" of these memoirs (the fictionalizing to which all autobiography is subject[4]) that turns whatever weakness of memory or historical accuracy there may be into all the more eloquent exercises in self-imaging.[5] Derzhavin's and Dashkova's memoirs not only offer striking evidence of the Russian classicist autobiographical self, but also exemplify the ocularcentric cultural imperative to make virtue visible.[6]

Dashkova and Derzhavin were leading literary and cultural representatives of Catherinean Russia, a period when visibility, and the visibility of virtue, took on an especially important role in cultural consciousness.[7] Simon Dixon has contrasted Foucault's analysis of Bentham's "panopticon" as a model for the nineteenth-century state's control of its citizens by surveillance to the early modern world of Catherine the Great where "it was the sovereign rather than the subject whose visibility mattered most."[8] The visibility of virtue was a particular priority for Catherine, who came to the throne as a usurper, regicide, non-Russian, a woman, and someone born out of the faith. As Anthony Lentin has written, "A good reputation was not just flattering to her ambition; it was essential to her security. It was for this reason that Catherine was among the first rulers in modern times to place propaganda—the deliberate cultivation of a public image—in the forefront of her policy, and the first ruler to employ the press on a continental scale in support of this image."[9] Virtually her entire reign may be seen as a quest to justify her right to rule, which was founded on the Enlightenment argument that put merit and virtue above all other qualifications and insisted on their transparency.[10] Furthermore, self-advertising served not only a legitimizing function, but also may be seen as a key to the moral values of the age, the staking of a claim to greatness and immortality.[11]

Dashkova and Derzhavin were of the cohort that made their careers during Catherine's rule. They were almost exact contemporaries, born in 1743 less than four months apart, and their fame and fortune were famously linked with Catherine, Dashkova by having helped her seize the throne in 1762, and Derzhavin by his poetry of the 1780s dedicated to the empress, which brought him literary renown and important government offices.[12] Princess Dashkova had been born into the highest nobility, goddaughter to Empress Elizabeth and Peter III, and made her reputation early by participating in Catherine's coup; Catherine later appointed her the first woman head of the Academy of Sciences and founder of the Russian Academy. Derzhavin's path to success, in contrast, was slow and difficult, starting from modest beginnings and followed by long years of obscurity including eleven years in the army. Dashkova and Derzhavin's memoirs were both written late in life, less than ten years apart, and offer elaborate retrospective justifications of their lives and actions, attempting to rescue their public images from slander and misrepresentation. Dashkova's memoir is a triple defense: it is a vindication of Catherine the Great as a truly "great and enlightened empress"; an affirmation of Russian Enlightenment culture; and, not least, a justification and clarification of Dashkova's own character and historical role.[13]

In classicism, autobiography's tendency toward offering an idealized portrait of the writer dovetailed with the new philosophically informed view of the individual. As Monika Greenleaf has argued in her analysis of Catherine the Great's autobiographical writings, "autobiography was perhaps the crowning genre in the Enlightenment system of genres, a strictly verbal proof of the power of individual reasoning to overcome external obstacles, examine its own consciousness, and submit a unified vision of life to the reason of the public. It has been regarded as the site where the Western individual, liberated now by Enlightenment reason and tolerance, came fully into view."[14] Autobiography was thus an ideal arena for describing the Great Man, and both

Dashkova and Derzhavin subscribed to its ethos. Struggling to describe the "peculiarities & inextricable varietys" of Dashkova's contradictory character, Catherine Wilmot observed that "For my part I think she would most be in her element at the *Helm of the State*, of Generalissimo of the Army, or Farmer General of the Empire. In fact she was born for business on a large scale which is not irreconcilable with the Life of a Woman who at 18 headed a Revolution & who for 12 years afterwards govern'd an Academy of Arts & Sciences."[15]

This is also quite evident from *Mon histoire*. Dashkova constructs and defends a powerful, charismatic, intellectually impressive public persona. Dashkova fully subscribes to the ideal of her age, defining herself in terms of the great soul or Great Man as encountered in tragedy. As the label indicates, the serious, public role she chose to emulate was culturally gendered as male; indeed, as noted earlier, the classical Roman heritage that was one of its main sources preserved an etymological linkage between the male (*vir*) and virtue (*virtus*).[16] As in classicist tragedy, greatness comes both from a lofty sense of self-conscious virtue and from fulfilling the great responsibilities that come with great power.[17] Hence the main drama of both Dashkova's and Derzhavin's life writing centers on their actions for the public good, their life of service to Russia, to the throne, and to divine truth. As in tragedy, the conflicts mostly revolve around the king and court intrigues, and involve overcoming serious obstacles so that the truth may triumph. In autocratic Russia, the profession of virtue could easily be seen as staking a claim on political power, and both Dashkova and Derzhavin had repeated minor clashes with Catherine and her other courtiers over what they perceived as ignoble, unworthy, or dishonest behavior; unlike Catherine, they scorned the politics of favoritism and compromise.[18]

Dashkova's memoir arguably centers on her public life and public image, while Derzhavin's *Zapiski* provide a painstaking defense of the writer's rocky career primarily as soldier and administrator.[19] Like Dashkova, Derzhavin insists on a strict interpretation of virtue and continually clashes with those around him who do not live up to his standards or conspire to besmirch his righteousness. Richard Wortman's comments on Derzhavin's memoirs are equally applicable to Dashkova: "their most striking characteristic for the historian . . . is Derzhvin's ego, his limitless confidence in himself, the wonderful naïve sense that his personal progress and success are identical to the cause of justice and the national well-being. This boundless self-certainty, which would be lacking in memoirs of a later era, provides the central unity and verve of the *Zapiski*."[20] Derzhavin refers to himself in the third person in the *Zapiski*, creating the impression that he is admiring himself in a mirror, and underscoring the paradoxical combination of self-effacement and self-promotion also seen in Dashkova.[21] This is more than quaint idiosyncrasy, however, as Wortman seems to suggest; like Dashkova, Derzhavin subscribes to the impossible demands of the great soul, which is marked by purity of intention, blamelessness, incorruptibility, and the absence of self-interest.[22]

## The Defense of Pride

In Enlightenment ethical thought, the desire for approbation immediately raised the specter of sinful pride. Sumarokov's short essay "Letter on Pride" ("Pis'mo o gordosti") of 1759 outlines the problem. Here is the entire text:

> Pride is the mother of all vices, both in nature and according to the revelation of Holy Writ. Because of this the enemy of God and of the human race has been deprived of mercy for all time. Pride is the daughter of self-love [*samoliubie*], which is the basis for all of our actions, good and bad. Virtue is the source of the love of fame [*slavoliubie*], while vanity comes from pride. It has only the same appearance [*edinyi vid*] as the love of fame. All admirable deeds are born of the love of fame, while vanity gives birth to shameful deeds. From the first comes utility, from the second injury. The fame-loving person is a friend to his neighbor, while the vain one is his neighbor's enemy. The first does not bar the way to well-being for other worthy people, while the second hates [*nenavidit*] worthiness, and as far as he can obstructs the path to well-being. The first is intent on service to the fatherland, the other—like Aesop's ass dressed in a lion skin, forgetting his natural condition—tries to shine based on nothing. The first serves the fatherland, and encourages others to do so, [while] the other is a parasite, and makes useful activity repugnant to people, so that they too try to get their daily bread for nothing. A rational person, even if in the highest station, cannot have pride; for it is not characteristic of good sense, but rather the first mark of illegal and insane behavior. What under the sun is greater than the Emperor? Can a person have less pride than Peter the Great and His Daughter? Yet there are people on the lowest level who are puffed up with pride like bubbles with air. Deference [*sniskhozhdenie*] in people produces zeal and love, while arrogance [*spes'*] creates repugnance and produces hatred. Improper haughtiness and immoderate baseness, like atheism and superstition, are while different in appearance nonetheless extremely similar vices; both are ignoble. And so the prideful person does not imitate the one in whose image he was created, but follows the one who, perturbed by pride, rose up against

the All-Sovereign One who possesses unbounded deference, philanthropy, and toleration; and is cast down into hell by the Master of the universe, and into eternal bondage.[23]

Sumarokov here lays out two diametrically opposed attitudes toward the prideful self. The first presents what might seem a very traditional moralistic critique of pride as "mother of all vices," worst of the seven deadly sins, ascribed at both start and finish to the devil ("the enemy of God and of the human race" and "the one . . . perturbed by pride"). Indeed, throughout the odes and the tragedies, as well as many other eighteenth-century Russian writings, pride as such—*gordost'*—has an explicitly negative meaning.[24]

Yet Sumarokov's essay almost immediately turns from the condemnation of pride as a deadly vice to a discussion of virtue, based on "the love of fame" (*slavoliubie*). Both kinds of concern for reputation derive from self-love (*samoliubie*), but even though the two may have "the same appearance" (*edinyi vid*), they are otherwise opposite. (The problem of distinguishing between the two may be a serious one, both in tragedy and in autobiography.) Self-love may give birth either to *gordost'* (bad pride, vanity, arrogance) or to a good type of pride (the love of fame) that emerges as an unequivocal good. The eighteenth-century terminology for these different brands of self-regard is slippery and inconsistent.[25] To start with, the notion of self-love—*samoliubie*—may mean a variety of things, including *amour de soi*, *amour-propre*, self-love, and even selfishness or greed, and may carry either positive or negative connotations.[26] The terms relating to "good pride" are also various and inconsistent—*slavoliubie* (the love of fame or glory), as in the essay above, and also, more commonly, *liubochestie* or *chestoliubie* (both meaning "the love of honor" and "[positive] ambition"). These terms, which are no longer used in Russian, in some cases may also carry a negative connotation.

A fundamental point Sumarokov is making in his essay is the vindication of the love of fame or of honor. While self-love (*samoliubie*) may produce the evil passion of pride (as vanity, *tshcheslavie* [literally, "vain-glory"], and social parasitism), *liubochestie* or *chestoliubie* produces "utility," "service to the fatherland" and "all admirable deeds," opening the way to "well-being for other worthy people." Similarly, in his popular *Rhetoric* (*Short Guide to Oratory*), first published in 1748 and revised in 1765, and republished seven times during the eighteenth century, Lomonosov gave detailed instructions on how to arouse in one's audience its passion for honor (both *chestoliubie* and *liubochestie*), which he defines together with honor itself as "the enjoyment of the good opinion people have of us." Among the arguments he lists to support this idea are that "esteem is the best reward for magnanimity and noble behavior; . . . all great people love honor and praise; . . . without this passion great undertakings would not be carried out, and . . . no great deed would be brought to conclusion; . . . and there is nothing, however great or difficult, that the love of honor [*chestoliubie*] cannot bring into being."[27]

Adam Smith's *Theory of Moral Sentiments* (1759), written in the same year as Sumarokov's essay on pride, offered a similar argument in defense of "good pride." Like Sumarokov, Smith asserted that self-love "frequently . . . may be a virtuous motive of action," and defended it against the charge of sinful vanity: "The desire of doing what is honorable and noble, of rendering ourselves the proper objects of esteem and approbation, cannot with any propriety be called vanity. Even the love of well-grounded fame and reputation, the desire of acquiring esteem by what is really estimable, does not deserve that name. The first is the love of virtue, the noblest and the best passion in human nature. The second is the love of true glory, a passion inferior no doubt to the former, but which in dignity appears to come immediately after it."[28] Smith clearly rates love of fame lower than love of virtue-for-virtue's-sake—yet not by very much, as long as this is "love for true glory" and for "well-grounded fame" and for "what is really estimable." (Like Sumarokov, Smith is aware of the potential for confusion between the two kinds of pride.)

In Sumarokov's essay, however, the Russian author makes an even more direct and optimistic equation between the love of fame and the love of virtue by opposing them to their sinful opposite (*gordost'*), and in the posthumously published essay, "On Godlessness and Inhumanity," he even more explicitly defends the good kind of pride. He declares that while "Bias is the tool of injustice, and the source of evildoing; the love of honor [*liubochestie*] is the tool of righteousness, and the source of virtue."[29] In the same essay Sumarokov attacks evil self-love (*samoliubie*), and connects it with the vice of *pribytochestvo*—another word no longer in use, which may mean "self-aggrandizement" or "the desire for (or act of making) profit." As opposed to the virtue of loving honor, this vice is labeled "the cause of inhumanity and all of our disquiet," a blanket assertion that seems to recall his description of pride as the mother of all vices. What links *gordost'* (bad pride) and *pribytochestvo* (the desire for gain) is precisely their common element of selfishness, self-love in the bad sense. Thus Sumarokov can connect "inhumanity, self-love and love of money" ("bezchelovechiia, samoliubie, i srebroliubie") as all the result of *pribytochestvo*, which in this instance might be better translated simply as "selfishness."

A particularly Russian aspect of Sumarokov's Enlightenment moralizing may be noted here. The notion of a larger good arising from potentially evil passion (self-love) was widely accepted during the Enlightenment, and was used to validate various modern social practices, in particular, the spread of commercial capitalism.[30] This was famously the case in Bernard Mandeville's *The Fable of the Bees or Private Vices, Publick Benefits* (1714). Mandeville's poem argued that "private vice" (selfishness) could and did serve the "public good," and even though his harsh satire, which seemed to offer an apologia for venality, put many people off, his basic argument was taken up by later thinkers from Voltaire and Pope to Kant and Adam Smith, including the latter's notion of the "invisible hand," his famous argument in defense of capitalism that the common good could result from individual self-interest.[31] In contrast to Mandeville and Smith, Sumarokov rejects the notion of "profit-making," which he considers a manifest evil that cannot lead to the public good. He thus both evinces a cultural bias against capitalist enterprise that opposes "service to the fatherland" to personal gain, and manifests the kind of zero-sum value system present in the tragedies—a view of self-love as either totally good (altruistic) or evil (selfish).

Dashkova's moral writings express much the same argument, although without the theological scaffolding. Virtue is defined as what is good for society and social good is based on enlightened self-love. In her essay "On Genuine Well Being" of 1783, for example, she wrote:

> Ranks and power are things to which self-love and the love of honor [*samoliubie i liubochestie*] invincibly attract people. The natural desire to extend one's well-being forces people to seek the means to this end, and they usually hope to find these means in ranks and power, and they are not mistaken in this, if their dispositions are righteous and lean toward true utility; in the opposite case power and ranks bring them either ruin or shame and obloquy. . . .
>
> The rules [of virtue] consist not in the annihilation of natural human desires but in learning to use the good we receive according to reason for the good of ourselves and society. It does not prohibit the desire for wealth, ranks, power, etc., but only proscribes their misuse. . . . From this explanation we see that virtue is nothing other than the true duty of the good citizen, who not only for the general but for his own utility is obliged to promote the private and common good with all of his powers.[32]

While Dashkova could support this argument on the basis of Baron d'Holbach's *La politique naturelle* (1773), in which morality was based in nature and not in divine forces, this distinction did not signal a rift between the two in the Russian context, as it did in the French.[33] Rather, reason and revelation were held to dovetail in the virtuous self. As Sumarokov put it in "Letter on Pride," the ideal of the self he was describing is grounded "both in nature and according to the revelation of Holy Writ"; the "Letter" begins and ends with references to Satan, as the opposition of good and bad pride is thus framed as a zero-sum clash between God and the Devil. Characteristically, for both Dashkova and Sumarokov, the tsar is both the prime example of the virtuous person and also the key figure in bringing about the well-being of others. Sumarokov asks: "What under the sun is greater than the Emperor? Can a person have less [bad] pride than Peter the Great and His Daughter?" On the one hand, Peter the Great may be seen as the golden mean, the correct balance between pride and humility, but on the other he (and Elizabeth) contrasts with the Devil in absolute terms, as God's representative on earth.

In the "Letter on Pride" this opposition is also described using terms of traditional Russian Orthodox anthropology—the iconic notion of man as created in God's "image and likeness" (Genesis 1:26): "And so the prideful person does not imitate the one in whose image he was created, but follows the one who, perturbed by pride, rose up against the All-Sovereign One . . . and is cast down into hell by the Master of the universe, and into eternal bondage."[34] Similarly, the attack on pride, pridefulness, and self-aggrandizement echoes the traditional Orthodox call to *kenosis*, "emptying" of the self, the supreme exemplar of which is Jesus's self-abnegation.[35] To manifest one's divine image requires becoming like God (Jesus's self-sacrifice), and eliminating all selfish desires; traditional Orthodox thinking posits the basic obstacle to this as pride. It is here that Enlightenment and Orthodox discourses blend, substituting a species of good pride for bad, deference in place of humility, and glorification of true worth for vainglory. The ideal that in the medieval tradition had been reserved for God now devolves upon the ruler, and on humanity in general. Humility is no longer something to be exclusively encouraged (and in the eighteenth century traditional Orthodox asceticism had to retreat underground).[36] Moral philosophy gave a theological stamp of approval to the new kind of self-assertion and positive self-consciousness.

Paradoxically, self-promotion—alien to traditional notions of Orthodox humility and self-abasement—could be defended by asserting selfless altruism. As in the kenotic tradition, the ideal self is conceived as the purposeful rejection of the private, individualistic, and "selfish" interest as a way of attaining the higher, true, collective, "selfless" and divine Other (a higher self). On the one hand then, the approbative imperative suggests a rejection of traditional Christian values; a new justification of pride to replace the older primacy of humility, as loyalty to God and faith yields to service to tsar and fatherland. On the other hand, it also may be seen as a kind of secularized (but not secular) version of kenotic humility, as the claim for glory is asserted in the name of a selfless, supra-individual ideal. Self-love is equated with love for one's neighbor and with love of God. If vanity and love of honor may have "the same appearance" and be wrongly confused, excessive debasement and elevated conceit are "while different in appearance nonetheless extremely similar vices," and likened to superstition and atheism. Approbativeness is next to godliness, and to reject the proper glorification of virtue is to ally with Satan.

In this connection it is suggestive that in Russian, the word commonly used to translate "fame" is "*slava,*" which also translates as "glory," fame's close equivalent (as the common phrase "fame and glory" suggests in English), but the semantic and conceptual differences between the terms are significant. Starting with the term for Russian Orthodoxy—*Pravoslavie* ("correct glorifying" or "glorification")—glory suggests something immortal and divine.[37] Correct glorification is a primary moral and cultural imperative. In contrast, the Latin word "*fama*" (Greek φήμη) that may mean report, rumor, saying, talk, or tradition as well as fame, reputation, and public opinion, never took hold in Russia except in Latin inscriptions. In the classical and the later Western tradition, "fame," even when allegorized as a divinity, has an exclusively earthly function, to spread information or reputation among humankind; furthermore, fame often comes uncomfortably close, or may even turn into, infamy (gossip, rumor, slander).[38] Like everything in the mortal realm, fame is fleeting and subject to ambiguity and corruption. Glory, on the other hand, retains its divine associations, as fame in its highest aspect, suggesting the Platonic trinity of the good, the true, and the beautiful. Glory is an attribute of God, fame of the (merely) famous. In English as in Russian, glory has an active, verbal function that fame does not (in English one can defame but not fame someone)—as opposed to "to glorify," or "make famous" (in Russian: *slavit'*, *proslavit'(sia)*, *proslavliat'(sia)*, *slavoslovit'*, etc.). Glory may be personified, or attached to a person, as fame can be, but fame, like fickle fortune (*fortuna* in eighteenth-century Russian is often translated "*shchastie*"/"*schastie*"—also "happiness" or "luck"), follows its own often accidental and often perverse logic, without moral trappings. Furthermore, *Slava* is the name of the pre-Christian Slavic mother goddess, and folk etymology has often linked it to the name "Slav" itself. (Of course, in the Holy Scriptures, "Glory" may also be synonymous with the Judeo-Christian God, e.g., Exodus 40:34.) In Russian, the word "*Slav*" is more properly connected etymologically to "word" (*slovo*) and *slyt'*, "to be named, to be called, to be known (as)," thus suggesting a basic identity between the "Slavs" and "being named" (being known), i.e., having recognized existence.[39] From all of this it may be suggested that despite obviously modern elements, the discourse of honor and fame in Russia had strong indigenous roots in the Orthodox tradition that may also suggest a heightened eschatological expectation of virtue revealed.

What may seem strange in eighteenth-century autobiography, particularly to a modern sensibility, is the extent to which the virtuous self is equated with universal and "natural" merit and with the eradication of the "personal." Dashkova, like Derzhavin, insists on the total disinterestedness of her behavior, in which she expresses confident pride, disclaiming any ulterior personal (selfish) motives. As in tragedy, the personal or private element, if not in line with the demands of family, society, and nature, is ascribed to the dark side. Dashkova, like Derzhavin, is a strict constructionist. To be virtuous is to act unselfishly, disinterestedly, and without regard for the consequences. Private merit can only consist of impersonal virtue, and to act primarily in one's own self-interest—selfishly—is to act in an evil way. Altruistic self-sacrifice is the measure of goodness, although as apparent in Dashkova's essay "On Genuine Well-Being," aligning private and common good is at least a possibility. The following passage, in which Dashkova describes the consolations of pride in the face of suffering, is characteristic: "I never pursued either my personal interests or the criminal elevation of my own family . . . [I] gathered support from the feeling of my own innocence, the purity of my conscience, and a certain moral pride which gave me strength and courage, but which I had never previously suspected in myself and which, after giving the matter much thought, I could only attribute to resignation, a sentiment proper to every rational being."[40]

On the one hand, Dashkova asserts a complete disinterest suggestive of the Orthodox "kenotic" self. On the other, her quasi-Stoic stance engenders "a certain moral pride which gave me strength and courage," especially in retrospect, as her alleged "resignation" includes a big dose of self-satisfaction based on rational virtue.[41] The working of her rational pride is also clearly evident in a key passage in which Dashkova defends her relationship with Catherine the Great and asserts the complete transparency of her motives for writing:

> I want to disguise nothing in this narrative. I shall tell of the little differences that cropped up between Her Majesty and myself, and because I shall hide nothing the reader will see for himself that I never fell into disgrace, as has been claimed by several writers who wanted to harm her interests, and that

if the Empress did not do more for me, it was because she had an intimate knowledge of me and was quite aware that every form of self-seeking was entirely alien to my nature.

Besides, my heart remained, in the midst of Court life, so artless, so unspoilt, that I forgave even those who showed black ingratitude, egged on as they were by my all-powerful enemies who managed to turn against me those I had done all I could to help. I have waited forty-two years before venturing to reveal the whole of my experience of human ingratitude, which, however, never made me tired of doing all the good of which I was capable, often at the cost of great financial inconvenience, for my means were more than modest.[42]

This remarkable passage offers striking insight into the workings of Dashkova's self-image. On the one hand, she offers herself as totally virtuous, disguising nothing, someone for whom "every form of self-seeking was entirely alien"; her heart is pure, "artless," "unspoilt" and stoically forgiving. She will tell of the "little differences" she had with the empress (that is, there were no big ones), and "because I shall hide nothing the reader will see for himself," and all will be revealed. Yet this mask of stoic virtue and all-forgiveness is immediately undercut by the fact that the entire reason for writing, it emerges, is precisely to get back her own, to set the record straight, to reveal "the whole of my experience of human ingratitude" stored up over the course of 42 years—that is, from the time of Catherine's ascension to the throne in 1762 to the time she finished writing in 1805. This second, vehemently self-righteous and hyperbolically defensive posture threatens to undercut the pose of artless simplicity, and forces the reader (especially modern critical one) to take her pronouncements with some skepticism.[43] From Dashkova's perspective, though, the writing of the text is motivated by the conviction that "virtue must advertise"—if only after holding back for 42 years. Autobiographical writing allows the memoirist what may have been lacking during the life itself: the opportunity to have the last word.

While Dashkova also invokes the deity, her brand of stoicism is largely absent in Derzhavin. Be that as it may, both memoirs offer a public stage on which greatness of soul may be displayed, often in the context of dangerous confrontations with power; indeed, the great soul seeks out such confrontations when he/she sees virtue in peril, despite the possible personal cost.[44] In contrast to Dashkova, who as high nobility had a sense of natural entitlement, Derzhavin constantly emphasizes the difficulties of his rise from "nothingness" to greatness, from oblivion to public visibility. On the one hand, this rise is accredited to Derzhavin's merit (his greatness of soul), but on the other, to divine Providence (*Bozhii Promysl*).[45] If there is pride here then it is justified in terms of the great soul's pure and holy mission—to Russia, to the empress, to God.

## The Vagaries of Virtue

Greatness of soul, as in tragedy, stands out in sharp relief against the background of the fallen, anti-utopian world that is fraught with enemies and mortal dangers at every turn. As in tragedy, virtue confronts vice with no possible compromise between them. Hence the language of both Dashkova's and Derzhavin's memoirs is consistently hyperbolic, with choices posed in all-or-nothing, life-or-death terms. As in Russian classicist literary discourse, there was only one right way, that of the truth, that brooked no contradiction.[46] To deny that truth meant either stupidity, impaired judgment, or malicious intent, which both memoirists perceive all around them.

Dashkova's description of the crisis that followed Catherine's death starkly illustrates her sense of virtue under siege. The new emperor Paul, who wished to vindicate the honor of his deposed father, ordered her to leave Moscow and retire to her place in the country, where she was instructed to "ponder on the events of the year 1762" (that is, Catherine's coup), and to await his decision on her further fate. Dashkova writes:

> I left Moscow on 6 December. My health was reduced to a struggle against death. Every other day I wrote to my brother and other members of my family, who also wrote very regularly to me. Several of them, including my brother, told me that Paul I's behavior toward me was dictated by what he thought he owed to his father's memory, but that at his coronation he would change our fate. I shall quote my reply to my brother as one of the many prophecies I have made which have come true:
>
> "You tell me, friend, that after his coronation Paul will leave me alone. You do not know him then. Once a tyrant begins to strike he continues to strike until his victim is totally destroyed. I am expecting persecution to continue unabated, and I resign myself to it in the full submission of a creature to its Creator. The conviction of my own innocence and lack of any bitterness or indignation at his treatment of me personally will, I trust, serve me in place of courage. Come what may, and provided he is not actively malevolent to you and those near and dear to me, I shall do or say nothing that will lower me in my own eyes. Goodbye, my friend, my well-beloved brother. All my love."[47]

The scenario of virtue under siege offers a striking microcosm of Dashkova's memoir as a literary and psychological document. She presents herself like a heroine of tragic drama or a sentimental novel, a Great Man displaying the transparency of her virtue for all to appreciate.[48] Dashkova's life in this sense emulates art, and constitutes a performance of virtue. She stands tall on the stage of history, describing innocence and virtue pitted against relentless malice, as her forthright response puts her courage and self-possession into sharp relief. By quoting the letter Dashkova helps establish the documentary nature of the moment—its historical truth—and at the same time reflects her exalted, extremely "literary" self-image. It frames the scene as if Dashkova were reciting a tragic monologue or contemplating herself at a remove, as in a mirror.

While Dashkova's dramatic stance might seem appropriate considering the real threat from Paul, similar extreme oppositions—a continual struggle between life and death, salvation and destruction, approbation and opprobrium—operate throughout the text. They characterize Dashkova's understanding of the self as in a constant struggle between absolute virtue and vice whose outcome has highly serious, even metaphysical, consequences. Dashkova presents herself as totally virtuous, and she makes no secret of the pride and self-satisfaction she feels in her virtue. Once again, while her submission to God's will may have something in common with kenosis, Dashkova's language stresses more her adherence to an Enlightenment conviction—echoing classical Stoicism—of righteousness founded on reason and superior self-knowledge. This submission is not humility in the traditional religious sense, born of a sense of sinfulness or guilt, but a defense of pride and self-esteem as an enduring virtue.

Furthermore, Dashkova at one point describes herself as "an unhappy princess over whom a wicked wizard had cast an age-long spell," and this is an apt characterization of the tragic heroine's self-image.[49] Hers is a Cassandra-like tragic self-consciousness of frustrated virtue. The tragic element in some sense represents the objective elements of reality that always intrude to frustrate the happy ending, forcing the princess to remain unhappy. Indeed, the absolute terms in which the conflict is framed tend to turn the world into a huge conspiracy to frustrate the heroine's virtuous strivings. No one (with some minor exceptions—like her husband or the Wilmots)—not Catherine the Great, and certainly not her own children—are able to live up to her exacting, altruistic standards. Dashkova casts herself in the role of a victim so pure, innocent, and virtuous that the world is eternally ungrateful, and failure simply serves to confirm virtue.[50] On the one hand, Dashkova judges herself in the court of self-opinion, allowing no word or action "that will lower me in my own eyes"; the ultimate criterion may be said to be conscience, related back to "the full submission of a creature to its Creator." On the other hand, the notion of silent resignation, of virtue for its own (undisplayed) sake, is undercut by the very fact that it is mentioned so often. In the episode under discussion, Dashkova describes her virtuous resignation in a private letter, which she thereupon makes public in her memoir. She offers up testimony not only to herself, as if she were apart from herself (an attempt at objectifying self-imaging), but also to her brother, the audiences noted above, and ultimately to posterity.

Derzhavin's life writing relates a similar high-stakes battle against evil, surprisingly devoid of that "humorous Russian style" ("*zabavnyi russkii slog*") that made his name as a poet. Like Dashkova, Derzhavin is surrounded by pitiless enemies (*goniteli, nepriateli, nedobrozhelateli*) and constantly threatened by conspiracies meant to undermine his virtuous position and reputation. As a courtier and high official pledged to uphold the law and the public good, he is the constant target of slander, lies, malicious falsehoods, envy, foul innuendo, fiendish plots, cavils, insults, hatred, evil machinations, and so on. At the same time, he is also besieged by negligence, ignorance, or neglect of the law, and "the stupidity and abomination of bias"; like Dashkova, Derzhavin is not one to suffer a fool gladly.[51] Even in the earlier parts of the *Zapiski*, before Derzhavin becomes involved in court intrigue, he is repeatedly involved in life-threatening situations from which he miraculously escapes (e.g., a hunting accident, violent physical clashes, a carriage smash-up, a fall, threats of being murdered [for good deeds], the victim of false arrest, and so on). In contrast to Dashkova, whose stance of high virtue leads to a Cassandra syndrome in which she rightly predicts that her virtue will not be rewarded, Derzhavin is on the whole more positive that he will win out in the end.

Approbation demands more than simply receiving passive recognition— the kind of recognition, say, that a humble Christian saint might desire from God. Virtue for its own sake (despite protests to the contrary) is insufficient. Stoic self-assurance aside, to be a great soul requires public validation— both that others recognize and esteem its virtue, and also that the great soul itself recognize and render honor to others' virtue. Virtue had to be seen and celebrated; even more, the very act of praising virtue and making virtue evident were themselves praiseworthy, held to confer merit. To honor others represents a visual and symbolic marker of selflessness and personally disinterested virtue. Approbativeness, then, requires reciprocal approbation. Conversely, if you fail to advertise, or if you hide your candle under a bushel, you throw doubt on your righteousness. Seeing is believing.

Significantly, the term that Sumarokov and others often use for what might be said to mean the virtue of approbation (Lovejoy's "approbativeness"), *liubochestie*, comes from Church Slavonic, and is in turn a calque from the classical Greek φιλοτιμία, *philotmia*, "the love of honor." The Slavonic term means not only the desire to excel and to be esteemed but also the desire to render honor and esteem to others.[52] In a speech addressed to Catherine of 1764 concerning the re-inauguration of the Academy of Arts, Lomonosov describes the satisfaction of both doing good deeds and being recognized for them: "It is a great joy in life to turn one's mental gaze [*umnoe zrenie*] on the actions of one's good deeds, to see the general benefit and pleasure they cause, to see the happiness of those under one's care and to see their jubilant faces, and to hear their exclamations of gratitude."[53] This inner spiritual (or mental) satisfaction comes not only from contemplating the good one has caused people but also the result of their outwardly expressed visual and vocal appreciation, in which category Lomonosov's speech itself may be counted; to give praise to others' virtue (e.g., in odes and speeches) is not only giving justice its due, but it also reflects honor and pleasure back on the one who honors in a mutual mirroring. While the discourse of visual virtue centers on the ruler, as the one most worthy of praise and most able to render praise to others, this pleasure seems to devolve onto the poet-orator, as the giving and receiving of praise become mutually reinforcing. Lomonosov illustrates the notion of *liubochestie/chestoliubie* by quoting from Cicero's "Pro Archia Poeta" ("On Archias the Poet"), in which the love of honor extends to a desire for immortality through verbal commemoration:

> Virtue demands no other reward than praise and honor. If that is absent, then what profits us that we be burdened by so many labors in this life? And in truth, if we are unable to see the future and if the end of our life sets a limit to all of our designs, why then burden ourselves with so many labors and torture ourselves with such pains, deprive ourselves of sleep at night and cause our lives to be spent in distress? But in every noble soul there is a certain hidden force which urges our heart on to honor, emboldens us, and always reminds us that the memory of our name must not end with our death but must be spread to our most distant descendants.
>
> Or are we all so faint-hearted like those in the republic who spend their time involved in labors and legal troubles so that we cannot, to our last hour, catch our breath in peace and quiet, and think that everything will die together with us? If many great people have striven to leave behind sculptural representations, which have the appearance of a body but no soul, should we not try all the

more to leave behind a representation of our mind and our virtues, created and
ornamented with eloquence by people skilled in this?[54]

This passage has several interesting implications. First of all, from the point
of view of the virtuous person, if "virtue demands no other reward than praise
and honor," that means that it *does* demand praise and honor; virtue must
be made visible.[55] It adds a further dimension to *liubochestie* ("the certain
hidden force which urges our heart on to honor") as motivated by the desire
for earthly immortality (fame, perhaps, rather than glory), rather than by
the social good or religious motivations. As David Griffiths has argued, the
"quest for immortality" was a major motivation for Catherine the Great, and
the same impulse motivated what Anna Lisa Crone has called "the institution
of leading poet in Russia," in particular, for Derzhavin's claim for the poet's
moral independence later in the century.[56] This "Roman" theme of earthly
immortality, deriving principally from Cicero and Horace, might conflict with
Christian arguments about virtue, but in eighteenth-century Russia they were
mutually reinforcing; as already noted, the problem of pride usually shifted to
evaluating the true or false nature of the claim to fame.[57] The Roman model
helped shape the Russian cult of civic virtue and the cultural imperative that
insisted "*Contemtu famae, contemni virtutes*" ("Condemn fame, condemn
virtue").[58] Virtue must be seen, paraded onto the world stage and appreciated,
for it to be considered genuinely virtuous.

The imperative to make virtue visible also had major implications
concerning rulership and the best system of government.[59] Here too the
classical Roman precedent provided a striking model that insisted on the
constant display of virtue. To borrow terms from anthropology, this was a
"shame culture" rather than a "guilt culture," whose social psychology
revolved around preserving one's honor in the eyes of the community rather
than an inner sense of righteousness.[60] John Adams perhaps best described
this genius of the Romans to "regulate this passion" (the love of honor) and
turn it into "a principal means of government":

> Has there ever been a nation who understood the human heart better than the
> Romans, or made a better use of the passion for consideration, congratulation
> and distinction? . . . *Distinctions of conditions*, as well as of ages, were made
> by difference of clothing. . . . The chairs of ivory; the lectors; . . . the crowns
> of gold, of ivory, of flowers; . . . their orations; and their triumphs; everything
> in religion, government and common life, was parade, representation and
> ceremony. Everything was addressed to the emulation of the citizens, and
> everything was calculated to attract the attention, to allure the consideration,

and excite the congratulations of the people; to attach their hearts to individual citizens according to their merit; and to their lawgivers, magistrates, and judges, according to their rank, station and importance to the state. And this was in the true spirit of republics, in which there is no other consistent method of preserving order or procuring submission to the laws.[61]

Rome, then, was the model of institutionalized virtue, externalized and made public, which put emulation—inspiring the love of honor in its citizens—at the heart of the polity, although for eighteenth-century Russia the model was primarily Imperial rather than Republican Rome.[62] The respective merits of republics, empires, monarchies, and democracies was a long-standing debate, and in *The Spirit of the Laws* (1748), Montesquieu had ascribed the best setting for inspiring the love of virtue (even arguably as "false honor") to monarchies as upholders of aristocratic values.[63] In his *Ancient Russian History* of 1766 Lomonosov argued for the superiority of Imperial to Republican Rome as a model for Russian autocracy (*samoderzhavie*), and in *Dimitrii the Pretender* Sumarokov criticized aristocratic or oligarchic rule for Russia, defending monarchy (autocracy),[64] which he framed specifically in terms of false pride (*gordost'*) as juxtaposed to the love of honor (*liubochestie*):

Самодержавие—России лучша доля.
Мне думается, где самодержавства нет,
Что любочестие, теснимо, там падет,
Вельможи гордостью на подчиненных дуют,
А подчиненные на гордых негодуют.
[. . .] Правленья таковы совсем России новы,
Коль нет монарха в ней, власть—тяжкие оковы.
Несчастна та страна, где множество вельмож:
Молчит там истина, владычествует ложь.
Благополучна нам монаршеска держава,
Когда не бременна народу царска слава. (DS 272)[65]
[Autocracy is Russia's best destiny. / I think that in those places where it does not exist, / The love of honor (*liubochestie*), persecuted, declines; / Grandees arrogantly oppress (*gordost'iu duiut*) their subordinates, / And subordinates become indignant against the proud (*gordykh*). / (. . .) This kind of rule is completely new for Russia. / If there is no monarch there, power turns into grievous shackles. / Unhappy is that country that has a multitude of grandees: / The truth falls silent, falsehood reigns. / Monarchial power is beneficent for us / When the people is not weighed down by the tsar's glory.]

Sumarokov provides a further exemplary discussion of approbativeness as a central aspect of good rule in *Sinav and Truvor*, when Gostomysl offers advice to his daughter on how to act as future queen in terms of false pride versus proper sight and true glory:

> Возшед на трон, будь мать народа своего.
> Когда ты отстаешь любовныя забавы,
> Ищи утех среди величества и славы.
> Не гордости тебе отец искать велит,
> Престол не тем людей великих веселит,
> Но чтоб ты сеяла повсюду добродетель,
> На то имеет власть над обществом владетель.
> Он все с высокого седалища страны,
> Которы от богов ему поручены,
> Объемля взорами, брежет и учреждает,
> Искореняет ложь и правду утверждает.
> [. . .] В сей пышности себя между богов не числи,
> И смертна будучи, как смертная и мысли. [. . .]
> Превозноси людей, ко правде прилепленных,
> Разумных и честных, искусством укрепленных,
> Премудрости во всех последуй ты делах
> И спутницей имей ее во всех путях.
> Покровом будь сирот, прибежищем вдовицы:
> Яви ты истину под именем царицы
> И добродетель здесь, гнушаяся тщеты,
> Яви во образе девичьей красоты.
> Надеждой веселись, что ты себя прославишь
> И подданным своим златые дни восставишь. (DS 117)

[Having ascended to the throne, be a mother of your people. / When you abandon the amusements of love, / Seek satisfaction in greatness and glory. / Your father does not command you to seek pride / —That is not how the throne should make great ones happy— / But rather you should sow virtue everywhere; / It is for this that the sovereign has power over society. / From the country's high seat of power, / Entrusted to him by the gods, / Embracing everything with his sight, / He protects and sanctions, / Roots out falsehood and asserts the truth. ( . . .) / In this pomp do not count yourself among the gods, / But, as one who is mortal, think like a mortal person. ( . . .) / Raise up those who are committed to the truth, / Rational and honest people, fortified by their art. / Follow wisdom in all your actions / And have her as your companion in all travels. / Be protection to orphans and refuge for widows, / Manifest truth in your name as tsaritsa, / And, abhorring vanity, manifest virtue / In the image of maidenly beauty. / Be joyful in the hope that you will glorify yourself, / Resurrecting the golden age for your subjects.]

## The Quest for Recognition

The need to make virtue visible helps explain the fact that in their memoirs Derzhavin and Dashkova obsess over receiving appropriate rewards for their virtuous actions. Both, but especially Derzhavin, chronically complain of financial need, treading a fine line between protestations of disinterest in personal enrichment and insistent demands that virtue be properly acknowledged and rewarded. In Derzhavin's case, he was acutely aware of his lack of money and personal connections that were a prerequisite for advancement, but his constant self-promotion was not only a practical necessity; it was also a value in itself. Virtue may be priceless, and thus incommensurate with material compensation, but it nevertheless demands acknowledgement as the external, visible mark of inner worth. If, as Tiberius held, "to despise fame is to despise merit," conversely, to strive for fame is to evince merit.[66] Both Dashkova and Derzhavin spend many pages describing not only the marks of honor that accrue to them, but also the many incidents in which they deserved distinction but were slighted or passed over. Like Dashkova, for Derzhavin ingratitude is a cardinal sin (and one from which most people unfortunately suffer).[67] Furthermore, the preoccupation with reward extends on the one hand to an acute sensitivity to inflated pride and self-promotion in potential rivals in virtue, and on the other hand, to criticism of those who fail to recognize and reward virtue (which in many cases turns out to be Catherine). Several examples from Dashkova's and Derzhavin's memoirs illustrate the working of this moral and psychological conundrum.

Dashkova insists on the disinterestedness of her motives, a leitmotif of *Mon histoire* that, as noted, was often connected with a position of quasi-Stoic moral resignation. It also repeatedly comes into play in her relations with Catherine, as she claims, for instance, that "my love for her was quite disinterested, for I had been passionately fond of her at a time when she was not Sovereign yet, and I was in a position to be of far greater service to her than she was to me."[68] Here Dashkova denies any material reciprocity of their relationship, but at the same time recalls Catherine's debt to her. The "receipt of a bounty" as Dashkova puts it—material awards—"went against my principles" as something that could—or could seem to—contradict this disinterestedness.[69]

The problem of receiving "bounty" from Catherine comes up repeatedly during and after the coup that brought her to the throne. There is tension over the degree to which the empress owed her success to Dashkova, and thus over what honors and rewards the princess was due.[70] At one point during the coup, Dashkova describes helping to prepare Catherine to go out and lead the troops, making sure that the new sovereign replaces the Order of St. Catherine she had been wearing with the blue ribbon of the Cross of St. Andrew. These were the two oldest Russian orders, both established by Peter the Great, and the switch signaled Catherine's elevation to sole ruler, as the Order of St. Catherine was a women's honor created for Catherine I, whereas the order of St. Andrew indicated the highest, heretofore male power.[71] (Catherine wears the St. Andrew Cross in virtually all of her official portraits.) Dashkova held on to the Order of St. Catherine for the new empress after she took it off, and when she returned it to her shortly thereafter, the empress offered it to Dashkova herself, in part, it seems from her account, to placate Dashkova's anger over the troops that had been stationed at her father's house after the coup.[72] Catherine tries to soothe her:

> "Now, now, let's leave it at that. So much for your quick temper and this"—making a move to pin on my shoulder the Order which I had returned to her—"is for your services."
>
> Far from kneeling to receive the decoration, I said to her: "Forgive me, Your Majesty, for what I am to say to you. You are approaching the moment when, for all you may wish to the contrary, truth will be banished from your ears; I implore you not to confer this Order on me, because if it is meant as an ornament you know that I set no store by such things; if it is for my services, then, however mediocre they may appear to some people, in my own eyes they cannot be repaid because I am not to be bought, nor ever shall be, at any price."
>
> Her Majesty embraced me, with the words: "At least let friendship enjoy its rights."
>
> I kissed her hand.[73]

Dashkova accepts the order on her own terms. It cannot be taken as payment, she argues, insofar as virtue and the desire for profit (recall Sumarokov) are incommensurate, opposites. There can be no material quid pro quo as payment for services rendered, for "in my own eyes"—in the eyes of virtue—such things "cannot be repaid." As a thing of material value (and the Order of St. Catherine was covered with diamonds), the order, as a signifier, cannot approach the signified, as virtue is beyond such signification and its price beyond evaluation, Dashkova implies.[74]

The meaning of the proposed Order of St. Catherine is also problematic even when seen as the coin of symbolic currency. On the one hand, Dashkova notes that it might simply be dismissed "as an ornament"—an empty sign that has no correlation with inner worth—like the ass in the lion's skin, trying "to shine based on nothing." On the other hand—and this seems to be Dashkova's presumption in accepting the order—its symbolic quotient is potentially limitless, and represents maximal recognition. This is certainly the fundamental idea of orders, which were corporate honor societies modeled on medieval chivalric orders, and had their own elaborate rituals, practices, uniforms, holidays, charitable institutions, schools, and even dedicated churches. The exchange between the two women ends with an embrace and hand kissing, suggesting that Dashkova accepts the order as a friend to Catherine and equal in honor, and as someone—as her elaborate foreword makes clear—who does not relinquish the right to boldly speak the truth. Dashkova thus both defines the significance of, and her credentials for, receiving such a mark of honor. Yet at the same time she leaves the fact that she did accept the award unspoken, creating the impression of a humble and magnanimous renunciation of this honor. This is far from the case, and Dashkova will soon try to use it to get a good seat at Catherine's coronation, displaying it as something that has "for the past fifty years been considered the greatest distinction the State could confer."[75] Portraits of Dashkova, even those of her in exile, in humble clothing and surroundings, invariably show her with the Order of St. Catherine on her left breast.[76]

Concern over proper recognition is also a constant preoccupation in Derzhavin's *Zapiski*. Three episodes will serve to illustrate his continual struggle for acknowledgement in the memoir: one concerns his part in the Pugachev uprising, which he believed was insufficiently appreciated, and two concern his later role as poet and high official to Catherine the Great, which he strove to defend against the suggestion that he owed his success to flattery.[77] The first passage describes Derzhavin's disagreeable reception in Moscow after his return from service against Pugachev. It is quoted at length to give some sense of the rather long-winded and pedantic style characteristic of the memoir:[78]

[U]pon his arrival in Moscow he found circumstances in the regiment just as new for him as they were unpleasant, because all of the former commanders had been changed; Prince Potemkin and Major Tolstoi were in charge, and they did not know him. The former, possibly, [was not well disposed to him] due to cold remarks by General Potemkin, and the latter due to the slanders of his favorite, the officer Tsurikov, who even before his expeditionary mission had been at odds with Derzhavin, so that Major Tolstoi received him without any attention at all, and he was ordered simply to sign in, as if he had come back after a leave or from some totally insignificant errand. This extremely irritated the young officer who had served zealously in dangerous exploits, and who had earned extraordinary praise from many generals and from Potemkin himself, in many orders and letters, so that many of them had promised to present him directly to the imperial throne; but when it came to making good on their promises, they hid themselves away with their patronage [s svoimi protektsiiami], and did not want, or were not able to do anything to help him, and this included Prince Golitsyn. On the contrary, the next day he was assigned to sentry duty at the palace. And while he had been away, by command of the Empress's favorite, Count Grigorii Aleksandrovich Potemkin, who later was a prince, the parade-ground regulations for the regiment had been changed, and he, knowing nothing about this, made an error, and instead of ordering the platoon simply to "march right" according to the new system he said "left, halt, right march" as it was formerly; and that caused me [sic] trouble, which was considered even more unforgiveable because the regiment assigned to sentry duty was dressed up like dandies in new uniforms by Prince Potemkin and was supposed to march by platoon in front of Fieldmarshal Count Rumiantsev-Zadunaisky who had arrived from Moscow for the peace celebrations, and who was looking down on them from a window of the palace. For this innocent mistake, when the regiment was released to the encampment at the Khodynka [River], the officer who had made the misstep was assigned to disciplinary sentry duty. This all the more stung his ambitious soul when he recalled to himself how recent it had been that he had been entrusted with such an important assignment and had been able to have the corps of generals moved on his orders, take as much money from cities as he wanted, send out scouts, conduct executions, prevent the evildoers from crossing the Irgiz in spring into the inner, completely unguarded provinces, and had defended, by himself alone, so to speak, all of the foreign colonies lying on the meadow side of the Volga from being despoiled by the Kirghiz, by which taken together he had saved both the Empire and the glory of the Sovereign Empress, who, having summoned them [the foreign colonists] from abroad, had taken them under her protection and promised to arrange their more solid prosperity than they had known in their homelands. But for all of this instead of rewards he received degradation [unichizhenie] before his brothers in arms, the guard officers, who had been awarded villages, and he alone was left without any respect, but like a good-for-nothing was assigned to punitive duty.[79]

The peculiar syntax of this last sentence suggests the ambiguity or possible equivalence between relating his being "left alone without any respect" and being treated like "a good-for-nothing," on the one hand, and not being awarded villages, on the other. Derzhavin's "ambitious soul" (*chestoliubivaia ego dusha*) still stings with the insult to the young officer being ignored and treated "as if he had come back after a leave or from some totally insignificant errand," to the point that his irritation leads him to disregard the conceit of speaking of himself in the third person. Derzhavin seems to be arguing with posterity as if it were his unjust commanding officer who is morally obliged to acknowledge his services, and he feels compelled to enumerate in detail both the many factors unfairly working against him (from changed parade-ground commands to unfair second-hand rumors and broken promises), as well as his own extraordinary feats. As his situation becomes more desperate, his "zealous service in dangerous exploits" that earns "extraordinary praise" expands to become the single-handed salvation of "both the Empire and the glory of the Sovereign Empress."

In another episode, many years later, Derzhavin is similarly frustrated, even though he is now being promoted to senator and given a medal rather than assigned to guard duty:

[I]t may have been that either because of the unceasing calumnies of his detractors or that the truth was annoying [*pravda naskuchila*] [to the empress], on Sept. 8, [1793,] the day of celebrating peace with the Turks, although Derzhavin publicly announced from the throne the reward of several thousand serfs to those officials who had distinguished themselves during the war; for all of his labors, for all of his wide-ranging, important, constant and noteworthy deeds, not one serf, not one red cent [*ni polushki*] was given him as a reward, but he was promoted to senator in the surveying department, and, among many others, got a cross of St. Vladimir second class, a bunch [*tucheiu*] of which were given out to the worthy and unworthy alike. But not long before that he had had the hope of receiving something more outstanding.[80]

Again Derzhavin demands recognition, at least on a par with others of his cohort singled out for achievement, but hopefully something even better, and a cross "given out [indiscriminately] to the worthy and unworthy alike" means nothing. Like Dashkova, he wants rewards and recognition on his own symbolic, grand terms. Even serfs and other financial boons are arguably secondary to the appreciation of his "wide-ranging, important, constant and noteworthy" labors. The "something more outstanding" Derzhavin had hoped for here refers to the possibility of being appointed general-procuror, a powerful position roughly equivalent to minister of justice; he would have replaced his former mentor turned nemesis Prince A. A. Viazemsky. Catherine's current favorite, Platon Zubov, tried to sound Derzhavin out on this appointment but Derzhavin's principles stood in the way:

> During the course of this conversation, the favorite [Zubov] stared intensely into his eyes, as if prompting him to ask about this; but Derzhavin from the start of and during his entire service had made it his unchanging rule never to ask anyone for anything, never to thrust himself forward, but, on the other hand, never to refuse anything, and when charged with some service, to fulfill it with complete fidelity and honor, according to justice and the law, as far as his strength allowed (basing this rule on Holy Scripture: that no one receives honor except [those] called by God [Hebrews 5:3], and that a good pastor does not climb over fences, but goes in through the door and pastures the sheep entrusted to him, reckoning on his soul [John 10:1–11]); and when he is summoned to something, God will help him fulfill the most difficult tasks easily and successfully; but if he pushes himself forward with intrigues, he will have to carry the entire burden on his shoulders. . . . [The passage continues for about as long again.] In a word, he held back from asking for the place of general-procuror, even though he deserved it more than anyone else. . . . [He explains why, specifically.][81]

Derzhavin's attitude recalls that of Margarita toward Woland (the Devil) from Bulgakov's *Master and Margarita*: "You're absolutely right!" says Woland. "Never ask for anything! . . . especially from someone who's more powerful than you are. They will offer and grant everything themselves."[82] Any trace of selfish interest represents surrender to the evil forces. As with many passages in the *Zapiski*, the "action" here takes place internally, within Derzhavin's thoughts, and the writer's *velikodushie* only comes to light in their pages, many decades later. As with Dashkova, autobiography offers an unequalled opportunity to have the last and uncontradicted word.

In the final episode, Derzhavin sums up Catherine's reign at the time of her death. Derzhavin's famous statements in the *Zapiski* about his disenchantment with Catherine and consequent inability to write poetry in praise of her "on order" are well known, and echo his equally famous poetic lines about "speaking truth to tsars with a smile" ("istinu Tsariam s ulybkoi govorit," from "Pamiatnik" ["Monument"] of 1796, an emulation of Horace's last ode of Book 3, "Exegi monumentum"). The following passage, which sums up and reiterates their problematic relations, sheds a somewhat different light on the problem, as it focuses specifically on the problem of virtue and rewards:

> But as concerns him [Derzhavin], having begun to serve her, as seen above, from having been a soldier, for more than 35 years, he rose to eminent ranks, having executed all of the responsibilities laid upon him irreproachably and unselfishly, was worthy of attending her personally [as her state-secretary], and of being entrusted in a significant way with receiving and fulfilling her commands; but he never received outstanding favor and for his faithful service was not given any special reward (as did others of his cohort—Troshchinsky, Popov, Gribovsky and many others; he even requested at the time he was released from [serving as] state-secretary that, because of his extreme need, his salary be extended into a pension, but even this was not done)—neither villages, nor expensive things or sizeable sums of money, apart from, as noted earlier, that he was granted 300 serfs in Belorussia for saving the colonies [during the Pugachev uprising], from which he never received more than three silver rubles per serf, that is, 1000 rubles, and later up to 2000 paper rubles; as well as at various times presents for his poetry, i.e., a gold snuff box with 500 chervontsy [gold coins] for the ode Felitsa, another gold snuffbox for [the ode] on the taking of Izmailov, and for a report [*za tarif*]—a snuffbox with diamonds left to him that had a note in her hand signed "To Derzhavin" that he received from Emperor Paul after her death. But in all justice he had to acknowledge that the most priceless of all rewards was that she, for all of the persecutions of his many strong enemies, did not deprive him of her protection and did not let them, so to say, strangle [*zadushit'*] him; but on the other hand she did not let him publicly triumph over them by proclaiming his righteousness [*spravedlivost'*] and faithful service, or by some other special trust that she showed to others. To sum up, this wise and powerful sovereign, if in the strict judgment of posterity will not keep the name of the Great for all eternity, it was only because she did not always hold to sacred justice but played up to those around her, and the more so to her favorites, as if she were afraid of annoying them; and therefore virtue could not always, so to speak, force its way through this thicket [*chesnochniak*], and ascend to its proper greatness [*velichie*]. . . . Insofar as Derzhavin's spirit was always disposed to morality, if he wrote verses in praise of her triumphs, he always however used allegory or some other subtle method [to depict] the truth, and therefore she was not always pleased with him in her heart. But be that as it may, let the memory of such a monarch under whom Russia flourished, and who will not soon be forgotten, be blessed.[83]

For Derzhavin and Dashkova, Catherine's achievement as a ruler—whether she deserves the title "Great"—hinges on her acknowledgement of *their* greatness. This passage is perhaps most notable for its significant equivocations. Even while appreciating Catherine's patronage as "the most priceless of all rewards," without which Derzhavin's rise would almost certainly never have happened, and which preserved him from his enemies, he is left to reckon up the meager rewards he did get. He lists them in painful detail, perhaps to emphasize their inadequacy, in that this was all he had to show for 35 years of service (with no pension!), or perhaps to demonstrate his scrupulous accuracy.[84] Similarly, Derzhavin is equivocal in his homage to Catherine, characterized as a "wise and powerful sovereign" under whom virtue was not always able to "force its way" through the thicket of special interests that surrounded her and "ascend to its proper greatness," and hence whose memory is less than immortal. Finally, this less than wholehearted tribute tries to defuse the specter of sycophancy in his poetic praise of the empress by reference to his adherence to truth in life and art, to which Catherine's annoyance and her very failure to acknowledge him attest. On the other hand, in the classicist genre of autobiography as described here, the author's own virtue is presumed to be obvious, a peculiarity of the epoch that may make more sense in light of the discussion in the chapter that follows.

# CHAPTER SIX

# The Seen, the Unseen, and the Obvious

"Видимый нами мир сей уверяет о безконечной мудрости Божие.
[The world that is visible to us convinces us of God's infinite wisdom.]

Вся природа проповедует нам бытие Божие.
[All nature proclaims God's existence to us.]"
—Phrases illustrating the words "visible" and "nature" in the *Dictionary of the Russian Academy* (1789)

"My first question is this. After saying that this part of your discourse needed no elaboration because it was obvious and universally agreed that the gods exist, why did you labor the point at such length?"
—Cotta, critiquing the Stoic position in Cicero, *On the Nature of the Gods*

In this chapter, the ideal associated with true vision will be asserted and challenged in two types of mostly poetic works. The first group exemplifies the discourse of "physicotheology," which asserted that the visual evidence of the physical world attests to the rational structure of the universe and proves the existence of God. The second group, associated with the Book of Ecclesiastes, took a more skeptical stance, describing vision in a minor key; these works might promise ultimate knowledge in heaven but throw doubt on the efficacy of vision in this world. This latter group may be seen as a counterpoint to the reigning optimistic, ocularcentric trend, at times complementary and at times antagonistic to it, questioning although ultimately supportive of the dominant visual paradigm.

Illustration to Derzhavin's poem "The Proof of [God's] Creative Being" ("Dokazatel'stvo tvorchesk-ogo bytiia") of 1796, a paraphrase of Psalm 18 (Psalm 19 in Western Bibles). It depicts "a wise man [*starets*] with one hand pointing to creation and with the other indicating a book thrown open before him, resting on a cubical stone with the inscription 2 x 2 = 4, signifying the true and undeniable proof of God's existence." The artwork was carved on wood and signed by the St. Petersburg engraver G. V. Gogenfel'den some time after 1795 for an edition of Derzhavin's works that was not published. From *Sochineniia Derzhavina*, edited by Ia. Grot (St. Petersburg: Akademiia nauk, 1864), 1:726–27.

## Nature as an Open Book

Sumarokov's historical tragedy *Dimitrii the Pretender* of 1771 opens with a short debate between the false tsar Dimitrii and Parmen, his advisor and eventual nemesis, over human beings' ability to perceive divine wisdom. The scene serves as overture to the play's main action and touches on the main thematic oppositions of pretendership versus legitimacy, tyranny versus monarchy, and Russian national self-determination versus foreign overlordship, all of which are framed in terms of the larger political and theological clash between Russian Orthodoxy and Catholicism. In representing a specific era of Russian history, the early seventeenth century's "Time of Troubles," the play has been seen as a step in the direction of greater historicism, but this exchange clearly reflects contemporary eighteenth-century Enlightenment Orthodox concerns.[1] Mid-eighteenth-century ideas are projected back more than a century and a half, not only confirming the peculiar "presentist" nature of early modern Russian historical consciousness, but also testifying to an ocularcentric value system that had become so normative as to be taken for granted as universally valid.

Dimitrii and Parmen argue over whether or not divine wisdom is accessible to individual mortals. Parmen contrasts modern rational religious thinking to Dimitrii's "Catholic" mistrust of human reason:

Пармен
[. . .] Разумный человек о Боге здраво мыслит.

Димитрий
Во умствовании не трать напрасно слов.
Коль в небе хочешь быть, не буди философ!
Премудрость пагубна, хотя она и льстивна.

Пармен
Премудрость вышнему быть может ли противна?
Исполнен ею, Он вселенну созидал
И мертву веществу живот и разум дал.
На что ни взглянем мы, его премудрость видим.
Или, что в Боге чтим, в себе возненавидим?

Димитрий
Премудрость божия непостижима нам.

Пармен

Так Климент оныя не постигает сам.

К понятию ея ума пределы тесны,

Но действа божества в творении известны.

И если изострим нам данные умы,

Что папа ведает, узнаем то и мы.[2]

[*Parmen*: A rational person can think about God in a sensible way. / *Dimitrii*: Do not waste words intellectualizing. / If you want to go to heaven, do not be a philosopher! / Wisdom is harmful, though too it is also seductive. / *Parmen*: Can wisdom really be offensive to the Most High? / Filled with it, He created the universe / And gave life and reason to dead matter. / Wherever we look, we see His wisdom. / Or should we hate in ourselves that which we revere in God? / *Dimitrii*: Divine wisdom is inaccessible to us. / *Parmen*: Then (Pope) Clement himself cannot access it either. / Our mind's limits make understanding difficult, / But divine actions in creation are known. / And if we develop the intellect that has been given us, / What the Pope knows, so too can we.]

This argument covers many issues, from wisdom and the ability to know the world, to the authority of the Catholic Church, to the relationship between the divine and human. It is also an argument about the nature of seeing and not seeing. Dimitrii voices the Russian perception of Catholicism as he defends the Church's dominion over interpretation: God's reason is hidden and inaccessible, and hence one must obey the dictates of authority. For this reason an interest in philosophy is vain as well as politically subversive and corrupting. In rejecting the exclusivity of the pope's knowledge, Parmen discounts decisions made by the single anointed leader alone, who expects all others to follow blindly. By analogy, the pope, like Dimitrii, is a "pretender"—*samozvanets*, literally, one who is "self-proclaimed." Throughout the play, Catholicism's sway is maintained by fear and deception, things that also characterize Dimitrii's arbitrary and despotic rule.

Parmen counters Dimitrii's argument with the ocularcentric position: divine truth is immanent in the world, and hence may be seen and understood by all. Needless to say, Parmen's position has almost nothing in common with early seventeenth-century Orthodox views, indeed Dimitrii's views are far closer to the Russian position of that era, as the Counter-Reformation had been perceived in Russia as corrupted by the disease of philosophy and rationalism. Parmen's post-Cartesian argument is based in part on the premises that underlay early modern science, presuming both a universe governed by rational (divine) law, and the capability (also, arguably, divine) to "develop (sharpen) the intellect that has been given us" in order to see God's wisdom. "Whatever we look at, we see His wisdom. / Or will we hate in ourselves that which we value in God?" The divine both informs ontology—the nature of the visible world as divinely rational—and epistemology—reason as a divinely validated tool. It also defines anthropology, as Parmen's question suggests, on the one hand connecting love and sight-knowledge, and on the other love of God and love of self. (This couplet's rhyme—*vidim*/*voznenavidim* [we see/we will hate]—stresses the connection between evil and not seeing.) Parmen's position suggests parity between God and man, a human mirroring of divine reason, while Dimitrii offers a thin rationalization for his claim to despotic power.

Parmen argues that the right to look and decide does not belong exclusively to the Church, but is shared by everyone, pope and individual believer alike, so that no one has a monopoly over truth. The truth is evident and accessible to all.[3] Once it is accepted that "the divine actions in creation are known" and may be seen wherever one looks, the gates are open to free investigation, both scientific and philosophical, with all of the attendant intellectual and political ramifications. What is most remarkable, perhaps, about the eighteenth-century tradition as a whole, is the widespread belief in sight as a key to philosophical and theological truth, and the relatively quick jump from an argument about the universal accessibility of wisdom to the conviction that the truth is obvious. This ocular optimism was buttressed by an array of arguments that validated vision, grounding it in the certainty of faith supported by reason.

The common use of the traditional biblical image of the book of nature in eighteenth-century poetry illustrates this new perspective, one that contrasts sharply with the older baroque understanding of the same trope. The image itself brings together sight and reading, ocular- and logocentrism, and recalls the connection and contrast between the start of Genesis (the *fiat lux*—"let there be light") and the beginning of John, "in the beginning was the Word." As in Parmen's debate with Dimitrii, the image involves conflicting hermeneutics, that is, varieties of interpretation. In such baroque poems as Simeon Polotsky's "The World Is a Book," "Book," and "Writing," the meaning to be found in the book of nature is emblematic and allegorical, not empirical, and not easily accessible to sight; thus it requires authoritative interpretation of the kind Dimitrii upholds.[4] While the world is still God's creation, His Word, it can only be seen through a glass darkly.[5] The unlearned and uninitiated may easily misunderstand what they see and be led astray. Thus in the poem "Writing," Polotsky compares written words to a rushing river: one is in jeopardy of seeing only the flickering surface, missing the deeper truth that may elude the untrained eye (*prekhodiashcha zrenie neiskusna oka*), and drowning. One must look beneath superficial reality to find the often esoteric, hidden, higher truth, and for this one needs training and careful instruction; the book of nature is not easily accessible. To the contrary, the eighteenth-century ocularcentric view held that (in Parmen's words) "whatever we look at, we see His wisdom," and the image of the "world as a book" was used to underscore that the truth to be read in the book of nature is obvious and open to everyone without any preparation. As if in response to Polotsky, in his ode entitled "Reading," for example, Kheraskov asserted that

Всегда у нас перед очами
Отверзта книга Естества;
В ней пламенными словесами
Сияет мудрость Божества.[6]
[Before our eyes the book / Of Nature is always open; / In it, in flaming words, / Divine wisdom shines.]

Similarly, when the eponymous protagonist of Elizaveta Urusova's *Polion* (1774) asks his quasi-divine heroine-mentor what books have made her so wise, she answers:

Те книги [. . .] которы я читаю,
Суть вещи зримые, меж коих обитаю;
Печатаны они рукою Божества,
Не в буквах состоят, в глаголах Естества;
Хотя учеными бывают и презренны,
Но каждому они из смертных отворенны[7]
[Those books that I read (. . .) / Are the visible things among which I dwell; / They are printed by the hand of the Deity, / Made up not of letters [but] of Nature's verbs; / Though they may be disdained by scholars / They are open to any mortal person]

Many similar examples could be cited. Metropolitan Platon (Levshin), the leading churchman of Catherinean Russia, elaborated on this point in his sermon on the empress's ascension to the throne, published in 1782: "Knowledge of God is of the most accessible [*udobneishikh*] kind because it is the most necessary. This book is open to the entire universe. It is written in letters which the educated and uneducated can understand, and all of the peoples on earth, who speak different languages, can read them without difficulty and without preparation [*bez nauki*]. It is enough to open one's eyes and see the Creator and Ruler of all things."[8] Vision makes the highest and most necessary values accessible in a way that transcends national, linguistic, and educational limitations, offering a theological support for Enlightenment universalism. The fact that sight was considered universally accessible to all regardless of national origin or cultural background must also have contributed to the appeal of such ideas to younger literary traditions like the German and Russian.

The simple opening of the eyes, while clearly a moment of revelation, is nevertheless not the same kind of ecstatic experience described in Lomonosov's odes, which drew on mystical Orthodox ideas about "uncreated light." The visual revelation here, and in the material analyzed in this chapter, is grounded rather in rationalist-Enlightenment theology that argues the validity of knowing God through creation, using our sensual and mental faculties. In terms of the "threefold division" of Orthodox spirituality discussed in chapter 3, this theological position may be described as the second level, the contemplation and knowledge of created things, and as a kind of middle way between pure empiricism or logic and true mystical knowledge, based on the conviction that faith and reason are fully compatible.[9]

## Physicotheology: Self-Evident Truths

As the image of the open book of nature suggests, the starting point for much of Russian philosophical and theological thinking in the eighteenth century was quite simple and basic: that to any unbiased observer, the truth is obvious. The senses—in particular "the noblest of the senses," vision—offer incontrovertible proof of the rational structure of the universe, and hence of God's existence. The connections between seeing and knowing, sight and truth, and being seen and having an independent existence were taken as positive truths and their implications embraced. Such ideas underwrote the Enlightenment's fundamental belief in reason. They were central to what was known in the eighteenth century as "physicotheology," the idea that the existence of God and the rational structure of the universe are self-evident in the visual evidence of the physical world.[10] As the compound label itself suggests, "physicotheological" works sought to elaborate (and to celebrate) God's design as manifested in the material, scientifically measurable world, so that no boundary or contradiction was to be recognized between science and theology, literature, and philosophy, or between "natural philosophy" and "natural theology" (*estestvennoe* or *natural'noe bogoslovie*). To quote Thomas Saine, "in the first half of the eighteenth century, a flood of physicotheological works, by scientists, divines, and laypeople alike, contrived to see God's hand and His design for the universe in every creature, every rock, and every blade of grass."[11] This was truly a monumental tide that hit Europe in the later seventeenth and eighteenth centuries, but that almost completely ebbed at the time of the French Revolution and the intellectual sea-change it brought about.[12]

Scholars have usually looked at physicotheological works in the context of the Enlightenment as a product of the struggle to domesticate the "Newtonian-Copernican Revolution"—what Russian scholars refer to as the new "Scientific Picture of the World" (*NKM, Nauchnaia kartina mira*)—and to reconcile it with traditional theological notions about man's place in the universe.[13] Saine and others, however, have argued that emphasis should be placed not on the conflict of traditional religious thought with the new science, but rather on these works' assertion of faith in their reconciliation. That is, the physicotheological movement did not represent a conservative backlash against "the shock of the new rationalism," as some have argued, but reflected a generally held confidence among scientists and clergymen alike that the new approaches to the world offered a triumphant validation of traditional theodicy.[14] The physicotheological tradition in Russia has been virtually unstudied, but was abundantly present as a generally accepted part of Russian Enlightenment Orthodoxy and of Russian culture in general, constituting a popular visual theology.[15]

Physicotheological discourse and ideas may be found in numerous Russian scientific, religious, and philosophical texts, in poetry (religious as well as what is often referred to as "natural-philosophical" verse), as well as in sermons and other religious works. Physicotheology was not only a meeting ground for heterogeneous genres—works of natural science, poetry, sermons, philosophy—but also a melting pot of chronologically disparate trends. It manifested a peculiarly early modern blend of classical, Christian—both Eastern and Western—and Enlightenment ideas, and offers a striking example of the seamless blending of heterogeneous traditions in Enlightenment Orthodoxy.

The most ambitious physicotheological work produced in Russia must be Trediakovsky's long poem *Feoptiia*. Although Trediakovsky was unable to publish this work (the poem first saw print in 1963), it is a valuable document for inquiry insofar as it offers a formulation of the explicitly visual basis for theology.[16] In writing a philosophical tract in verse, Trediakovsky emulated

Alexander Pope's *An Essay on Man* (1733–1734), which he read in a French version; Pope's *Essay* was one of the most famous moral poems of the age, and Trediakovsky aspired to compose "an essay on God."[17] The main philosophical and textual source for *Feoptiia* was François Fénelon's *Traité de l'existence et des attributs de Dieu* (1712, 1718), a prose work that was translated and published repeatedly throughout the eighteenth century.[18] A decade before Trediakovsky, Kantemir had written a paraphrase of Fénelon's treatise, also in prose, entitled "Letter on Nature and Man" (1743), which like the *Feoptiia* remained unpublished (it finally appeared in P. A. Efremov's edition of 1868).[19] Trediakovsky focuses on what may be seen as at the core of all of these works—their dependence on sight.

A fundamental change in perspective wrought by early modern science, and in particular by the works of Newton, was to reconceptualize the physical universe as an image of the divine, and not its opposite (i.e., it was not made up of "fallen" matter), and to identify previously metaphysical concepts like infinity with the newly revealed physical universe.[20] The invisible was now made potentially visible and accessible, as the ancient association of God and His creation took on new and powerful scientific support.[21] In the words of *Feoptiia*:

> Твердо по премногу может тварь, что создана,
> Божиих зерцалом совершенств быть названа. (IP 312)[22]
> [With abundant certainty can the things that have been created / Be called the mirror of God's perfections.]

Trediakovsky's work foregrounds an explicitly "visual theology" based on a rationalist conception of sight. This is how the title's neologism *Feoptiia*, made up of *Feos* (theos) plus *optos*, the Greek roots for God and the visible, may be interpreted. The Russian appears to be derived from the Greek Θεόπτία, "divine vision."[23] The title, in full, is: *Feoptiia ili dokazatel'stvo o bogozrenii po veshcham sozdannogo estestva*, meaning "Feoptiia or proof of the knowledge of God via sight [*bogozrenie*] on the basis of created nature," whose subtitle may be paraphrased as "proof of God's existence by means of visual evidence from natural creation." *Bogozrenie* is a rare Slavonic word, meaning "the contemplation, cognition of God" (*sozertsanie, poznanie Boga*) which suggests both sight or knowledge of God and the process of knowing God via sight.[24] It is arguably a synonym for *bogovidenie*, which in the Orthodox tradition was occasionally used to mean "theology," and perhaps may thus be taken as another rendering of *feoptiia* itself. As the discussion of the second and third stages of spiritual vision in chapter 3 showed, there is some inherent tension between physical and spiritual knowledge-sight, and there is the suggestion in Trediakovsky's title that the proof of the divine through vision (*dokazatel'stvo o bogozrenii*) is based on empirical evidence (*po veshcham sozdannogo estestva*), that divine vision of God will come via physical vision of the created world. Hence the subtitle may also be paraphrased as: "a defense of God's existence by means of visual proofs." Trediakovsky mentions Leibniz's *Theodicy* (*Theodicée*, original in French, 1710) in the preface as one of the works he emulated, and like *Feoptiia* the word "theodicy" was a neologism, of Leibniz's invention (from the Greek *theos* plus *dike* [God plus justice]).[25] With these titles, Leibniz and Trediakovsky may also have gestured toward the tradition of classical cosmological works titled with neologisms going back at least to Hesiod's *Theogony*. Still, Trediakovsky acknowledged the difference between his didactic popularization in verse and Leibniz's work, a serious extended philosophical treatise. They are theodicies of a different order. One scholar rightly points out apropos of the *Traité de l'existence* that "Fénelon's theodicy . . . , unlike that of Leibniz, is not a justification of God, but rather a demonstration of his existence through the spectacle of nature's wonders," and the same is true for Trediakovsky's poem.[26]

Physicotheological works espoused a modernized version of Scholastic cosmology dependent on quasi-Aristotelian teleological arguments about the orderly, hierarchical nature of the universe; this is true, for example, in the works of Christian Wolff, which were authoritative in eighteenth-century Russia.[27] They also offer a striking example of Enlightenment faith in reason, both the imperative to justify religion via philosophy, and the special nature of Enlightenment logic. Enlightenment thought was caught in a kind of ontological and epistemological loop going back to the way Descartes had posed the central problems of modern philosophy. Descartes's ultimate criterion for knowledge, the well-known formula of "clear and indubitable truth," was self-verifying, as it posited an inner faculty ("the light of nature," which in turn depended on Scholastic proofs of God's existence). If sight is divinely underwritten, it follows logically that what is obvious—what is seen, what is visible—is true. Such proofs of the objectivity of sight-reason necessarily depend to some degree on individual subjective perception.[28] This problem, known by historians of philosophy as the Cartesian Circle, is clearly present in *Feoptiia*, which echoed Descartes's position presented in Fénelon's *Traité de l'existence et des attributs de Dieu*. As one eighteenth-century French critic of the *Traité* charged, "Fénelon has fallen into the same vicious circle as his leader [Descartes]: Reason is to demonstrate the existence of God, and God to guarantee the validity of Reason . . . they presuppose what they set out to justify."[29] Reason is the tool "natural theology" uses to prove God's existence and goodness, but without God's existence reason cannot be validated; otherwise one is left in the solipsistic cul-de-sac of Descartes's "*cogito ergo sum*," with no way to validate anything outside the self.

Physicotheological faith-based support of reason of the kind in *Feoptiia* also drew on ancient and more modern Christian and Orthodox sources, and the very notion of the divine light of nature or of reason could easily be transposed into theological terms. While there are basic differences in perspective between Palamas's defense of the personal experience of the divine and Trediakovsky's physicotheological conclusions allegedly based on universal, impersonal logic, the mystical tradition of vision defended by Palamas also formed a background on which Trediakovsky's physicotheological arguments could rest. They may also be seen in terms of the threefold division of spiritual ascent as its second stage: the knowledge or contemplation of created things in which discursive reason (*dianoia*) combines with spiritual intellect (*nous*) and ascends toward—or partakes in—divine vision. In this sense, the difference in outlook reflects the contrast between the mystical and moderate rationalist currents in Orthodox theology.

The first and most basic assertion of *Feoptiia* is that sight is a valid tool of cognition. As in the case of the open book of nature, Trediakovsky claims in the prose summary of the second epistle that "in order . . . to demonstrate the truth incontestably and clearly, . . . it is not necessary to use great subtlety of argument, but one simple glance [*edin prostyi vzor*] at all things, taken together however with some general reasoning and attentiveness in scrutinizing things, is alone sufficient" (IP 211). This passage paraphrases Fénelon's opening sentence: "I cannot open mine eyes without admiring the art that shines throughout all nature; the least cast [i.e., glance] suffices to make me perceive the hand that makes everything [that exists]."[30] The truth is so clear and unmistakable, all one has to do to be convinced is to open one's eyes.[31] For all of the asserted simplicity, however, there is a palpable element of equivocation in Trediakovsky's formulation, marked by the distance between the "one simple glance" that "alone is sufficient" and the clause introduced by "however" ("taken together however with some general reasoning and attentiveness in scrutinizing things"). The need to bridge this gap marks the challenge, the need to defend faith (or Cartesian subjectivism) in terms of reason. Trediakovsky marshals many strategies to bolster the "simple, self-evident truth" and to ward off the cracks and fissures of doubt.

The power of vision to immediately take in and reveal the truth is a leitmotif of *Feoptiia*:

Единственно простый доволен токмо взор (IP 213)
[A simple glance alone is sufficient]

Видите вы сами:
Я свидетельствуюсь в том всенадежно вами. (IP 201)
[See for yourselves: / I bear completely reliable witness of this through you.]

Может явственно всяк зреть (IP 201)
[Anyone can see this distinctly]

Всяк, едва на твари с примечанием воззрит,
То творцом премудрым разум свой и озарит. (IP 203)
[Anyone who merely glances at creation with attention / Will have his mind illuminated by the most wise Creator.]

Едва кто всех вещей воззрил на всяк конец (IP 212)
[One who has but glanced at anything in any direction]

*Feoptiia* insists that when one opens one's eyes to the world and to the "light of nature" (*prirodnyi svet*) or the "light of reason," one sees God's hand at work everywhere. The proofs of His existence as Creator and Prime Mover are seen, for example, in the structure of the heavens:

[Д]ругие чудеса
Взор поражают наш; а те суть—небеса.
Огромностям дивясь пречудным, познаваю
Всесильну руку я: ту в них усмотреваю,
Которая свод сей в окружности такой,
Что равную понять не может здесь ум мой,
Над нашими с верьхов главами утвердила
И чашею к бокам в пространстве ж ниспустила. (IP 227)[32]
[Other miracles / Strike our vision, and these are the heavens. / Amazed by the most marvelous magnitudes, / I recognize the all-powerful hand. In them I see that / Which established the vault in this circumference, / Whose equal my intellect cannot conceive, / And set it above our heads from above / And lowered it like a chalice upside down in space.]

The "simple act of vision" is richly laden with meaning, both in terms of what is seen—the miracles of nature—and of its impact. Seeing that which the "intellect cannot conceive" produces feelings of wonderment, ecstasy, joy, and an awareness of beauty, which to some degree replicate the emotional response to Lomonosov's odes, but belong to the lower, second level of the "spiritual intellect."

The response to the "simple act of vision" substitutes wonder for logical proofs in order to draw some sort of conclusion from the things that the "intellect cannot conceive." Following Aristotle, wonder has traditionally been interpreted as a special category of cognition, an emotional response that results from the ways in which the unknowable is experienced and assimilated. Wesley Trimpi, explicating Aristotle's discussion in the *Metaphysics*, describes the correlation between the degree of an object's familiarity or knowability and the "degrees of astonishment" that are evoked. Wonder in these terms occurs in inverse proportion to understanding, that is, wonder decreases as knowledge expands, and the greatest wonder results from the things least comprehensible, in a progression from "things knowable relative to us" to those that are "foreign, uncommon, and unexpected," the highest of which are divine.[33] The Aristotelian emphasis on delimiting wonder, the drive "to domesticate the marvelous" in terms of knowledge, contrasts to that of Longinus (a.k.a. "Pseudo-Longinus"), who in his tract "On the Sublime" argued for a wonder that was irreducible to reason and logical knowledge, which he called the sublime. According to Longinus, "the effect of genius is not to persuade the audience but rather to transport them out of themselves [i.e., ecstasy]. Invariably what inspires wonder casts a spell on us and is always superior to what is merely convincing and pleasing. For our convictions are usually under our control, while such passages exercise an irresistible power of mastery," scattering "everything before it like a bolt of lightning."[34] This distinction between Aristotelian wonder and Longinus's sublime offers another way of distinguishing between the rationalist and mystical Orthodox approaches to visible reality. On the one hand, there is wonder that reconciles itself into knowledge via reason, as the objects of wonder are assimilated. On the other there is an irreducible species of wonder that overcomes all rational limits, a paradoxical "lack of knowledge that is higher than knowledge, and knowledge that is higher than understanding" (as Palamas described the experience of uncreated light, quoted in chapter 3).

This distinction is thus also compatible with one Lossky makes between the revelatory ecstasy of "the early stages of the mystical life"—associated with the odes—and the process of acclimatization to "the constant experience of the divine reality.[35] The differentiation may help to distinguish Lomonosov's odes from *Feoptiia* as two kinds of ocularcentric work, both involving wonder as a characteristic response to the divine, but differing in their concepts of vision and "degrees of astonishment." The ecstatic vision of the odes results from a revelation of the unknowable and inexpressible, and their emotional response is correspondingly charged. Notably, Boileau's translation of "On the Sublime" (1674), which initiated discussions of the concept in modern European literature, served as a theoretical basis for Lomonosov's odic practice.[36] Wonder in the *Feoptiia*, on the other hand, deals with "the familiar things close at hand" in a style that is "concerned with the meticulous scrutiny (by the eye) of things and events, most suitable for scientific investigation."[37] Still, in the *Feoptiia* Trediakovsky often resorts to the rhetoric of emotional effusion and explicitly describes how the reader-viewer is expected to react:

> Всё долженствует нас сие всех приводить,
> Дивящихся, в восторг и ум наш просветить
> Строением во всем премудрости толики,
> И благости творца, и силы превелики (IP 251)
> [Everything should bring all of us, in amazement, / Into ecstasy and illuminate our mind / So great is the wisdom in the world's whole structure, / And the Creator's goodness, and His most great powers]

Even while the wonder, amazement, and ecstasy cited here and elsewhere in *Feoptiia* suggest a connection to mystical vision, Trediakovsky's physicotheological argument concerns not primarily the mystical experience of theophany but an explanation of how sensual-intellectual faculties prove God's existence. *Feoptiia*'s approach is more didactic than experiential, more intellectual than psychagogic (to use Trimpi's term), and its heavy philosophical discourse lacks emotional power. There are many moments that do suggest that divine sight underwrites the mind and senses, for example:

> Сотворивший очи на видение нам дня
> Искры в них небесны и небесного огня
> По щедроте положил, да и красотою
> Возвеличил, ничему б не равняться с тою.
> Сии суть зерцала: образ всяк в них естества
> Начертан бывает мудростию божества;
> Всю природу видит ум светлыми очами,
> Света подают ему свет зарей лучами.

Чудно! (IP 272)

[The one who created our eyes for us to see the day, / Placed heavenly sparks of divine fire in them / Out of generosity, and exalted them with beauty / Which nothing can equal. / These are mirrors: every image of nature is inscribed / In them with divine wisdom. / The mind sees all of nature with bright eyes, / They bring the light of sunrise's rays to it. / Marvelous!]

If creation is the mirror of divine perfections, the eyes and vision are also divine both as conduits of wisdom ("the mind sees all of nature with bright eyes") and also as receptacles of "sparks of divine fire" that are themselves "inscribed with wisdom." The world is reflected or contained in the eyes, not as a subjective, solipsistic self-mirroring, or as an ecstatic visionary experience, but as an objective image-microcosm of all creation.[38] This is both the "mind's sight" and the external light of nature, suggesting a unity of inner and outer vision.

As in Palamas, the "one single glance" may grasp everything instantaneously but nevertheless remains in the dark about the essential nature of the experience:

Весь неба, солнца, звезд толь красный в вид убор,—
Единым взглядом се мой постигает взор.
Почто ж мне нужно есть учиться, да познаю,
Откуду двиг во мне, того не постигаю? (IP 293)

[The whole attire of the heavens, suns and stars, so beautiful to see / My vision grasps in one single glance. / Why do I need to study this, indeed I comprehend it, / [But] from whence this change in me, that I cannot explain.]

Palamas describes the experience of uncreated light in very similar terms: "by means of some supernatural knowledge he [a person] knows precisely that he is seeing light that is higher than light, but how he sees, he does not know at that time, indeed he cannot penetrate the nature of his vision due to the unanalyzable character of the spirit by which he sees."[39] Yet unlike Palamas, who tries to confirm that the experience of the divine is real, Trediakovsky's goal here is to prove the existence of God by means of reason and the senses.[40]

## The Argument from Design

To look out into the universe (to cite Young's *Night Thoughts* again) is to find system, order, and in them, a more certain faith:

> To look on *Truth* unbroken, and intire;
> Truth in the *System*, the full Orb; where Truths
> By Truths inlightene'd, and sustain'd, afford
> An Arch-like, strong Foundation, to support
> Th' incumbent Weight of absolute, complete
> *Conviction*; Here, the more we press, we stand
> More Firm; Who most examine, most Believe.[41]

For Young, looking here is of a more solid and sustained kind than mere eye opening, and the main issue is that it reveals so clearly and obviously the arch of system, and thus "Truth in the *System*" itself. Another contemporary French critic of Fénelon reduced this idea to what might seem its most absurd syllogistic form—"il y a de l'ordre, donc il y a un Dieu"—but that did not lessen the fact that for many this remained an extremely convincing argument.[42] (The notion was reiterated in the famous line from Pope's *An Essay on Man* that so impressed Trediakovsky: "Order is Heav'n's first law." In Popovsky's translation: "Poriadok pervyi est' sozdatelev zakon."[43]) This idea derived from the Aristotelian argument that assumed that this order or system a priori necessitated a First Cause, a Prime Mover. The logic seemed ironclad, the proofs of God's existence irresistible, to the point that even entertaining doubts seemed unthinkable. As Trediakovsky put it in his preface to the *Feoptiia*:

> All created things, material and non-corporeal, overwhelmingly prove His existence; and it seems in no way possible that a person of healthy and undoubted mind could not only assert that THERE IS NO GOD, but not even entertain any doubt about whether He exists or if He could be the way He is [*takovyi i tolikii*]. It would be strange to even think, not to speak of hearing it asserted by someone, that this world is mere necessity, and therefore consists only of itself, not demanding a cause which would have produced it by means of infinite power; and that the motion of things comes from itself, according to laws of necessity. [To be] such a so-called speculative atheist, it would seem, is completely impossible [*vsemirno byt', mnitsia, nevozmozhno*].[44]

The basic proof is taken for granted as universally understood and accepted, as something obvious; it is simply a question of being "of healthy and undoubted mind." The reasoning seemed incontrovertible and the alternative out of the question, suggesting chaos, the supremacy of blind, senseless chance.

The proof here, the core of the physicotheological position, is based on the so-called "argument from design" that deduced God's existence from the astonishing order and interconnectedness of the physical universe.

Lomonosov laid it out very clearly in his *Rhetoric* in a seven-page proof of God's existence based on Cicero's dialogue *On the Nature of the Gods*. It was also meant as an exercise in formal logic, the illustration of a "conditional syllogism" (*uslovnyi sillogizm*). This syllogism goes as follows: "If something consists of parts, of which each one depends on another for its existence, [that means that] it was put together by a rational being. The visible world consists of such parts, of which each one depends on another for its existence. It follows that the visible world was created by a rational being."[45] The ideas expressed in this tripartite argument—two premises and conclusion—had far-reaching influence in the eighteenth century, and provided a basic theological framework for the physicotheological argument and faith in the validity of the visible world. *On the Nature of the Gods*, which has been termed Cicero's *summa theologica*, had a major impact on both the medieval Christian tradition (via St. Augustine and Thomas Aquinas), as well as on the growth of modern philosophy from Grotius and Descartes to Montesquieu, Locke, and Hume.[46] Cicero's logic concerning interlocking parts deriving from a rational being, as well as its application to the question of God's existence—the argument from design—was generally accepted by the later Christian tradition, which found additional support for it in Holy Writ. These ideas made a dramatic comeback in the early modern period in the wake of challenges to the old medieval view of the cosmos. As Saine has noted, with the demise of Aristotelian-Ptolemaic cosmology, the even older Epicurean atomist model that it had displaced, and whose arguments had long seemed scientifically discredited as well as morally repugnant, now suddenly took on dangerous new plausibility. Seemingly outmoded and long-resolved arguments against the Epicurean position assumed new relevance.[47] Texts like *On the Nature of the Gods*, which iterated the position of the Sophists against the Epicureans, many of whose arguments had been taken up by the Church Fathers centuries before, also took on new relevance. This was especially true in Russia, where the Newtonian system was only beginning to take a firm hold and where the Aristotelian Scholastic theological framework had not been completely displaced even among modern scientists.[48]

Lomonosov's working out of the second premise of the syllogism—the inter-connectedness of the visible world—closely parallels the argument in *Feoptiia*: "But let us take a look at the marvelous enormity of this visible world and at its parts: do we not see everywhere the mutual connection of things whose very being benefits one another? Do not the mountains' height and the valleys' inclination serve so that the water that comes together from their springs creates streams and finally unites in rivers? And do not rivers themselves stretch out over the broad earth like the manifold branches of a thick tree, small and large united, so as to water and bathe the inhabitants spread out over the land and with its movement to connect the human race for its mutual benefit?"[49] The discussion of water circulation continues for several pages, covering the role of the heavenly bodies, plants, seeds, and then the arrangement of the human body and its sense organs. Similarly, more than half of *Feoptiia* is taken up with cataloguing the many (potentially infinite) things that demonstrate the universe's structure and logical purpose, arguing that it could not have come into being by necessity or blind accident. The second epistle, for example, covers the earth, the sun, moon, stars, and planets as well as the four elements (earth, water, air, fire); the third the animal kingdom ("natural history"); and the fourth the human body.

Cicero's *On the Nature of the Gods*, which provided direct material for Lomonosov's "mutual connection and benefits" argument, also offered a model of such catalogues, which were a staple of physicotheological works.[50] Part of the efficacy of the argument about the interconnectedness of physical reality evidently came from the sheer mass of examples and variations on a theme. While such repetitions may seem annoyingly redundant and naïve to a modern reader, their effect on a premodern reader may have been to underscore both the newly discovered variety of the natural world and the fact that it was amenable to reason and analysis. The argument from design proceeded in good Aristotelian fashion from the magnificence of the universe to an appreciation of the grand designer. Cicero, Fénelon, and St. John of Damascus alike liken God to an artist, and the universe to an ever-astonishing work of art—an epic, a classical sculpture, a painting. In *Feoptiia* God is described as the "supreme artist" (*khudozhnik* or *ver'khovneishii zograf*, literally, "painter"). Looking at the *Iliad*, for example, Trediakovsky (after Fénelon), asks: "Who could believe that chance made order / Out of the mix of all these letters and created such a unity?" ("Kto poverit' mozhet, chto pripadok vsekh bukv smes' / V tot privel poriadok i soiuz sostavil ves'?") (IP 203). Cicero had used Ennius's *Annals* as his example. Similarly,

Мира здание сие, обще всеми зримо,
С разумом как можно дерзновенно утверждать,
Что оно припадком возмогло в порядок стать?
Можно ль сомневаться впрямь, что свет не всесильным,
Не всемудрым сотворен, не всеизобильным? (IP 205)
[How could anyone with any sense impudently claim / That the edifice of the world, universally visible to everybody, / Could have assumed order by chance?

/ Can anyone really doubt that the world was created / By something not all-powerful, not all-wise, not all-bountiful?]

One of the most common dramatizations of this second syllogistic premise describes the moment when the viewer looks out into the dark, starry sky and is overcome by the sublime order of the universe. The prototype of this epiphanic experience may also be traced to Cicero's *On the Nature of the Gods*, which quotes the following passage from Aristotle's lost treatise *On Philosophy*:

> Imagine that there were people who had always dwelt below the earth in decent and well-lit accommodation embellished with statues and pictures, and endowed with all the possessions which those reputed to be wealthy have in abundance. These people had never set foot on the earth, but through rumor and hearsay they had heard of the existence of some divine power wielded by gods. A moment came when the jaws of the earth parted, and they were able to emerge from their hidden abodes, and to set foot in this world of ours. They were confronted by the sudden sight of earth, seas, and sky; they beheld towering clouds, and felt the force of winds; they gazed on the sun, and became aware of its power and beauty, and its ability to create daylight by shedding its beams over the whole sky. Then, when night overshadowed the earth, they saw the entire sky dotted and adorned with stars, and the phases of the moon's light as it waxed and waned; they beheld the risings and settings of all those heavenly bodies, and their prescribed, unchangeable courses through all eternity. When they observed all this, they would certainly believe that gods existed, and that these great manifestations were the works of gods.[51]

The episode described here is comparable to the parable of the cave in *The Republic*, only in this version people escape not into the transcendent realm of truth and light but out into the physical world, whose unvarying natural movements embody eternal truth. Aristotle's underground visitors experience a vision of divine power and beauty that may also be seen to exemplify Aristotle's conception of wonder, discussed above, that sparks philosophical inquiry and aspires "to domesticate the marvelous."[52] The truth is both something to be physically felt (the force of the wind, the power of the sun, the process of seeing) and also logically deduced, as the people from beneath the earth scrutinize and become aware of the regular and eternal motions of nature.

Aristotle's story also recalls and contrasts Symeon the New Theologian's description of what divine ecstasy is like, related above in chapter 3, when a man born in a dark prison suddenly gets a glimpse of a sunlit landscape through a chink in the wall.[53] Symeon himself further contrasts this kind of initial ecstatic moment of revelation to the man's gradual acclimatization to the sun, just as (according to Lossky) "the soul which progresses in the spiritual life no longer knows ecstasies" but "has the constant experience of the divine reality in which it lives."[54] In describing the ecstatic experience, neo-Palamist theologians distinguish between the Catholic view that conceives of it as something "created," the "supernatural" action of grace totally under God's control and conferred at specific moments, and Orthodox ecstasy as spiritual ascent, partaking in the divine, eternal, uncreated energies—a grace that is always accessible to the pure in spirit. One can also distinguish between levels of ecstasy: the initial ecstatic shock as opposed to accommodation to it (which Lossky describes as an end to ecstasies). These may correspond to the two varieties of wonder described above and the differing "degrees of astonishment." Aristotole's earth dwellers seem to experience the more "rational" kind of revelation, systematically surveying the earth, sea, stars, phases of the moon, and so on, over an extended period of time. This contrasts to ecstasy of the more radical sort, described in terms of a sudden shock, loss of consciousness, out-of-body experience, and irrational extremes (e.g., divine darkening, blinding, being struck down).

This motif of revelation of the glory of the physical universe, experienced by gazing up into the sky, often appears in eighteenth-century Russian religious and meditative poetry. One lesser-known example is Sumarokov's reworking of Psalm 13 (Psalm 14 in the Western Psalter, beginning: "The fool says in his heart, 'There is no God'"):

> Безумный говорит: творца вселенной нет;
> И что состроился собой пространный свет.
> Такое здание устроится ль собою?
> Безумный зря! везде создатель пред тобою.
>  Воззри на небеса,
> На солнце, на луну, на звезды, ко ефиру,
> И к обитаему нам созданному миру,
> На горы, на луга, на воды, на леса:
> Воззри и на свое ты собственное тело;
> Незапности ль одной сие премудро дело?[55]
>
> [The fool says that the universe has no creator, / And that the spacious world was formed on its own. / Could such an edifice be fashioned by itself? / Senseless prattle! The Creator is everywhere before you. / Look at the heavens. / At the sun, the moon, the stars, the ether, / And at the inhabited world made for us. /

At the mountains, pastures, waters, forests, / Look too at your very own body; / Could something so wise [appear] right out of the blue?]

As L. F. Lutsevich notes, there is nothing resembling these lines in the original psalm—this is a "completely independent" authorial interpolation.[56] Sumarokov's direct address to the doubter of God, nowhere in the original psalm, reiterates the logic of the physicotheological argument, centering on God's role as Creator, knowable by His creation.

Another example is verses Lomonosov included in an addendum to his 1761 essay on Venus's passing across the sun, a free and incomplete paraphrase of the first eleven lines of Claudian's "Against Rufinus":

Я долго размышлял и долго был в сомненье,

Что есть ли на землю от высоты смотренье;

Или по слепоте без ряду все течет,

И промыслу с небес во всей вселенной нет.

Однако, посмотрев светил небесных стройность,

Земли, морей и рек доброту и пристойность,

Премену дней, ночей, явления луны,

Признал, что божеской мы силой созданы. (8:695 and 4:376)

[I meditated a long time and was in doubt / Whether or not something watches over us from on high / Or whether everything flows blindly, without sequence, / And there is no Providence anywhere in the universe. / However, having looked at the harmony of the heavenly luminaries, / And the goodness and rightness of the earth, seas, and rivers, / The succession of days and nights, the appearance of the moon, / I recognized that we have been created by divine power.]

As in Sumarokov's psalm paraphrase, this is a calm and serious scrutiny of the natural world. The poem contrasts Providence and blindness, as gazing into the sky inspires a reassuring conviction of the harmony, goodness, and rightness or propriety (*pristroinost'*) of both heaven and earth. But this was not merely a "poetic" notion; in the addendum to the scientific paper of 1761, Lomonosov defended the practice of modern science, especially astronomy, in the same terms: "While the indescribable wisdom of God's deeds is clear [*iavstvuet*] if only from meditations on the whole of creation [*o vsekh tvariakh*] to which the study of the physical [world] leads, astronomy more than anything else gives a sense of His majesty and power [*velichestva i mogushchestva*], demonstrating the order of heavenly bodies' motions. . . . We imagine the Creator the more distinctly the more precisely our observations accord with our predictions; and the more we achieve new discoveries, the louder we glorify Him."[57]

Understandably in the context of a scientific paper, vision is presented here as a rational process of looking and meditation, a continual exercise of reason that is nevertheless accompanied by a sense of wonder and awe at God's majesty and power. Lomonosov repeats the basic physicotheological argument about God revealed through His creation, and goes on to ground his position on the authority of Holy Writ, the "inspired prophetic and apostolic books" by "the great teachers of the church." In particular, he cites the authority of St. Basil's *Hexaemeron* ("In Six Days," in Russian *Shestodnev*), sermons that examine the six days of creation as described in Genesis and attempt to accommodate science to scripture. Lomonosov also refers to St. John of Damascus's "Exposition of the Orthodox Faith" (part three of the *Fount of Knowledge*, a kind of *summa theologica* for the Eastern Orthodox). Notably, the "Exposition" begins with a guarded defense of reason, necessary not only for scientific pursuits, but also for theological speculation itself. SS. Basil and John of Damascus were important figures in the tradition of "moderate theological rationalism," and together with Gregory of Nazianzus (Grigorii Bogoslov), were among the main Eastern Orthodox writers who contributed to the physicotheological tradition and to the moderate rationalist Enlightenment Orthodoxy espoused by eighteenth-century Russian hierarchs like Metropolitan Platon. Notably, all three of these church fathers were famous both as theologians and as poets or orators, and were revered in the East and West (although Lomonosov contrasts their enlightened position to the anti-scientific bias of Western Christian thought).[58]

Many physicotheological works returned to the ideas and structure of the *hexaemeron* genre that posited a basic connection between the universe's being (ontology) and the process of its creation (cosmology); many physicotheological compositions were conceived as cosmologies for the modern era.[59] Some traced the movement from night to day (as in Lomonosov's "Evening" and "Morning Meditations") or reiterated the six days of creation. Like Basil the Great's *Hexaemeron*, in which each sermon relates to one day of creation, *Feoptiia* is divided into six parts, six "conversations" (*besedy*, notably, also a term for "sermon").[60]

## The Problem of Those Who Do Not See

To what extent God's signs are obvious in the material world is a question resolved somewhat differently by various physicotheological writers. For many, like Trediakovsky in *Feoptiia*, this problem is not admitted, because the truth (with some minor qualifications) is held to be self-evident, and the argument from design logically unimpeachable. The question of the "perishable eye" (the physical capacity of vision) aside, the degree of obviousness also depends on the nature of the one who looks. In the 1761 addendum cited earlier Lomonosov argued that God created "the visible world . . . so that a person, looking upon the immensity, beauty and harmonious construction of the edifice, would recognize divine omnipotence, to the extent of the understanding given him [po mere sebe darovannogo poniatiia]."[61] The final caveat accords with traditional Orthodox teaching (as in Palamas, for example) that one's capacity to see and understand depends on the moral purity of one's soul. For other and more secular-minded Enlightenment physicotheologists, this depended rather on one's education and capacity for reason. Where for the former the ability to see truly characterizes the saint, for the latter this privilege is given to the geniuses of natural science.[62]

*Feoptiia*, however, insists that to the unbiased viewer the truth is obvious, self-evident, unmistakable, and universally accessible to everyone:

На весь чин естества вперяя внешний глаз,
Представлю ону внутрь я божества показ.
Такая мудрость всем всегда есть не закрыта,
Да разве от страстей в жар может быть забыта.
Едва кто всех вещей воззрил на всяк конец,
Не может не узреть, что их премудр творец . . . (IP 212)
[Directing my external eye to the entire order of nature, / I imagine within the manifestation of the divine. / Such wisdom is never hidden from anyone, / Although it may be forgotten when passions are kindled. / Anyone who has even taken the least glance at all things / Cannot fail to see how very wise is their Creator . . .]

That is, one cannot help but see the truth, either by looking outward into nature or inward at its reflection within; inner and outer vision are in perfect balance. There is a certain slippage between "directing one's eyes" and wisdom that is "never hidden," between "the entire order of nature" and the finite self, between "the least glance" and taking in "all things," but Trediakovsky suggests that anyone who does not see this truth must be blind: literally blind, ignorant, or blinded by passion.

If seeing means believing, not to see may represent an intentional refusal to accept the truth, and those who do not see are thus to be pitied or scorned, but (obviously) not to be taken seriously. In this context, reason taken too far, reason in excess (in philosophical terms, either the skepticism of a Hobbes or the Deism of a Spinoza), also becomes an obstacle to the truth. This is sight that is tantamount to blindness, the inverse of sublime "darkening." Examples may be multiplied:

И не ослепленный грубых заблуждений тьмой,
Весь в природном свете пребывающий с собой,
Гнусными ниже страстьми сердца восхищенный,
Ни пороками, ни злом скотства развращенный,
Не возможет тотчас Бога жива не познать,
А безбожных мыслей из среды той не изгнать; [. . .]
Можно ль, коль бы вам во мрак слепо ни стремиться,
Чтоб от истинных зарей в том не просветиться:
Разве вы нарочно восхотите затворить
Очи внутрь душевны, света б правды вам не зрить.
Инако преодолеть нельзя всем предлога,
Кой доказывает вам присносущна Бога,
Разного от мира, миру здателя сему,
Всяких благ начало и виновника всему. (IP 197–98)
[And one who has not been blinded by the darkness of coarse error, / Who fully abides with himself in nature's light, / Not enthralled by vile passions of the heart, / Nor by vices, nor perverted by the evil of bestiality / Cannot fail to recognize the living God immediately, / And to expel godless thoughts (. . .) / Is it possible that however blindly we strive in the gloom / We can never be enlightened by true sunrises? / Do you really purposefully want to shut / Your spiritual eyes within, so as not to see the light of truth? / Otherwise no one could overcome the proposition / That proves to you the ever-existing God, / (Who is) different from the world, Creator of the world, / Source of all good things and cause of everything.]

То промысл я такой в нем самом ясно зрю,
Что оного не зреть—быть должно ослепленну
И всеконечно уж вовек обезумленну. (IP 249)
[I see such Providence in this so very clearly, / That in order not to see one must be blinded, / Completely and forever bereft of reason.]

Смотрение его толь ясно зримо есть,
Что не возможет скрыть от нас никая лесть
И что без слепоты извольныя не можно

Не видеть нам везде того, что есть неложно. (IP 251)
[His oversight is so clearly visible / That no kind of flattery can hide it from us, / And it is impossible without intentional blindness / For us not to see what truly exists all around us.]

Мудрости в сем вышни, в мудрованиях нелеп,
Точно кто не видит, и с очами тот есть слеп;
Тот не токмо назван быть может малоумным,
Но бессмысленным совсем и страстями шумным. (IP 272)
[(One who has) wisdom within, but is foolish with sophistries / Is like one who does not see, who has eyes but is blind; / Such a person may be called not only weak of intellect, / But completely senseless, (overcome) by strident passions.]

Не вем, как можно быть толикой слепоте
Безбожия, при сей созданной лепоте?
Нечестие сие в себе есть толь порочно,
Что так слепотствовать не можно ненарочно.
Поистине здесь всяк божественну зрит власть,
Но отрицает кой ту чрез извольну страсть,
Котора Бог быть отнюдь бы не желала,
Чтоб, мести не бояс, бесчинием пылала. (IP 302)
[I do not know how atheism can be so blind / In the presence of such beauty that has been created. / This impiety is so perverted in itself / That to be thus blind cannot but be on purpose. / In truth everyone sees the divine power / But can deny it only through willful passion, / Which would not want there to be a God at all, / So as to blaze with mayhem, not fearing retribution.]

In contrast, in Lomonosov's "Evening" and "Morning Meditation on God's Greatness," the crisis of the lyric persona stems not from blindness due to passion or vice but from a consciousness of the limitations imposed by our "mortal sensations" (*brennykh chuvstv*). The "Meditations" are among Lomonosov's most famous lyrics and have been described as prototypical physicotheological works.[63] In contrast to the syllogistic logic of the *Rhetoric* and to Trediakovsky's *Feoptiia*, which like Fénelon's work is conceived as a proof of God's existence and attributes, the genre of meditation dramatizes the process of seeing and gaining understanding. Here the "one simple glance" is not quite so simple, but subject to doubt and questioning, as discussions of the rational structure of the universe yield to questions of gnoseology and epistemology. In epistemological terms, vision is not so unambiguously perfect, and what we see is defined by how "our perishable eye" functions.[64] The "Meditations" connect the epistemological problem to various natural-scientific theories (the nature of the Northern Lights and the sun's surface) and contemplate the limits of vision as a tool for knowing the physical universe.[65] In terms of gnoseology, the optimistic view of vision as divine runs up against the fact that God is fundamentally unknowable, unproveable, unseeable—beyond the limits of human comprehension.

The opening lines of the "Evening Meditation" set the tone, plunging us into darkness and confusion:

> Лице свое скрывает день.
> Поля покрыла мрачна ночь,
> Взошла на горы чорна тень,
> Лучи от нас склонились прочь.
> Открылась бездна звезд полна;
> Звездам числа нет, бездне дна.
>
> Песчинка как в морских волнах,
> Как мала искра в вечном льде,
> Как в сильном вихре тонкой прах,
> В свирепом как перо огне,
> Так я, в сей бездне углублен,
> Теряюсь, мысльми утомлен! (8:120–21)[66]

[Day hides its face. / Gloomy night has covered the fields, / A black shade has ascended the mountains. / The rays (of sunlight) have disappeared. / An abyss full of stars has opened up; / The stars are without number, the abyss bottomless. // Like a speck of sand in the sea waves, / Like a small spark in eternal ice, / Like fine dust in a powerful whirlwind, / Like a feather in a fierce fire, / So I, deep in this abyss, / Lose myself, wearied by thoughts!]

All is dark, confused, mysterious, and the "baroque" poetics (sound and word play, e.g., *bezdna . . . bezdne dna*) dramatizes the persona's sense of dislocation and contrasts with the desire for "classicist" transparency and understanding.[67]

Nevertheless, the truth upon which the "Meditations" meditate and the point to which they ultimately arrive is the validation of sight. The "Evening Meditation" offers several hypotheses on the nature of the Northern Lights,[68] but concludes with a continuing series of questions, as the poet's doubts seem to remain:

Сомнений полон ваш ответ
О том, что окрест ближних мест.
Скажитеж, коль пространен свет?
И что малейших дале звезд?
Несведом тварей вам конец?
Скажитеж, коль велик Творец? (8:123)
[Your answer is replete with doubts / About the places nearest man. / Pray tell us, how vast is the world (or: light)]? / What lies beyond the smallest stars? / Is creatures' end unknown to you? / Pray tell how great is God Himself?]

The "you" here refers to "the most wise men" (*premudrykh*), possibly natural scientists, but it also seems to include Lomonosov himself and his own scientific hypotheses. To some extent, the last question is also an answer, insofar as it is rhetorical, and insofar as defining the majesty of God is equal to defining His nature in general.[69] God exists, but how can one determine how great He is, and what are the limits to our understanding?

The tone of the "Morning Meditation" is far more affirmative than that of the "Evening" and we may consider it as offering a direct answer to the questions of the first.[70]

Чудяся ясным толь лучам,
Представь, каков Зиждитель сам! [. . .]
Велик Зиждитель наш господь! (8:117-18)
[And marveling at such radiant beams, / Just think how God Himself must be! (. . .) / Our Lord Creator is great!]

Nevertheless, the truth is not so obvious even in the "Morning Meditation." The picture of the sun's surface that makes up the scientific center of the poem's interest, describing Lomonosov's theory in verse, is presented not simply as a spontaneous act of sensation and understanding but also as an act of imagination:

*Когда бы* смертным толь высоко
*Возможно было* возлететь,
Чтоб к солнцу бренно наше око
*Могло*, приближившись, воззреть (italics mine) (8:117)
[*If it were only possible* for mortals / To fly so high above the earth / So that our perishable eye / *Could see* the sun, having come close to it]

As traditionally acknowledged by theologians and philosophers, the act of sight, for all its seeming immediacy, nevertheless involves mental processing, memory, thought (meditation), and imagination. The complex nature of human understanding was a central issue in Enlightenment thought, which also posed the question of the interaction between the physical and the spiritual, and material sensation and mental activity.[71] From an Orthodox perspective, this could be seen in terms of the second stage in the "threefold division" of spiritual ascent in which, as noted, the rational knowledge of created things (*dianoia*) combines with spiritual intellect (*nous*).

The resolution of the epistemological problem comes in the final stanzas of the "Morning Meditation," which may be taken as the denouement of both poems taken together.[72] First the difference between inner and outer vision is noted and the weakness of sensual sight before God's divine insight is recognized:

> Светило дневное блистает
> Лишь только иа поверхность тел,
> Но взор твой в бездну проницает,
> Не зная никаких предел. (8:119)
> [The luminary of day shines forth / But only on the surface of bodies; / But Your gaze penetrates the abyss, / Not subject to any limits.]

The poet's potential crisis of vision is resolved in the final stanza, which brings the poem close to a prayer by addressing God directly: "Tvorets! pokrytomu mne t'moiu / Prostri premudrosti luchi." ("To me, Creator, covered in darkness / Extend the rays of [Your] wisdom!") (8:119). "The rays of wisdom" serve as the culminating image of the entire poem (or cycle), combining the "two lights"—divine, spiritual light and real, physical light.[73] This is both a prayer for help and a reassertion of sight's grounding in divine wisdom. It thus arrives at fundamentally the same point as that which *Feoptiia* takes as its basic premise, the validation of vision as the path to God.

Trediakovsky, like Lomonosov, employs various rhetorical modes of discourse to re-create the sublime experience by verbal means, overwhelming logic by emotional effusion. This moment is sometimes portrayed in the *Feoptiia* as a darkening of the rational faculties that is also an enlightening (a marker of revelation):[74]

> Мятется разум наш, к сим высотам паря,
> На множество и тел и на далекость зря.

Се виды каковы! и зрим мы их колики!

Различные те коль! и разно коль велики!

Поистине на то, как древний муж сказал,

Бог человека сам единственно создал,

От прочих тварей всех отменна и отлична,

Чтоб красоту небес ему, зря, знать коль слична,

Свободно очи выспрь возможет он возвесть

И видеть над его главою, что там есть. (IP 227)

[Our reason falters as we soar to the heights, / Seeing the multitude of bodies and the distances. / What views these are! And how many do we see! / How much variety! And how variously great! / Truly it is as the ancient wise man said, / God himself created man only / To distinguish and privilege him before all other creatures, / So that he, seeing the beauty of the heavens, / Could know how (all is) joined, / Could freely raise his eyes upward / And see what is there above his head.]

As often in *Feoptiia*, Trediakovsky reverts to exclamations. He uses the collective "we" as the subject, and substitutes the experiential for the philosophical, the aesthetic for the rational. The "ancient wise man" might be a reference to Cicero, whom Fénelon mentions by name in the passage Trediakovsky is adapting (Breitschuh suggests a specific subtext from *On the Nature of the Gods*), or as I. Z. Serman suggests, to David the psalmist.[75] The confusion itself is significant. The psalms were one source of physicotheological inspiration, as we saw in Sumarokov's case, and Trediakovsky, like many physicotheological poets, wrote paraphrases of the Psalms, echoes of which may be found in the *Feoptiia*.[76] A similar exclamatory mode takes over in passages like the following, with 17 exclamation marks in 10 lines:

Колико зримых Солнц! Земель колико нижных!

Колико тварей всех! родов коль непостижных!

Счетаний коль взаем! колик исправный чин!

Различных сколько действ! и коль вторых причин!

Всему един чертеж! но коль по виду разно!

О! промысл, всё ж со всем не втуне и не праздно!

А под одною всё то хлубию на взгляд!

Объемлется одним тот обыдом весь ряд!

Разлитие то всё! прекрасное убранство!

Темнеет свет ума: нет сил обнять пространство! (IP 232)

[How many Suns are visible! How many lower planets! / How many creatures of all kinds! Unimaginable how many sorts! / How many combinations! How precise the order! / How many different movements! / And how many secondary causes! / And only one blueprint for everything! But how visually diverse! / Oh, Providence, all this is not in vain, not idle! / Yet beneath it all, it looks to be an abyss! / The entire sequence taken in a single daily cycle! / All abundance! Beautiful adornment! / The mind's light dims: one has not enough power to embrace this space!]

Again a darkening signals an enlightening, and there is no fear of being misled, no dysfunction between inner and outer vision, reason and faith; what you see is what you get, and what you get is good.

If the exclamatory mode substitutes forceful assertion for argumentation, a further common rhetorical strategy, which Lomonosov also employs both in the syllogism and the "Meditations," is to shower the reader with questions, to which no answers are supplied (they are presumed to be obvious). One function of both the interrogatory and the exclamatory mode is to emphasize by repetition the overwhelming obviousness of God's existence. Objections are countered with more questions:

Я напротив спрошу: кто ж он, толико сильный,
Который естеству закон дал толь обильный?
Толь постоянный тот? и нужный толь закон?
Да сказывают мне, премудрый, кто есть он?
Устав, которым всё чиновно толь вертится,
Без наших мыслей сам на пользу нам трудится!
[. . .] Хранение кому ж мы всех вещей присвоим?
Кого началом всех уставом удостоим? (IP 233–34)
[On the contrary, I will ask: who then is he, so powerful, / Who gave nature such a lavish law? / So constant? so necessary? / And they say to me: who is this all-wise one? / The law by which everything turns so regularly, / That which labors for our benefit, / Without any reasoning from us! / (. . .) To whom then do we relegate the preservation of all things? / To whom do we vouchsafe the basis, the regulation of all things?]

Кто легионам звезд места дал пригвожденны?
А ниже вкруг послал планеты учрежденны?
Измерил точно всё, как оным расстоять?
От злата тем велел, сим от сребра сиять?

Кто чашам оным двиг разложистым собщает?

И свод огромный весь кругом нас обращает?

Но буде небо есть состав из жидких тел,

Какой в родстве себе наш воздух возымел,

То твердые тела на чем там пребывают?

Как в тягости своей ко дну не утопают?

И меж собою как не токмо не сплылись,

Но ни от стезь своих намало подались?

И то ж еще веков чрез многи толь округи

Отнеле же свой свет нам подают в услуги? (IP 231)

[Who had the legions of stars fastened to their places? / And who sent the planets beneath to be established in orbits? / And precisely measured where everything should be placed? / Who ordered that this (be made) of gold, and that to shine of silver? / Who imparts motion to these extensive chalices? / And directs the huge vault all around us? / And if the sky is a compound of liquid bodies, / Of the kind the air was made up of at its birth, / Then on what do the solid bodies then rest? / Why do they in their heaviness not sink to the bottom? / Or why do they not only not break up from their groupings / And fly apart, but do not depart at all from their paths? / And also after so many ages and revolutions / How can they still provide us the service of their light?]

Question and exclamation marks seem almost interchangeable. For comparison, consider also the following passage that makes the same basic argument, using the same rhetorical strategy, from John of Damascus's "Exposition of the Orthodox Faith," which both Lomonosov and Trediakovsky cite as a source for their works:[77]

Who is it that gave order to things of heaven and things of earth, and all those things that move in the air and in the water, and what existed before all this, heaven and earth, air and the elements like fire and water? Who combined and separated these things? Who set these in motion and keeps them on their unceasing and unhindered course? Was this not an Artist, who set out the law for all these things, according to which everything is done and guided? Who then is the Artist of this? Is it not the one who created it and brought it into existence? We cannot attribute such a power to blind chance, for, supposing this all came into being by chance, who [then] brought it all into such order? And we can give way on this point too, if you please, but who then observes and preserves those laws, according to which everything was once created? Someone else, of course, and not blind chance. And who is this other than God?[78]

Trediakovsky's lines also recall Lomonosov's paraphrase of Job ("Oda, vybrannaia iz Iova, Glava 38, 39, 40 i 41" ["Ode Taken from Job Chapters 28, 29, 40 and 41"]) of 1751, although in this poem, as in the original, the tone is harsh, threatening, and ironic, as when God asks:

Где был ты, как я в стройном чине
Прекрасный сей устроил свет,
Когда я твердь земли поставил
И сонм небесных сил прославил,
Величество и власть мою?
Яви премудрость ты свою! (8:387–88)[79]

[Where were you when in harmonious order / I established this beautiful world, / When I created the dry land / And the multitude of heavenly powers / Glorified by my greatness and power? / Show me *your* great wisdom!]

Lomonosov's syllogism-paraphrase of Cicero ends with a formal "Conclusion" that offers a gloss on the epiphanic experience of vision of the kind that we traced back to Aristotle's parable of the earth-dwellers. It begins:

> Hence there is no doubt at all that this visible world has been constructed by a being possessing reason and that, apart from this most marvelous and magnificent enormity, there is some force that has delimited [*sogradila*] it, a force that is immeasurably great, so as to create such an immeasurable edifice; a force so inconceivable and most wise so as to make it so well shaped, so harmonious, so magnificent; a force so inexpressibly generous that it established and confirmed the mutual utility of all these creations. Is not this immeasurably great, inconceivably wise, inexpressibly generous power none other than that which we call God and revere as immeasurably great and all-powerful, inconceivably wise, inexpressibly generous?[80]

The logic rests on a recognition of what is beyond logic, the distance between a perfect force (that which is "immeasurable," "inconceivable," "inexpressible," "immeasurable") and the human limitations of perception. The force here represents something like "nature" and also "none other than that which we call God"—a category itself beyond categorization.[81] Like Aristotle's earth-dwellers or Lomonosov's meditating lyric persona, the subject looks out and up at the heavens and natural landscape and is overcome by wonder: a special category of knowledge that may be taken for—or perhaps, better, as a substitute for—logical "proofs."[82]

Lomonosov's "Conclusion" ends:

> And you who are privileged to gaze into the book of unshakable natural laws, raise up your minds to the One who constructed them, and with extreme reverence thank the One who revealed to you the theater of His most wise deeds, and the more that you comprehend of them, the greater the awe with which you will extol Him. The tiniest of vermin [*gady*] proclaim His omnipotence to you, and the vast heavens announce, and the numberless stars demonstrate, His greatness that passes understanding. O how blind you are, Epicurus, that in the presence of so many luminaries you do not see your Creator! Sunk because of barbaric ignorance or carnal pleasures in the depth of unbelief, rise up, bethink yourself, having considered that the One who once shook the earth's foundations may throw you down alive into hell, the One who caused seas and rivers to overflow will drown you with His waters, the One who set mountains aflame with His touch will exterminate you with fire, the One who covers the heavens with storm clouds will strike you down with lightning. The One Who casts down lightning, He Is. Atheists, tremble![83]

This is a rich passage, that may perhaps even recall the Petrine scenario on a larger cosmic scale, revealing the theater of God's creation—a revelation of ultimate truth and being by means of "the simple glance." This is both physical sight—another reading of "the book of nature"—and a spiritual "raising up" of mental vision. It is a wonder that continues and increases, as "the more that you comprehend . . . , the greater the awe with which you will extol" the Creator. It also returns to those who do not see, and who hence pose a threat to the notion of the sufficiency, or the efficacy, of the "simple glance." The harshness of invective against Epicurus is noteworthy, as largely absent from Cicero's dialogue, which presents viewpoints both pro and con.

Like the added section to Sumarokov's psalm paraphrase and the preface to *Feoptiia*, atheists are a prime target; as discussed above, Trediakovsky directed his work "not only at those who may assert that THERE IS NO GOD, but [at those who] *might even arrive at a certain measure of doubt*" (my italics).[84] While there certainly may be other motivations for such polemical ardor, it suggests the need to defend the image of the ideal self and to fight back against a dangerous threat to psychic wholeness. Characterizing one's detractors as godless atheists beyond the pale of reason seems one unambiguous way to stave off internal misgivings.

## That Which Is Not So Obvious: The Ecclesiastes Paradigm

Nevertheless, for all of the insistence on the obviousness of divine truth, the gnoseological problem—the extent to which God in His "absolute unknowability" may nevertheless be known—remains. The physicotheological tradition emphasizes that the distance between man and God may be overcome, as both the physical world and the senses themselves may partake in the miracle of transfiguration, deification, or union with the divine. A contrasting traditional view—for example, that of Simeon Polotsky, also characteristic of the baroque—emphasizes the epistemological difficulty of seeing and knowing that stems from the sinfulness of human life and the deceptiveness of "external" sensations. Poetic works on this theme continued to be written, forming a counterpoint to the reigning optimistic, ocularcentric tendency, at times complementary and at times antagonistic to it.[85] An argument about the visual dominant would not be complete without taking these counter-examples into consideration.

We may for convenience refer to this secondary model of vision as the "Ecclesiastes paradigm," since many of its themes and motifs may be traced directly or indirectly back to Ecclesiastes, supplemented by various Psalms. Ecclesiastes, which famously focuses on the vanity of life, is one of the most difficult and debated books of the Bible, as it offers an ambiguous resolution to the problem of human existence somewhere between an apodictic demand to follow God's law (without rational or revelatory argument) and a philosophical determinism that some consider influenced by Stoicism.[86] Although sometimes taken as the metatext or master metaphor of the baroque, the Ecclesiastes theme, especially that of *vanitas vanitatum* (*sueta suet*), inspired a significant corpus of Russian classicist poetry as well.[87] The most obvious works connected to Ecclesiastes are the many poems that directly address the "vanity of vanities" theme, including those by Sumarokov, Kheraskov, Rzhevsky, Maikov, Kapnist, and Derzhavin, as well as a large number of Psalm paraphrases and poems that denounce a spectrum of vain pursuits (wealth, fame, beauty, etc.).[88] Where the function of triumphal odes was panegyric, poems on the Ecclesiastes theme were explicitly didactic, like much of eighteenth-century poetic production.[89]

In the Ecclesiastes paradigm, death and suffering are the only sure things, and unlike the situation described in *Feoptiia*, the world is ruled by accident (fortune), whether good or bad, and not by virtue. The cluster of thematic components associated with this paradigm include death, suffering, the inconstancy of fortune, the fleeting nature of time, the unreliable nature of rewards and punishments, the hegemony of the passions and vanity, and the fundamental futility of life. Vision is deceptive—likened to smoke, dreams, shadows, phantoms, and even blindness—and understanding the positive goods in life (happiness and pleasure), however fleeting and limited, constitutes wisdom, which in eighteenth-century Russian poems is usually presented in didactic terms as virtue (*dobrodetel'*), suggesting correct behavior. As with physicotheology, this is a mode of vision and a discourse that is not limited to particular genres.[90] It may also function as a contrast or counterpoint within a particular work.

On the philosophical-theological level, the Ecclesiastes paradigm dramatizes the futility of human endeavor and weakness of sight. Among the ethical problems it raises are: What is wisdom? How should one respond to the world's vanity and immorality? And how can the existence of God be reconciled to the world's evil (i.e., the question of theodicy)? These questions are not given conclusive answers in Ecclesiastes apart from the suggestion that such attempts at ultimate wisdom are themselves worthless, or the simple instruction to obey God's commandments and to trust in His justice. Given the lack of reference to an afterlife, immortality, or revelation, the reader remains primarily in the realm of negative truths. Russian poems in the Ecclesiastes paradigm offer a spectrum of responses to these issues. For example, wisdom may be seen as attaining spiritual tranquility (*spokoistvie*) amid the changing vicissitudes of life, either as the ideal of moderation (*umerennost'*), enjoyment of the pleasures of life as they present themselves (e.g., Voltaire's Epicurean cultivating of one's own garden), or keeping faith in God and divine commandments in spite of evil and misfortune (a quasi-Stoic cultivation of virtue amid vice).

The Ecclesiastes paradigm rejects or inverts the optimistic, ocularcentric paradigm that presumes the immanence of divine goodness in the world, in which the divine light of reason reveals good and evil for what they are. In contrast, the Ecclesiastes paradigm functions within the context of the dark mirror, the "fallen world," and either shows the inability to see (blindness or deception caused by sinfulness) or condemns intentionally evil vision. These poems stress the divergence between inner and outer, divine and human sight; they contrast deceptive, deceiving, transient human vision to God's perfect and all-comprehending sight. Rzhevsky's "Stans" ("Stanza") of 1761 may be taken as representative:

> Наполнен век наш суетою,
> Нигде блаженства в нем не зрим;
> Единой только мы мечтою
> Прельстясь, от истины бежим. [. . .]

Всяк то блаженством почитает,
К чему страсть ум его влечет,
И правды в слепоте не знает,
И суеты блаженством чтет.[91]

[Our age is full of vanity, / We do not see happiness anywhere; / Ensnared by a mere fancy / We flee from the truth. (. . .) // Every person considers happiness / That which his passion dictates, / And in blindness does not see the truth, / And considers vanities happiness.]

This poem describes a dark, fallen age, ruled by vanity and passion, in which sight misleads or blinds. As in Ecclesiastes, there is a tension (or contradiction) between the denial that happiness exists (in the first cited stanza) and the suggestion in the second that it exists but is not recognized. On the one hand, "we flee from the truth" and on the other we are blinded and cannot see it. Life is a dream, an illusion, and "man is like a breath; his days are like a fleeting shadow" (Psalm 144 [143]—the psalm chosen for translation in the competition over versification between Trediakovsky, Lomonosov, and Sumarokov in 1744).[92] People themselves are highly flawed, and a cardinal sin or error is vanity—to overrate one's value, power, and ability. This traditional moralism is an inversion of the defense of *liubochestie*—good pride—and contradicts the anthropology of the triumphal ode and classicist tragedy that celebrates the virtues of the Great Man and her or his *velikodushie*, equating heroism with divine qualities. In the Ecclesiastes paradigm the pursuit of power is also vanity, and this criticism may extend to the corruption and oppressiveness of rulers, although this theme is mostly confined to Psalm paraphrases (e.g., Derzhavin's paraphrase of Psalm 81 [82], for which he earned Catherine's displeasure).[93] Taken further, the Ecclesiastes paradigm may suggest the uselessness of all human endeavors in a metaphysical nihilism (e.g., Kheraskov's ode "Nichtozhnost'" ["Nullity"]).[94] Even the material world, including the heavens—whose permanence was such an important source of inspiration for the physicotheologists—is subject to decay and collapse, as here in Sumarokov's "Ода на суету мира" ["Ode on the Vanity of the World"]:

Во всем на свете сем премена,
И всё непостоянно в нем,
И всё составлено из тлена:
Не зрим мы твердости ни в чем;
Переменой естество играет,

Оно дарует, отбирает;

Свет—только образ колеса.

Не грянет гром, и ветр не дохнет,

Земля падет, вода иссохнет,

И разрушатся небеса.[95]

[Everything on this earth is subject to change, / And everything in it is inconstant, / And everything is made up of decay. / We see stability in nothing; / Nature plays with change, / It gives and takes away; / The world is but the image of a wheel. / Thunder will not strike and the wind will not die, / The earth collapses, the waters dry out, / And the heavens collapse.][96]

In the Ecclesiastes paradigm, the power of reason is undermined and subject to misuse, a tool of selfish passions and irrational will. The critique of reason is double-edged, however. On the one hand, there is a strong anti-rationalist streak; a harsh, satirical criticism of the pretensions masked under the guise of objectivity; criticism that taps into traditional Christian discourse on the seductions of vanity. On the other side, the anti-rationalist discourse of the Ecclesiastes paradigm is itself strongly tinged with a skeptical, critical rationalism that questions ultimate values without offering a solution in terms of the afterlife or immortality. Here arguments about the vanity of human endeavor and of the passions often echo Stoic and Epicurean moral discourse that asserts the positive value of virtuous behavior in this world, either in moderation and enjoyment of the passing pleasures of this life, or in achieving a dispassionate wisdom and tranquility in the face of inevitable suffering and death.[97]

Voltaire's poetic paraphrase of Ecclesiastes (the *Précis de l'Ecclésiaste* of 1759) dramatically posed this challenge to philosophical optimism, which he had attacked, most famously, in his poem on the Lisbon earthquake in 1755 and in *Candide*, also written in 1759.[98] Ecclesiastes provided Voltaire a unique opportunity (as one scholar put it) "to quote *bona fide* Scripture to support his own anti-biblical philosophy," and as another notes, it "offered Voltaire the peculiar luxury of sacred scepticism . . . , a scepticism, at least in the *Précis*, free from the destructive presence of barbed satire."[99] Despite various inflammatory statements Voltaire made about Ecclesiastes, his paraphrase was neither unfaithful to the biblical text nor in any way blasphemous, and tended toward a resolution of the problem of theodicy in Deist-Epicurean terms.[100] Ecclesiastes accorded with his skepticism toward dogmatic theology and his attempts to define the limits of God's action in an evil world.[101] As in *Candide*, he addressed the problem of how to find a way to exist morally in an immoral world without self-deception, and "cultivate your own garden," which was not so far from the message of Ecclesiastes.

Comparing the ending of Voltaire's *Précis de l'Ecclésiaste* both with the text of Ecclesiastes and with the adaptations (largely based on Voltaire) by Kheraskov (1765, revised 1779) and by Karamzin (1797) helps gauge the Russian recension of the Ecclesiastes paradigm.[102] The last sentences of Ecclesiastes offer a curt summary of the book: "Vanity of vanities, saith the preacher; all is vanity. . . . And further, by these, my son, be admonished: of making many books there is no end; and much study is a weariness of the flesh. Let us hear the conclusion of the whole matter: Fear God, and keep His commandments: for this is the whole duty of man. For God shall bring every work into judgment, with every secret thing, whether it be good, or whether it be evil" (King James Version).

These verses have long challenged interpreters. The terse ending reduces "the whole matter" to keeping God's commandments, putting a heavy burden of faith onto the last sentence. No other hint of otherworldly recompense is suggested. Not all readers have felt that these lines, which biblical scholars take to be the addition of an editor, mitigate the relentless refrain of "vanity of vanities, all is vanity." Voltaire himself wrote provocatively in the *Philosophical Dictionary* (published in 1764) that Ecclesiastes expressed "the sentiments of a materialist, at once sensual and digested, who appears to have put an edifying word or two on God in the last verse, to diminish the scandal which such a book must necessarily create."[103] Yet Voltaire's ending to the *Précis de l'Ecclésiaste* echoes the pious tone of the biblical text: "L'homme est un vil atôme, un point dans l'étendue: / Cependant du plus haut palais éternels, / Dieu sur notre néant daigne abaisser sa vue: / C'est lui seul qu'il faut craindre, & non pas les mortels" ("Man is a vile atom, a speck in the universe. / And yet, from the highest of eternal palaces, / God deigns to look [down] upon our nothingness; / It is He alone that we must fear, and not mere mortals").[104]

While "vile atom" recalls the explicitly Epicurean argument that Voltaire saw in Ecclesiastes, this ending seems true to its generally negative picture of humankind ("our nothingness") and the simple exhortation to trust in God. It is skeptical of human folly but this is sacred skepticism, that is, it preserves faith in a divine principle, however undogmatc. In contrast, Kheraskov's paraphrase of Ecclesiastes (as noted, itself a paraphrase of Voltaire), ends on a somewhat more reassuring note, going from a series of moral admonitions on how to live the good life to the comforting assertion of God's protective sight:[105]

Безсовестных людей беседы убегай;
На щастие людей зависно не взирай;

Не оскорбляйся ты злодеев клеветою:
Бог зрит дела твои, и Сам везде с тобою.

Пылинка человек, и точка в мире сем,
Но от пресветлаго, небеснаго чертога,
Взирает на него, печется Бог о нем.
Не бойся никого, о смертный!—бойся Бога. (7:14)[106]
[Shun conversation with dishonest people, / Don't look upon other people's happiness with envy, / Don't be insulted by the slander of evildoers: / God sees what you do and is everywhere with you Himself. // Man is a speck of dust, a dot in this world, / But from His most luminous, heavenly palace / God watches over him, cares for him. / Fear no one, mortal!—fear God.]

Human vision may fail, but God's does not. The ending of Karamzin's version (which draws on both Voltaire and Kheraskov's texts) is even more positive:

Не только для благих, будь добр и для коварных,
Подобно как творец на всех дары лиет.
Прекрасно другом быть сердец неблагодарных!
Награды никогда великий муж не ждет.

Награда для него есть совесть, дух покойный.
(Безумие и злость всегда враги уму:
Внимания его их стрелы недостойны;
Он ими не язвим: премудрость щит ему.)

Сияют перед ним бессмертия светилы;
Божественный огонь блестит в его очах.
Ему не страшен вид отверстыя могилы:
Он телом на земле, но сердцем в небесах.[107]
[Be kind not only to the good, but also to the deceitful, / Just as the Creator pours out gifts on everyone. / Readily be a friend to ungrateful hearts! / A great man never expects reward. // Reward for him is his conscience, a tranquil spirit. / Insanity and malice are always the enemy of reason; / Their arrows are unworthy of its attention; / It is not wounded by them: wisdom is its shield. // The immortal luminaries shine before him; / Divine fire sparkles in his eyes. / He is not frightened by the view of an open grave: / His body is on earth, but his heart is in heaven.]

Here the Ecclesiastes paradigm is itself basically upended as the optimistic narrator offers a portrait of a Great Man in the likeness of God the Creator, rather than a pitiful speck of dust or vile atom. He is wise, deserving but not expecting reward, a man of reason and conscience whose eyes are not clouded with fear of death or a sense of the vanity and worthlessness of earthly endeavor. The "immortal luminaries" (a phrase that can do double duty as a reference both to astronomy and as a metaphor for God) shine before him and their "divine fire" sparkles in his eyes. Body and soul, inner and outer self, are in perfect balance.[108] In contrast to Kheraskov's poem, which is more generalized, didactic, and less hedonistic (Epicurean), and to Voltaire's, which is truer to Ecclesiastes's downbeat tone, Karamzin stresses a more positive Stoic approach to life's choices and the ideal of tranquility. This is also suggested by the title "Solomon's Practical Wisdom, or Thoughts Selected from Ecclesiastes" ("Opytnaia Solomonova mudrost', ili Mysli, vybrannye iz Ekkleziasta"). His version includes the (original) lines:

> Привычки, склонности и страсти
> У мудрых должны быть во власти:
> Не мудрым цепи их носить.
>
> Нам всё употреблять для счастия возможно,
> Во зло употреблять не должно ничего;
> Спокойно разбирай, что истинно, что ложно:
> Спокойствие души зависит от сего.[109]
> [Wise people must be in control of their / Habits, inclinations, and passions; / The wise do not wear their chains. // We can turn everything to our happiness, / (But) we must not use anything for evil; / Calmly examine what is genuine and what is false. / Tranquility of soul depends on this.]

Karamzin's more positive attitude toward the problems raised in Ecclesiastes is also suggested by a footnote to the first publication. In reference to a line about the unsolved secret of the afterlife, Karamzin noted that Solomon (titular author of Ecclesiastes, commonly referred to as "Kohelet" [the Preacher]) had not been privy to Christian revelation.[110] Still, Karamzin's "Solomon's Practical Wisdom" refers back to earlier poems of the Ecclesiastes paradigm from the 1760s—including those by Rzhevsky and Kheraskov—in which the Stoic-moralist interpretation was foregrounded. It was possible, as Voltaire suggested, to interpret the issue in Stoic/Epicurean, non-metaphysical terms, as a problem of moral philosophy (self-interest). For example, Rzhevsky's "Stans" quoted above concludes with an ideal of spiritual tranquility similar to Karamzin's:

> Уму кто волю подвергает,
> А ум в ком правде покорен,
> Тот мудростию обладает,
> И тот премудр и совершен.
>
> Душа в спокойствии вседневном,
> Его ничто дух не страшит.
> В одном спокойствии душевном
> Блаженство наше состоит[111]

[One who can subordinate one's will to reason, / And in whom reason is obedient to truth, / Possesses wisdom. / This person is most wise and perfect. // The soul, tranquil in daily life / Nothing can disturb its spirit. / Our happiness consists / In spiritual tranquility alone]

In many cases it was possible, as Andrew Kahn has suggested, to see the Stoic discourse of tranquility in Russian Orthodox terms, although in some poems the transcendental answer is far more explicit than in others (e.g., references to the afterlife or the Last Judgment).[112] This is the case with several of Sumarokov's poems on the vanity theme, and in his "Oda o dobrodeteli" ["Ode on Virtue"] (1759), the poet explicitly rejects the Stoic position:

> Всё в пустом лишь только цвете,
> Что ни видим, - суета;
> Добродетель ты на свете,
> Нам едина красота! [. . .]
>
> Чувствуют сердца то наши,
> Что природа нам дала,
> Строги Стоики! не ваши
> Проповедую дела.
> Я забав не отметаю,
> Выше смертных не взлетаю:
> Беззакония бегу[113]

[Everything is drained of color, / Whatever we see is empty and vain; / You, virtue, are / Our one delight on earth! (. . .) // Our hearts feel / What nature has given us. / Stern Stoics! I do not / Preach your cause. / I do not reject pleasure; / I do not try and fly above mortals; / I shun lawlessness]

The Stoics' denial of the passions ("what nature has given us") and the material pleasures of the world ("I do not disregard pleasure") are rejected as well as their prideful superiority ("I do not try and fly above mortals").

By way of conclusion, two further examples of the Ecclesiastes paradigm in eighteenth-century literature will be examined, one that downgrades the ocularcentric discourse of vision, and another in which it is seriously questioned. The first is Sumarokov's drama *The Hermit* (*Pustynnik*), whose treatment of the Ecclesiastes paradigm parallels what we have just seen in his "Ode on Virtue" of the same year. *The Hermit* is Sumarokov's single "drama" and is also unique in terms of its subject matter—the defense of a king's ascetic withdrawal from the leadership of his kingdom. Despite this surprising departure from classicist and Enlightenment thematics, in other ways the play conforms to the dramatic model of Sumarokov's tragedies.[114] The protagonist Eumenius (Evmenii), whose name, from the Greek, means "gracious" or "merciful," has renounced the throne of ancient Kiev and his family in order to seek spiritual peace in the wilderness.[115] His rejection of the world and its vanity might be seen as contradicting classicist moral imperatives, but it fully accords with the lessons of Ecclesiastes (which, like *The Hermit*, is presented from the point of view of a burned out, retired king, traditionally taken to be Solomon). Eumenius reiterates the Ecclesiastes paradigm:

> Забавы здешние утоплены в слезах,
> И светлостию тьма мечтуется в глазах:
>   Век краток здесь, а смерть ужасна;
> Прелестна жизнь; однако и несчастна.
> Для нас, не ради бед земля сотворена;
> Но нашим промыслом бедам покорена.
> Повергли идолов в стране мы сей прехвально;
> Однако и поднесь еще живем печально.
>   Нам чистый дан закон,
> Но мы не делаем, что предписует он.
>   Грехами поражены,
> Мы в тину прежнюю глубоко погружены.[116]

[Worldly amusements are drowned in tears / And darkness parades like light in the eyes. / Our span is short and death horrible; / Life has charms but is also wretched. / The earth was created for us, not for misfortunes, / But we are subjected to them by our own actions. / Most laudably we have toppled the idols in this land; / However, to this day we still live in sadness. / A perfect law was given us, / But we do not do what it prescribes. / Afflicted with sins, / We are deeply mired in the former slime.]

"And darkness parades like light in the eyes"—more literally, darkness is perceived in a dreamlike fashion, that is, incorrectly, as light—vision deceives. Visible pleasures may hold some charms but are ultimately vain, masking pain and suffering, "drowned in tears," and Eumenius rejects the vanities of society, politics, and family life in favor of the life of ascetic withdrawal, among the most revered practices of traditional Eastern Orthodox culture. This contrasts with classicist tragedies, including Sumarokov's own, that uphold duty to the state as the prime directive. *The Hermit*, however, endorses Eumenius's choice of a higher duty to God and rejects the other characters' criticism that he is being selfish and socially irresponsible; they demand he heed his duty to family and society, an ethical imperative that prevails in the tragedies. Unlike most Russian classicist tragedies, *The Hermit* is explicitly framed in terms of Christianity, as Eumenius refers directly to Russia's conversion ("we have toppled the idols in this land"; "A perfect law was given us"). The play's unexpected defense of asceticism both contradicts mainstream Western Enlightenment criticism of monasticism (e.g., that of Voltaire), and also reverses the common image of monasteries in Western European drama as places of imprisonment or as a means to separate lovers.[117] The official state Enlightenment position since Peter the Great had also been disapproving of monasticism, especially of the eremitic type, and just a few years after Sumarokov's play church property was nationalized and many monasteries closed. Nevertheless, *The Hermit* explicitly defends this venerated type of traditional Orthodox behavior and suggests its parity with, if not supremacy over, classicist Enlightenment virtues. In its critique of the world's vanity and deception and its advocacy of withdrawal rather than self-display, *The Hermit* inverts the ocularcentric suppositions of tragedy. In terms of the larger visual dominant of eighteenth-century Russian culture, it carves out a special complementary or alternative role for non-ocularcentric values.

The Ecclesiastes paradigm also plays a key role in Derzhavin's poetry—our second and final example. Derzhavin's verse embodies the conflict between the two opposing anthropological models and paradigms of vision outlined above as it invokes and undercuts the ocularcentric ideal of the Lomonosovian ode and other works that endorse transparency and a perfect balance between inner and outer truth, vision and reality. In Derzhavin's poetry the Ecclesiastes paradigm often intrudes, as the lyric "I" is highly aware both of his own shortcomings, as well as the painful distance between the ideal and the reality, the visible and the true. What Derzhavin's ode "Felitsa" famously satirizes—the failings of Catherine's courtiers—has a serious, even tragic potential, as it cites Psalm 116:11 (Psalm 115 in the Slavonic Psalter), "But every man is a lie" ("No vsiakii chelovek est' lozh'"). (Compare Ecclesiastes 7:20: "There is not a righteous man on earth who does what is right and never sins.") Here the alternative anthropology represented by the Ecclesiastes paradigm undercuts assertions of transparency and virtue. As in the case of Kniazhnin's *Vadim of Novgorod*, discussed in chapter 4, this sentiment could threaten the image and authority of even the most virtuous absolute ruler; Derzhavin's own doubts about Catherine's greatness were considered in chapter 5.[118]

The often stark juxtaposition of high ideals and human weaknesses in Derzhavin's poetry—the distance between the Great Man and man as a lie—undercuts high classicist moral pretensions and highlights the deceptiveness of visual reality, the dysfunction of inner truth and outward façade. This is the case in many of his major programmatic works like "Vel'mozha" ("The Grandee")—"Ne mozhno vek nosit' lichin, / I istina dolzhna otkryt'sia" ("One cannot forever wear a mask / And the truth must be revealed")—which parallel the final lines of Ecclesiastes (12:14): "For God will bring every deed into judgment, including every hidden thing." Derzhavin's poetry may thus be squarely situated in the spectrum of visuality suggested in this book, as his poetry engages directly with the problem of correct versus deceptive seeing.[119] As Anna Lisa Crone has demonstrated, Derzhavin's central ethical concerns translate into the ongoing opposition in his verse between high and low styles, in which stylistic and moral qualities are sharply contrasted. Thus high odic discourse may be undercut by its corrupt content, as when high-style language describes morally low behavior, or when low lexicon can assume a high moral function.[120] On the one hand, Derzhavin's lyric persona upholds truth and justice. On the other, it may also be implicated in the all-too-human behavior it decries in others, as in "Felitsa," where the poet's lyric mask is that of a slothful Persian *mirza*. Furthermore, as in Ecclesiastes, two menacing forces haunt Derzhavin's poetic universe—death and fortune. The first threatens to render all human endeavors empty and vain, and the second turns morality (or rather, its proper recognition and reward) into a game of chance.[121] In the case of Radishchev (the subject of chapter 8), the serious, tragic potential of seeing through deceptive reality is played out most fully, but as in Derzhavin's case, while the ocularcentric ideal comes under harsh criticism, on some basic level it is ultimately vindicated.

# CHAPTER SEVEN

# The Icon That Started a Riot

$A$ttitudes toward vision are examined in this chapter—not as expressed in literary or philosophical works, but as they clashed at a particular historical moment, during Moscow's infamous Plague Riot (*chumnyi bunt*) of September 15–17 (old style), 1771, that was sparked by the struggle for control of an icon. The riot, in which a murderous mob rampaged through the Kremlin and other parts of the city, claimed the life of the city's celebrated Archbishop Amvrosii (Zertis-Kamensky), who had tried to take control of the image. The riot posed a serious challenge to the authorities not only as a violent public disturbance in the midst of a large-scale health crisis, but also as a potentially ugly blot on Russia's image in Europe. The clash over the icon starkly demonstrated the cultural divide separating two "scopic régimes,"—the state-imposed, official Enlightenment code of visual values and behavior, in conflict with the older but still vital mode of vision embodied in icons, which insisted on their miraculous efficacy in a literal way.[1] While the discussion so far has presented a spectrum of ways in which the Orthodox religious tradition underwrote eighteenth-century Russian ocularcentrism, overtly or as a covert subtext, in the Plague Riot competing versions of the Orthodox tradition— Enlightenment and premodern—came into physical confrontation.

## The Official Narrative and the Need to Police Icons

Catherine the Great, who was concerned to uphold Russia's reputation as a land under enlightened rule, wrote to Voltaire about the riot, sending him something of a press release outlining the official version of events. Catherine presented the incident as an object lesson in what modern values should and should not be:

St. Petersburg, 6th/17th October 1771

Sir,

I have a small supplement to the article on *Fanaticism* for you, which would also not be out of place in the article on *Contradictions*, which I read with the utmost satisfaction in *Questions sur l'Encyclopédie*. This is what it is about.

Disease is rife at Moscow: there is an epidemic of various fevers, which are causing numerous fatalities, despite all the precautions which have been taken. The Grand Master, Count Orlov, asked as a favor to be allowed to go there, to ascertain on the spot what measures would be the most suitable for checking the outbreak. I agreed to this request, such a fine and zealous one on his part, not without feelings of acute anxiety over the risks he would run. He had hardly been gone twenty-four hours, when Marshal Saltykov [governor-general of Moscow] sent word of the following catastrophe, which took place at Moscow between the 15th and 16th September, old style.

Archbishop Ambrose [Amvrosii] of Moscow, a man of intelligence and ability, learned that vast crowds of people had for several days been gathering before an image which was supposed to heal the sick—these were in fact dying at the holy Virgin's feet—and that people were bringing large sums of money to this shrine. He therefore had the money taken under his official charge, in order to use it later on in various charitable causes, a financial measure which every bishop is fully entitled to take in his diocese. It is to be supposed that he intended to have the image removed, as has been done more than once, and that the confiscation of the money was the preamble to this. Certainly, this horde of people gathered together during an epidemic could only help it to spread. But note what happened. Some of the rabble began shouting: *The Archbishop is going to steal the holy Virgin's treasure; let us kill him.* Others took the Archbishop's side. From words they came to blows. The police tried to separate them, but the ordinary police could not manage on its own. Moscow is a world of its own, not just a city. The most frenzied made for the Kremlin; they broke down the gates of the monastery where the Archbishop resides; looted the monastery, got drunk in the cellars, where many merchants store their wines; and having failed to find the man they were looking for, some went off to the Donskoy monastery, from where they dragged the old man, and killed him without mercy; the rest stayed behind to fight over the spoils. At last Lieutenant-General Yerapkin [Eropkin] arrived with about thirty soldiers who very soon put them to flight. The ringleaders were taken. The famous Eighteenth Century really has something to boast of here! See how far we have progressed! But I do not need to speak to you on this score: you know mankind too well to be surprised at the contradictions and excess it is capable of. One has only to read your *Questions sur l'Encyclopédie* to be persuaded of your deep understanding of men's minds and hearts.

I owe you a thousand thanks, sir, for your kind allusions to me in various parts of this book; I am astonished to find my name so often at the end of a sentence where I least expected it.[2]

This is a remarkable document in many respects. To begin with, it is a prime example of Catherine's basic cultural program—a continuation of the Petrine project of making Russia part of Enlightenment Europe. Her description of the riot is framed at both ends by discussion of the *Encyclopédie*, presented here as the authoritative source on mankind and its foibles. Voltaire had inscribed the empress into this blueprint for universal progress, and Catherine writes the Plague Riot into this script, offering the episode as further illustrative material, as an object lesson with a clear moral to be drawn—under the heading "Fanaticism" or "Contradictions."

The letter thus functions as part of Catherine's quest for legitimization in European public opinion that especially marked the first decade of her rule, as she attempted to put a special spin on a potentially embarrassing event.[3] Catherine imposes a clear narrative scheme on the material, with sharply delineated characters, visual markers, and philosophical geography—features of an Enlightenment "scopic regime" par excellence, particularly if one associates the term with visual values imposed from above. Catherine the Great continued and extended Peter's mission of utterly transforming Russia's external appearance—from sartorial fashions and regulations; to the showcase of St. Petersburg and the construction (and reconstruction) of Russian cities to a uniform pattern on an empire-wide scale; to building gardens, theaters, and new public spaces; to accumulating and displaying the finest collections of European art; and to promoting the modern arts and letters to compete with those of Europe. In the case of the Plague Riot, Catherine is at pains to depict it as an anomaly, an unpleasant blot (a "contradiction") on Russia's otherwise exemplary advancement toward modernity and taking its place among enlightened nations. Catherine's parable of the Plague Riot includes a martyr, the upright Archbishop Amvrosii, who was indeed a leading Russian enlightened cleric, and it also has heroes, Orlov and Eropkin, who dash in to save the day. The wise empress remains in the background, orchestrating calm, rational measures against the villainous rabble, repository of superstition and backwardness. The event is thus couched in a black and white Enlightenment discourse as a zero-sum opposition in which the Plague Riot appears as something totally opposed to reason and modernity. This is a heroic Enlightenment scenario, a clash of two worlds.[4] Exclaiming "See how far we have progressed!," Catherine defines the event historically in terms of Russia's connection to—and distance from—"the famous Eighteenth Century" and the march of progress or reason. She maps it geographically in terms of the distance between Moscow and Petersburg, loci of the old and the new, the world of Peter's imperial order, of sober reason, hygiene, justice, humanism, civilization—and violent, misinformed, fanatic, infectious, corrupt, murderous, drunken Moscow—"a world of its own, not just a city."

Moscow is particularly marked in Catherine's mind as an unpleasant, frightening place "full of symbols of fanaticism, churches, miraculous icons, priests, and convents, side by side with thieves and brigands," as she wrote in her *Memoirs.*[5] Notably, she groups together "churches, miraculous icons, priests, and convents" as what would seem to be almost interchangeable symbols of fanaticism and places them all as part of a series that concludes with thieves and brigands. She thus suggests an opposition between secular and religious, in which religious is synonymous with ignorance, fanaticism, and the spread of illness. Notably, in her letter to Voltaire, Catherine carefully avoids use of the word "plague" (this was in fact an outbreak of black or bubonic plague); she refers instead to "disease" and "an epidemic of various fevers." Plague was stigmatized in Enlightenment discourse as the marker of ignorant, uncivilized regions such as Asia or Africa that lacked medical science and public health systems.[6] Catherine was widely celebrated for having had herself and the Grand Duke Pavel Petrovich inoculated against smallpox in October 1768 by the English physician Thomas Dimsdale.[7]

Catherine could also be seen as contrasting good and bad images of religious behavior, with calmness, reason, order, health, justice, and civilization allied with true religiosity and the fulfillment of duty. Indeed she scripts Archbishop Amvrosii as a hero, a martyr to Enlightenment, "a man of intelligence and ability." Like Orlov, he came into a chaotic situation to impose legitimate control, to dispel the threat to both health and order posed by the mob and to dispose of the charitable donations in a proper fashion ("a financial measure which every bishop is fully entitled to take in his diocese"). In this sense the riot was a clash between premodern Orthodoxy and its modern Enlightenment version. Significantly, the event took place over a visual artifact, a "miraculous icon." Catherine's picture of the episode as presented to Europe was one of rational public order imposed from without—to curb violence, infection, and superstition. At the same time, Catherine was far from denying the value of icons as religious and cultural objects, at least for her Russian subjects, although official regulations had long been directed at controlling their influence.

Pietro Antonio Novelli (1729–1804), *Count Gregorii Orlov Visiting Plague Victims in Moscow* (black ink and watercolor on off-white antique laid paper, 32.1 x 49.4 cm). Novelli offers a perfect illustration of that heroic image of the plague that Catherine the Great described in her letter to Voltaire. Count Orlov grandly gestures to the suffering masses, two of whom in the center reach out to him for salvation, as imperial servitors help with the sick. The cart on the left, in the shade, appears to be piled with the dead. Courtesy of the Harvard Art Museums/Fogg Museum, Gift of Jeffrey E. Horvitz, 2006.

It is suggestive that in her catalogue of Moscow's unfortunate traits Catherine includes "miraculous icons," one of those "symbols of fanaticism," a metonym for Moscow, for religion (in its worst sense), and for everything that was evil and backward in Russia. Yet in the Orthodox tradition, icons by definition partake of the divine and are hence all potentially miraculous, although the ones associated with miracle-working (*chudotvornye ikony*) have traditions of special veneration.[8] Icons are commonly referred to as "holy icons" (although there are no icons that are not holy), which habitually caused the official church troubles in dealing with unsanctioned assertions of icons' miraculous feats.[9] This issue gained new urgency during the Enlightenment, when the very existence of miracles came under attack, most famously by David Hume in his *An Enquiry Concerning Human Understanding* of 1748.[10] In Russia, at least since the time of Ivan IV and the Stoglav Council, church law had been concerned with regulating the production and use of icons, and attempts at regulation continued through the eighteenth century. Under Peter the Great, ukases of 1710 and 1711 designated a superintendent over icon production and called for him to classify icons into three categories, each with its own tariff, and required icons to be signed, dated, and attested.[11] During the Petrine era there were also controversies over the issue of icons' miraculous nature, in some cases due to the influence of Protestant iconoclastic ideas, and the abuses of popular belief in icons continued to be a special concern on the part of the authorities.[12] The Petrine charter of the reorganized Russian Orthodox Church, the *Spiritual Regulation* (*Dukhovnyi reglament*) of 1721, warned against attributing "false miracles" to icons and condoning such superstitions, threatening harsh punishments (including hard labor for life) to discourage them.[13] By the middle of the century, state regulation of icons seemed mostly concerned with halting the proliferation of inexpensive and poorly painted icons and woodcut *lubki* (popular prints) of icons.[14] One problem with such works was that they violated traditional iconographic canons. A ukase of 1744, for example, forbade icons that were "absolutely contrary to the Holy rules" ("pravilam Sviatym ves'ma protivno").[15] Similarly, a ukase of November 6, 1760, referring back to those of 1744 and 1745, approved the confiscation of prints of Dimitrii Rostovsky depicted as miracle-worker that were being sold "at the Spassky Bridge" (the main marketplace for *lubki*) and at other places in Moscow and Petersburg, in part on the grounds that Rostovsky had not yet been canonized; the order reasserted the church's right to certify all such images.[16]

More pronounced than the demand for canonicity, however, was the concern not with the theological content of these images, but rather with their poor quality ("ves'ma neiskusnoi raboty"), which, it was believed, could lead people astray. For example, a ukase of March 16, 1759, approving the confiscation of offending icons from kiosks, churches, and monasteries (and even from iconostases!), ordered that they be repainted "skillfully" (*iskusno*) "so as not to perpetrate such ugliness and corruption" ("daby kakovago neblagolepiia i soblazna proizoiti ne moglo").[17] Ugliness and corruption were linked together, but not to any specific style, aesthetic, or religious system, as church and state merely demanded "greater beauty" (*luchshago blagolepiia*, also suggesting more grandeur, higher quality).[18] A further concern here, which had been voiced since the start of the century, and even by Peter the Great himself, was the reaction of foreigners (*inovernykh*, people of other faiths) to shoddy work, something repeatedly mentioned in other official documents concerning icons.[19] Policing icons promoted positive self-display, as the invocation of the foreign audience confirms.

Further regulation over icons repeated the insistence on "attentive . . . supervision" ("pristoinoe . . . nadsmotrenie") over icon painters and purveyors and the need to stem the proliferation of low-quality prints.[20] While these regulations may have reflected the imperial scopic regime's impulse toward the panopticon, such "policing" only began to give way to a regime of discipline and punishment toward the very end of the eighteenth century.[21] Still, to maintain the proper level of decency and external visual decorum was clearly a major concern. That such ukases had to be repeated many times suggests that they did little to prevent the proliferation of cheap and "indecent" icons. Notably, the ukase of 1759, cited above, reported that "in due course of confiscating these unskillfully painted icons there occurred some measure of opposition" from "the people" to the clerics undertaking the confiscations, and they called for "the secular authority" to prevent "offenses" (*obidy*, also: insults) against them. This, the only case of resistance to the state's measures to police icons noted in the regulations, presaged the conflict that broke out in 1771.

Catherine the Great herself took an active interest in the propriety and seemliness of church art. A ukase of August 24, 1767, conveyed her shock over an icon that had been presented to her during her trip down the Volga that "depicted the Holy Trinity with three faces and with four eyes," causing the empress to ask, "was painting such images [really] permitted?"[22] The ukase firmly repeated the injunction against any "strange," "corrupting," and "ugly" "indecencies" (*strannye, soblaznitel'nye, nelepye* [also, absurd] *nepristoinosti*) such as this. On the same trip, on June 13, she visited the Cathedral of the Assumption in Vladimir and was dismayed by its state of disrepair. She quickly had 14,000 rubles allocated to have it remodeled. The ancient iconostasis was replaced by a massive carved and gilded one in grand baroque style, and its icons were replaced (excluding the ancient icon of the Bogoliubskaia Mother of God, but including several by Andrei Rublev). New ones were painted by a "former full time Episcopal worker" ("iz byvskikh prezhde Arkhireiskikh shtatskikh sluzhitelei") named Vladimir Strokin. The new carved and gilded iconostasis featured columns of every order, with carved angels on the cornices and the Lord of Hosts surrounded by cherubim rising up in the center. A huge matching gilded baldachin was erected on the spot where Catherine had stood during the service as a monument to her visit, and an icon of St. Catherine was placed on the bottom tier of the iconostasis opposite the spot.[23] Frescoes painted by Rublev and Ikonnikov in 1408 that were found to be in poor shape and out of synch with the newly painted icons were covered over with new ones in the new style.[24] Although some later historians have criticized Catherine for this alleged desecration of the old sacred art, in her rescript to Bishop Pavel announcing the money for repairs, she entrusted them to his supervision and recommended "that you preserve the ancient quality (*drevnost'*) of the building and preserve it in the best possible way."[25] However, the desire to modernize apparently trumped historical sensitivity. The incident is indicative of the lack of consciousness of the stylistic and cultural differentiation in church art that became so sharp in the later tradition.[26]

## The Bogoliubskaia Icon and Its Origins

The icon at the center of the Plague Riot was an image of the Virgin, the Moscow *Bogoliubskaia Bogomater'* (Bogoliubskaia God-Mother), that depicts Mary in a specific way and context. The narrative that accompanies (and is depicted by) the icon serves as its verbal counterpart, much like a saint's life or miracle tale, which themselves often include stories about wonder-working icons.[27] The holy nature of Russian icons includes belief in their miraculous origins, which in many cases—as in that of the Moscow icon—is also inscribed into their visual and accompanying textual narratives.

The history of what came to be known as the "Bogoliubsky" type of icon is rather complex and obscure, going back to the creation of an icon for Prince Andrei Bogoliubsky in the twelfth century. Oral and possibly lost written tradition connected the Moscow icon all the way back to this icon, possibly the only surviving Russian-made icon from before the Mongol invasion.[28] The creation of the Bogoliubskaia Mother of God as well as the narrative that came to be connected with it were associated in turn with the most famous and revered icon in Russia, of Byzantine origin, the Vladimir Mother of God (also known in English as the Vladimir Virgin).[29] The Vladimir Mother of God, which was designed as a processional icon, came to Kiev from Constantinople early in the twelfth century. Held by tradition to have been painted by St. Luke himself, the Vladimir Mother of God played a role in several of the most dramatic turning points in Russian history. Among its many reputed marvels are having protected Moscow from Tamerlane in 1395, from the Tatar Khan, Akhmat, in 1490, and from Polish and Swedish invaders during the Time of Troubles. Stories of its miracles began to be compiled in the late twelfth century on the order of Andrei Bogloliubsky, who had moved his seat of power from Vyshegorod to Vladimir-Suzdal in 1158, taking the icon with him (which is how it came to be known as the Vladimir Mother of God).[30] The transfer of the icon to Vladimir was part of Prince Andrei's unfulfilled plan to bolster his power in the north and to establish a second Russian see there. According to V. K. Onasch, Bogloliubsky meant for the Vladimir Mother of God to serve as the Russian counterpart to the Eleousa Mother of God, which was venerated by the Byzantine imperial family in Constantinople, and it played an important part in the local cult of the Mother of God (*Theotokos*) that Prince Andrei sponsored.[31]

The church Andrei had built—the Church of the Most Holy Mother of God's Birth (Khram Rozhdestva Presviatyia Bogoroditsy)—became the center of a new monastery, which became known as "Bogoliubsky" after him. Andrei had the Bogoliubskaia Mother of God painted between 1158 and 1174, the date of his assassination. It is in the standard Byzantine Hagiosoritissa pose, typical for a deisis icon in the iconostasis, depicting a full-length Mary slightly turned to the right, holding out both hands in supplication toward Jesus, who appears in a small rounded segment in the upper right corner. The Bogoliubskaia Mother of God also has its own small-scale deisis painted on the upper frame, thought to have been added in the thirteenth century.

The fact that the Vladimir Mother of God was accompanied by an ever-increasing compilation of stories about its miraculous acts reflects the importance of narratives concerning icons' origins and marks their complexity as cultural artifacts. In the case of the Bogoliubskaia Mother of God, surprisingly, the first surviving written narratives telling of its origin only date from the eighteenth century. The first mention of this is apparently in the vita of Andrei Bogoliubsky, composed in connection with his canonization in 1702.[32] The reasons for his canonization at this time, more than five hundred years after his death, are unclear.[33] In connection with the canonization, Bogoliubsky's tomb was opened and his relics examined; and in 1774, when the completion of the Cathedral's renovation sponsored by Catherine the Great was celebrated, the northern end of the church was rededicated in his honor.[34] The most detailed narrative concerning the miraculous origins of the Bogoliubskaia Mother of God is from a "Chronicle of the Bogoliubov Monastery from 1158 to 1770 . . . Compiled by the Father Superior of this monastery, Hegumen Aristarkh, in 1767–1769," that is, not long after Catherine's visit.[35]

The "Chronicle" begins with a story that directly connects the creation of the Bogoliubskaia Mother of God to Andrei Bogoliubsky's transfer of the Vladimir Mother of God to Vladimir. According to the "Chronicle," in 1158, Prince Andrei was on the way from Kiev to Rostov, travelling with the precious icon. When his company reached the left bank of the Kliaz'ma River seven courses (*sedm' poprichsh*) from Vladimir, the carriage carrying the famous icon became stuck and could not be budged despite all efforts. Profoundly disturbed, Andrei ordered prayers to the icon and tearfully promised to build a stone church on the spot. The Holy Virgin then appeared to Andrei while he was praying in his tent. She held a scroll in her hand and asked that her icon not be taken to Rostov, but remain in Vladimir; that a stone church be built on the spot in honor of her birth; and that a monastery also be founded there. Andrei gladly fulfilled her wishes, and in addition "he summoned the most skillful painters and ordered them to paint an image [icon] of the Most Holy Mother of God in the likeness in which she had appeared to him" (that is, the Bogoliubskaia Mother of God). Shortly thereafter he built a stone church (the Church of the Most Holy Mother of God's Birth), and June 18 (old style), the day commemorating the holy martyr Leontii, was established as the day for the icon's yearly celebration.[36] According to the "Chronicle," Prince Andrei was then christened Bogoliubsky (God-Loving) and the place named Bogoliubov (or Bogoliubimoe, Beloved of God) in honor of the miracle.[37]

The icon that sparked the Plague Riot was called Bogoliubskaia, but despite the shared name, represents a different type than the twelfth-century icon. This newer type developed in the fifteenth and sixteenth centuries and only subsequently acquired the label "Bogoliubsky," probably due either to Mary's similar pose as in the twelfth-century work, or based on elements of the above narrative.[38] Over the centuries it became popular in other parts of central Russia and the Balkans, and also made its way to Mount Athos.[39] This icon adapted the figure of Mary Hagiosoritissa of the twelfth-century icon, adding several other elements that associate it with the iconography of the Virgin Paraklesis (*zastupnitsa*, intercessor).[40] It became known in the sixteenth and seventeenth centuries as the "Mother of God of Supplication" (*Bogomater' Molebnaia*) or "Supplication (Prayer) for the People" (*Molenie o narode*), probably for its connection to the intercession service, and from the later seventeenth and early eighteenth century also began to be labeled "Bogoliubskaia Mother of God."[41] The icon type had long-standing ties to the Moscow ruling family. In the fourteenth century, Moscow Grand Prince Ivan I (Kalita) is thought to have founded the Vysokopetrovsky Monastery, near (now in) Moscow, and he or Dmitrii Donskoi dedicated a cathedral there in honor of the Bogoliubskaia Mother of God. About a century later Grand Prince Vasilii II had a copy of the icon made for the palace Sretenskaia Church in the Kremlin.[42] Several episodes also connect the icon type with Peter the Great, who is thought to have been the one who had the Moscow Bogoliubskaia Mother of God that sparked the riot hung on the Varvarskie Gates.[43] In 1690 Peter visited the Bogoliubsky Monastery and obtained a copy of the Bogoliubskaia Mother of God for a new church dedicated to the Bogoliubskaia Mother of God at the Vysokopetrovsky Monastery. This church was built over the graves of Peter's uncles Ivan and Afanasii Naryshkin, who had been killed during the Streltsy revolt.[44] It was roughly in this period, around the time of Andrei Bogoliubsky's canonization, that the June 18 celebration of the Bogoliubskaia

The Vladimir Bogoliubskaia Mother of God, twelfth century (185 x 105 cm), one of the only surviving pre-Mongol Russian-made icons. The icon has been restored many times; the text on Mary's scroll ("Most Merciful Sovereign, Lord Jesus Christ, hear my prayer . . .") was added in the eighteenth century. Uspenskii Sobor, Kniaginina Monastery, Vladimir.

Mother of God became accepted in the Russian Orthodox Church as a whole; the oldest copy of the service dedicated to the Bogoliubskaia Mother of God dates to 1704 and was connected with the Vysokopetrovsky Bogoliubskaia Mother of God Church.

That the written narrative was codified in writing just a year or two before the Plague Riot suggests that the miraculous nature of the Bogoliubskaia Mother of God was very much part of contemporary cultural consciousness. Indeed, it seems likely that the "Chronicle" story was more or less based on the icon's visual narrative and accompanying oral tradition as they had developed in recent times rather than on any historical records.[45] This blurring of boundaries between history and miracle tale was conditioned by the nature of icons as artifacts, insofar as they represent images of (identity with) the divine.

The Moscow Bogoliubskaia Mother of God—the version of the Bogoliubskaia Mother of God icon of the "Supplication for the People" type—contains four basic elements: Mary standing with a scroll; Jesus (often also with a scroll); an architectural representation and/or a cliff or mountain landscape; and supplicants. Each element deserves closer consideration:

(1) The first, commanding element of the icon is the full-length Mary on the left, standing in partial profile, gesturing toward the right. Mary is usually dressed in the fashion of traditional Byzantine icons, in a dark red cloak or *maforia*, decorated with "assist" (gold highlights), and in a darker (blue) tunic or undergarment (*chiton*); there are golden stars (or marks) on her forehead and shoulder. In her left hand Mary holds a scroll (*khartiia*), at the same time gesturing toward the supplicants at her feet, while her right hand points in the direction of the upper right corner of the icon, toward Jesus. Mary's pose is similar to the Hagiosoritissa type icon, while the scroll is common in Virgin "Intercessor" icons. Of all Russian icons those of the Mother of God were the most venerated and the most apt to earn the status of "miracle-working." There exist between two and four hundred types of Mary icons depending on how they are classified, and "[Russian] Orthodox life was famed for the exceptionally great number of wonder-working icons of the Virgin Mary."[46] This was true of Moscow in particular, and the city's great number of shrines dedicated to Mary (including those to the Bogoliubskaia Mother of God), starting in the fourteenth century, led to the popular notion that the city, and by extension Russia, was itself dedicated to the Virgin Mary.

(2) Jesus is the second basic compositional element of the Bogoliubskaia Mother of God icon. He appears in the sky or on a cloud, "in glory" (i.e., in a clearly delineated aureole, sometimes referred to as a *mandorla*, although these are by definition almond in shape), usually in the upper right corner or

middle of the top of the icon, and gestures with his right hand either to Mary, to the supplicants before her, or to both, and also holds or unfurls a scroll in his left hand. There is thus both in gesture and written words a dialogue in progress between Mary and Jesus. The texts on the scrolls vary somewhat, but basically, Mary requests grace and mercy from her "God and Son" for "your people," for the Orthodox, or for the world; and Jesus acknowledges her intercession for the sinners.[47]

(3) Third, many of the Moscow Bogoliubskaia Mother of God type icons, although not the Moscow icon itself, contain an architectural representation of what in the "Chronicle" narrative corresponds to the church (monastery) that Mary requested be constructed.[48] It may thus be considered part of Mary's vision to Andrei Bogoliubsky, or perhaps more accurately, the vision *within* his vision. In many of the icons of this type, a prominent mountainous terrain surrounds the architectural representation, sometimes also running along the bottom of the icon or framing Mary. This may also substitute for the architectural representation, perhaps suggesting the isolated spot in which it is to be erected. A recent mass-produced Moscow version of the icon substitutes the entire Kremlin in miniature, including its three main cathedrals, Ivan's bell tower, walls, and tower-gates, sitting atop a mountain (see p. 209). The architectural element connects the Bogoliubsky icon type to so-called "monastic icons," in which a founding saint or saints (rather than Mary) ask intercession for the institution they founded. For example, the icon of St. Gennadii of Kostroma, in the Hillwood collection, contains all of the three elements described so far—an outsize figure of the saint holding an unfurled scroll; God in glory, possibly at one point having held a scroll, surrounded by angels in a cloud (in the upper left hand corner); and the Liubimsky Spaso-Gennadiev Monastery in the foreground at the level of St. Gennadi's knees.[49] One well-known variant of the Bogoliubskaia Mother of God done at or for the Solovetsky Monastery in 1545 shows the monastery's founders SS. Zosima and Savvatii, standing, and other monks kneeling in front of the monastery that towers above them.[50]

(4) The final element—in the lower right hand quadrant, and, like everything else in most versions of the icon, on a much smaller scale than Mary— are supplicants who turn to her in various degrees of petition or adoration (bowing, kneeling, standing, with outstretched arms). Some variants of the icon have Andrei Bogoliubsky alone, some only a couple of figures; other versions may have dozens. Scholars note that during the course of the sixteenth and seventeenth centuries the group of supplicants grew larger and more complicated, developing into a kind of mini-iconostasis within the icon, with a hierarchical ordering of saints and supplicants. (One late seventeenth-century

The Moscow Bogoliubskaia Mother of God, late seventeenth century (?) (128 x 105 cm). This was the icon that sparked the Plague Riot. By some accounts this copy of the Bogoliubskaia Mother of God was ordered by Peter the Great and placed by him on the Varvarskie Gates in Moscow. The supplicants in the lower right include Moscow Metropolitans Petr, Aleksii, Iona, Filipp; holy fools (Saints) Vasilii and Maksim; St. Paraskeva; St. Basil the Great; the apostle Peter; Aleksei "Man of God"; the apostle Simeon, and the martyrs Paraskeva and Evdokiia. Church of Peter and Paul on Kulishki by the Iauza Gates, Moscow.

version in the Russian Historical Museum has approximately 70 supplicants in multiple rows![51]) The supplicants may include the royal patrons of the icon; the trio of SS. Basil, Gregory, and John Chrysostom (authors of the liturgy); saintly elders; local saints and fools in Christ; national and local church leaders; as well as Andrei Bogoliubsky. Moscow variants of the Bogoliubskaia Mother of God may include: St. Filipp, Moscow Metropolitan and victim of Ivan IV, and Patriarch Hermogen, hero of the Time of Troubles; holy fools with ties to Moscow (St. Vasilii the Blessed, St. Maksim the Blessed, and possibly St. Ioann Bol'shoi Kolpak); St. Aleksei ("Man of God"), St. Paraskeva, St. Evdokiia, the apostle Simeon; and others.[52] Some icons of this type, often explicitly labeled "Supplication for the People" (*Molenie o narode*) may also include a crowd representing the "simple folk," as does the Plague Riot icon. In some cases, the various audiences may be connected to local ceremonies of icon veneration that began in the fifteenth or sixteenth centuries.[53] Thus a royal version of the Bogoliubskaia Mother of God in which the patrons (three members of the Muscovite ruling family) are making a personal request for intercession may also be taken as a request for divine intervention on the part of the people as a whole, whether explicitly (as when the *narod* is depicted) or synecdochically through its royal leaders who join the ranks of the saintly intercessors, and indeed are themselves depicted with halos. Among other things, such images affirm the traditional religious connection between tsar and people, and also recall the homogeneity of Russian culture that was being

Commercially produced palm-sized contemporary icon of the Bogoliubskaia Mother of God.
Moscow, 2000.

eroded in the eighteenth century by modernizing trends. Including local saints among the supplicants functions much the same way as the architecture, reaffirming the divine as well as the locally grounded function of the image.

The final two elements of the Bogoliubskaia Mother of God type icon thus directly link the image to its specific geographical setting and traditions. Indeed many other Russian cities created their own variants of the Bogoliubskaia Mother of God, including Kozlov, Uglich, Usman', Zimarovo, Pechory, Rostov, Tarusa, Elat'ma, Iur'ev, and Tula. There were also new ones created in Moscow. Each has its own pictorial and local variations; all are connected with salvation from disease. The "optional" elements of the Bogoliubskaia icon thus make explicit what is presumed in the scopic regime of all icons, powerfully connecting the time and space of the viewer to that within the image. In accord with the originary narrative, the architectural element (church, monastery,

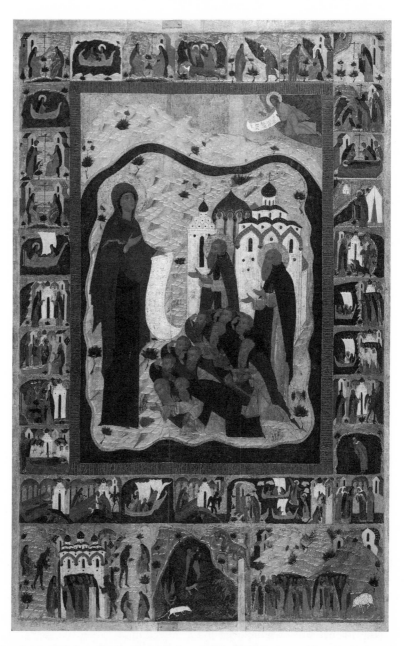

Bogoliubskaia Mother of God with scenes from the Life of SS. Zosima and Savatii of Solovetsky [Monastery], 1545 (Solovetsky Monastery, 160 x 126 cm). This was created on the order of Metropolitan Filipp (Kolychev). Moscow, Kremlin Museum.

kremlin) represents both an ideal vision of the monument to be erected and its realized, physical manifestation. The building demonstrates the icon's salvific power: the fact that the structure has actually come to exist stands as testimony to the truth of the vision and the protective power of its image. The physical, geographically specific space (Bogoliubovo or Moscow or some other place) is the location where the icon resides and thus represents a projection or function of the icon's own existence, part of the metaphysical reality it depicts and to which it bears witness. The icon thus projects (and is in some sense the source of) the physical reality within which the viewer abides and looks. It is not the depiction of some preexisting place but an image of transcendent reality. It may be significant from this point of view that in the Orthodox tradition, uniquely, churches are often created and named in honor of specific icons. As noted, Ivan Kalita is thought to have erected a church in honor of the Bogoliubskaia Mother of God icon (also after a vision), and other churches dedicated to icons in Moscow have included some of its most important shrines, for example, the church dedicated to Our Lady of Smolensk in the Novodevichii Convent, the Znamensky Cathedral and St. Basil's in Red Square, as well as a host of smaller churches and chapels (as of 2011 at least 24, of which most are dedicated to various icons of Mary).[54] From this point of view, icons define and subordinate physical, geographical space to the metaphysical reality they project. The power of icons works in both directions: it is not only the viewer-supplicants who seek entry to otherworldly glory, but also there is power that emanates from icons—like sunlight emanating from the ruler in Lomonosov's odes—that can give life, overcome evil, or vanquish disease.

The icon's scopic regime also defines the nature of time. Icons may be said to be both in time—that is, describing a specific place in an historical, chronological progression, for example, marking the establishment of Bogoliubovo or of Moscow—but also outside of time, as image-visions (in a special order of *kairos*, or divine time). Hence in some icons St. Luke is present painting a portrait of Mary and the baby Jesus, and in the Bogoliubskaia Mother of God icons the monastery or kremlin exists both as-it-will-be (as a vision) and as-it-actually-is, both historically concrete and part of divine reality. In the case of the supplicant-intercessors, the icon depicts a chain of intercessions: a group of local intercessors pleads for intercession from Mary, who in turn intercedes with Jesus. The supplicant-intercessors themselves, as a historical progression of saints, separated in some cases by many centuries, may also be presumed to have interceded—or be in the process of doing so—for each other. The primary dialogue depicted is obviously that between Mary and Jesus, but the larger dialogue extends both to the viewer-supplicants within the icon and also to those beyond the bounds of the image, the icon's viewers. Presumably the intercessors depicted in the icon are making supplication in the name of their fellow Russians, who themselves make supplication before the icon. Just as the story within the icon promises or affirms that the vision or prophecy it makes will come to pass, that the church will be erected, so too the icon's promise of the miraculous force of faith extends outside its spatial and temporal bounds to its observer-supplicants. The icon thus inscribes believers and their surrounding reality into its own metaphysical space and time. What the authorities might picture as an unmanageable "horde," invading and disfiguring what should be an orderly, properly policed and maintained public sphere, is here imaged (imagined) as a divinely ordered community of believers transcending time and space. Furthermore, the Russian Orthodox Church calendar is structured in part on the veneration of a succession of Mary icons; the current church calendar notes 91 specific Mary icons that are celebrated on 67 individual days (as noted, the twelfth-century Bogoliubskaia Mother of God is celebrated on July 1 [June 18 o.s.], together with the Uglich and Kozlov Bogoliubskaia Mother of God icons).[55]

A further important element of the icon's function as intercessor that came to be associated specifically with the Bogoliubskaia Mother of God was its power against disease. This ancient function of icons and relics, reaching back to the earliest history of Christianity, was very much alive in early modern Russia.[56] During an outbreak of the plague in 1654, for example, various miraculous Mary icons were sought out and believed to have protected believers from infection in Kazan, Tikhvin, and Uglich.[57] The belief in the Bogoliubskaia Mother of God's efficacy against plague in 1771 led to a proliferation of Bogoliubskaia Mother of God icons, some of which explicitly referred to the event. One, for example, contains a text in a cartouche thanking the sainted Moscow metropolitans and Mary "for delivering this city and all cities and the country from the death-dealing plague [*iazva*] with your prayers."[58] Another gold-embossed icon bears the inscription: "This icon was painted in time of plague in Moscow and other cities of Great Russia in 1772."[59] Thus the episode of 1771 became another miracle to add to the Bogoliubskaia Mother of God's chain of divine actions as well as a new originary miracle, stimulating the creation of new icons commemorating the event.

From Catherine the Great's perspective, however, the public worship of the Bogoliubskaia Mother of God icon during the plague represented not only superstition (intellectual deficiency), but also physical menace, caused both by the unhygienic congregation of people and their physical contact with the icon itself ("an image which was supposed to heal the sick—these were in fact dying at the holy Virgin's feet"). Everyday Orthodox religious practice, including the performance of the liturgy, prescribed several types of regular ritualized physical contact with icons, including carrying them in processions and kissing them.[60] According to Dr. Charles de Mertens, a doctor from Brussels working at the Foundling Home in Moscow at the time, during the Plague Riot people broke into hospitals to conduct religious ceremonies at the bedside of the sick using icons, which, he noted, "every person present kisses in rotation." He also reported that people dug up and reburied recent plague victims to whom the authorities had forbidden traditional last rites, which included washing and kissing of the corpse.[61]

Making physical, tactile contact with an icon—a divine object—is equally if not more important for many believers than making visual contact, and also played a direct role in the clash over the Bogoliubskaia Mother of God. The very term for "veneration," *poklonenie* (also, in eighteenth-century Russian, *preklonenie*) in the Russian as in the Greek (*proskinesis*), literally means "bowing down to," "getting down on one's knees," and refers to the physical gesture of ritual submission rather than to the exercise of sight.[62] The main acts of icon veneration were kissing and honoring them with a procession. On the yearly celebration of the Moscow Bogoliubskaia Mother of God, for example, "a triumphal service was performed in front of this icon, after which it was taken down from its usual place and for three days placed in a special tent-roofed chapel (*palatka*: tent or tabernacle). During this time traffic through the Varvarskie Gates ceased because the entire square was filled up with worshippers wanting to press themselves up against [*prilozhit'sia*—could mean: to kiss] the Miraculous [icon]."[63] These were clearly the actions that led up to the Plague Riot.

A further mark of reverence that was clearly on the mind of the rioters in 1771 is to provide an icon with metal decorations or a full cover of silver or gold, sometimes with inlaid pearls or precious stones—an icon's "raiments" (various types include *basma*, *riza*, *riznitsa*, and *oklad*)—through which only the face, body, or body parts (hands, feet) of the painted surface may show. Sight of the underlying image, though often repeated in the metal cover, is minimized, reduced to the spiritually most essential (the fleshly, already unclothed parts of the body—most crucially, the face), which show through as a kind of synecdoche or essence of the icon as a whole. However, it has been argued that the cover, with its precious stones and often elaborate decorative floral motifs, "augments the sacred value of the holy image" rather than reduces it, on the one hand representing a "materialized prayer . . . profoundly rooted in the reality of this world" (that is, stressing the material value of the

A gold-embossed Bogoliubskaia Mother of God, Moscow, 1772 (36 x 29.2 cm). An inscription reads: "This icon was painted in time of the plague in Moscow and other cities of Great Russia in 1772." Russian Historical Museum, Moscow.

object), and on the other, "magnifying" the icon's spiritual power, its shining surface symbolizing the uncreated light in which the saints dwell and the floral decorations representing paradise, the eternal flowering enabled by this light.[64] The cover itself thus may itself function as an icon, "a kind of fragile bridge which attempts to connect heaven and earth."[65] As one scholar describes it, the "creaturely brilliance [*tvarnuiu blesk*] and the shining of the precious materials manifest the visible, universally comprehensible image of the Divinity."[66]

The two aspects of the icon—as spiritual image and physical object—become problematic when the icon is encased, as doing honor to the icon's "creaturely brilliance" threatens to overshadow its spiritual essence.[67] For skeptics, treating icons as tactile objects with miraculous powers and adorning them with silver and jewels has suggested idolatry and fetishism. On a semiotic level, doing public honor to an icon in this way—bestowing visible, physically manifested marks of honor upon it—is no different from Catherine's casting a medal or building a triumphal arch in honor of Orlov's quelling the Plague Riot (on which see below), or having the decrepit iconostasis painted by Andrei Rublev and Daniil Chernyi replaced by a gilded baroque one in order to do proper public honor to the famous cathedral in Vladimir. Indeed, Catherine herself, like Russian rulers before her, together with building churches and contributing to their decoration and upkeep, also made public veneration to icons and donated rich covers for them. Prince Andrei Bogoliubsky himself had been one of the first to model this practice in Russia, as he had a cover made for the Vladimir Mother of God that reportedly used about eleven pounds of gold (*tridesiat' griven*) as well as silver, precious stones, and pearls.[68] And "in 1768, before having herself and Grand Prince Pavel Petrovich inoculated against smallpox during an outbreak, Catherine made pilgrimage to the Mother of God icon 'Joy to All Who Grieve' (*Vsekh skorbiashchikh radost'*) that Peter I's sister Natalia Alekseevna had brought to St. Petersburg in 1710 or 1711. Natalia Alekseevna had had a silver cover made for it, adorned with imperial family jewels as well as particles of holy relics, and under Catherine a new cover was also made for the icon."[69] In the same year, during a pilgrimage to the Kazan Mother of God Monastery, Catherine donated a small diamond-encrusted crown to decorate the cover of the famous Kazan Mother of God icon and gave another crown for a local icon of the Savior.[70]

Critics disagree on the extent of Catherine's religious feeling, and there may be possible ambiguities in such practices. In these cases, the Enlightenment ocularcentric directive to display found direct support in traditional religious custom. Like the creation of the elaborate baroque iconostasis in Vladimir, decoration of an icon by means of a cover served not only as a way to do honor, but also to modernize; covers had assumed baroque features in the seventeenth century and retained them through the nineteenth. In the case of icon covers, this tension is particularly striking insofar as the older, perhaps discredited style may be simultaneously respected and replaced (or policed, that is, put into a new and more acceptable aesthetic framework).[71]

This was one of many ways in which the imperial scopic regime may have been influenced by, and benefited from, traditional Orthodox mystical faith in the transcendent power of vision. From an opposite perspective, and in specific reference to icons, it is suggestive to consider the "Protestant" and "iconoclastic" aspects of Russia's Enlightenment scopic regime. Byzantine iconoclasm of the eighth to ninth centuries, with its attack on images, relics, and the cult of saints, and its generally anti-monastic, pro-humanist outlook, has been described as a kind of proto-Reformation (albeit a failed one).[72] Its program has many points in common with those of Peter and Catherine, who likewise fought to curtail the power of monasteries and manifestations of popular piety. On a broad functional level, the Enlightenment was the era when the church was definitively subordinated to the state—a process that began in the West roughly during the Reformation and the era of religious wars that followed. On the theological level, it was during the Reformation that critical reason began to take primacy over established tradition in religious affairs. In contrast to Western Europe, where the Protestants split with the Catholic Church because it refused to modernize, the late seventeenth-century schism in the Russian Orthodox Church was a protest *against* official reforms, protests carried out in the name of the "Old Belief," as the official Church gravitated toward proto-Enlightenment practices and trends. This was paralleled by the growing mistrust of the miraculous on the part of the official Church in the early modern period, including the suspicion of wonder-working icons, arguably as part of a mild Enlightenment Russian brand of iconoclasm.[73] Given the central place of the icon in Russian Orthodox theology and everyday practice, however, such suspicion of icons could probably never have been more than mild, a wariness of extremes and abuse. But as in the case of the Plague Riot, there was ample distrust of the kind of popular veneration of the Bogoliubskaia Mother of God being practiced in the streets of Moscow.

## Amvrosii, Enlightenment Martyr

Notably, the specific conflict over the Bogoliubskaia Mother of God that started the riot began with the idea of honoring the icon with a silver cover. People began to congregate near the icon at the Varvarskie Gates in Moscow, buoyed by rumors that it would prove an effective guard against the plague. According to some versions of the story, which followed a familiar pattern, Mary had appeared to certain people in dreams and demanded that the icon be venerated. According to others, miraculous action of the Bogoliubskaia Mother of God against the plague in Vladimir provided the impetus to venerate the Moscow icon.[74] In any case, it was decided to raise money to have a cover made for it and a considerable sum was collected in a short period. The police, stretched thin, were unable to cope with the large crowd that included several priests who came on their own to conduct round-the-clock services before the icon, and they called on Archbishop Amvrosii to help. His plan was to disperse the crowds by ordering the priests to leave, removing the icon to a nearby church, and having the money given to the Moscow Foundling Home where Amvrosii was an *opekun* (trustee). The Foundling Home was one of the state's most prominent charitable projects, founded by Ivan Betskoi and a pet project of Catherine's; it housed a hospital and was one of Moscow's main public health facilities.[75] Amvrosii himself was both a leading figure in the church and an outstanding representative of Russian Enlightenment Orthodoxy. Educated in the Kiev and Lviv academies, he had helped found the Alexander Nevsky Monastery Seminary in St. Petersburg and had served as its prefect. He was a member of the Synod as well as a scholar, and had translated numerous works, including Hugo Grotius's *Treatise Against Atheists and Naturalists* from the Latin.[76]

According to witnesses, the people gathering around the Bogoliubskaia Mother of God protested that "we are putting our last rag toward its decoration in order to make a silver cover and in return to receive healing from the dangerous disease, but the Archbishop wishes to give the money to the Foundling Home."[77] The crowd was intent on defending the icon and hotly resisted having the money they had collected taken for a state-sponsored, secular, Enlightenment institution (even if it went to health care). From their point of view this amounted to (quoting Catherine) "stealing *the holy Virgin's treasure.*" According to the rioters, they were standing up "to defend the true faith," although the line between true faith and bartering for a miracle was clearly thin. Amvrosii acted, and was seen to be acting, not only as a high-ranking member of the official church, but also as a partner with the secular authorities, whose extreme mismanagement of public health care, it should be noted, had greatly contributed to the plague and to the mounting toll that added up to over 50,000 fatalities, and possibly double that.[78] Amvrosii himself had been actively involved in the city's anti-plague measures, which included prohibitions against traditional burial rites, burial near city churches (bodies had to be taken and buried outside of the city), congregating in large crowds, and holding religious processions. Notably, the mob of worshippers at the Varvarskie Gates included out-of-work clerics (so-called unregistered "crossroads priests"), vagabond monks who were victims of Catherine's sharp reduction in the number of Russian monasteries, as well as Old Believers—that is, people who already felt victimized by the official church and state authorities.[79]

Much of the popular wrath became focused on Amvrosii, who in the course of the riot was systematically tracked down and violently murdered. Furthermore, the way he was killed merits comment. The eyewitness account of the writer F. V. Karzhavin offers some intriguing details. On the second day of the rioting, the morning of September 16, the rioters, having failed to find Amvrosii at his residence in the Kremlin at the Chudov Monastery, hunted him down at the Donskoi Monastery. They found him there just after he had "confessed and, having taken the sacrament, listened to the evening service" ("ispovedyvalsia i, priobshchaias' sviatykh tainstv, slushal obedniu"), hiding in the church "behind the iconostasis in the chorus" ("skrylsia v tserkve za ikonostasom na khorakh").

> From there the scoundrels [zlodei] dragged him out, however at his request allowed him to kiss the images [prilozhit'sia k obrazam]. Then, having dragged him into the courtyard, one scoundrel hit him on the top of the head with a stake, due to which he dropped down, but suddenly some others shouted, "do not beat him in the monastery, and do not defile a holy place with his blood." So they hauled him outside of the monastery, where the leaders—one inn-keeper [tseloval'nik], and another person of Mr. Raevsky's—hit him on the head with pikes while the others all began to beat him, poked out his eyes, cut up his face, ripped out his beard, stabbed his chest, broke his bones. In other words, his entire body was one big wound. While theft and destruction [was going on] in the Kremlin, in the Chudov Monastery this was continuing in the same way: the window frames [okonnitsy] were all smashed, the pictures [kartiny] shredded, the furniture all smashed and ripped, and the library—which consisted of a select group of church books and others relating to all the sciences and arts, in various languages, as well as rare manuscript volumes—was all destroyed or carried off, so that nothing remained; in the stable all of the carriages and coaches were smashed to smithereens. And when the monastery workers said to them, the robbers, that these didn't belong to the archimandrite but to the Chudotvorov [Monastery], they, the robbers, answered that the Chudotvorov people did not drive in them. In the house church the holy images were stripped, and the whole of their covers pried off [riznitsa rastashchena]; from the gospel book left on the altar the apostles were torn off and taken away, the communion cloth [antimist (sic)] ripped apart, the vessels all stolen, the painted images [obraza zhivopisnye] defaced [obrugany] by poking out of the eyes. They finally made it to the basement, and at last to the monastery's wine cellars

and storerooms, which belonged to the merchant Ptitsyn. . . . [There follows a description of the wines and drunken behavior.] They ravaged the consistory, robbed the monastery's staff, and took all of their property; they even made it as far as the monks' cells, but their attempt was useless. The rebels walked the streets in groups and gangs [*partiiami i artel'iami*], openly and without any fear denouncing the bishop [*arkhirei*], encouraging the mob [*chern'*] of whatever status they were, and threatening the officers and all those citizens who remained loyal to the fatherland.[80]

It is remarkable how the incident described here is played out in relation to icons and their human counterparts (especially eyes and faces), and how the rioters debate the line between reverence and sacrilege. Amvrosii's own actions, performing canonical acts of ritual piety, recall those of one of the most revered of Russian saints, St. Boris the Passion-Bearer, who also sings the liturgy and addresses an icon before his death. Amvrosii's acts include the physical act of icon veneration. The rioters, on the other hand, frame their actions as a defense of the faith. They consider their actions as in some sense protecting the holiness of the monastery—"do not beat him in the monastery, and do not defile a holy place with his blood." This may mean that they considered Amvrosii to be evil, or that the act of shedding blood was improper to a holy place, or both. The line between a sacred act of vengeance and one of profanation is obscured. This issue comes up again with the question whether or not to destroy the carriages, as the mob justifies its action by asserting that "the Chudotvorov people did not drive in them," suggesting also an element of class anger against the well-off church hierarchs.[81] While by the end the mob seems ever more clearly out for financial gain and pleasure—stealing or destroying property and getting intoxicated—there is also an explicitly "ideological," markedly semiotic and symbolic logic to their acts. Mutilating Amvrosii's body begins with his head, his face and particularly his eyes, suggesting the necessity to "deface" evil (as when images of evildoers and Satan have their eyes scratched out in medieval manuscripts); notably, when Patriarch Nikon had protested against the use of European-style painting for icons in the previous century, he had the eyes scratched out before having the works burned.[82] This is a symbolic rejection of evil that makes explicit the evildoer's loss of the divine image ("icon") within, to which the eyes provide passage (windows to the soul). Pulling off the beard—given the beard's marked semiotic significance in post-Petrine Russia—has a similar function. It is suggestive that Amvrosii's pictures (*kartiny*—which probably means modern paintings or prints, but in any case not holy images), are targeted for shredding and that later "the painted images" (*obraza zhivopisnye*)—again quite explicitly not icons— are "defaced [*obrugany*] by poking out of the eyes." If an icon invites divine looking, evil demands blinding. Amvrosii's library as a locus of modern learning ("a select group of church books and others relating to all the sciences and arts, in various languages, as well as rare manuscript volumes") is also targeted. On the other hand, tearing off and stealing icon covers as well as the (metal or ivory?) apostles on the cover of a gospel book and destruction of the communion cloth all suggest more wanton destruction.

If the epoch in question was a time of rapprochement between secular and religious values, the clash of cultures represented by the Plague Riot was the opposite—a clash of competing narratives that were mutually exclusive and uncomprehending.[83] On the one hand, Catherine celebrated Orlov's success in suppressing the riot and controlling the plague with various visual marks of honor. She commissioned a triumphal arch in Tsarskoe Selo designed by Antonio Rinaldi (the Orlov Gates, 1777–1782) and had a commemorative gold medal and marble medallion minted; paintings and poems were also composed in his and Eropkin's honor.[84] On the other hand, at the very same time as the riots were taking place in Moscow, in several other central Russian cities threatened by plague local prelates did not hesitate to call on the healing power of Bogoliubskaia Mother of God icons. The following modern retelling of the story of the Kozlov Bogoliubskaia Mother of God replicates the basic features of the ancient narrative. The Bogoliubskaia Mother of God first

> became known as a worker of miracles in the year 1771. In that year throughout Russia, and especially in the city of Kozlov, plague was rampant. The city residents did not know what to do, seeing no help from any quarter. On the gate of the home of a certain merchant in Kozlov there hung an icon of the Bogolyubskaya Icon of the Mother of God. It was revealed to a pious priest named John that he was to remove the icon from the gates and carry it in a procession of the cross—after which the plague disappeared. In commemoration of this miracle, the grateful citizens decided to have processions of the cross around the city every year on October 23, the day on which they were miraculously delivered from the plague. The grace-filled icon was placed in a silver and gilt frame decorated with various stones, and was installed in an elegant shrine. A chapel dedicated to the miraculous image was built onto the Protection Cathedral, and later a magnificent cathedral dedicated to the Bogolyubskaya Mother of God was erected.[85]

This salvation story, a variant of the "Chronicle" tale discussed above, is clearly still very much alive. All of the basic elements of the medieval narrative are present: an initial crisis; revelation of the remedy by supernatural means; carrying out of the remedy (having to do with proper treatment of the icon); miraculous deliverance; and subsequent commemoration (through further veneration of the icon, construction of a church, and a yearly celebration that situates the event in mythic, divine time extending to the present).[86] Just as the message of the Bogoliubskaia Mother of God icon is that the vision (promise, prophecy) it depicts will come to pass (i.e., that the church or monastery will be erected), so too the icon (and icon narratives) promise that the miraculous force of healing faith will extend outside its frame to its observer-supplicants.

At the same time as troops were quelling the Plague Riot in Moscow, several other cities commissioned new copies of the Bogoliubovo Mother of God icon—in Elat'ma, Iur'ev, Tula—in emulation of those in Moscow, Kozlov, and elsewhere, where it was believed that the image had provided another kind of salvation from disease. These cities instituted their own practices of veneration (as in the Kozlov narrative), and in the later eighteenth century many new copies of the Bogoliubskaia Mother of God continued to be painted. The icon's history of miraculous healings and protection from disease continued throughout the nineteenth century (e.g., during outbreaks of cholera in 1831, 1848, 1853, 1860, and 1870–1871 and 1892, when copies of the Bogoliubskaia Mother of God were again invoked or created anew).[87] The two cultural models and narratives examined in this chapter—Catherine's letter to Voltaire and that of the Bogoliubsky icons—were at ideological extremes, and may seem to exist in different worlds. On the positive end, these were the extremes of reason and faith, the modern and the medieval, science and religion, and on the negative side, incompetent administration and bad medicine versus superstition and mob violence. If both eighteenth-century Russian Enlightenment and traditional Orthodoxy culture may be seen as ocularcentric, this was a moment where their possible convergences also serve to underscore the immense social, cultural, and political divide between the two, separating the mass of the population from the numerically small Europeanized elite.

# CHAPTER EIGHT

# The Dialectic of Vision in Radishchev's *Journey*

"But this is the misfortune of mortals on earth: to go astray in the full light of day, to fail to see what stands directly before their eyes."

—Radishchev, *Journey from Petersburg to Moscow*

If the triumphal odes offered a comforting vision of greatness; and Russian historical tragedies validated virtue in extreme circumstances; if memoirs and essays on ethics defended the love of honor and self-affirmation; and physicotheological works confirmed the obviousness of virtue; if Catherine's politics argued for political transparency and merit as the cornerstone of enlightened Russian politics; with Alexander Radishchev's *Journey from Petersburg to Moscow* the hidden tensions and anxieties of the optimistic ocularcentric self came dramatically to the fore.[1] Like other works that have been examined so far, the *Journey* is preoccupied with sight and the problem of correct seeing. But here the desperate desire to justify sight came up against a major impediment stubbornly and cruelly embedded in Russian reality: serfdom.[2] When Radishchev held his mirror up to the world (a metaphor for truth-seeking in the *Journey*) he glimpsed Russia not as a utopian paradise but as a vale of tears. Serfdom represented the horrible, shameful, unseen, ignoble, and ignored underside of the beautiful utopian imperial façade and threatened to eclipse all of the nation's great accomplishments. The mirror Radishchev held up to Russia reflected a total inversion, reversal, and negation.

Radishchev centers his attention precisely on the problem of vision. He vacillates between the values of the classicist self that claims and demands a perfect balance between inner virtue and external appearance, and a profound anxiety over whether such a balance is possible, both in the world as a whole but also within the self. Lurking alongside or beneath the jubilant image of the noble, magnanimous, virtuous self was the threat of its failure, the possibility that the projected self was just that, a mere projection, contradicted by reality. The enslaved Russian peasant seemed to reveal all those things that the jubilant self was not: miserable, poor, ignoble, ignorant, downtrodden—those aspects of Russian life that were ignored and unseen but that threatened to undermine the entire edifice of the new Russia. This harshly negative perspective, which confirmed the Ecclesiastes paradigm's dire outlook, was matched by an equally immoderate sentimentalist idealization of the peasant as the embodiment of blissful, un-self-conscious, natural virtue.

Radishchev's *Journey* is permeated with deep anxiety, as the threat to Russia's self-image—as well as to Radishchev's personal safety— was immediate and palpable. Radishchev was arrested for his book and sentenced to death, but subsequently instead exiled to Siberia, and came to be considered an archetypal revolutionary martyr and intelligentsia hero for later generations. The *Journey from Petersburg to Moscow* was a direct and personal challenge to Catherine, and Radishchev's declaration that the king was wearing no clothes was an act of unheard-of civic daring, an insistence on the rights of the public sphere. The Radishchev affair marked both the logical fruition and the unhappy demise of Catherine's enlightened absolutism, insofar as Radishchev had insisted on carrying through the very program of political transparency and human rights that Catherine had promoted at the start of her reign as spelled out in the *Nakaz* (the *Instruction to the Legislative Commission* of 1767).[3] As in the case of the classicist self, for Radishchev the personal and political dramas were inseparable. Exposing the falsehood of the state façade not only threatened the basic political beliefs of the era, but also put the very possibility of self-knowledge in doubt, threatening the cohesion of the self as a psychic whole. While new sentimentalist trends in the *Journey* are obvious and have been well studied by scholars, Radishchev's goal is not knowledge by means of absorption in the self, which could lead to a solipsistic moral and emotional dead end. On the contrary, Radishchev strives to break out of this blind alley and to validate the universal, collective ideal, the selfless self defined in terms of the welfare of others, of the Russian masses, as a reflection of eternal laws of nature.

The *Journey*'s dedicatory piece offers a microcosm of the book's intensive scrutiny of the process of sight and miscognition. Here is the entire passage:[4]

I looked about me—my soul was stung [*uiazvlenna*] by the sufferings of humanity. I turned my eyes inward—I saw that man's woes arise in man himself, and frequently only because he does not look straight at the objects around him. Is it possible, I said to myself, that nature has been so miserly with her children as to hide the truth forever from him who errs innocently? Is it possible that this stern stepmother has brought us into the world that we may know only misfortunes, but never happiness? My reason trembled at this thought, and my heart thrust it far away. I found a comforter for man in himself: "Remove the veil from the eyes of natural feeling—and I shall be happy!" This voice of nature resounded loudly within me. I arose from the despair into which sensitivity and compassion had plunged me; I felt within me strength enough to withstand delusion, and—unspeakable joy! I felt that it was possible for anyone to be a collaborator in the well-being of others like myself. Such is the thought which moved me to sketch out what you are going to read.[5]

It may be noted first of all that there is an intense preoccupation with sight and the variety of words for vision (*vzglianul, obratil vzory, uzrel, vziraet,* etc.). The passage begins with the moment of crisis, looking and being "stung." Here in a short and pointed way the question is posed as to whether people are able "to look directly on the objects that surround them" ("vzirat' priamo na okruzhaiushshie predmety"), and the dedication outlines the basic stages of vision that are played out in the course of the narrative. In brief, the stages of Radishchev's dialectic of vision consist of visual shock, in which an initial stasis—based on the ocularcentric idyll of the sort pictured in Lomonosov's odes—is overturned, leading to a nihilistic depression; then a turning inward, marked by self-questioning and heeding an inner voice of truth (as opposed to visual deceptions); a moral awakening, involving the rejection of occluded vision; and a resolution to take action.

The dedication presents all of the stages of this dialectic except for the first, the starting point. It begins in medias res with a moment of crisis: "I looked about me—my soul was stung [*uiazvlenna*] by the sufferings of humanity." The image of the world that is thrown into crisis—the context for the stinging—is that picture of universal happiness, freedom, and well-being that was long familiar from the rhetorical tradition of the panegyric ode. This was the reigning discourse of the enlightened, imperial, classicist Russia of Catherine the Great. Radishchev provides a dramatic example at the start of his chapter "Khotilov: A Project for the Future":

We have brought our beloved country step by step to the flourishing condition in which it now stands; we see science, art, and industry carried to the highest degree of perfection which man can achieve; we see that in our realm human reason, spreading wide its wings, freely and unerringly soars everywhere to greatness. . . . With inexpressible joy we can say that our country is an abode pleasing to the Deity because its order is not based on prejudice and superstition, but on our inward perception of the mercy of our common Father. . . . Born in this freedom, we truly regard each other as brothers, belonging to the same family, and having one Father, God.

The torch of learning, enlightening our legislation, now distinguishes it from the legislation of many countries. The balanced separations of powers, the equality of property, destroy the very root of civil discord. Moderation in punishment causes the laws of the supreme power to be respected like the commands of tender parents to their children, and prevents even guileless misdeeds. Clarity in the ordinances concerning the acquisition and protection of property prevents the outbreak of family disputes. The boundary that separates the possessions of one citizen from another is deep and visible to all [*vsemi zrima*] and sacredly respected by all. Private offenses are rare among us, and are settled amicably. Popular education has taken pains to make us gentle, peace-loving citizens, but above all, to make us human beings [*prezhde vsego da budem cheloveki*].[6]

This may be taken more or less as a summary of the vision of Russia examined previously in this book, expressing joy in the display of Russia's virtue, greatness, and reason; the harmony between inner and outer perception, civil and divine law; political transparency and equality (here likened to a respectful family); all contributing to the supreme goal of being truly human. These things are obvious, "visible to all." We hear the high-style approbatory discourse familiar from Lomonosov's odes that was also echoed in drama, political and moral writing, and other genres.[7] There are many comparable passages in the *Journey*, in which Radishchev casts the reader in the role of a subject who unquestioningly accepts the paradisiacal, ocularcentric vision of Enlightenment Russia that is now to be harshly interrogated.

Everything, it seems, is self-evident. But Sumarokov warned in his essay on pride that it may not be so easy to distinguish good from evil self-interest, and it turns out that this is only an appearance of well-being; what had seemed so firm and obvious turns out to be a lie, a mirage. Hence the visual shock that begins the dedication: "I looked about me—my soul was stung by the sufferings of humanity." The second stage of the dialectic of vision is crisis, as the outer world is revealed as a place not of joy and gladness but a vale of tears. The sentence that directly follows the passage cited above from "Khotilov" represents an analogous moment of crisis. The sentence starts out like a simple continuation of what went before: "Enjoying inner peace, having no external enemies, and having brought society to the highest state of happiness based on civil association"—but ends up as a cry of despair that totally undercuts the previous exaltation: "will we really be so alien to human feeling, so alien to the emotions of pity, so alien to the kindness of noble hearts, so alien to fraternal love that we will let remain before our eyes as an eternal reproach and as a thing of shame [*ponoshenie*] for our descendants [the fact that we are abandoning] an entire third [sic][8] of our fellows, our equal citizens, beloved brethren in nature, to the heavy bonds of slavery and unfreedom?"[9] The jubilant delight in Russia's glory gives way to a crescendo of despair and self-censure. This new vision of human misfortune turns the world upside down. Serfdom now takes center stage as something that remains "before our eyes as an eternal [*vsegdashniuiu*] reproach." The picture of universal joy and well-being gives way to a shameful spectacle: "The bestial custom of enslaving one's fellow men, which originated in the hot regions of Asia, a custom worthy of savages, a custom that signifies a heart of stone and a total lack of soul, has quickly spread far and wide over the face of the earth. And we Slavs, sons of glory [*slava*], glorified in both name and deed among earth-born generations, benighted by the darkness of ignorance, have adopted this custom, and, to our shame, to the shame of past centuries, to the shame of this age of reason, we have kept it inviolate even to this day."[10] This image of Russia resembles that of its harshest European critics: savage, soulless, ignorant, barbaric. Radishchev plays upon the popular etymological connection between *Slav* and *slava* (glory), and upon archaic formulas ("imenem i delami slovuty v kolenakh zemnorodnykh") in order to emphasize the demise of glory and its replacement by shame, shame, shame. With bitter irony this Russia is geographically grouped not with Enlightened Europe but with "the hot regions of Asia," and serfdom also reflects back and taints not only "this age of reason" but also the past, as a practice that Radishchev caustically notes has been "kept inviolate" (i.e., that Peter's reforms have failed to affect). From this perspective, the previous vision of Russia as "an abode pleasing to the Deity" can only have been a result of self-serving flattery or blindness.

The dedication opens with this very unpleasant visual shock, the sight of something heretofore unseen that now becomes "an eternal [sic] reproach" "before our eyes." Similarly, in "Vyshnii Volochok," the narrator realizes that the earth's seemingly happy abundance may bear witness "to the heavy lot of its inhabitants" and that "if at first glance my spirit was delighted at the sight of this prosperity, upon second thoughts my joy soon waned."[11] The signified belies the signifier. Here the narrator's shock of miscognition comes while he is enjoying a cup of coffee: "'Remember,' my friend once said, 'that the coffee in your cup, and the sugar dissolved in it, have deprived a man like yourself of his rest, that they have been the cause of labors surpassing his strength, the cause of tears, groans, blows, and abuse. Now dare to pamper your gullet, hard-hearted wretch!' The sight of his disgust as he said this shook me to the depths of my soul. My hand trembled, and I spilled the coffee."[12] Notably, in this instance the shock of new vision comes not from looking at some physical evil per se (e.g., seeing slaves suffer, or imagining the coffee bathed in sweat and tears), but from seeing the disgust reflected in his friend's face. To see the Other as unhappy is painful, a dethroning of the divine signification of the world outside and an inner fall from self-complacency. It is a moment of acute consciousness in the sense of Dostoevsky's "underground man," brought on and defined by pain. The evil that a sensitive person sees in the external world is felt internally.

The horror of being stung by the vision of human pain and suffering leads at first to an extremely negative, even nihilistic, picture of existence. The external world now appears as a place of unrelieved sorrow, and the pain of others is internalized by the viewer as depression, anxiety, guilt, despair (*skorb', terzanie, otchaianie*), and even rage. This stage of vision—or rather, the eclipse of vision—corresponds to the Ecclesiastes paradigm, which inverts or reverses the main features of classicist ocularcentrism. As with the coffee incident, there are many passages in the *Journey* that cast doubt on the objects of vision in the material world. The fame and glory of this world are also repeatedly questioned in the *Journey* as transient and superficial, and not only that of individuals but also of whole civilizations, whose grandiose constructions, from pyramids to magnificent empires, all crumble to dust with time. The negative vision of material reality embraces political oppression, as the nihilist view of a comfortless, fallen existence easily segues into political oppositionism and revolt.[13]

A similar reversal from good to bad vision, also instigated by serfdom, serves as the crux of Vassili Kapnist's "Ode to Slavery" ("Oda na rabstvo," written 1783), which might more properly be called an anti-ode, insofar as the poet can offer Catherine only "unflattering speech" (*nelestnu rech'*) until such time as she fulfills her duty to bring freedom and happiness to her subjects:

Куда ни обращу зеницу,
Омытую потоком слез,
Везде, как скорбную вдовицу,
Я зрю мою отчизну днесь [. . .]

Воззрите вы на те народы,
Где рабство тяготит людей,
Где нет любезныя свободы
И раздается звук цепей:
Там к бедству смертные рожденны,
К уничиженью осужденны,
Несчастий полну чашу пьют;
Под игом тяжкия державы
Потоками льют пот кровавый
И зляе смерти жизнь влекут.[14]

[Wherever I turn my eye, / Everywhere I see my fatherland / Drenched with tears, / Like a sorrowful widow. (. . .) // Look you at those nations / Where slavery oppresses people, / Where there is no precious freedom, / But only the sound of chains. / There mortals are born to misfortune, / Condemned to degradation, / And drink a full cup of miseries. / Under the yoke of terrible state power / They pour a stream of bloody sweat / And drag out a life worse than death.]

As in the *Journey*, the image of horror is connected with drinking "a cup full of miseries." The Ecclesiastes paradigm poses a direct challenge to the Lomonosovian panegyric ode, overturning its generic and stylistic presuppositions by praising something so manifestly evil. In Kapnist's poem the promise of odic praise is denied, or withheld, since it remains as a potential should Catherine fulfill the enlightened promise and put an end to serfdom.[15]

This stage in the dialectic of vision, when one sees the evils of the world most clearly, is painful. Radishchev is "stung"; like the "eye doctor" Clear-of-Eye (*Priamozvorova*) from "Spasskaia Polest'," he seems eaten up with negativity: "she is a very dangerous witch who carries venom and poison, and gloats over grief and affliction; she is always frowning, and she scorns and reviles everyone; in her abuse she spares not even thy sacred head."[16] These words strikingly recall Catherine's criticism of the author of the *Journey* himself as a man eaten up by jealousy and bile.[17] Princess Dashkova used a similar image of a "wretched oculist" as a defense of serfdom. When challenged by Diderot about "what he believed to be our peasants' slavery," among other things she argued was that without the necessary "knowledge and understanding which produce freedom" nothing would result except "anarchy and confusion." She offered an allegorical description of

> a blind man on a steep cliff surrounded by a yawning chasm. He is unaware, thanks to his defect, of the dangers of his situation, and being unaware of them he is gay, he eats and sleeps with perfect unconcern, he listens to the singing of birds and sometimes sings himself. And then up comes a wretched oculist who gives him back his sight without being able to save him from his plight. So there is my poor man, his sight fully restored, feeling as unhappy as could be. He sings no more, he hardly eats or sleeps, he is afraid of all—of the abyss that surrounds him, of the waves which lash against the rock and which before he knew nothing about—and he ends by dying in the flower of his youth from fear and despair.[18]

Blindness here is a good thing, a protection against truths that are too hard to see and digest.[19]

This is just the difficult step that Radishchev took—to open his eyes to the myriad instances of poverty, slavery, the sale of serfs, unequal marriages, prostitution, and venereal disease with which the *Journey* is filled. But this nihilistic vision does not mean, as some scholars conclude, that Radishchev is a materialist, utilitarian, and revolutionary.[20] The negation of false vision and a sharp awareness of the material limits of the visible are important, but are only one stage of an ongoing dialectic. Radishchev's skepsis has definite limits.

As the dedication continues a new stage of vision begins to emerge: "I turned my eyes inward—I saw that man's woes arise in man himself, and frequently only because he does not look straight at the objects around him." The crisis that follows opening one's eyes to suffering leads to a turning inward, and the initial pessimism changes into a new, positive, more critical understanding of correct and incorrect vision. In contrast to Dostoevsky's "underground man," for whom "acute consciousness" becomes more and more painful and tragic, for Radishchev the sensation of pain may play a positive role. The word often used for this pain, a "stinging" (*uiazvlenie*, and forms of the verb *iazvit'/uiazvit'*, to wound or sting), has several important associations in the *Journey* and suggests some of the complexity of coming to consciousness. In eighteenth-century usage *iazvit'* could signify physical wounding, as in the case of a soldier wounded in battle, and also (as in later usage) a spiritual wounding, a stinging or biting that involves the tongue, most commonly via words. Forms of this verb are often associated with harsh satire or caustic speech (e.g., *iazvitel'naia rech'*); as in the dedication, it is also possible for one's soul to be "stung" (*dushu uiazvlenna stala*).[21] Seeing, hearing, touch, or any other contact with evil—spiritual or physical—is dangerous, and its bites and stings may penetrate and leave a dangerous residue, turning the victim into a callous, indifferent, evil oppressor himself. There are various metaphors for this kind of incipient blindness, including "veils" (e.g., the ones that are removed in the dedication) and the "cataracts" (*bel'ma*) Clear-of-Eye removes from the narrator's eyes, which she also describes as "a thick scab, like a horny substance" that obscures "natural vision" (*estestvennyi vid*).[22] A further metaphor for this blockage is an "opaque curtain" that keeps us from sympathy for the "most stinging afflictions and wounds, and even death itself" when they occur to other people, and that may scarcely evoke even "that momentary emotion which theatrical representations produce."[23] Truly evil people are the ones whose vision has been occluded by a "crust" (*kora*) that is both "impenetrable to light" and invulnerable to all other penetration, a smooth, hard surface that prevents the pricks and stings of conscience. The inner self, the heart, has become all surface, turned to stone, and is unable to be moved by other people's suffering or virtue. Thus Radishchev's dreamer in "Spasskaia Polest'" accuses his evil advisors of *okamenelost' zlodeianiia*, the "ossification of evil-doing." There may also be a connection—visual and auditory if not etymological—between Radishchev's notion of *kora* (crust) and of *koryst'* (profit or cupidity), which is his version of Sumarokov's *pribytochestvo* (the desire for profit) discussed earlier. The link between "crusts" and "profit-making" as things that blind is selfishness.[24] One may also be "stung" with a disease, *iazva* (from the same root as *iazvit'*; this may mean an ulcer, sore, the plague or infectious diseases generally, or, figuratively, a curse). "The example of the masters infects the higher-ranking servants, these infect the lower, and from these the pestilence [*iazva*] of debauchery spreads to the villages. [Bad] example is the real plague, for everybody does what he sees others do."[25] It is not so much venereal disease itself that infects, but the vision of evil behavior. Bad sight—bad example—is infectious, both on the spiritual and physical plane.

The stings of evil may provoke answering blows. In some sense this response to evil is completely logical and represents a natural reaction. On the level of ethics and politics this means resisting evil with an eye for an eye, even bloody rebellion and a defense of natural human rights by means of force.[26] But this is an extreme and undesirable course, because all participants may end up trapped in their shells, blinded. The results of such mutually escalating "stinging"—as in the case of the French Revolution—may be horrendous.[27]

However, the painful sting of negativity may also produce a positive result—a shock that leads to moral awakening and new vision. In his thoughts, the narrator warns Aniuta of "Edrovo" against hardening: "Let not your heart be troubled if a man steeped in debauch and grown gray in shamelessness should pass by and scorn [*prezrit*] you; do not attempt to bar his way with the solace of your converse. His heart is already stone; his soul is encrusted with a layer of adamant. The beneficent sting of innocent virtue cannot make any real impression on him. Its point will glide over the smooth surface of vice. Beware lest your sharp weapon be blunted against it."[28] The "layer [or crust] of adamant" (*almaznaia kora*) suggests hardness and smoothness, though not transparency; in contrast, "roughness" and "softness" (*nezhnost'*) may be "beneficent" as they indicate hearts "open everywhere for Thy coming"—ones that allow the sting of virtue to be felt, and hence the possibility of change.[29] An arrow or stinger may cause pain, but may also awaken a person from an evil, blind, or sleepy disposition.[30] The pain of being stung does not leave Radishchev's narrator stuck in an escalating cycle of sado-masochism, as it does for Dostoevsky's insular underground man.

The feminine ideal of divine virtue, innocence, and complete transparency offers a path to self-examination and repentance. In a confessional moment, Radishchev's narrator admits that "I love women because they embody my ideal of tenderness; but most of all I love village or peasant women, because they are innocent of hypocrisy, do not put on the mask of pretended love, and when they do love, love sincerely and with their whole hearts."[31] The woman plays the role of Other, the projection of a perfectly virtuous and transparent self. Of course, from the psychological point of view, this is but another fiction. In Radishchev's dialectic, however, this is the measure of correct vision, a vision of the heart or of the soul, which is also the counterpart of divine understanding. The narrator speculates that had he encountered Aniuta earlier in his life, "The influence of your living virtue would have penetrated to the depths of my heart, and I would have escaped the shameful acts which have filled my life. . . . O my Aniutushka! Be ever near us and teach us by your unconstrained innocence. I know that you will lead back into the way of virtue him who has begun to turn aside, and strengthen him who is tending to go astray."[32]

Thus for Radishchev's wanderer, the righteous sting leads him toward something outside of himself. The initial looking outward and being "stung" by the evil of the world leads to looking inward and seeking a new understanding, which in turn allows new outward-directed vision, the ability to look "straight at the objects that surround us." This process of turning inward and outward is not easy or simple, and vision is no longer obvious or automatic. The following stage of the dialectic of vision as represented by the middle section of the dedicatory piece consists of a series of complex and confusing questions that, it seems, the narrator himself cannot fully answer ("Is it possible . . . ? Is it possible . . . ?"). The transformation here, the move from inner to outer sight, from reason to feeling or faith, is on one level that of confession, the realization of error and complicity in evil, and is at times described in traditional terms of sin (*grekh*), "going astray" or "delusion" (*zabluzhdenie* or *bluzhdenie*) and repentance (*raskaianie*), although these are not emphasized, and the specially Christian aspect of confession as a sacrament is absent (see the chapter "Bronnitsy"). Radishchev's religious view is closest to theism.[33] Although Radishchev sometimes gives voice to the Hobbesian view of humanity in its "natural state," that is, in a constant struggle for existence (which corresponds to the nihilist stage of vision), this idea, like the Christian notion of primal sin, is secondary for him. The problem for Radishchev is not so much how to get rid of deeply rooted human evil (although this does concern him) as much as the question whether we, mortals, may physically free ourselves of delusion and "see directly." The impossibility of seeing directly is not only a moral but a practical issue: "Is it possible, I said to myself, that nature has been so miserly with her children as to hide the truth forever from him who errs innocently? Is it possible that this stern stepmother has brought us into the world that we may know only misfortunes, but never happiness? My reason trembled at this thought, and my heart thrust it far away." This problem of knowing exists equally for the morally innocent and for the guilty. If correct vision is impossible, there can be no guilty or innocent, insofar as one cannot fault a blind man for blindness. Is the truth forever hidden from us and our errors then inevitable if unintentional? Is true sight possible, or is this just another delusion, simply a fiction? If so, are we then condemned to ignorance and unhappiness? Radishchev questions the nature of "Nature," both the essence (ontology) of the external world and its knowability (epistemology). Morality is a function of epistemology; how and what we know determines how we act.

Yet as Radishchev's impassioned questions indicate, reason as a mode of knowing does not offer a satisfactory response; the answers that it gives are unacceptable. Recall:

> Is it possible, I said to myself, that nature has been so miserly with her children as to hide the truth forever from him who errs innocently? Is it possible that this stern stepmother has brought us into the world that we may know only misfortunes, but never happiness? My reason trembled at this thought, and my

heart thrust it far away. I found a comforter for man in himself: "Remove the veil from the eyes of natural feeling—and I shall be happy!" This voice of nature resounded loudly within me. I arose from the despair into which sensitivity and compassion had plunged me; I felt within me strength enough to withstand delusion, and—unspeakable joy! I felt that it was possible for anyone to be a collaborator in the well-being of others like myself.[34]

The narrator's experience is difficult and not fully clear. The notion of "nature" assumes at least three different aspects. First, it is as creator—as parent to her children (note that *priroda* is a feminine noun in Russian) and as "stepmother" who "brought us into the world." Second, it is "natural feeling" or sensation (*chuvstvovanie*)—which may mean either physical, material sensation or some inner spiritual capacity to feel; in this case it would be the first, the world of external physical existence. The third guise of nature here is the "voice of nature" as the expression of inner spiritual truth, which at various moments in the *Journey* is described as conscience or even the voice of God. Thus "nature" embraces both the physical and metaphysical aspects of human existence. The impassioned language of the dedication (and of the *Journey* as a whole) suggests that for Radishchev the ultimate criterion of truth is the "heart," which may be viewed as an intuitive, irrational principle, like God. God—or nature—represents no mere impassive material reality but a parent, implicated (indeed personally interested) in the well-being of her children.

The truth—while still something to be seen—is ultimately validated by hearing. The voice of nature puts an end to doubt and delusion, and gives instruction in how to "remove the veil" so as to "look straight at the objects surrounding" us and be happy. The very "sensitivity and compassion" that had earlier plunged the narrator into despair also make it possible to overcome alienating pain and reach a more valid happiness. He began in a state of "inexpressible joy" (*neizrechennogo radovaniia* ["Khotilov"]) and finished in "inexpressible happiness" (*veseliia neizrechennogo*). But the initial joyful seeing was only apparent, or perhaps it was only a state of blessed innocence like Adam and Eve before the Fall. "Sensitivity and compassion" allow the reconciliation with self and union with others. In some sense, the reader is returned to the ideal jubilant vision with which he or she started, or perhaps that paradisiacal ideal of a balance between inner and outer vision, between individual and communal well-being, has taken on a more conscious character. This new consciousness allows and demands action, both spiritual ("to be a collaborator in the well-being of others") and practical ("such is the thought which moved me to sketch out what you are going to read"). Thus the very writing of the *Journey from St. Petersburg to Moscow* in some sense represents the last stage of the dialectic of vision.

The dialectic of vision also serves to configure the *Journey*'s narrative structure, one of the most thorny and debated problems of the work.[35] The image of Radishchev as implied author is not clearly separable from the other narrative voices that may be taken as hypostases of a single aggregate authorial consciousness. These voices correspond to the various models or stages of vision that make up the dialectic, which taken together may be seen to constitute a single collective authorial consciousness. While few of the individual episodes in the *Journey* contain all of the various stages in the dialectic of vision, there is a larger cumulative unity of the *Journey* to which all of the voices taken together (that of Radishchev as implied author as well as the others) contribute. At the same time, this does not mean that the dialectic is complete once and for all. Vision remains "dialogical" in Bakhtin's sense, open-ended and unfinalizable.[36] The end of development (spiritual petrifaction and perhaps also the state of perfect bliss) spells death; identity is a process. The self is a site of continued struggle, and the dialectic of vision an unending process. This may be what gives many readers of Radishchev's *Journey* a sense of the text's fragmentary and contradictory character, and allows critics to offer diametrically opposing interpretations. On the one hand, a new synthesis, a new validation of sight, has become firmer than the seemingly unconscious vision at the start of the process, as the narrator has gone through a crucible of doubt and philosophical testing. On the other, the new "unspeakable joy" remains fragile, subject to the continual "stings" of surrounding reality, including the "eternal reproach" of serfdom and the threat of harsh retribution from Catherine. Both the joy and the reproaches are "eternal" and continue to assert their pull, and the *Journey* continually oscillates between two opposing poles, that of reassuring hope (faith in social justice and universal happiness), and anxiety (a sense of hopelessness and the expectation of inevitable retribution).

## The Problem of Resolution

The final stage of the dialectic of vision—in the dedication, the "sketching out" of the *Journey* and presenting it to readers—thus remains tentative and fraught with anxiety. To reach an endpoint means both confronting authority and finding some resolution to the moral and visual dialectic. The new synthetic self that has engaged with the external world may even suggest a way forward out of the mirror-stage into adulthood, yet it is not clear that this breakthrough has occurred. The "unspeakable joy" can neither put an end to speech, nor to anxiety. Hence the basic questions that the *Journey* raises, and that readers have long struggled with, remain. What is to be done about serfdom, and what course of action exactly is Radishchev advocating? What is the relationship between his new allegedly "unspeakable joy" and his position on serfdom? What are the practical consequences of "withstanding delusion" and "collaborating in the well-being of others"? The question may be narrowed down even further: what is the final balance between the two aspects of self-image—joyful and self-reproachful—that emerge at the end of Radishchev's visual dialectic? To explore these issues and flesh out the tensions of the dialectic of vision as they manifest themselves in the *Journey* is the task of the remaining pages of this chapter.

Dividing the twenty-six episodes of the *Journey from Petersburg to Moscow* (all but the first and last named for stops along the route) according to their "joyful" or "despairing" resolutions results in a near even split of about 14 to 12. While readers might dispute the classification in some cases, as not all episodes even have plots, the fact that there is such a more or less even split itself indicates the great tension in the work, its atmosphere of intense psychic anxiety. The episodes that end on a "despairing" note include several that present portraits of particular abuses and characters: in "Mednoe" the "shameful spectacle" of selling serfs, carried out before a foreigner; in "Chernaia griaz'" a forced marriage that brings not joy but grief; in "Gorodnia" a levy (enrolling men into the army); in "Tosna" a man who peddles aristocratic genealogies; in "Vyshnii volochok" an evil serf-owner who sets a bad, infectious example; in "Sofiia" a defense of suicide. Other episodes present a pessimistic view of history and describe various legal abuses ("Podberez'e," "Novgorod"). The fundamental political message to be derived from these "despairing" episodes is that if the system will not correct its injustices and abuses, the oppressed will eventually rise up and take vengeance. As the narrator puts it at the end of "Mednoe": "But all those who might be the champions of freedom are great landed proprietors, and freedom is not to be expected from their counsels, but from the heavy burden of slavery itself," that is, from spontaneous violence.[37]

Some of the most famous "despairing" episodes describe characters who finally decide to give up on the world as hopelessly evil and retreat into isolation. In "Chudovo," the narrator's friend "Ch—," disillusioned with those who would not rouse an official from bed in order to save people in danger of drowning, declares that he will never return to St. Petersburg, that "den of tigers," and removes himself to "where people do not go, where they do not know where man is, where his name is unknown" (compare the Hobbesian view of man in a state of nature in "Novgorod").[38] In "Zaitsovo," the hero Krestiankin eventually gives up a struggle to gain justice for serfs who had stood up against their owner's violence and rape. He retires to his home "to bewail the lamentable fate of the peasant class, and to relieve [his] weariness in association with [his] friends," a conclusion some critics have taken to suggest either Radishchev's own sense of frustration with the existing system, or a criticism of sentimentalism, and perhaps literature in general, as ineffectual and escapist.[39] In two other episodes the narrator directly implicates himself in the evil described, without further resolution. In "Liubani" he cries bitter tears over his treatment of a servant after having denounced a cruel serf-owner for what he sees as similar behavior, and in "Iazhelbitsy," which the narrator calls a "trial," he seems to hear his "own sentence pronounced" when he overhears a man in a cemetery lamenting having killed his son by "infusing slow poison into him at conception" due to venereal disease.[40] He frames the episode with the remark that "I was destined to witness a spectacle which sank a deep root of sorrow into my soul, with no hope of ever plucking it out."[41]

In contrast, the affirmative episodes, rather than suggesting escape from the evils of humanity, involve the newborn passion "to be a collaborator in the well-being of others." Even while these episodes may include harsh denunciations of evil, they also offer either inspirational twists at the end or concrete plans for reform, for example, on how to end serfdom in "Khotilov," a project to abolish ranks in "Vydropusk," and arguments to replace censorship with freedom of the press in "Torzhok."[42] In "Edrovo," as noted earlier, a meeting with the peasant girl Aniuta and subsequent "beneficent sting of innocent virtue" inspire principled self-criticism in the narrator, "Klin" teaches him about true charity, and in "Krestitsy" a father gives inspirational moral admonitions to his parting sons, ending with a prayer, "troubled but in firm hope" for the future. In "Peski," one of many episodes in which the reader is called on to look upon various evils, the narrator is stung by a peasant woman's comment that aristocrats who have sugar in their tea are "drinking peasants' tears," and do not care if the peasants starve. As with the coffee incident cited earlier, the narrator is shocked by another person's pain, and it changes his sight: "This reproach, not uttered in anger or indignation, but with a profound feeling of sorrow in her soul, filled my heart with grief. For the first time I looked closely at all the household gear of a peasant hut. For the first time I turned my heart to things over which it had only glided heretofore."[43] He now gives his surroundings—a miserable hovel and its near-naked inhabitants—detailed scrutiny, and sees that unpalatable inverted mirror-self described above, as the narrator's language switches from high odic to low and vulgar diction, a prototype for later naturalism. The narrator then turns to "hard-hearted" Russian landlords with a call to conscience, and a warning not against earthly but divine vengeance from a God who sees all:

> If there is no judge over you here, you will be answerable before the Judge Who is no respecter of persons, Who once gave you a good guide, conscience, but whom your perverse reason long ago drove from his dwelling place, your heart. But do not imagine that you will escape punishment. The sleepless watcher of your deeds will surprise you when you are alone, and you will feel his chastising strokes. Oh, if only they could be of some good to you and those subject to you!—Oh, if man would but look into his soul more frequently, and confess his deeds to his implacable judge, his conscience! Transformed by its thunderous voice into an immovable pillar, he would no longer dare to commit secret crimes.[44]

Sight is transformed, restored, as human vision comes into line with the divine. Heart and soul (almost interchangeable organs) take precedence over reason, whose tendency is to serve narrow self-interest—or rather, reason assumes its proper role in harmony with feeling.

Three other episodes that may be categorized as positive, joyful resolutions include what may be taken to be "meta-literary" commentary on Radishchev's own task as a writer, and reinforce the idea that writing is the ultimate fruit and justification of Radishchev's dialectic of vision, a spiritual going out into the world that can spark corporeal change. In "Tver'," Lomonosov's versification system is criticized as restrictive, even though Radishchev uses that very system in his "Ode to Freedom" (which ends on a very positive note). While the poem is itself severely faulted in aesthetic terms, the narrator nevertheless suggests that it is "better to make reasonable haste with post nags than to climb on Pegasus when he is mettlesome," a comment that may be applied to the *Journey* itself.[45] Indeed, the narrator is travelling on "post nags" (attaining fresh horses is a constant problem) and, as suggested in "Tver'," he has no inflated notion of his own talents, but is arguing for reasonable haste in assuaging his own, and Russia's, anguish.

"Zavidovo" presents a satirical attack on blustering, bullying grandees of "high dignity but without true worth," whom the narrator compares to quack sorcerers who make gullible peasants think they have supernatural powers. "But as soon as in the crowd that idolizes them someone turns up who has to some extent freed himself from the grossest superstition, their deception is laid bare, and they will not tolerate such clear-sighted men [*dal'novidtsov*] in the place where they work their wonders."[46] Here and elsewhere, it seems clear that Radishchev has chosen for himself the role of that someone in the crowd. Lastly, the "Eulogy on Lomonosov" that ends the *Journey*, while sharply critical of his odes as servile flattery and of other of his accomplishments, is nevertheless both a rousing defense of Russian literature as the voice of Russian society and a paean to Lomonosov as its founder and as a Great Man. Despite his faults, Lomonosov is one of those select in whom "the incorporeal acts upon the incorporeal and produces the corporeal," that is, who inspire others with true vision and thus effectively engage with—and produce material changes in—the world.[47]

The remaining two "joyful" episodes in the *Journey* are the farthest away from the mundane world and perhaps for that reason also offer the most positive resolution of the dialectic of vision. In the first, "Bronnitsy," the narrator has a spiritual vision in which he meets God. The second, "Spasskaia polest'," poses the political problem of *The Journey* most sharply as the protagonist directly confronts Catherine the Great in allegorical guise. Each to some extent recapitulates aspects of the dialectic of vision outlined above, and sheds further light on its religious and political aspects, respectively. The first episode, "Bronnitsy," offers commentary on the voice of nature that rouses the narrator "from the despair into which sensitivity and compassion had plunged" him and foregrounds the theological underpinnings of the dialectic of vision. The narrator journeys to a hill where before the coming of the Slavs a pagan temple had stood, housing an oracle, which had been replaced by a church. As he approaches the summit he has a mystical epiphany that reveals the divine nature of inner truth:

> As I climbed the hill, I imagined that I was transported into antiquity, and that I had come to have the future revealed to me by the Almighty, and to find peace from my perplexity. Divine awe seized my limbs, my breast began to heave, my eyes grew dull, their light was darkened. I heard a voice like thunder proclaiming: "Fool! Wherefore dost thou desire to pierce through the mystery which I have hid from mortals behind the impenetrable shroud of the unknown? Wherefore, audacious one, wilt thou learn that which only eternal thought can grasp? Know that thine ignorance of the future is in accord with the frailty of thy nature. . . . What seekest thou, foolish child? My wisdom has implanted in thy mind and heart all that thou needest. Appeal to them in the day of sorrow, and thou wilt find comforters, appeal to them in the day of gladness, and thou wilt find restraints upon thy presumptuous happiness.

Return to thy home, return to thy family; quiet thy troubled thoughts, enter into thine innermost soul, and there thou wilt find my Godhead, there thou wilt hear my prophecy."[48]

Perplexity gives way to peace, as the outward journey ends up as a journey within, a return: "My wisdom has implanted in thy mind and heart all that thou needest . . . enter into thine innermost soul, and there thou wilt find my Godhead, there thou wilt hear my prophecy." The light of his eyes is darkened as the revelation of truth is an oral, not a visual experience, a "Hebraic" rather than "Hellenic" mode of perception, an interior journey that would even seem to obviate the need for a *Journey* out into the world.[49] Radishchev addresses a universal deity seeking a pure vessel into which he may descend:

Thy mighty right hand extends invisibly in all directions and compels even him who denies Thy all-powerful will to recognize the architect and preserver of nature. If a mortal in his error calls Thee by strange, unbecoming, and bestial names, his worship nonetheless aspires to Thee, Ever-living Lord, and he trembles before Thy might. Jehovah, Jupiter, Brahma, God of Abraham, God of Moses, God of Confucius, God of Zoroaster, God of Socrates, God of Marcus Aurelius, God of the Christians, O my God! Thou art everywhere the same, the One. When mortals in their error seemed to be worshiping not Thee alone, they were deifying Thine incomparable forces, Thine inimitable deeds. Thy almighty power, felt everywhere and in everything, has everywhere and in everything been worshiped. The atheist who denies Thee, but recognizes the immutable law of nature, thereby proclaims Thy glory, lauding Thee even more than our songs of praise . . . Most gracious Father, Thou seekest a true heart and spotless soul; they are open everywhere for Thy coming. Descend, O Lord, and enthrone Thyself in them.[50]

The image of the divine force here is theist, both in its universality (an assertion of divine being, called by whatever name, and worshiped in whatever manner—by pagans or even atheists) and, unlike Deism, in its overpowering sense of the divine power's personal involvement in the world. The revelation of ultimate truth in "Bronnitsy" concludes with a contrast between the fragility of the visible world and that which is immortal: "I stood for a few moments, removed from the objects around me, lost in profound contemplation. Then, raising my eyes and glancing at the nearby dwellings, I cried, "Behold the miserable hovels of the downfallen, in the place where once a great city reared its proud walls. Not even the smallest trace of them remains. Reason, demanding conclusive and palpable [*chuvstvennykh*] evidence, refuses even to believe the story. And all that we see will pass away; all will fall to ruins; all will become dust. But a certain mysterious voice says to me, something will forever live."[51] An inner voice sounds to recoup faltering vision. The passage as a whole, and particularly the last sentences, clearly evokes the Ecclesiastes paradigm, giving it a final optimistic turn. The Book of Ecclesiastes itself ends with an analogous sharp contrast between the vanity of all earthly endeavors and a curt promise of final justice (see chapter 6 above).[52] Similarly, Radishchev's meditation on the transitory nature of existence illustrates both sides of his dialectical position; on one hand, a cosmic pessimism that sees the vanity of human endeavor and undercuts reason, and on the other an ultimate validation of theodicy (the revelation of good and evil) and an argument for faith in the face of despair.

Notably in this connection, Radishchev contrasts Lomonosov's odes that he criticizes for flattery to his "Evening Meditation," which he paraphrases in terms that suggest the Ecclesiastes paradigm:

> Умеряя глас трубы Пиндаровой, на ней же он воспел бренность человека и близкий предел его понятий. В бездне миров беспредельной, как в морских волнах малейшая песчинка, как во льде, не тающем николи, искра едва блестящая, в свирепейшем вихре как прах тончайший, что есть разум человеческий?[53]
>
> [Moderating the voice of Pindar's trumpet, on it he also sang the frailty of man and the immanent limits of his understanding. In the boundless abyss of worlds, like the smallest grain of sand in the sea waves, like a barely shining sparkle in ice that never melts, like the finest dust in a the most violent whirlwind, what is human reason?]

As with Lomonosov's "Meditation," here closely paraphrased, knowledge of the self is questioned but nevertheless is seen to possess some kind of enduring coherence and value.[54] As the father puts it in giving parting advice to his sons in "Krestitsy," nothing will pass away, everything will be seen clearly: "even if you disguise trickery, lying, disloyalty, avarice, pride, vengefulness, and bestiality under the semblance of the noblest acts of life, so that you blind your contemporaries with the bright light of your external glamour, and even if you do not find anyone who loves you enough to place before you the mirror of truth [*zertsalo istiny*], do not imagine that you can eclipse the All-seeing Eye [*zatmit' vzory prozorlivosti*]. It will pierce through the shining mantle of your deceit, and virtue will lay bare the blackness of your soul."[55] The translator renders the peculiar personification of vision *vzory prozorlivosti* as "the All-seeing Eye" (more literally, something like: sagacity's sight; *prozorlivost'* is from the verb *prozre(va)t'*, meaning "to see, to recover one's sight, to begin to see clearly," literally, "to see through"). The father continues: "Your heart will hate it [*voznenavidit*], and it will shrink from your touch like a sensitive plant—but only for a moment, for its arrows will soon begin to sting [*iazvit'*] and torment you from afar."[56] That is, Radishchev's faith in *prozorlivost'*, the divine renewal of sight that comes from within, causes motion within the world, and inspires change for the better.

This brings back the problem of dealing with intractable evil—like that embodied in serfdom. The realization of the vanity of human existence and that "all that we see will pass away" does not vitiate ethical action. Indeed Radishchev makes a connection between the false, selfish, prideful pursuit of external honors that allow corruption and the notion that "worldly honors are dust and ashes." He does not allow the "vanity of all things" argument to become an excuse for passivity, a reason not to fight delusion, undercutting any notion of true merit, leaving "inexperienced worth . . . fated to content itself with its own approval, in the conviction that worldly honors are dust and ashes."[57] This is clearly unacceptable, and Radishchev validates the active pursuit of truth, *chestoliubie*, as predicated on the principle of true honor.

## Radishchev's Confrontation with Power

The second "joyful" episode dramatically recapitulates the dialectic of vision and argues for just such heroic ethical action based on true vision. Radishchev's allegorical depiction of Catherine the Great in the chapter "Spasskaia Polest'" features a dramatic de-cloaking, a stripping away of the empress's image as enlightened monarch.[58] Even though in the narrator's dream, which comprises the second half of this episode, he imagines himself "a tsar, shah, khan, king, bey, nabob, sultan, or some such exalted being, sitting on a throne in power and majesty," both the text itself and Catherine's extreme reaction to it indicate that the allegory was completely transparent.[59] Indeed elsewhere in the *Journey* the author defends the practice of such direct "personal satire" (*satira na litso*), as opposed to the rather toothless satire of vice of the kind Catherine advocated.[60] The allegorical dream is doubly unusual in that Radishchev casts himself—the narrator—in the role of Catherine. This is a common didactic procedure, to try and convince the reader sympathetically, from within; it draws considerable power in the present case from the popular Enlightenment notion of the monarch as social engineer, which the dream dramatizes. Radishchev's device of putting himself in the ruler's shoes also concretizes and humanizes the problems of miscognition, highlighting the deeper concern throughout the *Journey* that the evil being confronted is not only something external to the narrator (or reader), but also his—our own common human—inner failing. The pattern of the dream—a ruler coming to grips with the evils of the world— also reiterates the general narrative situation of Ecclesiastes, in which a king looks back on the accomplishments and wisdom of his life and sees only emptiness and vanity.

The dream in "Spasskaia Polest'" replicates the basic steps of the dialectic of vision outlined above, isolating some of the mechanisms of miscognition, focusing on the problem from the point of view of the ruler and the things that allow bad pride to be mistaken for good. It is framed by a series of stories that emphasize the narrator's anxiety of vision. It is preceded by "Chudovo," one of the "depressing" chapters in which the narrator's friend ended up turning his back completely on Petersburg as a place of inhumanity and "a den of tigers." The two stories that preface the dream in "Spasskaia Polest'" itself similarly provide a suggestive context. First the narrator overhears an intimate conversation between a low-ranking official and his wife in an inn. The official complains about corruption in promotions, and his wife counters that he was probably passed over because he himself had not shared his own bribes. He tells her to hush, thus suggesting the difficulty of confronting evil not only in others but also in oneself. Then the narrator gives a ride to a man who turns out to be fleeing from the authorities. He tells a Job-like chronicle of innocent suffering, about how his trust in a dishonest man had led to his destruction—the premature birth and death of his daughter, followed by that of his wife, and his flight from arrest and legal persecution. This leads the narrator to a long series of painful, self-searching questions. He wonders about his belief that an autocratic system of government is the most just, insofar as "only the supreme power could be impartial." He doubts the functioning of the rule of law, asking what rights the man has, or should have, and wonders about his own right—"the right of suffering humanity"— to intervene; and lastly he questions divine justice, asking why "instead of threatening future punishment" to evildoers Jesus does not "torment their conscience in proportion to their wickedness" and thus realize justice in this world. These incidents and questions thus rehearse the narrator's basic problems and anxieties and frame the dream as a response.[61]

The dream itself begins with perhaps the longest and most detailed example in the *Journey* of the "abode pleasing to the Deity" mode, with special emphasis on physical sight and the effect of sight and sound on the narrator. The beginning is, in fact, an extended ekphrasis, a written transcription of the visual, offering a striking panorama of the emblems of Russian power. It appears as if the dreamer has been transported into a typical eighteenth-century Russian baroque-style allegorical court engraving or sculpture:

> My throne was of pure gold and, cleverly set with varicolored precious stones, it shone resplendent. Nothing could compare with the luster of my raiment. My head was crowned with a laurel wreath. Around me lay the regalia of my power. Here lay a sword on a column wrought of silver, on which were represented battles at sea and on land, the capture of cities, and other triumphs of this sort; everywhere my name could be seen on high, borne by the Genius of glory, who was hovering over all these exploits. Here one could see my scepter resting upon sheaves heavy with abundant ears of grain, wrought of pure gold and perfectly imitating nature. A pair of scales hung from a rigid beam. In one of the scales lay a book with the inscription "The Law of Mercy"; in the other likewise there was a book with the inscription "The Law of Conscience." The orb was carved from a single stone and was supported by a circlet of cherubim sculptured in white marble. My crown was raised above everything else and rested on the shoulders of a mighty giant, and its rim was supported by Truth. A serpent of enormous size, forged of gleaming steel, wound all about the foot of my throne and, holding the tip of its tail in its jaws, represented eternity.[62]

The regalia of power depicted here are not only in themselves typical baroque court emblems, many bearing their own inscriptions (as with the scales and book) or explained by the narrator (in the case of the snake by the throne). The thick significations, both the allegorical images requiring explanation and their material embodiment in gold, silver, precious stones, and marble, seem to far outweigh what is signified, suggesting visual wealth that overwhelms and dazzles rather than clarifies. Baroque language and form come into conflict with rational, classicist transparency.

The impact of the environment is seen through the narrator's eyes. Everyone at court is "timidly submissive and anxious to catch [his] glance," totally "subject to [his] will," and indeed sensitive to every facial twitch. When, "self-centered and bored to the bottom of my soul by the cloying monotony of existence," he "pays his debt to nature" and yawns, his courtiers react dramatically: "Suddenly confusion spread its somber veil over the face of joy, the smile flitted away from the lips of tenderness and the sparkle of merriment from the cheeks of pleasure. Twisted and furtive glances betrayed the sudden approach of terror and imminent misfortune. Sighs were heard, the stinging forerunners of grief; and groans, restrained by fear. Despair and mortal terror, more agonizing than death itself, rushed in with giant strides to take possession of all hearts." The narrator is "moved to the depths" of his soul, makes an effort to smile ("a twitch that resembled a smile") and sneezes loudly.

> Just so the midday sun breaks through the thick, dark, foggy atmosphere. Its vital heat disperses the condensed moisture, which, divided into its component particles, is in part lightened and swiftly borne into the immeasurable space of ether, while the rest, retaining in itself only the weight of its earthly particles, swiftly falls down. The darkness, which had prevailed everywhere before the radiant globe broke through, suddenly disappears and, hastily throwing off its impenetrable shroud, flies away on rushing wings, leaving no trace of its presence. Even thus my smile dispelled the looks of sadness which had settled on the faces of the assembled company; joy quickly filled the hearts of all, and not an oblique sign of displeasure was left. All began to cry: "Long live our mighty Sovereign! May he live forever!"[63]

On the one hand, this appears to be a serious attempt to trace the action of spirit and matter and to describe the intimate connections between the ruler and his courtiers, both their spiritual and physical responses. On the other, it seems a satire of the odic image of the ruler as the sun, as the sycophantic approval—and the ruler's vanity—increase exponentially. The assembled august audience breaks into prolonged panegyrics about the ruler's great deeds—in war, commerce, agriculture, legislation, philanthropy—and the ruler becomes increasingly self-absorbed: "Speeches like these, striking my eardrum, resounded loudly in my soul. To my mind the praises seemed true, since they were accompanied by outward expressions of sincerity. Receiving them as such, my soul rose above the usual circle of vision, expanded in its essence, and, embracing all, touched the threshold of divine wisdom. But nothing could be compared with my self-satisfaction [*s udovol'stviem samoodobreniia*] as I uttered my commands."[64] Odic exaltation is satirized as the courtiers' orgy of flattery makes the ruler feel as if his soul were soaring "above the usual circle of vision" to reach "the threshold of divine wisdom." The commands he utters relate to even more "great deeds," from military ventures to architectural undertakings, which include "founding vast cities in swamps and solitudes which surpass in magnificence the most famous cities of antiquity" (e.g., Kherson, founded by Potemkin in 1774 and meant to emulate ancient Chersoneses) and other specific projects that clearly echo Catherine's own.[65] His inappropriate (self-deceiving) love of fame (*chestoliubie*) is further inflated by the generous gifts and rewards that he showers on his agents.

Then from out of the crowd comes one person, "an oculist, named Clear-of-Eye" (*Priamovzorova*), dressed in rags, with an appearance of "scorn and indignation," who acts to end the joyous celebration (it is the ruler's birthday) and expose the falsehood of the grandiose façade.[66] Like the "removing of veils" in the dedication, she removes the "cataracts" from his eyes and "cleanses" his sight, restoring "natural vision" (*estestvennyi vid*): "'Thou seest,' she said to me, 'that thou hast been blind, stone-blind. I am Truth. The Almighty, moved to pity by the groans of thy subject people, has sent me down from the heavenly regions to drive away the darkness which impenetrably obscured thy vision. I have done so. Now everything will appear before thine eyes in its true form. Thou shalt see into the heart of things.'" Now that "the tumult of vainglory and the storm of ambition no longer disturb" the king's soul, his vision of a happy Russia is upended: "My glittering garments seemed to be stained with blood and drenched with tears. On my fingers I saw fragments of human brains; my feet were standing in slime. The people around me looked still more odious. They seemed all blackened and seared within by the dark flame of greed."[67] He now sees that all those things in which he had formerly taken pride are worthless, either empty gestures without content or counter-productive. He now realizes that everything he had previously taken as genuine was a sham, all exterior surface, and the inner truth is unbearably ugly. The cumulative force of juxtaposing the earlier descriptions of baroque court visuality to this ruthless stripping away of "splendid exteriority" (*pyshnaia vneshnost'*) makes these nihilist passages among the most powerful in the *Journey*.

The catalogue of horrors, stupidities, and failures (including military disasters covered up, false voyages of discovery, etc.) continues for several pages, making reference to various projects of Catherine's. Philanthropy and liberal-minded reforms are exposed as a self-serving, self-deceiving sham that produce no positive results. For example:

> The achievement of which, in my blindness, my soul was most proud, namely, the abolition of the death penalty and the granting of amnesty to prisoners, had hardly any visible effect on the vast complex of governmental activities. My commands had either been completely violated by being misapplied, or had not had the desired effect because of distorted interpretation and dilatory execution. Mercy had come to be bought and sold, and the auctioneer's hammer knocked down compassion and generosity to the highest bidder. Instead of being thought merciful by my subjects because of the amnesty I had ordered, I passed among

them for a cheat, hypocrite, and wicked play-actor. "Keep thy mercy," thousands of voices shouted, "do not proclaim it to us in high-sounding words, if thou dost not intend to carry it out. Do not add insult to injury, do not make our burden heavier by making us feel it more keenly. We were peacefully asleep; thou hast disturbed our sleep when we did not want to wake up, since we had nothing to wake up for."[68]

The subjects (serfs?) in the dream thus replay the nightmare scenario Dashkova had described to Diderot and that she thought would result in anarchy and confusion, although here the emphasis is on Catherine's own role in having advertised high-sounding enlightened principles and creating inflated expectations without following through on them.

If Radishchev plays the role of Catherine, he also, even more conspicuously, doubles for Clear-of-Eye, the truth-sayer, adding a further "meta-literary" gloss to "Spasskaia Polest'" as a description of the author's lonely and heroic task. Clear-of-Eye tells the ruler:

Whenever thou desirest to see me, whenever thy soul, besieged by the wiles of flattery, thirsts for the sight of me, call me from afar; wherever my harsh voice is heard, there wilt thou find me. Never be afraid of my voice. If from the midst of the people there arise a man who criticizes thy acts, know that he is thy true friend. With no hope of reward, with no servile trembling, with a sturdy voice he will proclaim me to thee. Beware and do not dare to put him to death as a rebel. Call him to thee, be hospitable to him as to a pilgrim. For everyone who criticizes the Sovereign in the fullness of his autocratic power is a pilgrim in the land where all tremble before him. Treat him well, I say, honor him, so that he may return and tell thee ever more truth. But such stout hearts are rare; hardly one in a whole century appears in the world's arena.[69]

She is evidently speaking of Radishchev, also "a pilgrim in the land where all tremble" before the absolute sovereign, and someone all too much in danger of being executed as a rebel. There is a strange merging or confusion of identities here, between the feminine Clear-of-Eye (also: the truth, *istina*, gendered feminine in Russian), and the "he" who proclaims "her" to the ruler. There seems to be a curious echo of this mysterious "he" near the end, after Clear-of-Eye is gone, and the narrator (the dream ruler), now repentant, calls his advisors to account: "'Unworthy criminals, evildoers! Tell me, wherefore have you abused your Sovereign's trust? Stand now before your judge. Tremble, ye who have grown hardened in evil. How can you justify your deeds? What can you say in excuse? Here he is; I will call him from his hut of humility. Come,' I called to an old man whom I saw at the border of my vast realm, half-hidden in a moss-covered hut, 'come and lighten my burden; come and restore peace to my anxious heart and troubled mind.'"[70] Nothing else is said about this mysterious "old man," but this passage suggests a hint at Belisarius from Marmontel's novel *Bélisaire*, which is a probable source of the entire episode.[71]

The irony here is greatly multiplied by Catherine's direct association with the novel. She herself had personally participated in translating it into Russian together with her royal entourage during the celebrated trip down the Volga in 1767.[72] This was an extravagant example of Catherine's self-advertising as an Enlightened monarch, insofar as the novel represented an outspoken denunciation of despotism, a call for religious toleration, and a defense of theism; the translation was made even more sensational by the fact that it was subsequently banned by the church authorities in France, which only served to increase its European-wide popularity.[73] Furthermore, in "Spasskaia polest'" Radishchev may have been paraphrasing passages out of the very chapter that Catherine herself had translated, the ninth, which contained some of the sharpest criticism of tyranny and despotism.[74]

The bulk of Marmontel's novel consists of the celebrated general Belisarius, unjustly disgraced and blinded by Emperor Justinian, giving lessons in virtue to the heir to the throne, Tiberius, and to Justinian himself. Belisarius does not know their identity until the last pages, when Justinian can no longer bear his guilt and shame before the virtuous man he had so grievously wronged. He then offers Tiberius's hand in marriage to Belisarius's daughter and insists that Belisarius accompany them back to Rome to be his advisor: "Come then, said the emperor, snatching him [Belisarius] eagerly to his heart, come, my friend! my genius! and my guide! Oh! come, and teach me to expiate my guilt! Come and exhibit it to my court in all its striking colors: and let your presence, while it is a living memorial of my crime, be a proof of my repentance also."[75] Belisarius, like Clear-of-Eye, is a figure of infallible, godlike virtue and clear vision (underscored in Belisarius's case by his physical blindness), put in the position of guide to an emperor. Like Radishchev's old man summoned from his "hut of humility" on the periphery, Belisarius is recalled out of humble retirement to assume a position of respect in the capital and to replace the evil advisors who have led the emperor down the garden path.[76]

Radishchev, recalling *Belisarius*, and following its model of boldly speaking the truth to sovereigns, regardless of consequences, underscored the fact that he was simply holding the empress up to the standards that she herself had set, especially in the *Instruction to the Legislative Commission. Belisarius* also offered a comforting fantasy-image of approbation; as in "Spasskaia Polest'," the grateful and repentant sovereign acknowledges the pilgrim's disinterested superiority and embraces his divinely inspired advice. In both cases the ruler's unjust actions are caused by miscognition rather than malice, and with the help of a disinterested guide, the possibility to see correctly—and put things right—is embraced.[77]

The *Journey*'s underlying ocularcentrism shines forth in another area, and that is its outspoken attack on censorship featured in the chapter "Torzhok." Here Radishchev champions the transformative power of vision to reveal the truth in the political arena. In this often overlooked chapter Radishchev takes Catherine the Great's own earlier program validating free speech and the rights of civil society, famously proclaimed in the *Instruction*, and extrapolates from it.[78] Citing the *Instruction*, Radishchev acknowledges the power of the courts to prosecute slander and abuses of free speech, and as in the *Instruction*, he stresses the importance of law and of equal justice under its auspices. At the same time, however, he totally denies to the state (or to any other body) the right of censorship, arguing for its complete and total abolition, even as regards blasphemous and pornographic writing.[79] He proclaims:

> Let anyone print anything that enters his head. If anyone is insulted in print, let him get his redress at law. I am not speaking in jest. Words are not always deeds, thoughts are not crimes. These are the rules in the *Instruction for a New Code of Laws.* . . . What harm can there be if books are printed without a police stamp? Not only will there be no harm, there will be an advantage, an advantage from the first to the last, from the least to the greatest, from the Tsar to the last citizen. . . .
>
> But why should not every aberration be permitted to be out in the open? The more open it is, the quicker it will break down. Persecutions have only made martyrs.[80]

Radishchev puts faith in total visibility—without censorship, truth and falsehood will be able to be revealed for what they are: "To prohibit foolishness is to encourage it. Give it free rein; everyone will see what is foolish and what is wise. What is prohibited is coveted. We are all Eve's children."[81] To Radishchev these arguments seem self-evident:

> It would seem that no proof of this is necessary. If everyone is free to think and to proclaim his thoughts to all without hindrance, then naturally everything

that is thought out and discovered will become known: what is great will be great, and truth will not be obscured. . . . The rulers of nations will not dare to depart from the way of truth, lest their policy, their wickedness, and their fraud be exposed. The judge will tremble when about to sign an unjust sentence, and will tear it up. He who has power will be ashamed to use it only for the gratification of his lusts. Secret extortion will be called extortion, and clandestine murder—murder. All evil men will fear the stern glance of truth. Peace will be real, for there will be no ferment [in society]. Nowadays only the surface is smooth, but the ooze that lies at the bottom is growing turbid and dims the transparency of the water.[82]

Radishchev charges that governments do not make use of censorship to protect society from socially harmful influences or ideas, but that "in prohibiting freedom of the press, timid governments are not afraid of blasphemy, but of criticism of themselves." They worry that "the freethinker who has been stirred to his depths will stretch forth his audacious but mighty and fearless arm to the idol of power and will tear off its mask and covering and lay bare its true character. Everyone will see its feet of clay; everyone will withdraw the support which they had given it; power will return to its source; the idol will fall."[83] In contrast, if that power "is founded on sincerity and true love of the common weal," will it not, he asks, "be strengthened when its foundation is revealed?"[84] The choice then is between honest righteousness (full transparency) that will strengthen the state and hypocritical deception (the concealment of evil) that renders it weak and susceptible to collapse, as "a word of truth will destroy it" and "a manly act scatter it to the winds."[85]

Radishchev's argument is based on the Enlightenment ideal of self-evident reason and faith in the public as the ultimate repository and judge of virtue. Radishchev uses the metaphor of the theater as an image of public authority:

[T]he censorship of what is printed belongs to society, which is the one that gives a writer a wreath or uses his pages for wrapping paper. Just so, it is the public that gives its approval to a theatrical production, and not the director of the theater. Similarly the censor can give neither glory nor dishonor to the publication of a work. The curtain rises and everyone eagerly watches the performance. If they like it, they applaud; if not, they stamp and hiss. Leave what is stupid to the judgment of public opinion [*na voliu suzhdenie obshchego*]; stupidity will find a thousand censors. The most vigilant police cannot check worthless ideas as well as a disgusted public. They will be heard just once; then they will die, never to rise again. But once we have recognized the uselessness of the censorship, or, rather, its harmfulness in the realm of knowledge, we must also recognize the vast and boundless usefulness of freedom of the press.[86]

Catherine herself had put forward the notion of the public—"society," "public opinion," "civil society"—as arbiter of the common good in her *Instruction*, but Radishchev takes it much further. His position suggests Jürgen Habermas's notion of "the public sphere" as an ideal independent space informed by the Enlightenment ideal of rational public critical debate in which "private people come together as a public" in order to determine their own best interests.[87] What is remarkable in Radishchev's argument is the unquestioned assumption that the Russian public was up to the task. As Douglas Smith puts it, Radishchev's position on abolishing censorship was "extreme, naïve, and unworkable, especially in a country like Russia."[88]

The concluding chapter of *The Journey*, the "Eulogy for Lomonosov" ("Slovo o Lomonosove"), may offer a key to Radishchev's idealization of the public, as here it is clearly associated with the creation and expansion of Russian literature, starting with Lomonosov. While the word "slovo" of the title may suggest "oration" or "eulogy," it also evokes Radishchev's exaltation of "the Word" in terms that foreshadow the logocentrism of the next century. Radishchev's verdict on Lomonosov is quite equivocal. On the one hand, this is far from a eulogy, as Radishchev faults Lomonosov for the sycophantic flattery of his odes as well as a host of other failings.[89] On the other hand, he lauds Lomonosov as a Great Man, the Moses of Russian literature, its demiurgic creator who led Russia to the promised land even if he was unable to enter. The oration concludes:

> Before the beginning of time, when existence had no firm support and everything was lost in eternity and infinity, everything was possible for the Source of power; all the beauty of the Universe existed in His thought, but there was no action, no beginning. And behold, an Almighty Hand thrust matter into space and gave it motion. The sun began to shine, the moon received its light, and the revolving bodies on high were formed. The first impulse [*pervyi makh*] in creation was all-powerful; all the wonders, all the beauties of the world are only its consequences. Thus do I understand the influence of a great soul upon the souls of its contemporaries or descendants; thus do I understand the influence of mind upon mind. Lomonosov is the first upon the path of Russian literature.[90]

Despite his criticisms, Radishchev's praise of Lomonosov is cosmic and transcendental, glorifying him as a great soul and demiurge who "thrust matter into space and gave it motion." Radishchev thus revises the Petrine *fiat lux*, with Lomonosov replacing Peter the Great in the role of Creator and Russian letters supplanting the state as vehicle of the common good. The mantle of service to society was now to be passed on to Russian literature.[91]

Furthermore, Radishchev's argument about the public good and the deleterious effects of censorship is framed in terms of Russia's need to achieve maturity. Ultimately, the way to learn—to create a society that sees straight—is to treat it as if it already did, to trust in the anticipated clear-seeing self and permit full visual discrimination. Both Catherine in the *Instruction* and Radishchev in the *Journey* relate excessive government control over society to weakness and old age.[92] While despotism leads to ossification and spiritual senility, this may also be seen as the result of remaining trapped in a state of infantilism. Censorship, which Radishchev describes as the "nursemaid [*nian'ka*] of reason, wit, imagination, and of everything great and enlightened," plays a central role in this process, impeding normal, healthy development:

> [W]here there are nurses, there are babies who go on leading strings [*na pomochakh*—or: with braces], which often lead to crooked legs; where there are guardians, there are minors and immature minds unable to govern [*pravit'*] themselves. If there are always to be nurses and guardians, then the child will walk with leading strings for a long time and will grow up to be an absolute cripple. Mitrofanushka [the famous title character from Fonvizin's comedy of 1782 *The Minor*] will always be a minor, will not take a step without his valet, and will not be able to manage his inheritance without a guardian. Everywhere these are the consequences of the standard censorship, and the sterner it is, the more disastrous are its consequences.[93]

Radishchev well understood that Catherine would hardly welcome his work with open arms, and the writing and publishing of the *Journey from St. Petersburg to Moscow* was clearly an act of exceptional courage that represents the last stage of the dialectic of vision.[94] Despite any possible oscillations, publishing the *Journey* should be seen as the result of the author's deliberate moral and psychological deliberations and as the assertion of his hard-won "adult" consciousness, that of educated Russians' right to defy censorship and govern themselves.[95] This was a declaration of selfhood in the name of independent Russian public opinion and of a commitment to practical action in the political arena; as in the case of Lomonosov's great soul, taking this first step was all-important, whatever the consequences.[96] While Radishchev recanted under interrogation, his act was seen in the later tradition as a prototypical heroic act of rebellion and his fate that of a martyr.[97] The subsequent inability of the tsarist state to moderate its autocratic, patriarchal role in the face of pressure from below closed avenues to the negotiation of a less idealized self-image on the part of Russian intellectuals, which condemned the country to a long-term pattern of repression and stagnation from above and passivity or rebellion from below. But that is another story.

# Conclusion

## *Russian Culture as a Mirage*

"Happy families are all alike; every unhappy family is unhappy
in its own way."
—Leo Tolstoy, *Anna Karenina*

"Чтоб истребил Господь нечистый этот дух.
Пустого, рабского, слепого подражанья."
[If only the Lord would eradicate this ignoble spirit / Of empty,
servile, blind imitation.]
—Alexander Griboedov, *Woe from Wit* (1824)[1]

Radishchev's successive stages of vision offer a striking
illustration of Latour's proposition, with which this book opened, that "a new
visual culture redefines both what it is to see, and what there is to see."[2] What
Radishchev saw—joyful images of Russian greatness alternating with visions
of misery and reproach—was defined by a complex negotiation between
inner and outer perception, moral and psychological understanding. What had
seemed the objective status of reality, its obviousness and certainty, dissolved
before his eyes, suggesting the fragility not only of the eighteenth-century
Russian self-image, but also of any cultural formation, liable, like Prospero's
conjured fictions, to melt "into air, into thin air: / And, like the baseless fabric
of this vision, . . . Leave not a rack behind."[3] Yet unless one subscribes to
the view that all is vanity or that every culture functions entirely on myths,
then it is clear that by the end of the eighteenth century Russia could count

numerous achievements to support its claim to be seen and acknowledged by the "society of political peoples." First of all was Russia's extraordinary political and material success: the establishment of the Russian Empire, with its military victories and extensive territorial gains. "By the time of Catherine's death," writes Martin Malia, "Russia . . . was not only the largest, but also the most populous state in Europe." But even here, Malia notes, "the decisive factor governing Russia's first century as a [continental] power remains this: her integration into the political concert of European states [that] was contingent on her assimilation into the cultural concert of dynastic-aristocratic Old Regimes," and on her acknowledged "legitimacy as a civilized state."[4]

The quest for such legitimacy also stimulated much of Russia's intellectual and cultural activity, and by the end of the century could claim significant success. The eighteenth century witnessed the birth and development of Russian civil society and an independent intellectual life. While as in the newly born American republic the problem of slavery (serfdom) was left unresolved, serf culture, for all its problematic sides, nourished the golden age of Russian aristocratic culture, including the development of the Russian country estate and a court culture that rivaled those of Paris and Vienna.[5] Intellectual life could boast new institutions that fostered a spectrum of arts, sciences, and scholarly pursuits—the Academy of Sciences; Moscow University; the Academy of Fine Arts; the Russian Academy; the Imperial Theater; the Free Economic Society and other learned associations; Masonic lodges; the Smolnyi Institute for Women; the Moscow Foundling Home and hospital; and a host of other educational and charitable establishments. Supported by a small but expanding reading public, the publishing industry, a fundamental pillar of civil society, made impressive strides, with the proliferation of newspapers and literary, scientific, and other specialized journals; the comprehensive catalogue of books published between 1725 and 1800 lists almost 9,000 book titles (more than 120 per year) and more than 520 journals.[6] Especially during the period of the Free Press Law of 1783–1796, these numbers were sustained by a series of institutional and private presses, most notably Novikov's Moscow University Press and Typographical Company. Among the century's most important achievements was the creation of a modern vernacular literary language—a key instrument of Russia's imperial power—that could boast of those supporting features that other modern civilized European tongues enjoyed: established rules of rhetoric and poetics, a grammar, an Academy dictionary, and, most important, a host of celebrated writers—Lomonosov, Sumarokov, Kheraskov, Fonvizin, Bogdanovich, Khvostov, Maikov, Nikolev, Kapnist, Emin, Ruban, Dashkova, Urusova, Kniazhnin, Derzhavin—and canonical texts.[7] Nikolai

Novikov's *Attempt at an Historical Dictionary of Russian Writers* of 1772 featured 317 authors; while this number included some pre-eighteenth-century and decidedly secondary writers, "The message could not have been clearer: Russians were living amid a literary cornucopia, an unprecedented flowering of the pen and the press."[8] Dashkova made a similar point with her *Russian Theater, or the Complete Collection of All Russian Theatrical Works* in 43 volumes (1786–1791, 1793–1794).

Within a generation all of this changed. In Pierre Bourdieu's terms, the eighteenth-century cultural field and the "symbolic capital" that it had accumulated underwent a catastrophic devaluation.[9] The years between the last period of Catherine's reign and the beginning of that of Nicholas I marked a major paradigm shift in European culture that was exceptionally traumatic for Russian intellectuals. By 1825 the culture of Enlightenment had already long been discredited across Europe, especially in light of the French Revolution and its aftermath, but perhaps nowhere were the repercussions of this repudiation as strongly felt as in Russia in the years following the 1812 invasion. Disillusionment came to a head for the younger generation that had fought all the way to Paris and back in the Napoleonic campaigns, as the surge of patriotism that accompanied the victory gave birth to secret political societies hoping for reform at home. The unsuccessful Decembrist Revolt of December 1825 was arguably the terminal point of Russia's "long eighteenth century." In the political sphere, the "Decembrist catastrophe" represented a final failure of the Enlightenment, "liberal" model of gradual reform based on a public sphere, to be replaced in the 1830s by the new state ideology of "Official Nationality" founded on ancien regime legitimacy.[10]

The long-term consequences of the collapse of Russian Enlightenment and of the mirror-imaged self traced in this book were profound, though difficult to pin down. If, to paraphrase Tolstoy, normal development is routine and more or less predictable, the far-reaching effects of unhappy psychic experiences are far harder to grasp. For many educated Russians, the post-Napoleonic malaise led to a sense of despair over the alleged bankruptcy of Russia's imitative, "pseudo-classicist" culture. The very success of Russian arms over the greatest European continental military power served to emphasize her distance from Western Europe as well as from her own national roots. The crisis of Russian cultural self-image that marked Nicholaevan Russia may be thought of as a kind of national nervous breakdown, which has marked Russian development ever since.[11] Many historians down to the twenty-first century have characterized Russian culture in terms of infantilism and psychic trauma; accepting the model of development suggested in this book, it is possible to speculate on the implications of its collapse for the body politic and on the chronic difficulty of modern Russian culture to achieve an adequate sense of national identity. The dizzying anticipatory heights Russian culture had reached for conditioned the hard shock of the fall. The focus of the remainder of this chapter will be on some of the main arguments that led to the rejection of the optimistic, ocularcentric cultural consciousness, analyzing aspects of their discourse (in particular, visual metaphors), and a consideration of some of their implications and reverberations for later Russian self-image.

## The Logic of "Servile Imitation"

The cultural debates of the 1820s reveal the sequence of thought that led to the vehement rejection of the eighteenth-century tradition. In a survey of Russian poetry of the previous decade, written in 1824, Wilhelm Küchelbecker (V. K. Kiukhel'beker) expressed his dissatisfaction with Russian literature by drawing a sharp distinction between "classicism" and "Romanticism":

> Freedom, invention, and novelty are what constitute the chief values of Romantic poetry, as opposed to the so-called Classical poetry of the modern Europeans. The ancestors of this allegedly Classical poetry are more the Romans than the Greeks. It abounds in versifiers, not with *poets*, who are as rare in literature as albinos in the physical world. In France this dull tribe long held sway: the finest, purest poets of that land—Racine, Corneille, Moliere, for example—had despite their inner loathing to play up to them, submit to their conventional rules, dress in their heavy robes, wear their immense wigs, and make frequent sacrifices to the deformed idols which they call "taste," "Aristotle," and "nature," bow down before the finicality, propriety, and mediocrity which these names hide. . . . Let's be grateful to Zhukovsky that he liberated us from the yoke of French literature and from the domination over us of the laws of La Harpe's *Lycée* and Batteux's *Cours*. But let us not permit him or anyone else, even should they possess a talent ten-fold greater than his, to impose upon us the fetters of German or English dominion! It is much better to have a native poetry. . . . But it is not enough—I repeat—to appropriate for ourselves the treasures of other tribes. Let there be founded for the glory of Russia a poetry truly Russian; let Holy Rus be the first power in the universe not only in the civic, but in the moral world![12]

Here classicism ("so-called Classical poetry") is used as a derogatory term, and contrasted to Romanticism as an opposition between derivative versus original, rule-bound versus free, foreign versus national, insipid versus inspired, Roman versus Greek—in all cases, bad versus good. "Imitation," which in the eighteenth century—and indeed for classical poetics in general—had been seen as emulation of the true and beautiful, and as an expression of the morally admirable desire for approbation, now became a term of condemnation, as the symbolic capital of the classical European greats themselves suffered a major fall in value.

From this time and for approximately the next hundred years, until the work of A. S. Orlov, G. A. Gukovsky, V. B. Shklovsky and other scholars working in the Soviet 1920s, Russian classicism (sometimes: neoclassicism) was almost completely relegated to the trash bin of history as worthless, servile imitation, and formally designated as "false-" or "pseudo-classicism" (*lozhno-klassitsizm, psevdo-klassitsizm*).[13] In his critique, Küchelbecker, a soon-to-be Decembrist rebel, poses the problem in implicitly political terms—liberation, slavery, domination, imposed fetters—and makes an explicit contrast between Russia's military might and desired moral (i.e., intellectual, cultural) authority. Küchelbecker and his cohort also posed the problem of Russian development in biological metaphors, describing the country's organic inability to emerge from infancy or its abortive attempt at adulthood having led to premature senility.[14]

As early as the sixteenth century, Europeans had begun to disparage Russians as alien, despotic, Asiatic, barbaric, servile, ignorant, and backward, as "a people born to slavery."[15] With Russia's dramatic rise to power and influence on the European political scene in the eighteenth century, the issue took on more pressing importance for European thinkers, as Russian cultural development became a test-case for various aspects of the Enlightenment program and politics. As noted in chapter 4, Rousseau made one of the most famous and influential statements of the anti-Russian position in *The Social Contract* of 1762:

> Russia will never be really civilized, because it was civilized too soon. Peter had a genius for imitation; but he lacked true genius, which is creative and makes all from nothing. He did some good things, but most of what he did was out of place. He saw that his people was barbarous, but did not see that it was not ripe for civilization: he wanted to civilize it when it needed only hardening. His first wish was to make Germans or Englishmen, when he ought to have been making Russians; and he prevented his subjects from ever becoming what they might have been by persuading them that they were

what they are not. In this fashion too a French teacher turns out his pupil to be an infant prodigy, and for the rest of his life to be nothing whatsoever.[16]

Both Dashkova and Catherine the Great made substantial efforts to combat this kind of Russia-bashing, as they were both heavily invested in defending Russia's enlightened image.[17] Significantly, this literature and its harshly negative image of Russia did not have a noteworthy impact on Russian intellectuals in the eighteenth century, buoyed as they were by that very optical optimism chronicled here. Nicholas I's legitimist politics together with the new wave of Western anti-Russian feeling in the post-Napoleonic era helped to actualize the negative self-image in Russian cultural consciousness that had been present but not taken seriously before. Rousseau's rhetoric clearly echoes in that of Küchelbecker and his cohort.[18]

The notion of "servile imitation" voiced by Decembrist critics and in such works as Griboedov's *Woe from Wit* (1824) had a long pedigree in Western European literature, going back at least to Horace. In the ninth epistle of his first book ("O imitatores, servum pecus" ["O you imitators, servile herd"]) and other passages, he advocated "a more discriminating poetics by explicitly rejecting mechanical, pedantic imitation of Greek verse."[19] In the development of modern vernacular European literatures the problem of Latin's relationship to Greek posed by Horace was transposed onto that of creating a modern literature on the model of the classics; here Latin literature was the positive model, having successfully fashioned itself on Greek. The danger of "servile imitation" of the classics arose as a modern issue in the late fifteenth century in debates over how best to learn Latin (e.g., Erasmus and the debate over Ciceronianism[20]), which in turn helped shape polemics in France over Ronsard, du Bellay and the Pléiade, who had championed a vernacular literature in French.[21] Malherbe and succeeding generations harshly rejected Ronsard, who was pigeonholed and dismissed through the nineteenth century precisely for his alleged servile imitation. The issue also became part of English poetic and critical discourse, for example in Thomas Carew's elegy on the death of John Donne of 1631: "The Muses' garden, with pedantic weeds / O'erspread, was purged by thee; the lazy seeds / Of servile imitation thrown away, / And fresh invention planted."[22]

The French critique of Ronsard for servile imitation (usually contrasted to Malherbe's originality, as having provided the fresh seeds for modern French literature), was canonized by Boileau and echoed by many writers, for example, the Abbé Dubos:

The [unfortunate] destiny of Ronsard's writings does not make me fear for the works of our [modern] French poets. These wrote in the same manner [*goût*] as good classical authors. They may have imitated them, but not as Ronsard and his contemporaries imitated them, that is to say, in a servile way, the way in which Horace says Servilius imitated the Greeks. This servile imitation of poets who write in foreign languages is the fate of writers who work at a time when their nation begins to want to break out of barbarism. But our good French poets imitated in the same way that Horace and Virgil imitated the Greeks, that is, following as others had done the genius of the language in which they were writing, and in taking, like them, nature as their first model.[23]

In Russia, this same historiographical scheme was applied to eighteenth- and then to early nineteenth-century literature, at first in order to emphasize that the nation had broken out of the barbarism that was stigmatized by its servile imitation. Initially the historical opposition of Ronsard and Malherbe as models of imitative and original poetry (good and bad literature) was transposed onto the opposition of Russian baroque and classicist poetry, with Lomonosov cast in the role of Malherbe, and then onto one between classicism and sentimentalism, with Karamzin cast as the reforming Malherbe.[24] By the 1820s, however, the perception of the lack of an independent, viable, original literature in Russia escalated sharply, echoing earlier harsh European condemnations of classicism, particularly of the French type, as "servile imitation" (e.g., those of Lessing and Herder), and threw a dark shadow over Russian letters. As in Küchelbeker, the debate over imitativeness played out in struggles to define "Romanticism" and its rival "classicism," a term that first began to be applied as a blanket term for eighteenth-century culture at this time, as a pejorative. This discussion was indicative of how new Romantic ideas about language and nationalism (e.g., those of Herder) quickly turned into metaphysical complaints over the insufficiencies of Russian culture.[25]

A further step in this reasoning was taken in an essay of 1826, written by the young poet Dmitrii Venevitinov shortly before his death. Venevitinov was from the other end of the intellectual spectrum from Küchelbecker, a member of the "Liubomudry" (the Slavonic term for "philosophers," specifically used instead of "filosofy" to indicate the group's nativist, proto-Slavophile position). Yet his complaint about the Russian situation, framed as a crisis over Russia's lack of firm philosophical principles, was even more radical and desperate:

Russia has obtained everything from without; hence that feeling of imitativeness which pays not awe, but servility, in homage to the true man of talent; hence the total absence of any freedom and real activity. How is Russia to be aroused from her pernicious dreaming? How is the lamp of inquiry to be lit in the midst of this wasteland? The origin and the cause of the sluggishness of our successes in enlightenment have been that very swiftness with which Russia has assumed an outward appearance of educatedness and erected a sham edifice of literature without any foundation, without any exertion of her own inner powers. . . . [A]lmost as if predestined to contradict the history of literature, we have acquired the form of literature before acquiring its essence. . . . [We] are unable to boast of a single monument which could bear the stamp of free enthusiasm and true passion for science. This is our situation in the world of literature—an utterly negative situation. Was it so long ago that the misleading judgments of the French about philosophy and the arts were revered in Russia as laws? And what is left of them? They are either lost in the distant past or they are scattered through a few works which strain with feeble obstinacy to portray the past as present. Russia's emancipation from the fetters of these conventions and from the ignorant self-confidence of the French might have been her triumph, if it were a result of independent reasoning; but unfortunately, it did not produce significant benefit. . . . We have cast off the rules of the French not because we could refute them with some positive system, but merely because we could not reconcile them with a few works of modern writers in which we took pleasure in spite of ourselves. Thus, erroneous rules were replaced by the absence of any rules at all.[26]

Venevitinov took Küchelbecker one step further: the goal of creating Romantic culture in Russia is just as misguided as the classicist attempt had been; Russian Romanticism is also *so-called Romanticism*—that is, it is also slavishly imitative. The rejection of classicist rules leads either to substituting a new set of shackles or to the chaos of no rules at all. Venevitinov further asserts that "the present course of Russia's literature must be completely halted" and as a remedy he suggests that "it will be necessary to remove Russia somewhat [!] from the present course of other peoples."[27] Just what this would entail is left unclear; despite the "utterly negative situation" in Russian letters, and specifically in journalism, Venevitinov proposed that a new journal could "present her with a full vision of the development of the human intellect, a vision in which she may discern her destiny."[28] Indeed the essay, which was published after Venevitinov's death, was originally intended as the leading editorial statement for such a journal and presaged the role of "thick journals" in mid-century literary and ideological debates.

The supreme statement of despair and the culmination of this critique of

Russian culture was Petr Chaadaev's famous "First Letter on the Philosophy of History," written in 1829. As is well known, its publication in 1836 caused a furor; the journal in which it appeared was closed down and its editor sent into exile, while Chaadaev was put under house arrest and declared officially insane. Chaadaev's letter expressed a profound, eloquent despair about Russian culture, taking the devastating critique of Russian letters voiced by such as Küchelbecker and Venevitinov to a logical extreme:

> But where are our wise men, may I ask, where are our philosophers? Who has ever thought for us, who thinks for us today? And yet, placed between the two great divisions of the world, between the East and the West, resting one elbow on China and the other on Germany, we ought to combine in ourselves the two great principles of human intelligence, imagination and reason, and fuse in our civilization the history of all parts of the globe. But that is not the role Providence has assigned to us. On the contrary, it seems to have given no thought to our destiny. Excluding us from its beneficent influence on the minds of men, it has left us entirely to ourselves; it would have none of us, and it has taught us nothing. The experience of the ages has passed us by; eras and generations succeed each other without leaving us anything of value. To look at us one might come to believe that the general law of mankind has been revoked in our case. We are alone in the world, we have given nothing to the world, we have taught it nothing. We have not added a single idea to the sum total of human ideas; we have not contributed to the progress of the human spirit, and what we have borrowed of this progress we have distorted. From the outset of our existence as a society, we have produced nothing for the common benefit of all mankind; not one useful thought has sprung from the arid soil of our fatherland; not one great truth has emerged from our midst; we have not taken the trouble to invent anything ourselves and, of the inventions of others, we have borrowed only empty conceits and useless luxuries. . . .
>
> If the barbarian hordes which turned the world topsy-turvy had not crossed the land we inhabit before invading the West, we would barely have furnished one chapter to world history. To be taken notice of at all, we have had to spread from the Bering Strait to the Oder. On one occasion a great man [Peter I] sought to civilize us; and, in order to give us a foretaste of enlightenment, he flung us the mantle of civilization; we picked up the mantle, but we did not touch civilization itself. Another time, another great prince, [Alexander I] associating us with his glorious mission, led us victorious from one end of Europe to the other; returning home from that triumphant march across the most civilized countries of the world, we brought back only ideas and

aspirations which resulted in an immense calamity, setting us back half a century [the Decembrist Revolt]. There is something in our blood that resists all real progress. In a word, we have lived, and we live now, merely in order to furnish some great lesson to a remote posterity that will come to know it; today, say what you will, we are a blank in the intellectual order.[29]

Chaadaev's complaint is remarkable both for its radical Eurocentrism, its idealization of Europe as vessel of "the progress of the human spirit," and its corollary, the dramatic picture of Russia as worthless, alone, uncivilized, and uncivilizable, damned by "something in its blood," by nature and biology. Paradoxically, even while Chaadaev and his cohort damned previous Russian culture for its imitativeness, they were equally if not more deeply implicated in projecting an idealized image of Other— of desired selfhood—onto Western Europe. In part Chaadaev's starkly negative judgment concerning everything Russian was a reaction to what he perceived as Nicholas I's hopelessly regressive cultural politics. On the other hand, he also repudiated Russian culture (and by extension, Russian intellectuals) as displaying "the puerile frivolity of the child who raises itself up [as in the mirror stage!] and lifts his hands toward the rattle [meaning: European culture] which the nurse shows to him," but is unable to appreciate and make good use of it.[30]

The Russian philosopher Boris Groys has offered a striking analysis of the profound national identity crisis that Chaadaev expressed, a crisis that led to a dramatic redefinition of "Russia" and its relationship to "the West." This identity crisis was framed in terms of German Romantic philosophy, which had dramatically articulated the loss of faith in universal Enlightenment reason and put a new premium on national originality and uniqueness. As Groys describes the problem:

At that very moment when Russia still believed that it was moving along the path of universal Enlightenment, the very idea of the Enlightenment collapsed, and the relatively easy task of becoming enlightened was replaced for Russia with the much more complex task of becoming original. . . . [Russian critics negated the past and] according to the philosophy of German Idealism, Russia could not produce anything original in the future as well. Historicism in philosophy, as is well known, considered itself to be an end of an original historical development. . . . From the moment when historical reflection made its appearance in German Idealism, all truth and cultural forms gained their relativity, so that authentic historical creativity became impossible. . . . With the acceptance of German idealistic philosophy Russia put itself in a desperate situation: it confronted the demand to be culturally original in what was already a post-history, when originality became unattainable.[31]

Chaadaev described "the devastating effects of [Russia's] total isolation from universal spiritual unity."[32] However, as Groys explains, "by the same move world history itself appears as imperfect, and the Hegelian Absolute Spirit gains an opposition in a purely material principle which is not an external object of scientific research, but the unconscious, unrepresentable mode of being that is alternative to any historicity. Such a model of being escapes any philosophical reflection by the very fact that it is unarticulated, unobjectified, and unoriginal in the context of universal world history."[33] Hence for Russians "the West" now came to stand for faith in abstract, logical, scientific reason which aspired to universal validity, while "Russia," excluded from the universal progress of mankind, embodied its irrational, unassimilatable, irreducible, material mode of being, the West's unconscious and life principle. "Russia" thus represented "a space where Western discourse about the Other was to be realized or materialized."[34] Groys traces the various attempts on the part of later Russian philosophers to define this space, at the same time reversing Chaadaev's negative evaluation, like the Slavophiles who "theologized" Otherness as a spiritual ideal, "a special case of Christian asceticism which allowed Russia to maintain intact the purity of its inner being."[35] As a further step in this process, attempts were made to envisage a synthesis of the Russian and Western principles, to bring life to the "dead end" of European civilization by means of Russia's spiritualizing force. This would also resolve the crisis experienced in Western philosophy, as defined by post-idealist thinkers who were also seeking alternatives to rationalism, like Schopenhauer with "his theory of the unconscious cosmic will, unobjectifiable and irreducible to the dialectical process of historical self-reflection" or Kierkegaard and his notion of "irreducible existence."[36] In this group Groys also includes Marx, who "discovered a whole class, namely the proletariat, which did not fit in with the Hegelian system, and which represented a principle of purely material existence. The function of this class, according to Marx, is to realize, or materialize, on the level of reality itself, the ideal synthesis of Hegelian dialectics."[37] Groys thus demonstrates how Russian culture inscribed itself into the discourse of modern philosophy and describes how the terms of the philosophically laden opposition between "the West" and "Russia," conscious and unconscious, self and other, played out in further modern Russian thought from Vladimir Solov'ev to Mikhail Bakhtin and even in Soviet Marxist dialectics.

Groys's analysis offers a key to the strange fate of eighteenth-century Russian culture, reduced in this scheme not only to being "Western" and "un-Russian" by definition, but also worthless, embodying the worst stereotype of Western Enlightenment (and Western thought in general), characterized by lifeless rationalism.[38] It also suggests a new set of terms to explain the extreme, culturally and psychologically traumatic divide separating the eighteenth and nineteenth centuries. This was not merely another one of those cyclical revolutions or conversion moments described by Billington, Florovsky, Lotman, and Uspensky that were considered in the preface, but a uniquely profound shock, a radical rupture in Russian culture that has yet to be healed.[39]

## Russian Culture as a Façade and Mirage

Together with "servile imitation," the language used to describe the cultural insolvency of eighteenth-century Russian culture, and by extension, Russian culture as a whole, often employed metaphors for other kinds of negative mirroring—as a mirage; an intentionally misleading false front, a "Potemkin village," or as a "façade."[40] The post-Enlightenment discourse of cultural identity was thus covertly or explicitly a function of Russia's earlier abortive ocularcentric self-image. As in the case of Radishchev, even by the end of Catherine's reign the cultural status of the visual was being questioned; and here, in a most dramatic fashion, Catherine retreated from her earlier claims of political tolerance and transparency. The French scholar Albert Lortholary entitled his cold war–era book on the image of Peter and Catherine the Great in France *Le Mirage russe en France au XVIIIᵉ siècle*, in which he argues that "enlightened Russia" was a false and misleading front addressed particularly to Western Europe.[41] Recently another scholar has also reduced the Enlightenment in Russia to merely "the mythological action of state power," an appearance devoid of content: "Russian Enlightenment was a Petersburg mirage. Some Russian Enlightenment figures truly believed in its existence and others were its involuntary participants, but this does not alter its mythological essence. Above the Neva hung Semiramida's gardens, Minerva after a triumphant public prayer service inaugurated a temple to Enlightenment, Fonvizin denounced vice, and the people dwelled in bliss. This mirage was that same prototype of universal transfiguration in whose context the Russian monarch was magnified into a figure of cosmic consequence. And it was this same mirage that was reduced to nothing by the end of Catherine's reign."[42] This passage is remarkable both as a restatement of the Catherinean cultural program (or myth) and for the way it adopts the myth's own terms.

The notion of Russian Enlightenment culture as a mirage, an optical illusion, unconsciously adopts and inverts the age's own value system described above, which had privileged the visual. The term "mirage" itself, appropriately, is a product of the eighteenth-century preoccupation with the science of light and vision. It was coined by the French mathematician Gaspard Monge, Comte de Péluse (1746–1818), to describe the peculiar atmospheric phenomenon he observed while traveling with Napoleon's Egyptian campaign in the late 1790s. He noted that he was adopting a term used by French sailors to describe an oceanic atmospheric phenomenon, and defined it as "an illusion which is sometimes cruel, more especially in the desert, because it tantalizes you with the appearance of water, at a time when you experience the greatest want of that element."[43] The newly defined phenomenon was discussed in several parts of Alexander von Humboldt's popular multivolume *Personal Narrative of Travels to the Equinoctial Regions of America, During the Years 1799–1804* (original in French). Humboldt noted that its occurrence had long been attested, and that it derived from Asia and the Orient:

> This phenomenon, the most anciently observed, has occasioned the mirage to receive in Sanscrit the expressive name of desire (thirst) of the antelope. We admire the frequent allusions in the Indian, Persian, and Arabic poets, to the magical effects of terrestrial refraction. It was scarcely known to the Greeks and Romans. Proud of the riches of their soil, and the mild temperature of the air, they would have felt no envy of this poetry of the desert. It was born in Asia. The oriental poets found its source in the nature of the country they inhabited; they were inspired by the aspect of those vast solitudes, interposed like arms of the sea or gulfs between lands adorned by nature with her most luxuriant fertility.[44]

By the 1840s, the word mirage had become commonplace in modern European languages, including Russian, but was used in a variety of negative figurative contexts, e.g., "moral" and "intellectual" mirage, referring to an illusion, deception, or self-deception, "something that appears real or possible but is not in fact so."[45] Its application to Russia and to Russian culture signaled a reversal of the cultural equation of the previous century, as the visual dominant was devalued in favor of other less rational types of cognition.

This was dramatically the case with the perception of St. Petersburg, built as Russia's "window to the West," and center of modern imperial culture. The "Petersburg text" appears in Russian literature of the first half of the nineteenth century, along with appearance of the new "Russian literature" itself—with the works of Pushkin, Gogol, and Dostoevsky.[46] The inner, hidden, mystical, murky, or unseen essence of the city now takes precedence over its magnificent façades, now considered deceptive, misleading, false, untrustworthy, evil. In the works of the Natural School, notably in Gogol's *Petersburg Tales*, naïve trust in external appearances leads to disaster.[47] Grigorii Kaganov notes that "toward the 1840s, the former visual values had suffered such a profound devaluation that inhabited space came to be organized by other, non-visual, criteria" and the city of St Petersburg, itself formerly perceived as Russia's premier showplace, was now depicted as a place of mere appearances hiding emptiness or terror within.[48] With the advent of German Romantic philosophy, attention turned inward, and Russian writers discovered (invented) a cultural treasure—"the Russian soul."[49] Broadly speaking, in the nineteenth-century classics, even in painting (the work of the Wanderers) and music (the "Mighty Five" and Tchaikovsky), the literary text—narrative or libretto—took precedence over the visual and the aural. The divinization of the Word— logocentrism—displaced the visual dominant.

The word "mirage" continues to be employed to describe the false, ephemeral, ersatz nature of Russian culture, perhaps also (as in Humboldt's description) suggesting its Eastern, Oriental, non-European character. Imperial Russia, Russian culture, Soviet Russia, Stalinist Russia, Russian economic policies, and even post-Soviet Russian democracy have all been characterized as a mirage.[50] The word has been not only used as a way of describing the inadequacy of Russia's cultural and political systems, but also as a dangerous deception for Western intellectuals.[51]

## Potemkin Villages

The deceptive aspect of Russia's political and cultural weakness took on conspiratorial overtones in the notion of "Potemkin villages," the final metaphor examined here. This phrase has gone from stigmatizing Catherine's allegedly deceptive politics to become a catchphrase both for Russian culture as a whole and for ideologically motivated false fronts, especially those perpetrated by Stalin.[52] The phrase itself goes back to Catherine's famous Crimean tour of 1787, orchestrated by Prince G. A. Potemkin, and is arguably one of the most effective slanders in history. The six-month, 6000-kilometer tour, which has been called "the grandest spectacle of her reign," celebrated Catherine's quarter century on the throne and Potemkin's recent conquests in the south, also suggesting Russia's further imperial designs on Constantinople (the so-called

"Greek project").[53] Potemkin staged an astonishing extravaganza for a variety of European heads of state, ministers, and foreign dignitaries, complete with a specially constructed magnificent flotilla down the Dniepr, a land caravan of 200 gilded carriages, spectacular fireworks displays, 80,000 fruit trees lining the streets of the newly built city of Kherson, the ceremonial launching of new ships, the laying of the cornerstone of the city of Ekaterinoslav ("Glory of Catherine") and its cathedral, majestic reviews of the fleet and of the troops, including a battalion of Greek "Amazons," and much more. Yet there was nothing clandestine about all this. The historian George Soloveychik traced the notion that sham villages were erected to dupe Catherine and/or her European guests to a biography of Potemkin written by Saxon diplomat Georg von Helbig (d. 1813), noting that "neither Helbig or anyone else has produced so much as a vestige of evidence in support of these vile accusations."[54] The smear, which as in English became "a stock phrase in colloquial German" (*Potemkinsche dörfer*), reflected Joseph II's apprehension and censure of Russia's imperial pretensions, especially as regards the Ottoman Empire.[55] As A. M. Panchenko noted, it was fabricated and circulated by Potemkin's domestic foes even before the start of the trip.[56] The phrase thus takes the eighteenth-century impulse toward visibility and display, so evident in Catherine's trip, and inverts it into a mark of political and cultural disapprobation.

The Stalinist connection deserves some further comment, insofar as it is often suggested that its highly cynical ideological manipulations found their prototype in Potemkin's alleged fraud.[57] More broadly, the ersatz official culture of Socialist Realism has been deemed close "in spirit and content" to that of the Russian eighteenth century, insofar as it was a state-sponsored literature that encouraged panegyrics and insincerity. This view was popularized in Abram Tertz's (Andrei Siniavsky's) famous dissident essay "What is Socialist Realism?"[58] While such a notion, like that of "Potemkin villages" itself, may express rhetorically powerful criticism of the totalitarian ideological impulse that some may trace back to the repressive last years of Catherine's reign, it also reflects the same kind of anachronistic bias that inverted the eighteenth-century desire for visibility and approbation into a despicable display of servile imitation, whether naïve or calculated. The "Potemkin villages" image thus reduces the eighteenth-century quest for selfhood to the level of a shameful political conspiracy, the attempt to pass off something false for the real thing. Yet the phenomenon of "Potemkin villages" and the psychological motivation for them seem far more appropriate for the syndrome of Stalinism than the age of Catherine.

Groys and others have argued that Stalinism may be seen as an attempt to realize the utopianism of the avant-garde, treating the state as a "total work of art" (*Gesamkunstwerk*) realized in the political terms that, arguably, were fundamental to avant-garde artists.[59] To some extent, Stalinist visual culture appropriated the ocularcentric utopian desire of the avant-garde "to make all things visible," to overcome history, and to reverse the pattern of interiorized identity suggested for the nineteenth century—to make the unconscious conscious. At the same time, as Vladislav Todorov has argued, the Party, informed by a conspiratorial, Nietzschean will to power, constructed an ideological vision that was a magnificent façade; he refers to "a radically exteriorized revolutionary self-consciousness . . . a resounding grand public exterior."[60] This façade or fictionalized ideological vision was, according to Todorov, completely a function of the Party's political power to project it, and the Party's conspiratorial conception of power inspired Stalin with persistent paranoid visions of its loss. And hence "the chronic urge to repeat constantly the take-over of the power he already had. . . . The fact that the will to vision (*der Wille der Schein*) degenerates from ideology into paranoia is a symptom of the increasing inability of the ideologist to survive in 'this' system of power. Totalitarian power marks the merger of a super-generative ideology and a super-degenerative paranoia. . . . When the Party doctrine was overthrown, the world of communism instantly disappeared. The strategic vision withered away and laid bare a wrecked reality. Ideology generated no real world but the effect of a world."[61] This degenerated "will to vision" suggests a grotesque, nightmarish caricature of the mirror-stage, in which the anticipated grandiose self is motivated by paranoia and enforced by violence, leaving behind nothing but a wrecked reality.

Stalinism, then, could be taken as a pathology resulting from the long-term national inferiority/superiority complex, itself arguably a consequence of the intelligentsia's radical rejection of the eighteenth-century model of self. Of course such an interpretation is subjective, but it does not contradict the conclusions of one of America's leading scholars of Stalin's terror, J. Arch Getty, who concludes that the state-sponsored violence of Stalinist bureaucrats was

> the political equivalent of a psychotic break. Like the maniacally depressed person who has lost control of his environment—as he defines it—and climbs a tower with a rifle, or a postal employee who enters his workplace with a machine gun, they began shooting wildly. Strong and confident governments, with efficient and loyal bureaucracies and confident of the support of most of the

population, do not need to resort to terror to accomplish their policies or to stay in power. . . . We are used to imagining and theorizing the Stalinists as larger-than-life monsters, confidently pulling the levers of a well-oiled totalitarian machine in order to implement their ideological plans. But they were also nervous little monsters, hysterically reacting to real threats caused by their disastrous policies or to imagined conspiracies by dark and sinister forces.[62]

This psychotic break resulted from a long-term national psycho-cultural imbalance, and suggests the nasty underside of the revolutionary impulse that distorts vision, for both the subject and the observer, causing them to see inflated images of power and control.

Groys asks: "by means of what kind of self-interpretation . . . can [Russia] prevent its total dissolution into the more dynamic cultural milieu"?[63] The future of Russian identity in the twenty-first century seems to depend on its new images of "the society of political peoples" whose company the country has recently rejoined. Is the mirror-imaging described in this book, both as a model of dialogical self-definition and as a chapter in Russian cultural history, to be overcome, to be assimilated and recuperated—insofar as history may be re-imagined and reclaimed, however contingently—or are Russians once again fated to face a repeating cycle of self-aggrandizement and destruction?

# NOTES

## Introduction

1. Bruno Latour, "Visualization and Cognition: Thinking with Eyes and Hands," *Knowledge and Society* 6 (1986): 10. Latour is discussing Svetlana Alpers's description of Dutch visual culture in the age of Rembrandt (*The Art of Describing: Dutch Art in the Seventeenth Century* [Chicago: University of Chicago Press, 1983]), and, more generally, trying to define the changes in visual understanding that define modern (post-Renaissance) scientific culture.

2. The term is Martin Jay's. See his *Downcast Eyes: The Denigration of Vision in Twentieth-Century French Thought* (Berkeley: University of California Press, 1993).

3. James R. Russell, "Truth Is What the Eye Can See: Armenian Manuscripts and Armenian Spirituality," in *Treasures in Heaven: Armenian Art, Religion, and Society*, ed. Thomas F. Mathews and Roger S. Wieck (New York: Pierpont Morgan Library, 1998), 160n1.

4. Bruno Snell, *The Discovery of the Mind: The Greek Origins of European Thought* (New York: Harper & Row, 1960). On the Greek tradition, see Andrea Wilson Nightingale, *Spectacles of Truth in Classical Greek Philosophy: Theoria in Its Cultural Context* (Cambridge: Cambridge University Press, 2004). On the relationship between seeing and knowing in Russian, see Maks Vasmer, *Etimologicheskii slovar' russkogo iazyka*, trans. O. N. Trubachev, ed. B. A. Larin, 3rd ed., 3 vols. (St. Petersburg: Azbuka, 1996), 1:283 and 312.

5. See, for example Marx W. Wartovsky, "Picturing and Representing," in *Perception and Pictorial Representation*, ed. C. F. Nodine and D. F. Fisher (New York: Praeger, 1979), 272–83. In the eighteenth century, George Berkeley came to a similar, and at the time a minority view, that vision is a language that must be learned; and (in C. M. Turbayne's words) "since vision is a language, it follows that a foreigner to visual language cannot at first understand it." C. M. Turbayne, introduction to *Works on Vision*, by George Berkeley (Indianapolis: Bobbs-Merrill, 1963), xxx.

6. See, for example Peter Burke, *The Fabrication of Louis XIV* (New Haven: Yale University Press, 1992), which focuses on "the place of Louis XIV in the collective imagination" (1). His place in the eighteenth-century Russian imagination awaits study.

7. Jean Starobinski, *Jean-Jacques Rousseau, la transparence et l'obstacle* (Paris: Plon, 1957); *L'oeil vivant: Corneille, Racine, La Bruyère, Rousseau, Stendhal*, rev. ed., Collection Tel 301 ([Paris]: Gallimard, 1999); Starobinski, *1789, les emblèmes de la raison* (Paris: Flammarion, 1973). See the discussion in Martin Jay, *Downcast Eyes*, 85–89.

8. See note 7.

9. See, for example, the essays in David Michael Levin, ed., *Modernity and the Hegemony of Vision* (Berkeley: University of California Press, 1993).

10. R. J. Snell, *Through a Glass Darkly: Bernard Lonergan and Richard Rorty on Knowing Without a God's-Eye View* (Milwaukee: Marquette University Press, 2006), chap. 1, esp. 11–12. On "intuitionism," Snell cites Giovanni Sala, *Lonergan and Kant: Five Essays on Human Knowledge*, ed. Robert M. Doran, trans. Joseph Spoerl (Toronto: University of Toronto Press, 1994), 81.

11. In the conclusion to his study of *The Petrine Revolution in Russian Imagery* (Chicago: University of Chicago Press, 1997), James Cracraft, after abundantly documenting Russia's "visual transformation" (294), cites the "immensely problematic" nature of determining "the importance of the visual as distinct from the verbal" as the reason why historians—himself included—have not attempted to do so. Hence for Cracraft, Russia's "visual transformation" remains mostly unexplained as anything other than Westernization.

Among the works on avant-garde visuality, see especially Gerald Janecek, *The Look of Russian Literature: Avant-Garde Visual Experiments, 1900–1930* (Princeton: Princeton University Press, 1984). Of the five collections of articles in English published on Russian visual culture in recent years—Alla Efimova and Lev Manovich, eds., *Tekstura: Russian Essays on Visual Culture* (Chicago: University of Chicago Press, 1993); Roger B. Anderson and Paul Debreczeny, eds., *Russian Narrative & Visual Art: Varieties of Seeing* (Gainesville: University Press of Florida, 1994); Catriona Kelly and Stephen Lovell, eds., *Russian Literature, Modernism and the Visual Arts* (New York: Cambridge University Press, 2000); D. M. Greenfield, ed., *Depictions: Slavic Studies in the Narrative and Visual Arts in Honor of William E. Harkins* (Dana Point, CA: Ardis, 2000); and Valerie A. Kivelson and Joan Neuberger, eds., *Picturing Russia: Explorations in Visual Culture* (New Haven: Yale University Press, 2008)—only the last includes material on the eighteenth century. On icons and literature, see especially Leonard J. Stanton, *The Optina Pustyn Monastery in the Russian Literary Imagination: Iconic Vision in Works by Dostoevsky, Gogol, Tolstoy, and Others*, Middlebury Studies in Russian Language and Literature, vol. 3 (New York: P. Lang, 1995).

Two notable exceptions to this lack of attention to the centrality of the visual in the eighteenth century are: Richard S. Wortman's *Scenarios of Power: Myth and Ceremony in Russian Monarchy*, 2 vols. (Princeton: Princeton University Press, 1995–2000), and Gennadii Vdovin's *Stanovlenie "IA" v russkoĭ kul'ture XVIII veka i iskusstvo portreta* ([Moscow]: Nash dom, 1999) and *Persona, individual'nost', lichnost': opyt samopoznaniia v iskusstve russkogo portreta XVIII veka* (Moscow: Progress-Traditsiia, 2005). Vdovin's goal is in some ways similar to that of this book: to describe the birth of the modern Russian self, with reference to the visual (in Vdovin's case the development of portraiture), and to understand the "psychohistory" of this process.

12. I. A. Esaulov, "Problema vizual'noi dominanty russkoi slovesnosti," in *Evangel'skii tekst v russkoi literatury XVIII–XX vekov: Tsitata, reministsentsiia, motiv, siuzhet, zhanr*, ed. V. N. Zakharov (Petrozavodsk: Petrozavodsk University, 1998), 2:42–53. Esaulov suggests that the Symbolists were the first to try to oppose this tradition and to champion "Renaissance" values.

13. That is, not as something primitive, inferior, and unworthy of analysis. For Florensky's pioneering essays on the icon, see Pavel Florensky, *Beyond Vision: Essays on the Perception of Art*, ed. Nicoletta Misler, trans. Wendy Salmond (London: Reaktion, 2003).

14. See, for example, William M. Ivins, Jr., *On the Rationalization of Sight, With an Examination of Three Renaissance Texts on Perspective* (New York: Da Capo Press, 1975).

15. See chapter 7, note 1.

16. Mikhail Maiatskii, "Nekotorye pokhody k probleme vizual'nosti v russkoi filosofii," *Logos* 6 (1995): 57. Maiatskii notes contemporary scholarship's "complete lack of consideration" of the problem of the visual in Russia (48). In Maiatskii's scheme, the European tradition followed Aristotle, while the Eastern preferred Plato with his greater mistrust of vision. See also Thomas Seifrid's contrast between the Russian and Western traditions in "Gazing on Life's Page: Perspectival Vision in Tolstoy," *PMLA* 113, no. 3 (1998): 436–48, and his "'Illusion' and its Workings in Modern Russian Culture," *Slavic and East European Journal* 45, no. 2 (Summer 2001): 205–15, whose roots he sees in "the cultural-symbolic practices of Peter the Great" (205).

17. The rejection of eighteenth-century Russian culture is discussed in chapter 1 and in the conclusion. The general neglect extends to Russian philosophy, whose very existence before Chaadaev is often implicitly or explicitly denied. See, for example, Mary-Barbara Zeldin, "Chaadayev as Russia's First Philosopher," *Slavic Review* 37 (September 1978): 473–80. Tat'iana V. Artem'eva makes the case for a significant philosophical tradition in eighteenth-century Russia. See especially her *Istoriia metafiziki v Rossii XVIII veka* (St. Petersburg: Aleteiia, 1996) and the ongoing series *Filosofskii vek*, ed. T. V. Artem'eva and M. I. Mikeshin, nos. 1–25 (St. Petersburg, 1996–2003).

18. On this phrase, see chapter 1, note 28.

19. E. R. Dashkova, *The Memoirs of Princess Dashkova*, trans. and ed. Kyril Fitzlyon (Durham: Duke University Press, 1995), 180–81.

20. James H. Billington, *The Face of Russia: Anguish, Aspiration, and Achievement in Russian Culture* (New York: TV Books, 1998), 16–17. This book is directed at a general audience, and is clearly not meant as a methodological model (as is Lotman and Uspensky's scheme analyzed below). It is cited as an example of a general tendency.

21. For example, "originality" only became a central cultural requirement in the Romantic period, and the notion of "civilization" is specific to the value system of the Enlightenment. On the application of the latter idea to Russia, see Larry Wolff's "mapping" of the term in *Inventing Eastern Europe: The Map of Civilization on the Mind of the Enlightenment* (Stanford: Stanford University Press, 1994).

22. This is most clearly evident in definitions of the Enlightenment focusing on France, e.g., in Peter Gay, *The Enlightenment: An Interpretation*, 2 vols. (New York: Knopf, 1966–1969).

23. Marc Raeff, "The Enlightenment in Russia," in *The Eighteenth Century in Russia*, ed. J. G. Garrard (Oxford: Clarendon Press, 1973), 45.

24. Iu. M. Lotman and B. A. Uspenskii, "The Role of Dual Models in the Dynamics of Russian Culture (Up to the End of the Eighteenth Century)," in *The Semiotics of Russian Culture*, ed. Ann Shukman (Ann Arbor: Dept. of Slavic Languages and Literatures, University of Michigan Press, 1984), 3–35.

25. The term is from Georges Florovsky, "The Problem of Old Russian Culture," *Slavic Review* 21, no. 1 (March 1962): 1–15.

26. Francis Butler disputes the generally held assumption that Prokopovich had Peter in mind in writing his play, although he confirms that the parallel became a durable part of the Petrine mythology. See his *Enlightener of Rus': The Image of Vladimir Sviatoslavich Across the Centuries* (Bloomington, IN: Slavica, 2002), chap. 6.

27. Lotman and Uspenskii, "The Role of Dual Models," 20–21 and 26.

28. Ibid., 25–26.

29. Iu. M. Lotman, "Russkaia literatura poslepetrovskoi epokhi i khristianskaia

traditsiia," in *Izbrannye stat'i: V trekh tomakh* (Tallinn: Aleksandra, 1993), 3:27.

30. See the discussion of the Russian Enlightenment in chapter 1.

31. Gary Saul Morson, *Hidden in Plain View: Narrative and Creative Potentials in "War and Peace"* (Stanford: Stanford University Press, 1987), 121–22, 132, referring to Tolstoy's *War and Peace*, book 10, chapter 7.

32. The notion of "transplantation" is D. S. Likhachev's. See Iu. M. Lotman, "'Ezda v ostrov liubvi' Trediakovskogo i funktsiia perevodnoi literatury v russkoi kul'ture pervoi poloviny XVIII veka," in *Izbrannye stat'i*, 2:22–28; and Simon Karlinsky, "Tallemant and the Beginning of the Novel in Russia," *Comparative Literature* 15, no. 3 (1963): 226–33.

33. Elise Wirtschafter, *The Play of Ideas in Russian Enlightenment Theater* (DeKalb: Northern Illinois University Press, 2003), 36. Wirtschafter reads eighteenth-century Russian dramaturgy, regardless of its Western European sources, as material that "expressed ideas, attitudes, beliefs, and emotions that, taken as a whole, represented the thinking and moral universe of Russia's educated service classes" (37).

34. Amanda Ewington, *A Voltaire for Russia: A. P. Sumarokov's Journey from Poet-Critic to Russian Philosophe* (Evanston: Northwestern University Press, 2010), 59.

35. On Corneille and his idealization of noble honor, the "great soul," glory, and their ostentatious display, see Paul Bénichou, *Man and Ethics: Studies in French Classicism*, trans. Elizabeth Hughes (Garden City, NY: Anchor Books, 1971), chap.1, which discusses these ideas as a throwback to feudalism; Jay, *Downcast Eyes*, 89; and Starobinski, *L'oeil vivant*, esp. 43 (note that the essay on Corneille is not included in the English translation, *The Living Eye*, trans. Arthur Goldhammer, Harvard Studies in Comparative Literature 40 [Cambridge: Harvard University Press, 1989]). On Sumarokov's views of aristocratic honor, see chapter 4, note 39.

36. Among recent works that attempt to describe the Russification of European literary forms and cultural models, see Joachim Klein, *Puti kul'turnogo importa: Trudy po russkoǐ literature XVIII veka* (Moscow: Iazyki slavianskoi kul'tury, 2005); N. Iu. Alekseeva, *Russkaia oda: razvitie odicheskoi formy v XVII–XVIII vekakh* (St. Petersburg: Nauka, 2005); V. M. Zhivov, *Language and Culture in Eighteenth-Century Russia* (Boston: Academic Studies Press, 2009); Ewington, *A Voltaire for Russia*.

37. On Western European views of Russia in the eighteenth century, see especially Albert Lortholary, *Les "philosophes" du XVIIIe siècle et la Russie: Le mirage russe en France au XVIIIe siècle* (Paris: Éditions contemporaines, [1951]), whose cold war–era perspective has recently been analyzed in Sergej Karp and Larry Wolff, eds., *Le mirage russe au XVIIIe siècle* (Ferney-Voltaire: Centre international d'étude du XVIIIe siècle, 2001). See also the works cited in the following note. On Western views as a problem for Catherine the Great and for Dashkova, see Marcus Levitt, *Early Modern Russian Letters: Texts and Contexts* (Boston: Academic Studies Press, 2009), chaps. 17 and 19, esp. 380–82, and the works cited in the next note.

The question naturally arises whether the binary pattern described by Lotman and Uspensky basically reflected a reaction to outside influences (e.g., Western dualism) or derived from a preexisting indigenous value system (e.g., Manicheanism, as Lotman and Uspensky speculate). To some extent, no doubt, this is a chicken-and-egg problem. My analysis in the conclusion suggests that the crisis of Russian self-image in the modern period and its violent dualism only began in the late eighteenth and early nineteenth century and was connected with the harsh rejection of the ocularcentric tradition.

38. I refer the reader to several major studies of the eighteenth-century Western image of Russia. These include Dimitri S. Von Mohrenschildt, *Russia in the Intellectual Life*

*of Eighteenth-Century France* (1936; repr., New York: Octagon Books, 1972); Lortholary, *Le mirage russe*; Francois de Labriolle, "Le *Prosveščenie* russe et les 'Lumieres' en France (1760–1798)," *Revue des etudes slaves* 45 (1966): 75–91; Nicholas V. Riasanovsky, *A Parting of Ways: Government and the Educated Public in Russia, 1801–1855* (Oxford: Clarendon Press, 1976), chap. 1; Isabel de Madariaga, "Catherine and the *Philosophes*," in *Russia and the West in the Eighteenth Century*, ed. A. G. Cross (Newtonville, MA: Oriental Research Partners, 1983), 30–52; Carolyn Wilberger, *Voltaire's Russia: Window on the East*, Studies on Voltaire and the Eighteenth Century 164 (Oxford: The Voltaire Foundation, 1976); Karp and Wolff, eds., *Le mirage russe*; and Wolff, *Inventing Eastern Europe*. See also the useful bibliographical essay in *Voltaire and Catherine the Great: Selected Correspondence*, trans. and ed. Antony Lentin (Cambridge: Oriental Research Partners, 1974), 178–86; and my discussion of the tradition in Levitt, *Early Modern Russian Letters*, chap. 17.

The Western perception of modern Russia is also often dated to the period in question. Martin Malia begins his recent political history *Russia Under Western Eyes: From the Bronze Horseman to the Lenin Mausoleum* (Cambridge: The Belknap Press of Harvard University Press, 1999) from 1700, "from the time Russia entered the modern European world under Peter" the Great (7). Malia seeks his understanding of Russia's position by looking "within the body politic of the West" (8). On earlier perceptions of Russia, see Lloyd E. Berry and Robert O. Crummey, eds., *Rude & Barbarous Kingdom: Russia in the Accounts of Sixteenth-Century English Voyagers* (Madison: University of Wisconsin Press, 1968); Marshall Poe, *A People Born to Slavery: Russia in Early Modern European Ethnography, 1476–1748*, Studies of the Harriman Institute (Ithaca: Cornell University Press, 2000); Poe, *Foreign Descriptions of Muscovy: An Analytic Bibliography of Primary and Secondary Sources* (Columbus, OH: Slavica, 1995); and Michel Mervaud and Jean-Claude Roberti, *Une infinie brutalité: L'image de la Russie dans la France des XVIe et XVIIe siècles* (Paris: Institut d'études slaves, 1991).

39. Edward Young, *Night Thoughts*, ed. Stephen Cornford (New York: Cambridge University Press, 1989), Night VI, lines 170–73 and 426–29. Vision's ability to "instantaneously take in the whole" may be taken as a physical and phenomenological argument in favor of its transcendent (in Snell's terms, intuitionist) truth-value. See Hans Jonas, "The Nobility of Sight: A Study of the Phenomenology of the Senses," in *The Phenomenon of Life: Toward a Philosophical Biology* (Evanston: Northwestern University Press, 2001), 135–56; and Snell, *Through a Glass Darkly*, 17–18.

40. Since the city's tercentenary (2003) and the years leading up to it there has been a profusion of monographs, conference proceedings, collections, and exhibit catalogues about St. Petersburg, its history, inhabitants, political and cultural traditions, and its art and architecture. Among notable works: T. V. Artem'eva, ed., *Peterburg na filosofskoi karte mira* (St. Petersburg: Peterburgskii nauchnyi tsentr RAN, 2002); Evgenija N. Petrova, *St. Petersburg: A Portrait of the City and Its Citizens* ([Bad Breisig]: Palace Editions, 2003); E. V. Anisimov, *Iunyi grad: Peterburg vremen Petra Velikogo* (St. Petersburg: Dmitrii Bulanin, 2003); E.V. Anisimov, et al., *Sankt-Peterburg: 300 let istorii*, ed. R. Sh. Ganelin (St. Petersburg: Nauka, 2003); Feliks M. Lur'e, *Peterburg, 1703–1917: Istoriia i kul'tura v tablitsakh*, 2 vols. (St. Petersburg: Zolotoi vek, 2000); Julie A. Buckler, *Mapping St. Petersburg: Imperial Text and Cityshape* (Princeton: Princeton University Press, 2005); Emily D. Johnson, *How St. Petersburg Learned to Study Itself: The Russian Idea of Kraevedenie* (University Park: Pennsylvania State University Press, 2006); and George E. Munro, *The Most Intentional City: St. Petersburg in the Reign of Catherine the Great*

(Madison, NJ: Fairleigh Dickinson University Press, 2008), which includes a survey of the jubilee literature on 18–21. Among other things, Petersburg was important as "the prototype of the modern planned city" in Russia (Munro, 17), the model for new cities created throughout the empire. Anthony Cross has also commented that "Peter the Great created St. Petersburg and St. Petersburg created tourism in Russia" (*By the Banks of the Neva: Chapters from the Lives and Careers of the British in Eighteenth-Century Russia* [Cambridge: Cambridge University Press, 1997], 353).

41. See Nightingale, *Spectacles of Truth*, who analyzes the Greek claim that "the supreme form of wisdom is *theoria*, the rational 'vision' of metaphysical truths" (3).

42. This may also be true to some extent for the other senses as well, but to a far lesser degree than for sight, the premier intellectual sense. Smell is probably the least mediated sense; hearing and taste, in that order, are to some extent subject to training; and touch can hardly compare to the other senses in the range of things it can communicate. On smell in literature, including Russian, see Hans Rindisbacher, *The Smell of Books: A Cultural-Historical Study of Olfactory Perception in Literature* (Ann Arbor: University of Michigan Press, 1992); O. Vainshtein, ed., *Aromaty i zapakhi v kul'ture*, 2 vols. (Moscow: Novoe literaturnie obozrenie, 2003); and Maksim Klymentiev, "The Dark Side of 'The Nose': The Paradigms of Olfactory Perception in Gogol's 'The Nose,'" *Canadian Slavonic Papers* 51, nos. 2–3 (June-September 2009): 217–36.

43. Wortman (*Scenarios of Power*, vol. 1, chap. 2) analyzes Peter's myth as reflected in his self-presentation.

## 1: Prolegomena

1. Andrei Sakharov, *Alarm and Hope*, ed. Efrem Iankelevich and Alfred Friendly, Jr. (New York: Alfred A. Knopf, 1978), 18.

2. Quoted in Grigory Kaganov, *Images of Space: St. Petersburg in the Visual and Verbal Arts*, trans. Sidney Monas (Stanford: Stanford University Press, 1997), 107.

3. V. Kondakov, "'Poteriannyi rai' russkoi literatury (Problema vozvrashcheniia)," in *Puti i mirazhi russkoi kul'tury*, ed. V. E. Bagno, M. N. Mirolainen, and A. V. Lavrov (St. Peterburg: Severo-zapad, 1994), 192. Cf. also O. M. Goncharova, *Vlast' traditsii i 'Novaia Rossiia' v literaturnom soznanii vtoroi poloviny XVIII veka* (St. Petersburg: Russkii khristianskii gumanitarnyi institut, 2004), 3–15.

4. Georges Florovsky, "The Problem of Old Russian Culture," *Slavic Review* 31, no. 1 (1962): 1–15.

5. In the last chapter I consider the weaknesses of the comparison between eighteenth-century and Soviet (Stalinist) culture.

6. Scholars have demonstrated Petrine Russia's profound links to the past. Ernest A. Zitser has explored the nature of Petrine political culture in *The Transfigured Kingdom: Sacred Parody and Charismatic Authority at the Court of Peter the Great* (Ithaca: Cornell University Press, 2004). V. M. Zhivov has shown that the "Slaveno-Russian cultural and linguistic synthesis" reintegrated the Church Slavonic legacy back into eighteenth-century Russian national consciousness in *Language and Culture in Eighteenth-Century Russia* (Boston: Academic Studies Press, 2009), esp. chap. 3. Harvey Goldblatt, in "Orthodox Slavic Heritage and National Consciousness: Aspects of the East Slavic and South Slavic National Revivals," *Harvard Ukrainian Studies* 10, nos. 3–4 (December 1986): 336–54, has also suggested that "the survival and resystematization of the Orthodox Slavic tradition

played a central part in the 'new secular nationalism' of post-Petrine Russia," and asserts "the existence of a premodern type of supranational spiritual solidarity [in Russia] . . . based on the common Orthodox Slavic heritage," which he describes as Petrine Russia's "Orthodox revival" (347 and 353). Thus scholars have demonstrated that the purely Westernizing perspective suggested by Petrine cultural mythology seriously distorts the historical record.

7. O. G. Ageeva discusses the creation and significance of the speech in "Imperskii status Rossii: K istorii politicheskogo metaliteta russkogo obshchestva nachala XVIII veka," in *Tsar' i tsarstvo v russkom obshchestvennom soznanii*, ed. A. A. Gorskii, A. I. Kupriianov, and L. N. Pushkarev (Lewiston, NY: Edwin Mellen, 2000), 105–30. According to Ageeva, the Senate and Synod together initiated the new imperial title (115).

8. *Polnoe sobranie zakonov Rossiiskoi imperii, 1649-1913*, 133 vols. (St. Petersburg: Tipografiia II Otdeleniia Sobstvennoi Ego Imperatorskago Velichestva Kantseliarii, 1830–1916), hereafter referred to as PSZ, followed by volume and page: PSZ, 6:445, available online at "Russkii obshcheobrazovatel'nyi portal," <http://historydoc.edu.ru/>. The speech was also published in a separate edition and in the protocols of the Synod; see Ageeva, "Imperskii status," 126.

9. Vladimir Ger'e, *Otnoshenie Leibnitsa k Rossii i Petru Velikomu po neizdannym bumagam Leibnitsa v Gannoverskoi biblioteke* (St. Petersburg, 1871), 134. See also: Konrad Bittner, "Slavica bei G. W. von Leibniz," *Germanoslavica* 1 (1931–1932): 3–32, 161–234, 509–557; and Liselotte Richter, *Leibniz und sein Russlandbild* (Berlin: Deutsche Akademie der Wissenschaften zu Berlin, 1946). Leibniz's remarks to Peter are remarkable in many respects, and describe Russia in terms very close to those of Golovkin's speech. Ageeva ("Imperskii status," 115) emphasizes the importance of Grotius, Hobbes, and Pufendorf for the idea of the emperor's power stemming from the will of the people.

10. Francis Butler shows how the imagery here—darkness to light, ignorance to glory—was directly indebted to descriptions of Vladimir and Russia's conversion to Christianity in 988. In particular, he cites other instances of the motif of emerging from oblivion in Petrine-era sermons by Prokopovich and Buzhinskii. See "Images of Missionaries and Innovative Rulers in East Slavic Literature from Early Times Through the Reign of Peter the Great" (PhD diss., University of California Berkeley, 1991), 276–80. See also Francis Butler, *Enlightener of Rus': The Image of Vladimir Sviatoslavich Across the Centuries* (Bloomington, IN: Slavica, 2002), 148–49.

11. See Peter France, *Politeness and its Discontents: Problems in French Classical Culture* (New York: Cambridge University Press, 1992), chap. 4.

12. Marc Raeff, *The Well-Ordered Police State: Social and Institutional Change Through Law in the Germanies and Russia, 1600–1800* (New Haven: Yale University Press, 1983). For "the development of civilized conditions," see Martin Malia, *Russia Under Western Eyes: From the Bronze Horseman to the Lenin Mausoleum* (Cambridge: The Belknap Press of Harvard University Press, 1999), 28.

13. V. M. Zhivov, "Kul'turnye reformy v sisteme preobrazovanii Petra I," in *Iz istorii russkoi kul'tury*, ed. A. D. Koshelev, A. F. Litvina, and F. B. Uspenskii (Moscow: Shkola iazyki russkoi kul'tury, 1996–), 3:550–51. Still, B. A. Uspenskii argues that from the point of view of the ceremonial of 1721, the conferral of the new titles was more of a cultural and political than a religious act (*Tsar' i imperator: Pomazanie na tsarstvo i semantika monarshikh titulov* [Moscow: Iazyki russkoi kul'tury, 2000], 48). On the "divinization" and "political theology" of the tsar-emperor, see V. M. Zhivov and B. A. Uspenskii, "Tsar' i Bog: Semioticheskie aspekty sakralizatsii monarkha v Rossii," in B.

A. Uspenskii, *Izbrannye trudy* (Moscow: Gnozis, 1994), 1:110–218; and Stephen Lessing Baehr, *The Paradise Myth in Eighteenth-Century Russia: Utopian Patterns in Early Secular Russian Literature and Culture* (Stanford: Stanford University Press, 1991).

The phrase "from non-existence into being" occurs several times in the daily Orthodox liturgy, both those of St. John Chrysostom and St. Basil, including in the prayer that comes before the central liturgical act, the Eucharist. The phrase appears as both "You . . . who from non-being hast brought all things into being" ("ot nebytiia v bytie vsia privel esi") and "Thou didst bring us from nonexistence into being," ("Izhe ot nebytiia vo ezhe byti privedyi vsiacheskaia"). These occur in the Trisagion hymn (*Trisviatoe, Agios o Theos*), the Praefatio (Preface, *Prefatsiia*) to the Anafora, and in the Seraphic Song (*Kheruvimskaia pesn'*). On the Trisagion hymn, thought to be one of the most ancient Christian prayers, see Vladimir Lossky, *The Mystical Theology of the Eastern Church* (Crestwood, NY: St. Vladimir's Seminary Press, 2002), chap. 5; Alexander Schmemann, *The Eucharist: Sacrament of the Kingdom* (Crestwood, NY: St. Vladimir's Seminary Press, 2003), chap. 9; and his *Of Water and the Spirit: A Liturgical Study of Baptism* (Crestwood, NY: St. Vladimir's Seminary Press, 1995), 46.

14. Cf. V. N. Toporov, *Peterburgskii tekst russkoi literatury: Izbrannye trudy* (St. Petersburg: Iskusstvo-SPB, 2003), 41–42; Toporov notes that for the nineteenth-century "Petersburg text" a catastrophic end (a return to chaos) is also implicit in this scenario.

15. This text is used, for example, as epigraph to volume 1 of Aleksandr Bashutskii, *Panorama Sanktpeterburga*, 3 vols. (St. Petersburg: Tip. vdovy Pliushara, 1834), whose frontispiece depicts the statue of Peter with arm outstretched over the Neva. See also Alexander M. Schenker, *The Bronze Horseman: Falconet's Monument to Peter the Great* (New Haven: Yale University Press, 2003).

16. In contrast, the New Testament counterpart to this passage, the famous opening to the gospel of John—"In the beginning was the Word, and the Word was with God, and the Word was God"—was a fundamental text for the logocentric nineteenth century.

17. See, for example, Vladimir Lossky, *Mystical Theology*, and *In the Image and Likeness of God* (Crestwood, NY: St. Vladimir's Seminary Press, 1974), as well as the considerable literature on icons. See also chapters 2, 5, and 6 below.

18. Adrian Fortescue, "Feast of Orthodoxy," in *The Catholic Encyclopedia*, vol. 11 (New York: Robert Appleton Company, 1911), <http://www.newadvent.org/cathen/11330b.htm11330b.htm>.

19. Jaroslav Pelikan, "The Senses Sanctified: The Rehabilitation of the Visual," in *Imago Dei: The Byzantine Apologia for Icons* (Princeton: Princeton University Press, 1990), chap. 4.

20. See chapter 3, in which I discuss the views of the fourteenth-century theologian Grigorii Palamas.

21. In recent decades Russian historians have successfully challenged the notion that the Russian church was completely under the thumb of the state, putting forward arguments in favor of a discrete tradition of "Enlightenment Orthodoxy" or "Orthodox Enlightenment." See Gregory Freeze, "Haidmaiden of the State? The Church in Imperial Russia Reconsidered," *Journal of Ecclesiastical History* 36, no. 1 (January 1985): 82–102; his remarks in *The Russian Levites: Parish Clergy in the Eighteenth Century* (Cambridge: Harvard University Press, 1977), passim, e.g., 15; Olga A. Tsapina, "Secularization and Opposition in the Time of Catherine the Great," in *Religion and Politics in Enlightenment Europe*, ed. James E. Bradley and Dale K. Van Kley (Notre Dame, IN: University of Notre Dame Press, 2001), 334–90; and her "Pravoslavnoe Prosveshchenie—oksiumoron

ili istoricheskaia real'nost'?" in *Evropeiskoe Prosveshchenie i tsivilizatsiia Rossii*, ed. S. Ia. Karp and S. A. Mezin (Moscow: Nauka, 2004), 301–13; and chap. 13 in Levitt, *Early Modern Russian Letters*. For a survey of contemporary scholarship on the church, see Olga A. Tsapina, "Beyond the Synodal Church: Problems and Perspectives in the Studies of Eighteenth-Century Russian Orthodoxy," *Imperskaia Rossiia/Classical Russia* 1 (2006), 19–53.

22. I take the phrase "moderate rationalist theology" from V. V. Mil'kov, who contrasts the Cappadocian and Antiochan traditions. V. V. Mil'kov and M. N. Gromov, *Ideinye techeniia drevnerusskoi mysli* (St. Petersburg: Russkii Khristianskii gumanitarnyi institut, 2001), 155. This type of theology is discussed below in chapter 6.

23. See G. P. Fedotov, *Sviatye drevnei Rusi (X-XVII v.)*, 3rd ed. (Paris: YMCA Press, 1985), chap.1; G. P. Fedotov, *The Russian Religious Mind*, vol. 1: *Kievan Christianity* (Belmont, MA: Nordland, 1975), 94–110; V. N. Toporov, *Sviatost' i sviatye v russkoi dukhovnoi kul'ture* (Moscow: Gnozis, 1995), vol. 1, chap. 3, section 4.

24. *The Russian Primary Chronicle: Laurentian Text*, trans. and ed. S. H. Cross and O. P. Sherbowitz-Wetzor (Cambridge: The Mediaeval Academy of America, 1973), 128.

25. Iu. M. Lotman, "Russkaia literatura poslepetrovskoi epokhi i khristianskaia traditsiia," in *Izbrannnye stat'i* (Tallinn: Aleksandra, 1993), 3:27.

26. On the changing views of Rome, see Andrew Kahn, "Readings of Imperial Rome from Lomonosov to Pushkin," *Slavic Review* 52, no. 4 (Winter 1993): 745–68.

27. See Richard S. Wortman, *Scenarios of Power: Myth and Ceremony in Russian Monarchy* (Princeton: Princeton University Press, 1995–2000), vol. 1, chap. 2; and Zhivov, *Language and Culture*, chap. 1, esp. 59–62.

28. Algarotti wrote of "questo gran finestrone, dirò così, novellamente aperto nel norte, per cui la Russia guarda in Europa." See Robert Bufalini, "The Czarina's Russia through Mediterranean Eyes: Francesco Algarotti's Journey to Saint Petersburg," *Modern Language Notes* 121, no. 1 (2006), 155; Maria di Salvo, "What Did Francesco Algarotti See in Russia?" in *Russian Society and Culture and the Long Eighteenth Century: Essays in Honour of Anthony G. Cross*, ed. Roger P. Bartlett, Lindsey Hughes, and Anthony Glenn Cross (Munich: Lit, 2004), 72–81; and the discussion of this image in Russian history and poetry in Ettore Lo Gatto, *Il mito di Pietroburgo* (Milan: Feltrinelli, 1991), chaps. 1 and 3.

29. See the discussion in chapter 5 below. On the Roman notion of civic virtue, see E. A. Judge, *The First Christians in the Roman World: Augustan and New Testament Essays*, ed. James R. Harrison (Tübingen: Mohr Siebeck, 2008), chaps. 3 and 4. On the importance of vision in Augustan Rome and Roman literature, see David Fredrick, ed., *The Roman Gaze: Vision, Power, and the Body* (Baltimore: Johns Hopkins University Press, 2002); and Riggs Alden Smith, *The Primacy of Vision in Virgil's Aeneid* (Austin: University of Texas Press, 2005), which, as the title suggests, relies on Merleau-Ponty. Notably, Russia under Catherine the Great was commonly compared to the Augustan age in the eighteenth century.

30. This was especially clear in the case of Catherine the Great; see David Griffiths, "To Live Forever: Catherine II, Voltaire, and the Pursuit of Immortality," in *Russia and the World of the Eighteenth Century*, ed. Roger P. Bartlett, Anthony Glenn Cross, and Karen Rasmussen (Columbus, OH: Slavica Publishers, 1988), 446–68. On Catherine's myth-making, including myths of gender, see Vera Proskurina, *Creating the Empress: Politics and Poetry in the Age of Catherine II* (Brighton, MA: Academic Studies Press, 2011).

31. J. G. A. Pocock, *Barbarism and Religion* (New York, 1999), 1:7. For a useful discussion of the problem of a "Russian Enlightenment," see David M. Griffiths, "In Search

of Enlightenment: Recent Soviet Interpretation of Eighteenth-Century Russian Intellectual History," *Canadian-American Slavic Studies* 16, nos. 3–4 (Fall–Winter 1982): 317–56.

32. Elise Wirtschafter makes a fruitful distinction between Russian "civil" society (in Habermas's sense) and "civic" society in *The Play of Ideas in Russian Enlightenment Theater* (DeKalb: Northern Illinois University Press, 2003), chap. 4. Cynthia H. Whittaker also argues for the power of civil society to offer a check on absolute power in *Russian Monarchy: Eighteenth-Century Rulers and Writers in Political Dialogue* (DeKalb: Northern Illinois University Press, 2003).

33. Malia, *Russia Under Western Eyes*, chap. 1.

34. A. I. Komissarenko, *Russkii absoliutizm i dukhovenstvo v XVIII veke: Ocherki istorii sekuliarizatsionnoi reformy 1764 g.* (Moscow: Izd-vo Vses. zaochnogo politekhnicheskogo instituta, 1990) focuses on the struggle over land ownership.

35. On the linguistic and cultural synthesis, see Zhivov, *Language and Culture*, chap. 3.

36. Hans Blumenberg, "Light as a Metaphor for Truth: At the Preliminary Stage of Philosophical Concept Formation," in *Modernity and the Hegemony of Vision*, ed. David Michael Levin (Berkeley: University of California Press, 1993), 52.

37. See the discussion in chapter 6.

38. Jacques Lacan, *Écrits: A Selection*, trans. A. Sheridan (New York: Norton, 1977), chap. 1. For an insightful discussion of the mirror stage, which influenced my reading, see Jane Gallop, *Reading Lacan* (Ithaca: Cornell University Press, 1985).

39. Lacan himself used the historical formation of modern self-consciousness in the post-medieval world as an illustration of his theory. See Ellie Ragland-Sullivan, *Jacques Lacan and the Philosophy of Psychoanalysis* (Urbana: University of Illinois Press, 1986), 7–12.

40. E. A. Grosz, *Jacques Lacan: A Feminist Introduction* (London: Routledge, 1990), 39.

41. Lacan, *Écrits*, 4. In contrast, Gennadii Vdovin's approach to "the formation of the 'I'" as traced in eighteenth-century portraiture emphasizes the parity of inner and outer self-image, the externalization of the soul (to paraphrase the Russian philosopher Gustav Shpet). He sees the "I" develop in three psycho-cultural stages—mirrored in portraits— which he calls persona, individuality, and personality (*persona, individual'nost', lichnost'*). At least theoretically, portraiture offers snapshots of the self-in-becoming, thus in some sense avoiding or mitigating the drama of miscognition foregrounded in the mirror-stage drama. See G. V. Vdovin, *Stanovlenie "IA" v russkoĭ kul'ture XVIII veka i iskusstvo portreta* ([Moscow]: Nash dom, 1999) and *Persona, individual'nost', lichnost': opyt samopoznaniia v iskusstve russkogo portreta XVIII veka* (Moscow: Progress-Traditsiia, 2005).

42. Gallop, *Reading Lacan*, 80–81.

43. Ragland-Sullivan, *Jacques Lacan*, 8.

44. Voltaire, *Russia Under Peter the Great*, trans. M. F. O. Jenkins (Rutherford, NJ: Fairleigh Dickinson University Press, 1983), 251. On Voltaire's view of Russia, see the works cited above in the introduction, note 38, especially Wilberger, *Voltaire's Russia*.

45. Marc Raeff, "The Enlightenment in Russia," in *The Eighteenth Century in Russia*, ed. J. G. Garrard (Oxford: Clarendon Press, 1973), 45.

46. See my discussion of Descartes and the "Cartesian Circle" in chapter 7.

47. See William M. Ivins, Jr., *On the Rationalization of Sight, With an Examination of Three Renaissance Texts on Perspective* (New York: Da Capo Press, 1975); and Bruno Latour, "Visualization and Cognition: Thinking with Eyes and Hands," *Knowledge and Society* 6 (1986): 1–40.

48. These may also be connected to the development of the nation-state and of early modern Russian nationalism in this period, which may be seen in terms of a tension between two larger models of development. On the one hand, Russia was following a Western model of state-building as an empire with a newly formulated national church, subordinated to the state, and a powerful army that made it a new major player in European power politics (as described by Malia, *Russia Under Western Eyes*). In terms of language, which was one of the most crucial markers of cultural consciousness, Peter broke with the Slavonic tradition in favor of a new, "Russian," explicitly "civic" script and a vernacular literary language. On the other hand, Russia still retained elements of the older self-consciousness as leader of the Orthodox world. This second role was, depending on one's point of view, either something that took longer to expire in the East (as various neighboring Slavic peoples formed their own national linguistic and ecclesiastical variants on the Russian model—e.g., Serbo-Slavonic and Bulgaro-Slavonic as counterparts to Slaveno-Russian) or as a differentiating, "Panslavic" cultural factor that distinguished the development of national consciousness in the East from that in the West; Catherine's "Greek Project" at the end of her reign offers an example. Similarly, the "Slaveno-Russian cultural synthesis" (Zhivov, *Language and Culture*, chap. 3) at mid-century was, on the one hand, a movement away from anticlerical leanings of the Petrine period, but on the other, and perhaps more fundamentally, an attempt to develop an early modern model of nationhood that integrated Orthodox culture into Russian intellectual life and modern national consciousness.

## 2: The Moment of the Muses

1. The Russian triumphal ode had a complex cultural pedigree; as L. V. Pumpianskii put it, "Russia received the classical ideal through perhaps the greatest number of refractions; thus Lomonosov's ode was a classical work [that came] via Malherbe, Boileau, and the Germans" ("K istorii russkogo klassitsizma: poetika Lomonosova," in *Kontekst 1982: Literaturno-teoreticheskie issledovaniia*, ed. P. V. Palievskii [Moscow: Nauka, 1983], 305). See N. Iu. Alekseeva's authoritative *Russkaia oda: Razvitie odicheskoi formy v XVII–XVIII vekakh* (St. Petersburg: Nauka, 2005).

2. Stephen Lessing Baehr, *The Paradise Myth in Eighteenth-Century Russia: Utopian Patterns in Early Secular Russian Literature and Culture* (Stanford: Stanford University Press, 1991); V. M. Zhivov and B. A. Uspenskii, "Tsar' i Bog: Semioticheskie aspekty sakralizatsii monarkha v Rossii," in B. A. Uspenskii, *Izbrannye trudy* (Moscow: Gnozis, 1994), 1:110–218.

3. Pumpianskii, "K istorii russkogo klassitsizma," 310; Pumpianskii's italics.

4. Ibid., 310–11.

5. Ibid.

6. Zhivov, *Language and Culture*, 130. Zhivov describes the central role of Lomonosov's odes in forming the new literary language in chapter 2.

7. To some extent, this reflects the process of Lomonosov's posthumous canonization; the fact that the Khotin ode was only first published in 1752 in a revised version that reflected the poet's mature style made this first effort seem the more miraculous.

8. A. N. Radishchev, *Puteshestvie iz Peterburga v Moskvu: Vol'nost'*, ed. V. A. Zapadov (St. Petersburg: Nauka, 1992), 119. Note the imagery of a child awakening.

9. References to the odes are to: M. V. Lomonosov, *Polnoe sobranie sochinenii*, 11 vols. (Moscow: Akademiia Nauk SSSR, 1950–83), citing volume and page number.

10. Calls to behold misery or hardship, on the other hand, occur infrequently (e.g., 8:224, 8:635, 8:657).

11. Edward Young, *Night Thoughts*, ed. Stephen Cornford (New York: Cambridge University Press, 1989), Night VI, lines 170–73 and 426–29.

12. Jacques Lacan, *Écrits: A Selection*, trans. Alan Sheridan (New York: Norton, 1977), 2.

13. Harsha Ram, *The Imperial Sublime: A Russian Poetics of Empire*, Publications of the Wisconsin Center for Pushkin Studies (Madison: University of Wisconsin Press, 2003).

14. This distinction was (and is now in contemporary Russia again) expressed in the use of "rossiiskii" to mean Russian in the imperial or civic sense and "russkii" in the ethnic and national meaning. See M. N. Tikhomirov, "O proiskhozhdenii nazvaniia 'Rossiia,'" *Voprosy istorii* 11 (1953): 93–96. For a discussion of this distinction and its importance for Russian historical development, see Geoffrey Hoskings, *Russia: People and Empire, 1552–1917* (Cambridge: Harvard University Press, 1997).

15. V. N. Toporov has described these as "geo-ethnic panoramas." See "K proiskhozhdeniiu i funktsiiam 'geo-etnicheskikh' panoram v aspekte sviazei istorii i kul'tury," in *Istoriia i kul'tura (Tezisy dokladov)* (Moscow: AN SSSR, Institut slavovendeniia i balkanistika, 1991), cited in Otto Boele, *The North in Russian Romantic Literature*, Studies in Slavic Literature and Poetics 26 (Amsterdam: Rodopi, 1996), 24.

16. See, for example, the prayer that ends the 1754 ode that thanks God for being the "Extender of Russia's borders" (Predelov rosskikh rasshiritel') (8:564).

17. L. I. Sazonova, "Ot russkogo panegirika XVII v. k ode M. V. Lomonosova," in *Lomonosov i russkaia literatura*, ed. A. S. Kurilov (Moscow: Nauka, 1987), 121.

18. Sean Homer, *Jacques Lacan* (London: Routledge, 2005), 21, discussing the ideas of psychologist Henri Wallon.

19. In Lacan's formulation, style is not only "the man himself" but also "the man to whom one speaks." That is, in the words of Judith Miller, "identity is divided between what style represents and the one before whom it is represented" (Judith Miller, "Style Is the Man Himself," in *Lacan and the Subject of Language*, ed. E. Ragland-Sullivan and M. Bracher [New York: Routledge, 1991], 147).

20. Homer, *Jacques Lacan*, 24.

21. For Lacan, there is always a necessary gap or lag in signification, in mirror-stage imaging as well as in language; it is in this sense that the unconscious, structured by language, is also profoundly marked by incompletion, "founded on nothingness." What is signified is always incomplete or missing, inevitably leading to what Lacan refers to as "chains of signifiers"—the substitution of one signifier for the next. See Lacan's brilliant reading of Edgar Allen Poe's "The Purloined Letter" in these terms. See also the texts and commentary in John P. Muller and William J. Richardson, *The Purloined Poe: Lacan, Derrida & Psychoanalytic Reading* (Baltimore: Johns Hopkins University Press, 1988).

22. N. Iu. Alekseeva argues that "in the panegyric ode an object thus appears not in its actual substance [*real'nost'*] but transfigured, ideally seen [*ideal'no uvidennym*]." She describes this representational strategy in terms of achieving the neo-Platonic "*eidos*," the ideal essence. Alekseeva, *Russkaia oda*, 190.

23. Jane Gallop, *Reading Lacan* (Ithaca: Cornell University Press, 1985), 81–82.

24. A calculation based on the twenty original odes (in volume 8, poems number 4, 21, 22, 24, 26, 28, 42, 43, 44, 141, 149, 176, 189, 213, 232, 238, 260, 261, 266, and 271). Only one ode, of 1741—number 22—has no direct mention of Peter, only allusions to his military campaigns.

25. Of course, "St. Petersburg" technically refers to St. Peter and not Peter I.

26. Lomonosov, *Polnoe sobranie*, 8:774, 8:780, 8:789. Catherine herself made much of this connection. See Karen Rasmussen, "Catherine II and the Image of Peter I," *Slavic Review* 37, no. 1 (1978): 51–69.

27. For example, in the 1747 ode to Elizabeth's ascension God sends Peter to save "Russia, trampled down by ignorance" (Rossiiu, grubost'iu poprannu); in an earlier version of this ode, published in 1751, this line was: "Russia trampled down by barbarism" (Rossiiu, varvarstvom poprannu) (8:200n).

28. The gates of war may also be opened (8:45) and the door opened to most glorious victories (8:50).

29. Iu. N. Tynianov, "Oda kak oratorskii zhanr" [1927], *Poetika, Istoriia literatury, Kino* (Moscow: Nauka, 1977), 227–52; James Von Geldern, "The Ode as a Performative Genre," *Slavic Review* 50, no. 4 (Winter 1991): 927–39. There is no hard evidence, however, that the odes were ever actually performed. On this see Alekseeva, *Russkaia Oda*, part 3, chap. 1, esp. 178–79.

30. See Stephen L. Baehr, "The 'Political Icon' in Seventeenth- and Eighteenth-Century Russia," *Russian Literature Triquarterly* 21 (1988): 61–79, and *The Paradise Myth*, chap. 2.

31. See Lomonosov's defense of heliocentrism in "Iavlenie Venery na solntse," 4:361–76. On his clashes with certain Orthodox clergymen over the issue, see B. E. Raikov, *Ocherki po istorii geliotsentricheskogo mirovozzreniia v Rossii: Iz proshlogo russkogo estestvoznaniia* (Moscow: Akademiia nauk SSSR, 1947), chap. 11.

32. I.e., on its way up to its apex.

33. "Ot rizy"—"riza" literally means robe or clothing, but may also refer to the metal covering of an icon.

34. Ioann III (also known as Ivan VI), was infant emperor under the regency of Anna Leopol'dovna from October 17/28, 1740 until November 25/December 6, 1741, when Empress Elizabeth seized the throne. Gostomysl was a legendary leader of ninth-century Novgorod whose historical role and very existence was debated by eighteenth-century historians.

35. Note also that the reference to the Riurikide dynasty (that ended in 1613) is poetic license.

36. V. K. Trediakovskii, *Izbrannye proizvedeniia* (Leningrad: Sovetskii pisatel', 1963), 394.

37. The "north" here is a cultural rather than geographical marker for Russia. See Boele, *The North in Russian Romantic Literature*, chap. 2, esp. 26.

38. Compare the verbs for seeing with the prefix "na" and reflexive ending: *nasmotret'sia, nagliadet'sia*, "to look one's fill at something or someone, to look until complete satisfaction."

39. Lomonosov's xenophobic attack on foreigners living in Russia in his ode of 1762 seems to be a special case.

40. Lomonosov, *Polnoe sobranie*, 8:886.

41. Cf. Robert Graves, *The Greek Myths* (London: Penguin Books, 1974), 1:131–33.

42. In the given case, the giants serve as an allegory of the evil reign that Elizabeth overthrew. Cf. 8:919.

43. The giant Enceladus was hit by Athena with a "vast missile" that "crushed him flat and became the island of Sicily" (Graves, *Greek Myths*, 132); Athena often serves in the odes as an allegorical stand-in for Elizabeth.

44. In at least one other passage, the word *basni* (fables) is not used pejoratively—see 8:84.

45. Radishchev, *Puteshestvie*, 121.

### 3: *Bogovidenie*

1. This is true for Gregory Palamas, discussed below (see Sv. Grigorii Palama, *Triady v zashchitu sviashchenno-bezmolvstvuiushchikh*, trans. and ed. V. Veniaminov [Moscow: Kanon+, 2003], 97 and 111). The word has also been used to translate several of the theologian Vladimir Lossky's works into Russian, i.e., *Bogoslovie i bogovidenie: sbornik statei* (Moscow: Izd. Sviato-Vladimirskogo Bratstva, 2000); and *Bogovidenie* (Moscow: Izd. Sviato-Vladimirskogo Bratstva, 1995). The latter is a translation of his *Vision de Dieu* (Neuchatel: Delachaux & Niestlé, 1962)—in English as *The Vision of God* (Crestwood, NY: St. Vladimir's Seminary Press, 1983). As we will see in chapter 5, Trediakovskii uses the word *bogozrenie* (vision, contemplation, cognition of God) in the subtitle of his visual theodicy *Feoptiia* as a synonym for God's existence, based on the equation of seeing and knowing.

2. For a catalogue of such references, see I. Solosin, "Otrazhenie iazyka i obrazov Sv. Pisaniia i knig bogosluzhebnykh v stikhotvoreniiakh Lomonosova," *Izvestiia Otdeleniia Russkogo iazyka i slovesnosti Akademii nauk* 18, no. 2 (1913): 238–93. I. Z. Serman cites several precursors for Lomonosov's use of biblical imagery (Polotskii, Iavorskii, Buslaev) but argues that for Lomonosov it serves non-religious ends. In the case of the "Maiden in the sun," "the apocalyptic image is torn from its context and receives a secular, literary significance," as the Maiden (Virgin Mary) functions as stand-in for the "earthly empress," i.e., Elizabeth; it serves as just a metaphor, a likeness; so that "mysticism disappears, but poetic ecstasy . . . remains" (I. Z. Serman, *Mikhail Lomonosov: Life and Poetry* [Jerusalem: Centre of Slavic and Russian Studies, Hebrew University of Jerusalem, 1988], 78). See the discussion in Marcus Levitt, *Early Modern Russian Letters* (Boston: Academic Studies Press, 2009), chap. 20, on which parts of this chapter are based.

As Vladimir Lossky notes in *The Mystical Theology of the Eastern Church* (Crestwood, NY: St. Vladimir's Seminary Press, 2002), 8–9, there is no theology without mysticism. I am using the term to distinguish the transcendent vision discussed in this chapter from what has been called Orthodox "theology of a moderate rationalist type," analyzed in chap. 6.

3. The "neo-Palamists" include Vladimir Lossky, John Meyendorff, Basil Krivosheine, Georges Barrois, Christos Yannaras, George Mahoney, Kallistos Ware, and others—virtually all modern Russian Orthodox theologians, who, following Lossky, maintain that "the theology of Light [elaborated by Palamas] is inherent in Orthodox spirituality: the one is impossible without the other. One can be completely ignorant of Gregory Palamas, of his role in the doctrinal history of the Church of the East; but one can never understand Eastern spirituality" if one misunderstands its "theological basis, which finds its definitive expression in the great archbishop of Thessalonica [Palamas]. . . . All the liturgical texts are impregnated with it" (Vladimir Lossky, *In the Image and Likeness of God* [Crestwood, NY: St. Vladimir's Seminary Press, 1974], 69). The return to Palamas has been marked by debates with Catholic theologians over his doctrinal acceptability, particularly concerning his metaphysics of light and the nature of revelation. See Jeffrey D. Finch, "Neo-Palamism, Divinizing Grace, and the Breach between East and West," in *Partakers of the Divine Nature: The History and Development of Deification in the Christian Traditions*, ed. Michael J. Christensen and Jeffery A. Wittung (Grand Rapids: Baker Academic, 2007), 233–49, and the works cited below.

For Palamas's views on vision, see especially his *Triads in Defense of the Holy Hesychasts* (*Triady v zashchitu sviashchenno-bezmolvstvuiushchikh*). See also the partial

English translation: Gregory Palamas, *The Triads*, ed. and intro. John Meyendorff, trans. Nicholas Gendle, preface by Jaroslav Pelikan (New York: Paulist Press, 1983), which is in turn based on Meyendorff's full critical Greek edition with French translation, *Défense des saints hésychastes*, ed. John Meyendorff, 2nd rev. ed. (Louvain: Spicilegium sacrum lovaniense, 1973). The main sources for Palamas's ideas include Clement of Alexandria, Dionysius ("the Areopagite" or "Pseudo-Areopagite"), and Symeon the New Theologian.

Major works on Palamas and Orthodoxy include Lossky, *Mystical Theology*; Lossky, *In the Image and Likeness*; and Lossky, *The Vision of God*; John Meyendorff, *A Study of Gregory Palamas* (London: Faith Press, 1964); Meyendorff, *St. Gregory Palamas and Orthodox Spirituality* (Crestwood, NY: St. Vladimir's Seminary Press, 1974); Meyendorff, *Byzantine Hesychasm: Historical, Theological and Social Problems; Collected Studies* (London: Variorum Reprints, 1974); George Maloney, *A Theology of "Uncreated Energies"* (Milwaukee: Marquette University Press, 1978); and Basil Krivocheine, *In the Light of Christ: Saint Symeon the New Theologian (949-1022)*, trans. Anthony P. Gythiel (Crestwood, NY: St. Vladimir's Seminary Press, 1986). Meyendorff's contention that Palamas's main opponent, Barlaam the Calabrian, represented the Byzantine humanist position rather than that of the Latin West has met with sharp criticism; see Rev. John S. Romanides, "Notes on the Palamite Controversy and Related Topics," *Greek Orthodox Theological Review* 6, no. 2 (1960–1961): 186–205; and 9, no. 2 (Winter 1963–1964): 225–70; and Bishop Auxentios of Photiki, "The Humanist Quest for a Unity of Knowledge and the Orthodox Metaphysics of Light: A Corrective to Father Meyendorff's Misunderstanding of the Theology of St. Gregory Palamas," *Orthodox Tradition* 9, no. 3 (1993): 7–17.

I have applied some of Palamas's ideas in *Early Modern Russian Letters*, chap. 16, although the current analysis revises my earlier argument.

4. Palamas's doctrinal position on the energies/essence distinction (on which see below) was upheld by a series of Constantinopolitan church councils in 1341, 1347, 1351, and 1368, that are considered ecumenical (universally binding) in the Orthodox Church; these decisions cemented the rift between the Orthodox and Catholic churches. Palamas is considered a central figure in the Orthodox tradition, but is often treated with some skepticism in the West. His is a saint in the Orthodox Church (not the Catholic), celebrated on the second Sunday of Lent. For defenses of Palamas and the Orthodox position against Catholic critics, or attempts to reconcile the traditions, see Leonidas Contos, "Essence-Energies Structure of St. Gregory Palamas with a Brief Examination of its Patristic Foundation," *The Greek Orthodox Theological Review* 12 (1967): 283–94; Georges Barrois, "Palamism Revisited," *St. Vladimir's Theological Quarterly* 19 (1975); 211–31; Kallistos Ware, "God Hidden and Revealed: The Apophatic Way and the Essence-Energies Distinction," *Eastern Churches Review* 7 (1975): 125–36 and "The Debate about Palamism," *Eastern Churches Review* 9 (1977): 45–63; Christos Yannaras, "The Distinction between Essence and Energies and Its Importance for Theology," *St. Vladimir's Theological Quarterly* 19 (1975): 232–45; David Coffey, "The Palamite Doctrine of God: A New Perspective," *St. Vladimir's Theological Quarterly* 32 (1988): 329–58; Gerry Russo, "Rahner and Palamas: A Unity of Grace," *St. Vladimir's Theological Quarterly* 32 (1988): 157–80; and Finch, "Neo-Palamism."

5. Lomonosov's writings show a significant knowledge of Orthodox theology (see the discussion in chapter 5), and Lomonosov may justifiably be seen as an apologist for the Orthodox cultural tradition. See, for example, Riccardo Picchio, "Predislovie o pol'ze knig tserkovnykh M. V. Lomonosova kak manifest russkogo konfessional'nogo patriotizma," in *Sbornik statei k 70-letiiu prof. Iu. M. Lotmana*, ed. A. Mal'ts (Tartu: Tartuskii universitet, Kafedra russkoi literatury, 1992): 142–52.

Although Palamas's yearly (calendar) service on November 14 had been discontinued during the Nikonian reforms due to the lack of analogue in the Greek Minei, Palamas continued to be celebrated as a saint on the second Sunday of Lent; he is included in all Russian typicons (listing of church services) after 1682, and his special service (the *Triodnaia pamiat'*) was part of the Lenten service book (*Triod' Postnaia*). Hence Lomonosov was probably familiar with at least who Palamas was. The only publication of Palamas in eighteenth-century Russia that I know of is as part of the *Philokalia* (*Dobrotoliubie*), a collection of Hesychast works translated into Slavonic under the supervision of Paisii Velichkovskii and published in Russia in 1791, long after Lomonosov's death.

6. This was originally formulated by Evagrius Ponticus (ca. 345–ca. 399); see his *Praktikos & Chapters on Prayer* (Piscataway, NJ: Gorgias Press, 2009), chap. 60.

7. Ware, "The Debate," 52.

8. Lossky, *Mystical Theology*, 69. Both Lossky and Ware base their argument on antinomies or paradox, which is contrasted to a strictly logical, neo-Platonist approach. See Lossky, *Mystical Theology*, 43, 46, 66, 69; and Ware, "The Debate," 46–50.

9. Ware, "God Hidden and Revealed," 127–28.

10. The notion of theology as a "framework and a method for the systematization of the revealed data . . . , an intellectual discipline, the distinctive principle and axiom of which is the supernatural faith in the divine revelation" is subordinate in Orthodoxy to its function as "a reflection of the faith-experience of the Christian . . . [whose] goal is no mere erudition; theology is a wisdom and points toward spiritual experience" (Barrois, "Palamism Revisited," 230).

11. This helps explain why the Psalter was the most popular and well known of the Old Testament books in Russia, and also why the ode that consciously appealed to its example became the leading genre of eighteenth-century Russian literature. On the Psalter and Russian poetry, see Alexander Levitsky, "The Sacred Ode in Eighteenth-Century Russian Literary Culture" (PhD diss., University of Michigan, 1977); the essays in *Vasilij Kirillovič Trediakovskii, Psalter 1753*, ed. Alexander Levitsky (Paderborn: Ferdinand Schöningh, 1989); and L. F. Lutsevich, *Psaltyr' v russkoi poezii* (St. Petersburg: Dmitrii Bulanin, 2002). This attitude also contributed to the cult of the poet-prophet that emerged in later eighteenth-century Russia and that reached its apogee with Pushkin.

12. See T. V. Artem'eva, *Istoriia metafiziki v Rossii XVIII veka* (St. Petersburg: Aleteiia, 1996), 265–68, who suggests that Russian odes represent an expression of the Orthodox apophatic tradition.

13. References to Lomonosov's works cite M. V. Lomonosov, *Polnoe sobranie sochinenii*, 11 vols. (Moscow: Akademiia Nauk SSSR, 1950–83), giving volume and page number.

The 1751 manuscript of these lines reads: "No ves' edva obemlet svet / Eia povsiudu gromku slavu: / Kak v stikh vmestiti Toia dezhavu?" ("But the entire world can hardly embrace / Her ubiquitous resounding glory: / How can verse contain Your power?") (8:83n).

14. On the problematic use of this formulaic phrase, which Catherine the Great banned in 1786, see E. V. Marasinova, "'Rab', 'poddannyi', 'syn otechestva' (K probleme vzaimodeistviia lichnosti i vlasti v Rossii XVIII veka)," *Canadian American Slavic Studies* 38 (2004): 83–104.

15. L. I. Sazonova, "Ot russkogo panegirika XVII v. k ode M. V. Lomonosova," in *Lomonosov i russkaia literatura*, ed. A. S. Kurilov (Moscow: Nauka, 1987), 121.

16. See Meyendorff, *A Study of Gregory Palamas*, part 1, for a history of Hesychasm.

17. As Hans Jonas notes, the physical act of vision "is incomplete by itself; it requires the complement of the other senses and functions for its cognitive office"; what we "see" results from "the formal articulation of the sense material through the categories of the understanding" (*The Phenomenon of Life: Toward a Philosophical Biology* [Evanston: Northwestern University Press, 2001], 135–36 and 152). Nevertheless, Jonas also notes the "long-dominant trend" in Western philosophy exemplified in Kant to ignore this complexity and to make an automatic connection between sight and truth or knowing (153), what Snell criticizes as "intuitionism" (see the introduction, note 10). Jonas mainly describes this problem of cognition in physical (phenomenological) terms, i.e., the way sight is dynamic and involves the perception of motion.

18. Lossky, *In the Image and Likeness*, 58–59. This is from the so-called "Hagioritic Tome," whose authorship is attributed to Palamas; Meyendorff refers to it as a "solemn manifesto" of Palamas's position (*A Study of Gregory Palamas*, 48–49). It was endorsed by the monks of Mount Athos, whose practices Palamas was defending. The "Hagioritic Tome" is thus also known as "The Declaration of the Holy Mountain in Defense of Those who Devoutly Practice a Life of Stillness." An English translation can be found in *The Philokalia: The Complete Text*, trans. G. E. H. Palmer, Philip Sherrard, and Kallistos Ware (London: Faber and Faber, 1998), 4:331–417; the corresponding passage is on 424.

19. Lossky, *In the Image and Likeness*, 59

20. See note 5.

21. Ware, "God Hidden and Revealed," 129.

22. Lossky, *Mystical Theology*, 86. This view of sight suggests an optimistic theological reading of the mirror stage as a "true" image of one's mysterious and unknown yet marvelous divine potential.

23. Mikhail Kheraskov, *Tvoreniia: Vnov' ispravlennyia i dopolnennyia*, 12 vols. (Moscow, 1796–1803), 7:25. Kheraskov's ode echoes both Lomonosov's triumphal odes and his "Meditations," although the given passage suggests the more rational, philosophical nature of his lyrics.

24. On so-called "cardiology" in Orthodox theology that is associated with the Hesychast "prayer of the heart," see V. V. Mil'kov and M. N. Gromov, *Ideinye techeniia drevnerusskoi mysli* (St. Petersburg: Russkii Khristianskii gumanitarnyi institut, 2001), 92–101. In Orthodox discourse "vision of the heart" may be equivalent to "*umnoe zrenie.*"

25. According to V. I. Dal'"s famous nineteenth-century dictionary, *dukh* usually implies something connected with the divine (*Tolkovyi slovar' zhivogo velikorusskogo iazyka*, 4 vols. [1880–1882; repr., Moscow: Russkii iazyk, 1978–1980], 1:503). *Dukh* shares the same root with *dusha* (soul) (from the Greek, *pneuma*, meaning wind, breath, spirit), which in Russian can also mean "psyche."

26. In Lomonosov's 1742 birthday ode to Grand Prince Petr Fedorovich, for example, some published versions have the line "Videnie moi *um* vozvodit" in place of "Videnie moi *dukh* vozvodit," i.e., "dukh" and "um" are virtually interchangeable (8:66n). See also the entry on "*dukh*" in L. V. Tychinina, ed., *Slovar' Akademii rossiiskoi 1789–1794* (Moscow: MGI im. E. R. Daskovoi, 2001–2006), vol. 2, column 802–4, esp. meaning 10, which cites Lomonosov himself as an example. A. M. Peskov notes that in poetic discourse *um* and *dukh* served as equivalents of the French *esprit*; see his "Sumarokov i Bualo," *Nauchnye doklady vysshei shkoly: Filologicheskie nauki* 2 (1982): 77.

27. Lossky, *Mystical Theology*, 21–25.

28. Lossky, *In the Image and Likeness*, 58–59 (from the "Hagioritic Tome").

29. See George C. Papademetriou, "The Human Body According to Saint Gregory Palamas," *Greek Orthodox Theological Review* 34, no. 1 (1989): 1–9. On deification, see G. I. Mantzarides, *The Deification of Man: St. Gregory Palamas and the Orthodox Tradition*, trans. L. Sherrard (Crestwood, NY: St. Vladimir's Seminary Press, 1984).

30. Palamas, *Triady v zashchitu*, 68.

31. Ibid., 93.

32. Ibid., 82.

33. Ibid., 63.

34. Ibid., 105.

35. Ibid., 82.

36. See N. Iu. Alekseeva's Platonic reading cited in chapter 2, note 22.

37. The latter according to St. Isaac the Syrian, cited in Lossky, *Mystical Theology*, 208. On differing varieties of wonder, see chapter 5.

38. In reference to the Hesychast goal of tranquility, see for example Lossky, *Mystical Theology*, 208. See also Christos Yannaras's discussion of ecstasy in regard to "The Distinction between Essence and Energies," 235.

39. Here the Orthodox tradition and Palamas in particular sharply part company with Platonism. For a discussion of the philosophical issues in relation to both the classical and Hebrew traditions, see Papademetriou, "The Human Body," 1–10. For the quotation, see Palamas, *Traidy v zashchitu*, 95; cf. 105.

40. This is what Stephen Baehr describes as Russia's "paradise myth," which he also attributes in large part to the Orthodox tradition. See Baehr, *The Paradise Myth*.

41. G. A. Gukovskii, *Rannie raboty po istorii russkoi poezii XVIII veka* (Moscow: Iazyki russkoi kul'tury, 2001), 47.

42. Ibid., 47.

43. Ibid., 46.

44. In the ode of 1754, there is no end to joymaking:

> Так ныне град Петров священный,
> Толиким счастьем восхищенный,
> Восшед отрад на высоту,
> Вокруг веселия считает
> И края им не обретает;
> Какую зрит он красоту! (8:558)

> [So today the holy city of Peter / Is enraptured with such happiness, / Having gone, joyous, to a height, / Considers the merrymaking all around / And is unable to find its limit. / What beauty it sees!]

45. Lossky, *Mystical Theology*, 222–23 and 208–9; cf. 35.

46. In the Slavonic: "восхищенъ бысть въ рай, и слыша неизреченны гл(а)голы, ниже не леть есть человеку глаголати"; in the Russian Synodal version: "восхищен в рай и слышал неизреченные слова, которых человеку нельзя пересказать." This moment of sudden revelation may also be experienced as being "captured" or stupefied. Cf. in Lomonosov such phrases as "Vostorg vnezapnyi um plenil" ("Sudden ecstasy has captured my mind)" (8:16) and "No speshno tol' kuda voskhodit / Vnezapno moi plenennyi vzor?" ("But to where so quickly is / My captive gaze suddenly raised?)" (8:66). Consider also Victor Zhivov's analysis of the Western ascetic and Eastern patristic roots of the related notion of "sacred intoxication" (from Boileau's "Ode sur la prise de *Namur*"), which played a crucial role in legitimizing the language and poetics of Lomonosov's odes (*Language and Culture in Eighteenth-Century Russia* [Boston: Academic Studies Press, 2009], 195–202).

47. Lossky, *Mystical Theology*, 209. Note in passing that "blindness" and "being struck down" may be analogues to illumination by divine light and being carried upwards. See Lossky, *Mystical Theology*, chap. 2, "The Divine Darkness."

48. Ibid., 209. Compare the scenario from Aristotle discussed in chapter 5.

49. The translation is from Palamas, *The Triads*, 38. According to Nicholas Gendle, this image comes from Plotinus (*The Triads*, 122n41). Palamas, *Triady v zashchitu*, 83.

50. Jaroslav Pelikan, *Imago Dei: The Byzantine Apologia for Icons* (Princeton: Princeton University Press, 1990), 102; on the importance of beauty in Orthodoxy, see Paul Evdokimov, *The Art of the Icon: A Theology of Beauty* (Redondo Beach, CA: Oakwood, 1996).

51. Palamas (*Triady v zashchitu*, 63) is paraphrasing St. Nilus of Sinai.

52. Ibid., 197. Translation from Palamas, *The Triads*, 57.

53. Palamas, *Triady v zashchitu*, 79.

54. On this unusual image, see E. Pogosian and M. Smorzhevskih, "'Ia devu v solntse zriu stoiashchu . . . ': Apokalipitcheskii siuzhet i formy istoricheskoi refleksii," in *Istoriia i istoriosofiia v literaturnom prelomlenii*, ed. A. A. Danilevskii, Studia russica Helsingiensia et Tartuensia 8 (Tartu: Tartu Ülikooli Kirjastus, 2002), 2–36 and Levitt, *Early Modern Russian Letters*, chap. 16.

55. V. M. Zhivov and B. A. Uspenskii, "Tsar' i Bog: Semioticheskie aspekty sakralizatsii monarkha v Rossii," in B. A. Uspenskii, *Izbrannye trudy* (Moscow: Gnozis, 1994), 1:174.

56. Palamas, *Triady v zashchitu*, 83.

## 4: The Staging of the Self

1. Jacques Lacan, *Écrits: A Selection*, trans. A. Sheridan (New York, 1977), 4.

2. As Jane Gallop puts it, the mirror stage "is the source not only for what follows but also for what comes before. It produces the future through anticipation and the past through retroaction. And yet it is itself a moment of self-delusion, of captivation by an illusory image. Both future and past are thus rooted in an illusion." *Reading Lacan* (Ithaca: Cornell University Press, 1985), 80–81.

3. Accordingly, the later phase of classicist tragedy, marked by Sumarokov's *Dimitrii the Pretender*, manifests a greater attempt at historical accuracy, which became a central concern with Romantic historical drama. On the play and its theme, see Birgit Osterwald, *Das Demetrius-Thema in der russischen und deutschen Literatur: Dargestellt an A. P. Sumarokovs "Dimitrij Samozvanec," A. S. Puškins "Boris Godunov" and F. Schillers "Demetrius,"* Studia Slavica et Baltica 5 (Munich: Aschendorff, 1982).

4. Jean-Jacques Rousseau, *The Social Contract and Discourses*, trans. and intro. G. D. H. Cole, rev. ed. by J. H. Brumfitt and John C. Hall (New York: Dutton, 1979), 198–99.

5. Gallop, *Reading Lacan*, 80.

6. The issue of evaluating "Russia before Peter" resurfaced as an especially sharp problem in the famous nineteenth-century debate between Slavophiles and Westernizers. On this, see Andrzej Walicki, *The Slavophile Controversy: History of a Conservative Utopia in Nineteenth-Century Russian Thought*, trans. Hilda Andrews-Rusiecka (Oxford: Clarendon Press, 1975).

7. Nicholas V. Riasanovsky describes this change both on the part of European views of Russia and Russian views of themselves in *A Parting of Ways: Government and the Educated Public in Russia, 1801–1855* (Oxford: Clarendon Press, 1976). On Russia's crisis of self-image see also Boris Groys, "Russia and the West—The Quest for Russian

National Identity," *Studies in Soviet Thought* 43, no. 3 (May 1992): 185–98. See the discussion in chapter 10 below.

8. On eighteenth-century Russian theater and the growth of the public, see Elise Wirtschafter, *The Play of Ideas in Russian Enlightenment Theater* (DeKalb: Northern Illinois University Press, 2003); and Murray Frame, *School for Citizens: Theatre and Civil Society in Imperial Russia* (New Haven: Yale University Press, 2006), chap. 1.

9. References are to M. V. Lomonosov, *Polnoe sobranie sochinenii*, 11 vols. (Moscow: Akademiia Nauk SSSR, 1950–1983).

10. Revealing aspects of nature and rendering praise to God are further functions. Feofan Prokopovich, *Sochineniia*, ed. I. P. Eremin (Leningrad: Akademiia nauk SSSR, 1961), 233 and 341. On the debt of Sumarokov's and classicist theater to Prokopovich and school drama, see, for example, E. A. Kasatkina, "Sumarokovskaia tragediia 40-kh–nachala 50-kh godov XVIII veka," *Uchenye zapiski Tomskogo pedagogicheskogo Instituta* 13 (1955): 213–61; Iu. V. Stennik, "Istoriosofskie aspekty soderzhaniia russkoi dramaturgii XVIII veka (Zhanr tragedii)," in *XVIII vek: Sbornik 19*, ed. N. D. Kochetkova (St. Petersburg: Nauka, 1995), 73–74; and K. A. Smolina, *Russkaia tragediia: XVIII vek; Evoliutsiia zhanra* (Moscow: IMLI RAN, 2001). This connection awaits full and balanced investigation. Consciousness of Prokopovich's importance for the later tradition fell victim to the Petrine myth of origins, as the codifiers of the "new" Russian literature—Trediakovskii, Lomonosov, and Sumarokov—mostly denied connection to the earlier baroque, syllabic poetic tradition.

11. V. I. Chernyshev, ed., *Slovar' sovremennogo russkogo literaturnogo iazyka* (Moscow: Akademiia Nauk SSSR, 1960), vol. 10, column 96–97. This is a common ambiguity in titles of medieval Russian works, characteristic of an era before the modern notion of "fiction." In modern Russian, the basic meaning of *povest'* is the genre of the short story.

12. As Cynthia Whittaker suggests, history writing of the era was considered as "a branch of literature or as a practical extension of philosophy." See chap. 5 in her *Russian Monarchy: Eighteenth-Century Rulers and Writers in Political Dialogue* (DeKalb: Northern Illinois University Press, 2003); this quote is from 120. On the "intergeneric" dialogue between history and fiction in the Russian tradition beginning in the eighteenth century, see Andrew Baruch Wachtel, *An Obsession with History: Russian Writers Confront the Past* (Stanford: Stanford University Press, 1994).

13. The "foreword" was both an influential restatement of the classicist stylistic hierarchy, and, no less important, a defense of the vulgar tongue as a literary language, whose strength Lomonosov located in its assimilation of the Slavonic, Orthodox religious heritage. Hence Ricchardo Picchio could also refer to this as "a manifesto of confessional patriotism." See Ricardo Picchio, "'Predislovie o pol'ze knig tserkovnykh' M. V. Lomonosova kak manifest russkogo konfessional'nogo patriotizma," in *Sbornik stat'ei k 70-letiiu prof. Iu. M. Lotmana*, ed. A. Mal'ts (Tartu: Tartuskii universitet, Kafedra russkoi literatury, 1992), 142–52. 14. The word *nevedenie* here may suggest either these peoples' profound ignorance (that *they* did not know) or the fact that others do not know of *them*.

15. From Horace's fourth book of odes, number 9. Horace has "Agamemnon," for which Lomonsov uses "Atrides," the equivalent of "son of Atreus" (Atreus being Agamemnon's father). Lomonsosov also used this name to represent the heroic in an early translation of Anacreon (1738; 7:14) and in passages translated from the *Iliad* (8:160–62). An echo of this passage also occurs in Ia. B. Kniazhnin's "K Kniagine Dashkovoi, Pis'mo

na sluchai otkrytie Akademii Rossiiskoi [1793]" in *Izbrannoe*, ed. A. P. Valagin (Moscow: Pravda, 1991), 338.

16. The corpus of tragedies analyzed in this chapter include Sumarokov's works plus selected plays by Lomonsov, Rzhevskii, Maikov, Kheraskov, Nikolev, and Kniazhnin, which form a coherent body of work. On this see especially G. A. Gukovskii's "O sumarokovskoi tragedii," which first attempted to define the features of the "Sumarokov system" and contrast it to that of French classicism (*Rannie raboty po istorii russkoi poezii XVIII veka* [Moscow: Iazyki russkoi literatury, 2001], 214–28); Gukovskii coined the term "Sumarokov school" in reference to the broader poetic tradition he began (40–71); on this, see also his *Russkaia literatura XVIII veka* (Moscow: Aspekt Press, 1998), chap. 4. While there are differences in various scholars' approaches to tragedy, and minor modifications to Sumarokov's model, as a group the plays nevertheless preserve formal and generic coherence. The critical works listed below also propose several periodizations and divisions and note developments within the tradition. Kheraskov's plays perhaps most stretch the limits of the tragic genre, but have been included insofar as they share fundamental features, representing what Michael Green has called "Sentimentalism in its Classicist Stage." See his "Diderot and Kheraskov: Sentimentalism in its Classicist Stage," in *Russia and the West in the Eighteenth Century*, ed. A. G. Cross (Newtonville, MA: Oriental Research Partners, 1983), 206–13.

On Russian classicist tragedy and the Sumarokov tradition, see V. N. Vsevolodskii-Gerngross, *Istoriia russkogo teatra*, ed. A.V. Lunacharskii, 2 vols. (Leningrad: Tea-kino-pechat', 1929); Hans-Bernd Harder, *Studien zur Geschichte der russischen klassizistischen Tragödie, 1747–1769* (Wiesbaden: Otto Harrassowitz, 1962); I. Z. Serman, *Russkii klassitsizm: Poeziia, drama, satira* (Leningrad: Nauka, 1973), chap. 6; Iu. V. Stennik, *Zhanr tragedii v russkoi literature: Epokha klassitsizma* (Leningrad: Nauka, 1981); Smolina, *Russkaia tragediia*; and Ioakhim [Joachim] Klein, *Puti kul'turnogo importa: Trudy po russkoi literature XVIII veka* (Moscow: Iazyki slavianskoi kuk'tury, 2005), 263–87 and 361–92. Stennik, *Zhanr tragedii*, 163–67, includes a useful listing of all Russian tragedies with dates of first staging and publication.

17. Cf. G. N. Moiseeva, *Drevnerusskaia literatura v khudozhestvennom soznanii i istoricheskoi mysli Rossii XVIII veka* (Leningrad: Nauka, 1980), 149. A very important indigenous prototype was Feofan Prokopovich's "tragicomedy" *Vladimir* (1705), whose importance for the later tradition deserves further study.

18. Moiseeva has examined this question in chapter 3 of *Drevnerusskaia literatura*, although her focus is almost exclusively on the written (historical) sources for Russian tragedy rather than the nature of writers' interest in that history.

19. Eleanor F. Jourdain, *Dramatic Theory and Practice in France, 1690–1808* (New York: B. Blom, 1968), 125–26; this refers to his two historical tragedies, *Zaire* and *Tancrède*. Jourdain cites a small number of other classicist historical tragedies on French themes by Chénier and Lemercier, acknowledging that it was Voltaire who pointed the way to the nineteenth century's flowering of historical drama (126, 138, 154). On *Zaire's* great popularity in Russia, see P. R. Zaborov, *Russkaia literatura i Vol'ter: XVIII–pervaia tret' XIX veka* (Leningrad: Nauka, 1978), 37, and Levitt, *Early Modern Russian Letters*, 362–64. On the Sumarokov-Voltaire-Shakespeare connection, see also "Sumarokov's Russianized 'Hamlet': Texts and Contexts," chap. 5 in the same volume.

20. Stennik, "Istoriosofskie aspekty," 71.

21. At the same time, as Wachtel notes, tragic dramatists made no claim to historical accuracy (*An Obesssion with History*, 21).

22. For a recent discussion of tragedy's "*antiistorizm*" or "*vneistorizm*," see Smolina, *Russkaia tragediia*, chap. 6. Smolina proposes a Christian reading as the key to the problem.

Because of this orientation on the present, many critics, especially in the Soviet period, have put undue emphasis on classicist tragedy as allegorical political commentary, focusing on those aspects that may be seen as critical of the state. While historical tragedies could offer commentary on contemporary political concerns, they were, first of all, fundamentally pro-government, reflecting the Petrine program of enlightenment from above and serving as what Cynthia Whittaker defines as "advice literature" addressed to the monarch (*Russian Monarchy*, 88–89 and passim). As in the odes, classicist tragedy aimed at self-assertion on a universal scale, and its audience was conceived more broadly than that small circle of cognoscenti to whom Aesopian hints would have been addressed. For an analysis of the Aesopian mode as a closed communicative system (based on material from the Soviet period), see Lev Loseff, *On the Beneficence of Censorship: Aesopian Language in Modern Russian Literature* (Munich: O. Sagner, 1984).

23. In 1802 Karamzin noted Sumarokov's poor reputation, but still tried to give him credit as a founding father. Among the weaknesses of his tragedies, Sumarokov "attempted more to describe *feelings* than to present *characters* in their aesthetic and moral truth . . . ; he did not attempt [*ne dumal*] to correlate their traits, deeds, or language with the character of their age" (N. M. Karamzin, *Sochineniia v dvukh tomakh*, ed. Iu. M. Lotman and G. P. Makogonenko [Leningrad: Khud. Lit., 1984], 2:170). On the problem of historicism as regards eighteenth-century Russia, with special emphasis on Karamzin, see *Problemy istorizma v russkoi literature konets XVIII–nachalo XIX v.*, XVIII vek 13, ed. A. M. Panchenko and G. P. Makogonenko (Leningrad: Nauka, 1981).

24. In chapter 5 I draw attention to this play's anachronistic framing of theological issues.

25. Stennik, "Istoriosofskie aspekty," 82; for a dissenting view, see Smolina, *Russkaia tragediia*, chap. 6.

26. Page references refer to: (1) "Trag." = V. A. Zapadov and P. E. Bukharin, eds. *Russkaia literatura, vek XVIII: Tragediia* (Moscow: Khudozhestvennaia literatura, 1991), available online at: <http://www.pushkinskijdom.ru/> under "Elektronnye publikatsii"; (2) "DS" = A. P. Sumarokov, *Dramaticheskie sochineniia*, ed. Iu. V. Stennik (Leningrad: Iskusstvo, 1990); and (3) "PSVS" = A. P. Sumarokov, *Polnoe sobranie vsekh sochinenii v stikhakh i proze*, ed. N. I. Novikov, 10 vols. (Moscow: Universitetskaia tipografiia, 1781–1782). In a few places I have made minor changes in the quotes from *Dramaticheskie sochineniia*, restoring the eighteenth-century punctuation; see, for example, note 34.

27. This perspective on the tragic protagonist is quite different from that of Racine, one of Sumarokov's important models, insofar as Racine's characters struggle with the shame and intractability of their own evil desires. Sumarokov's indebtedness to French classicist tragic models is clear, even while Gukovskii, Harder, Klein, and other scholars cited in note 11 have described differences in the Russian and French tragic systems (see also note 39 below). On the role of vision in Corneille and Racine, see the first two essays in Jean Starobinski, *L'oeil vivant: Corneille, Racine, La Bruyère, Rousseau, Stendhal*, rev. ed., Collection Tel 301 ([Paris]: Gallimard, 1999), which are absent from the English translation (*The Living Eye*, trans. Arthur Goldhammer, Harvard Studies in Comparative Literature 40 [Cambridge: Harvard University Press, 1989]).

28. G. A. Gukovskii's "O sumarokovskoi tragedii," in *Rannie raboty*, 214–28 remains the best formal analysis of Sumarokov's plays; see also the works cited in note 16.

On the contrast with baroque theatricalism, see also the discussion in Levitt, "Sumarokov's Russianized 'Hamlet': Texts and Contexts," in *Early Modern Russian Letters*, chap. 5.

29. See for example Lurana O'Malley, "Catherine the Great's Operatic Splendor at Court: 'The Beginning of Oleg's Reign,'" *Essays in Theatre/Etudes Théâtrales* 17, no. 1 (1998): 33–51, and her *The Dramatic Works of Catherine the Great: Theatre and Politics in Eighteenth-Century Russia* (Aldershot, England: Ashgate, 2006).

30. See the discussion in Gukovskii, *Rannie raboty*, 40–71, esp. 54.

31. Cf. in Sumarokov's *Hamlet*: "Ia bedstviem svoim khochu sebia iavit'" ("I want to manifest myself by means of my misfortune") (PSVS 3:3).

32. Cf. Gertrude in *Hamlet* (PSVS 3:82), a more explicitly "Christian" play, who notes that suicide is a sin, both against the law and "divine statute" (this in the context of considering suicide as an alternative to repentance).

33. A. N. Radishchev, *Puteshestvie iz Peterburga v Moskvu: Vol'nost'*, ed. V. A. Zapadov (St. Petersburg: Nauka, 1992), 55; translation based on Aleksandr Radishchev, *A Journey from St. Petersburg to Moscow*, trans. Leo Wiener, ed. Roderick Page Thaler (Cambridge, Harvard University Press, 1958), 123. Radishchev's reference is to Cato the Younger (95–46 BC), the Roman statesman, Stoic philosopher, and orator, who commits suicide rather than accede to Caesar's despotic rule. "The words of the dying Cato" most likely refers to Joseph Addison's tragedy *Cato* (1713), cited directly earlier in the text, but may also refer to Gottsched's *The Dying Cato* (1732), itself in part an adaptation of Addison's play.

This passage is a good example of the ethical system of tragic drama taken as a guide for civic behavior. Radishchev's own suicide, much debated in the scholarly literature, seems a prime example. See Iu. M. Lotman's discussion in "The Decembrist in Everyday Life: Everyday Behavior as a Historical-Psychological Category," in Iu. M. Lotman and B. A. Uspenskii, *The Semiotics of Russian Culture*, ed. Ann Shukman (Ann Arbor: Dept. of Slavic Languages and Literatures, University of Michigan, 1984), 71–124. In this passage, note also the issues of being a "man" and striving for "greatness" discussed below. Suicide also appears as a positive act of civic virtue in Ia. B. Kniazhnin's *Rosslav* and *Vadim Novgorodskii*.

34. The original text has no hyphen between "gde" and "libo," and suggests not that Ilmena will see Truvor "somewhere" but that it is possible she will see him in the afterlife (i.e., she has some doubt). See PSVS, 3:17.

35. Gukovskii, "O sumarokovskoi tragedii," 75.

36. In Maikov's *Femist and Hieronima*, for example, the heroine is to be put to death, but is saved; imprisoned, then let out of the dungeon, she escapes from the city, and then is captured by enemy forces; she is finally stabbed by her nemesis, the evil Magomet. As Klein points out in reference to Lomonosov's tragedies, this kind of tragic conflict hinges on changes in "external" circumstances (e.g., who is in power, what the king decides) rather than reflect conflicts that are personally connected to the inner lives of the characters, as they are, for example, in Racine (*Puti kul'turnogo importa*, 286–87). From the perspective of our analysis, the characters' inner crises are thus completely externalized and made evident. This privileging of "moral clarity" over psychological complexity (Klein, 286), where particularizing "psychology" itself is a mark of evil, is characteristic of classicist tragedy. On the denial of the "personal," see also chapter 5 (in regard to Dashkova and Derzhavin). On the externalization of the psyche as exhibited in eighteenth-century Russian portraiture, see Gennadii Vdovin, *Stanovlenie "IA" v russkoi kul'ture XVIII veka i iskusstvo portreta* ([Moscow]: Nash dom, 1999).

294 Notes to Pages 96–104

37. On Sumarokov's spare use of imagery, see Gukovskii, *Rannie raboty*, 54, and Zita D. Dabars, "The Similes of Sumarokov, Karamzin, and Derzhavin" (PhD diss., Indiana University, 1971), 18, 52, 63.

38. "Hades" would probably be a better translation, since these are explicitly pagan rather than Christian characters, and Sumarokov is not suggesting that Osnelda and Khorev are in any way evil.

39. Cf. Sumarokov's satires "O blagorodstve" and "O chestnosti" (PSVS 6:356–58 and 366–68); A. P. Sumarokov, *Izbrannye proizvedeniia*, ed. P. N. Berkov (Leningrad: Sovetskii pisatel', 1957), 189–91, 193–95. For Sumarokov and the dramatists analyzed here, the issues of "nobility" and "honor" often hinged on the problematic connection between noble birth and merit, with merit and social utility—true to the spirit of the Petrine reforms—defining true worth.

The complex of ideas associated with honor in eighteenth-century Russian social, political, and ethical thought still awaits full exploration. Nancy S. Kollmann has analyzed the crucial place of honor in pre-Petrine, sixteenth- and seventeenth-century Russia in *By Honor Bound: State and Society in Early Modern Russia* (Ithaca: Cornell University Press, 1999). Its transmutation in the new social and political realities of the eighteenth century, with their new European influences (e.g., the salon values of the "honnête homme") was clearly a complex one. Gukovskii and Serman connect the notion of "honor" in Sumarokov's tragedies to Montesquieu's *Spirit of the Laws*, which associates honor with monarchial systems of rule that are supported by an aristocracy (in opposition to despotism, which functions through fear and erodes aristocratic values); this distinction holds quite true for the plays analyzed in this chapter (Gukovskii, *Russkaia literatura*, 123–24; Serman, *Russkii klassitsizm*, 122–23). Gukovskii himself refers to tragedy as a "school of noble honor" (*Russkaia literatura*, 135–38). For a social-psychological approach to the issue of noble honor, see E. N. Marasinova, *Psikhologiia elity rossiskogo dvorianstva poslednei treti XVIII veka: Po materialam perepiski* (Moscow: Rosspen, 1999).

Another cultural-anthropological model that may be relevant is the notion of "guilt" and "shame" cultures, the latter being (as in classicist tragedy) concerned with external appearance and others' opinions. This distinction was first articulated by E. R. Dodds, applying "shame culture" to ancient Greek heroic culture (in *The Greeks and the Irrational* [Berkeley: University of California Press, 1951]); Ruth Benedict applied it to modern Japan in *The Chrysanthemum and the Sword: Patterns of Japanese Culture* (Boston: Houghton Mifflin, 1946). See chapter 5, p. 140.

40. Martial bravery (*muzhestvo*) is clearly gendered male (*muzh*), but in the play is contrasted not so much with female timidity (for example, Sumarokov, *Dramaticheskie sochineniia*, 345, war as gendered male, and women's hearts tremble in fear) but rather to *varvarstvo* (noble and enlightenment versus savage and tyrannical behavior).

41. This moral position, at times associated with pastoral retreat into a private sphere, began to become popular in the mid-eighteenth century, became widespread with sentimentalism, and reached a crescendo in the Romantic era (e.g., Pushkin's famous line: "Ty tsar'—zhivi odin"). For an interesting case study of the issue, see Thomas Newlin, *The Voice in the Garden: Andrei Bolotov and the Anxieties of Russian Pastoral, 1738– 1833* (Evanston: Northwestern University Press, 2001).

42. See, for example, the fifth epistle of Trediakovskii's *Feoptiia*, analyzed in the next chapter, which examines the nature of the soul and its connections to the body. For an attempt to rehabilitate eighteenth-century "psychological thought," see V. A. Kol'tsova, *Psikhologicheskaia mysl' Rossii: Vek prosveshcheniia* (St. Petersburg: Aleteiia, 2001). See also note 36.

43. On Lavater in Russia, see Edmund Heier, *Studies on Johan Caspar Lavater (1741–1801) in Russia*, Slavica Helvetica 37 (New York: Peter Lang, 1991). Lavater's physiognomy combines a faith in scientific positivism with profound mysticism, a combination also seen in many later eighteenth-century Russian intellectuals (e.g., Novikov's Freemasons, among whom his works were popular).

44. The use of deception and self-deception is a standard, traditional plot device in comedy, which, as David J. Welsh notes, was also the case in Russia (*Russian Comedy, 1765–1823* [The Hague; Mouton, 1966], 108). This is reflected in many titles such as *Pridanoe obmanom, Rogonosets po voobrazheniiu, Pritvornaia sumasshedshaia, Pritvornaia nevernost', Obmanschchik* (*Dowery by Deception, The Imagined Cuckold, The Pretend Madwoman, Sham Infidelity, The Deceiver*), etc. Russian comedy and satire offer a further rich area in which the ideas proposed in this chapter and this book may be further analyzed and refined. Of special interest are the comedies concerning the narcissistic personality and that of the vain, self-glorifying writer ("*samokhval*") and the analogous material from the Russian "satirical journals." On the former, see Joachim Klein, "Poet—samokhval: 'Pamiatnik' Derzhavin i status poeta v russkoi kul'ture XVIII veka," in *Puti kul'turnogo importa*, chap. 16.

45. This is the "fainthearted" response, as opposed to a purposeful ethically (and religiously) grounded retreat (cf. note 41). The conflict between these two positions is played out in Sumarokov's drama *The Hermit*, whose genre appellation clearly separates it from mainstream tragedy. See the discussion in chapter 6 below and in Levitt, *Early Modern Russian Letters*, chap. 6.

46. At the end, Gikarn saves Artistona, refusing to kill her and thereby lying to Femida: "Ia vzial to na sebia i lgat' byl prinuzhden" ("I took this on myself and was forced to lie") (Sumarokov, *Dramaticheskie sochineniia*, 186).

47. See, for example, David Hermann, "Being Untrue: The Pretence of Neoclassical Tragedy in Sumarokov's *Dmitrij samozvanec*," delivered at the December 29, 2001, AATSEEL National Convention, New Orleans (abstract is available at: <http://aatseel.org/program/aatseel/2001/abstracts/Herman.html>). Hermann confronts what he considers the "distinctly mixed message" of the play's attitude toward deception. My argument here developed in dialogue with Hermann's.

48. See also his monologue at the end of act 2, in which he declares his love—and hate—for his tormented self, and also speaks of wanting to escape from his murderous, self-destroying self.

49. F. M. Dostoevskii, *Polnoe sobranie sochinenii*, 33 vols.(Leningrad: Nauka, 1972–1990), 14:229. The ontological (aesthetic and ethical) status of evil is one of Dostoevskii's central preoccupations, and this is a key statement.

50. This underscores the character of classicist "tragedy" as fundamentally non-tragic (in the original or classical sense of the word), insofar as it realizes (externalizes, makes visible) the inalienable goodness of existence and relegates evil to oblivion. See the discussion in Levitt, *Early Modern Russian Writers*, 90, 95–97.

51. For two recent readings of eighteenth-century Russian theater and its relationship to the state that stress its positive, civic function, see Whittaker, *Russian Monarchy*, chaps. 6–7, and Wirtschafter, *The Play of Ideas*, chap. 6. Whittaker stresses the plays' function as "advice literature," addressed to the throne, while Wirtschafter explores drama's cognitive function for Russian noblemen, arguing that "Like children's play, eighteenth-century Russian theater allowed people to examine themselves and their society free of responsibility for the social dilemmas represented" (52). See also her discussion of the problem of asserting a Russian public sphere in "A State in Search of a People: The

Problem of Civil Society in Imperial Russia," in *Eighteenth-Century Russia: Society, Culture, Economy; Papers from the VII International Conference of the Study Group on Eighteenth-Century Russia*, ed. Roger Bartlett and Gabriela Lehmann-Carli (Munich: LIT-Verlag, 2007), 373–81.

52. An exception is Kniazhnin's *Vadim Novgorodskii*, which pits monarchial against republican government; see the discussion below.

53. For some recent discussions, see Philip J. Ayres, *Classical Culture and the Idea of Rome in Eighteenth-Century England* (New York: Cambridge University Press, 1997); David Walker, "Addison's *Cato* and the Transformation of Republican Discourse in the Early Eighteenth Century," *Journal for Eighteenth-Century Studies* 26, no. 1 (2003): 91–108; and Susan Maslan, "The Dream of the Feeling Citizen: Law and Emotion in Corneille and Montesquieu," *SubStance #109* 39, no. 1 (2006): 69–84.

54. In general, we may agree with Gukovskii's statement that Sumarokov's tragedies have "the character of a panegyric to individual virtues," and are "meant to inspire ecstasy in the viewer in the face of virtue, to act on his emotional receptivity, . . . to correct the viewers' souls and not their minds, and also not [to rectify] the state apparatus" (Gukovskii, "O sumarokovskoi tragedii," 220–21).

55. For a recent attempt to describe the change in Russian theater, see Catherine Schuler, *Theatre and Identity in Imperial Russia* (Iowa City: University of Iowa Press, 2009), who argues (we think, unfairly) that before the nineteenth century the theater "was marginal to Russian social and cultural life" (21).

56. *Russkii vestnik* 4 (1810): 119, as quoted in Zapadov and Bukharin, *Russkaia literatura, vek XVIII*, 710.

57. There is some ambiguity in the use of the word "*samovlastie*," a calque from the Greek "autocracy"; on the one hand, Catherine consistently reserved autocratic power for herself; on the other—as in this case—when wielded by tyrants the term takes on a negative connotation, and may even be translated as "despotism," which also implies power based in the individual. See also chapter 5, note 64.

58. See note 51.

59. These plays were: *Nachal'noe upravlenie Olega* (*The Start of Oleg's Reign*, 1787) and *Iz zhizni Riurika* (*From the Life of Riurik*, 1786). On them, see Lurana O'Malley's works cited in note 29.

60. Wachtel, *An Obsession with History*, 30. The stakes were raised by the fact that Riurik established the dynasty that ruled Russia until 1598, and that the "calling of the Varangians" depicted in the play was the subject of the so-called "Normanist controversy" (on which see note 71).

61. Wachtel, *An Obsession with History*, 27; cf. O'Malley, *Dramatic Works*, 141.

62. Wachtel's argument is that the similarities to her historical works were so great as to challenge her readers to compare versions.

63. Wachtel, *An Obsession with History*, 34.

64. E. R. Dashkova, *The Memoirs of Princess Dashkova*, ed. Kyril Fitzlyon (Durham: Duke University Press, 1995), 239.

65. The notion that a ruler's virtue and merit overruled dynastic or other legitimacy had been a staple of Russian classicist tragedy even before Catherine came to the throne, so what Catherine was doing was not new, although the self-referential nature of her allegory was.

66. Dashkova, *Memoirs*, 238. "The Hermitage" is a reference to Catherine's own palace theater built in 1783–1787. Of course, Dashkova had good reason to argue that

the play was innocuous, as Catherine's wrath fell directly on her for publishing the play.

67. William B. Edgerton, "Ambivalence as the Key to Kniazhnin's Tragedy 'Vadim Novgorovskii,'" in *Russia and the World of the Eighteenth Century*, ed. Roger P. Bartlett, Anthony Glenn Cross, and Karen Rasmussen (Columbus, OH: Slavica Publishers, 1988), 306–15; this passage is on 311.

68. Ibid., 308–9.

69. Ibid., 312–13. In the play's own terms, however, everyone (including Ramida) acknowledges her "sacred duty" to obey Vadim, that is, it is not seen in political terms.

70. The king versus the oligarchs is a central political conflict, for example, in A. A. Rzhevskii's *Podlozhnyi Smerdii* (*The False Smerdius*), in which a group of grandees plots to take over the usurped throne of Persia in the name of the people but without their involvement. In contrast, Sumarokov's *Dimitrii the Pretender* explicitly rejects rule by grandees in favor of autocracy. On this, see also chapter 5, note 65.

71. This was the subject of the famous "Normanist Controversy," when Lomonosov and historian Vasilii Tatishchev challenged German historians at the Academy of Sciences (Gottlieb Siegfried Bayer, Gerhard Friedrich Müller, and August Ludwig Schlötzer) who, citing the chronicles, argued for the "foreign" (Scandinavian) origins of Riurik and Russia's first dynasty. This gave the issues debated in Catherine's plays and *Vadim of Novgorod* even greater topicality. For a useful recent survey of the controversy, which has continued among Russian, Ukrainian, Polish, as well as non-Slavic historians and linguists, see Roman Zakharii, "The Historiography of Normanist and Anti-Normanist Theories on the Origins of Rus ': A Review of Modern Historiography and Major Sources on the Varangian Controversy and Other Scandinavian Concepts of the Origins of Rus '" (PhD diss., University of Oslo, 2002).

72. While the Russian ocularcentrism of the odes and tragedies implied an idealized model of human nature, and especially of the ruler, the alternative model of the "Ecclesiastes paradigm," described in chapter 6, took the more skeptical position that "there is not a righteous man on earth who does what is right and never sins" (Ecclesiastes 7:20).

73. In Lacanian terms the choice is between submitting to the comforting yet stifling control of the mother and to the illusions of the mirror-stage or facing the new challenges and anxieties of what Lacan calls the "Name-of-the-Father," the transition from the imaginary into the symbolic realm of adapting to social demands. In terms of Habermas's notion of a "public sphere," the question concerns moving from a "representative [that is, essentially symbolic] public sphere" to a "literary public sphere" and into a full-fledged political public sphere, which Russia arguably has never achieved. See Jürgen Habermas, *The Structural Transformation of the Public Sphere: An Inquiry into a Category of Bourgeois Society* (Cambridge: MIT Press, 1991). For the problem of its application to Russia, see Wirtschafter's discussion in the works cited in note 51.

74. It is suggestive that many of those who took part in the Decembrist Revolt had adopted a code of behavioral ethics taken in part from classical (and classicist) tragedy; see Iu. M. Lotman, "The Decembrist in Everyday Life." As argued in chapter 5, Princess Dashkova's stringent ethical demands and clashes with Catherine also reflected the values of tragedy, and gravitated in a similar direction as the Decembrists, toward a bid for political independence.

## 5: Virtue Must Advertise

1. "O istinnom blagopoluchii," *Sobesednik liubitelei rossiiskogo slova* 3 (1783), 24–34; quoted in E. R. Dashkova, *O smysle slova "vospitanie": sochineniia, pis'ma, documenty*, ed. G. I. Smagina (St. Petersburg: Dmitrii Bulanin, 2001), 130.

2. This argument about the early modern quest for "approbativeness" is indebted to Arthur O. Lovejoy, *Reflections on Human Nature* (Baltimore: Johns Hopkins Press, 1961).

3. H. Montgomery Hyde, *The Empress Catherine and Princess Dashkov* (London: Chapman & Hall, 1935), 261, cited in A. Woronzoff-Dashkoff, *Dashkova: A Life of Influence and Exile* (Philadelphia: American Philosophical Society, 2008), xxix.

4. See Patricia Ann Meyer Spacks, *Imagining a Self: Autobiography and Novel in Eighteenth-Century England* (Cambridge: Harvard University Press, 1976), chap. 1, esp. 13–16. As she writes, "one may feel that the central character of an autobiography has created a self, then written the book to validate the creation" (16). In the case of a false claim by Edward Gibbon, Spacks notes that the "power to reveal character increases if one realizes that the episode derives from imagination rather than memory" (2).

5. The very title of Dashkova's memoir, *Mon histoire*, which may mean both "My Story" and "My History," suggests the blurring of individual and historical perspectives.

6. This despite the fact that Dashkova's autobiography was written in French. See Kelly Herold, "Russian Autobiographical Literature in French: Recovering a Memoiristic Tradition (1770–1830)" (PhD. diss., University of California, Los Angeles, 1998); and Iu. M. Lotman and V. Iu. Rozentsveig, *Russkaia literatura na frantsuzskom iazyke: frantsuzskie teksty russkikh pisatelei XVIII–XIX vekov* (Vienna: Gesellschaft zur Förderung slavistischer Studien, 1994). The use of French, of course, may also be seen as an aspect of Dashkova's self-image, and may reflect one of her main goals: to defend Russian prestige in Europe, as part of the branch of literature that came to be known as "Russica." On the particular writers Dashkova challenges, see V. A. Somov, "'Prezident trekh akademii': E. R. Dashkova vo frantsuzskoi 'Rossike' XVIII veka," in *E. R. Dashkova i A. S Pushkin v istorii rossii*, ed. L. V. Tychinina (Moscow: MGI im. E. R. Dashkovoi, 2000), 39–53.

7. Volumes could be penned on the uses of display and the conscious manipulation of image and ideology during her reign. Catherine was arguably no less a formidable mythological influence than Peter the Great, although her myth and myth-making have only recently begun to attract scholarly interest. See Simon Dixon, *Catherine the Great* (Harlow, England: Longman, 2001), chaps. 3–5; Richard Wortman, *Scenarios of Power: Myth and Ceremony in Russian Monarchy*, vol. 1, *From Peter the Great to the Death of Nicholas I* (Princeton: Princeton University Press, 1995); A. L. Zorin, *Kormia dvuglavogo orla—: literatura i gosudarstvennaia ideologiia v Rossii v poslednei treti XVIII–pervoi treti XIX veka* (Moscow: Novoe literaturnoe obozrenie, 2001); and Vera Proskurina, *Creating the Empress: Politics and Poetry in the Age of Catherine II* (Brighton, MA: Academic Studies Press, 2011). See also K. Dianina, "Art and Authority: The Hermitage of Catherine the Great," *Russian Review* 63, no. 4 (2004), 630–54. These studies also help to chart the development of state ideology in Russia. While clearly to some extent an extension of Petrine cultural practices, one wonders about the qualitative changes of state doctrine under Catherine that contributed to the more explicitly proclaimed state ideology of "Official Nationality" in the 1830s–1840s, which was, paradoxically, predicated on a reversal of Catherine's Enlightenment practices.

8. Dixon, *Catherine the Great*, 41.

9. *Voltaire and Catherine the Great: Selected Correspondence*, ed. and trans. Antony Lentin (Cambridge: Oriental Research Partners, 1974), 10. The full story of Catherine's cultural politics has yet to be told. On the "construction of her image" in art see Erin McBurney, "The Portrait Iconography of Catherine the Great: An Introduction," *Study Group on Eighteenth-Century Russia Newsletter* 34 (2006): 22–27, and her forthcoming Columbia University dissertation.

10. Transparency in politics suggests openness, freedom of information, and accountability under the law, all of which Catherine publicly stressed. See the discussion in chapter 8. Catherine's insistence on virtue and transparency certainly contributed to her posthumous reputation as a "Tartuffe in skirts" (Pushkin's phrase) due to the dramatic shift in her political position in the later part of her reign.

11. On Catherine's quest for visibility, see David M. Griffiths, "To Live Forever: Catherine II, Voltaire, and the Pursuit of Immortality," in *Russia and the World of the Eighteenth Century*, ed. Roger P. Bartlett, Anthony Glenn Cross, and Karen Rasmussen (Columbus, OH: Slavica Publishers, 1988), 446–68; and Dixon, *Catherine the Great*, chap. 3.

12. See V. N. Alekseev, "Kniaginia E. R. Dashkova i G. R. Derzhavin: Istoriia vzaimootnoshenii," in *E. R. Dashkova i A. S. Pushkina*, 13–18; and Igor' Efimov, "Rossiei pravit' nelegko (Memuary Derzhavina i Dashkovoi, k 250-letiiu so dna rozhdeniia oboikh)," in *Gavrila Derzhavin, 1743–1816*, ed. Efima Etkind and Svetlana El'nitskaia (Northfield, VT: Russkaia shkola Norvichskogo universiteta, 1995), 330–40. On the basis of the memoirs, Efimov argues the identity of their political beliefs, although Derzhavin was more of a staunch backer of autocracy than Dashkova, who as an associate of the so-called "Panin Party" advocated some degree of power-sharing between the monarch and Russian aristocracy.

13. Notably, both Dashkova and Derzhavin idolized the early Catherine but subsequently had difficult relations with her; while in her memoirs Dashkova downplays their disagreements, Derzhavin—who immortalized Catherine in poetry—is at pains to avoid suspicions of flattery. On Dashkova's "triple defense," see Marcus Levitt, "Virtue Must Advertise: Dashkova's 'Mon histoire' and the Problem of Self-Representation," in *The Princess and the Patriot: Ekaterina Dashkova, Benjamin Franklin, and the Age of Enlightenment*, ed. Sue Ann Prince (Philadelphia: American Philosophical Society, 2005), 39–56, reprinted in Marcus Levitt, *Early Modern Russian Letters: Texts and Contexts* (Boston: Academic Studies Press, 2009), chap. 19; parts of this article are incorporated into the present chapter.

14. Monika Greenleaf, "Performing Autobiography: The Multiple Memoirs of Catherine the Great (1756–1796)," *The Russian Review* 63, no. 3 (July 2004): 407–26; this passage is on 410. This view might be somewhat revised in application to Russia, where individualism was moderated by subordination to state service, although as we will see this subordination seamlessly coincided with a staunch belief in universal Enlightened values. In these terms, autobiography was a privileged site at which individual achievement and enlightened social imperatives came together in a very public way.

15. *The Russian Journals of Martha and Catherine Wilmot, . . . 1803–1808*, ed. Edith Helen Vane-Tempest-Stewart and H. M. Hyde (London: Macmillan, 1934), 211. A "Farmer General of the Empire" is something like a minister of finances, the official in charge of taxes and revenue.

16. Judith Vowles contrasts Catherine the Great's ability to reconcile "the claims of worldly society and the intellectual life" to Dashkova's rejection of "feminine" social pursuits (e.g., the life of the salon) in favor of serious "male" interests. See "The 'Feminization' of

Russian Literature: Women, Language, and Literature in Eighteenth-Century Russia," in *Women Writers in Russian Literature*, ed. Toby W. Clyman and Diana Greene (Westport, CT: Greenwood Press, 1994), 40–44. Irina Savkina, however, sees a basic similarity in their memoirs as examples of "self-justification and self-assertion." See her *Razgovory s zerkalom i zazerkal'em: Avtodokumental'nye zhenskie teksty v russkoi literature pervoi poloviny XIX veka* (Moscow: Novoe literaturnoe obozrenie, 2007), 76–87.

17. In sharp contrast, Derzhavin's close friend and younger colleague I. I. Dmitriev (*Vzgliad na moiu zhizn'* [1895, repr., Cambridge: Oriental Research Partners, 1974]) apologizes from page one for comparing himself to "significant people" (*znachitel'nye liudi*) in writing his memoir and emphasizes that his writing is fulfilling a debt to his friends. He consistently professes his weaknesses and his "impudence" in wanting to write. For a comparison between Dmitriev's and Derzhavin's autobiographical writings and a useful discussion of Derzhavin's text, see Donald Loewen, "Placing the Poet in the Prose Autobiographies of Ivan Dmitriev and Gavrila Derzhavin," *Canadian Slavonic Papers* 47, nos. 1–2 (2005): 23–47; and his "Questioning a Poet's Explanations: Politics and Self-Presentation in Derzhavin's 'Footnotes' and Explanations," *Russian Review* 64, no. 3 (July 2005): 381–400.

18. As M. M. Safonov describes her predicament, "Dashkova had the courage to be a personality . . . at a time when only one person in this autocratic country had the right to be a personality—Catherine II" ("Ekaterina malaia i ee 'Zapiski,'" in *Ekaterina Romanovna Dashkova: Issledovaniia i materialy*, ed. A. I. Vorontsov-Dashkov [St. Petersburg: Dmitrii Bulanin, 1996], 21). This is the Dashkova who heroically challenged tyrants and who stood up for enlightened ideals. Dashkova's uncompromising insistence on her own moral authority itself reflected an uncomfortably authoritarian claim on virtue; see the discussion in Levitt, *Early Modern Russian Letters*, 386–87. However, Dashkova would not admit to any contradiction between Catherine's regime and the moral imperative, although as Safonov's argument suggests, Dashkova's "courage to be a personality" is not far from the Decembrists' bid for power.

19. For a different perspective on Dashkova, see Barbara Heldt, *Terrible Perfection: Women and Russian Literature* (Bloomington: Indiana University Press, 1987), 69–71, who stresses the "blending" of Dashkova's public and private selves. Savkina (*Razgovory s zerkalom*, 3) shrewdly notes that for Dashkova, "the retreat into private life is a kind of exile, a form of forcible *non*-participation in the public sphere ([thus] one might say that for Dashkova 'the private is political')." On the status of the private sphere for Dashkova, see below.

One manuscript of Derzhavin's *Zapiski* is labeled *Zapiska* (memorandum) (G. R. Derzhavin, *Sochineniia*, ed. Ia. K. Grot [1864–1883; repr., Cambridge: Oriental Research Partners, 1973], 6:413), which has led some commentators to consider Derzhavin's memoir a kind of bureaucratic document.

20. Richard Wortman, introduction to G. R. Derzhavin, *Perepiska (1794–1816) i "Zapiski"* (1871; repr., Cambridge: Oriental Research Partners, 1973), 2–3. Writers' insistence on equating personal and universal merit was also a central problem in establishing the norms of literary usage, and made literary critical discourse of mid-century Russia notoriously acrimonious. See my discussion in *Early Modern Russian Letters*, chap. 4.

21. On Derzhavin's use of the third person, see Loewen, "Questioning a Poet's Explanations."

22. Derzhavin, *Sochineniia*, 6:516, 6:621, 6:640, 6:673.

23. A. P. Sumarokov, *Polnoe sobranie vsekh sochinenii v stikhakh i proze*, ed. N. I. Novikov, 10 vols. (Moscow: Universitetskaia tipografiia, 1781–1782), 6:361–62. Henceforth references will be to "PSVS."

24. See, for example, the passage from Lomonosov, (*Polnoe sobranie sochinenii*, 11 vols. [Moscow: AN SSSR, 1950–1983]), 8:38, cited above in chapter 3, page 57. In this passage "cursed pride" is associated with deception, false reputation of the kind tragic villains might strive for, blindness, tyranny, and evildoing. As in Sumarokov's essay, it is also linked in the desire to "overtop supreme (or divine) power," and to the satanic, as those who refuse to take part in this deception are threatened with death. Also as in Sumarokov's essay, the supreme exemplar (good or bad) is the ruler.

25. V. M. Kruglov (*Imena chuvstv v russkom iazyke XVIII veka* [St. Petersburg: Institut lingvisticheskikh issledovanii RAN, 1998], 12–28) traces the development of a positive notion of *noble* pride (*blagorodnaia gordost'*) in the eighteenth century by considering how older negative connotations were overturned. Kruglov notes that the vocabulary of pride was influenced by French as calques (e.g., гордиться—être fier de, orgueil) and in some cases via the adaptation ("secularization") of slavonicisms.

26. In Sumarokov's "Artistona," for example, *slavoliubie* and *gordost'* are equated as bad things that pervert vision:

> О славолюбие! О гордость! Вы всему
> Причиной стали днесь несчастью моему!
> О, как прибыток злой, ты очи ослепляешь!
> Ты нрав и естество по воле превращаешь!
>
> [O glory-seeking! O pride! You have become / The reason for my current misfortune! / O, you evil (desire for) gain, how you blind my eyes! / You pervert customs and nature at your will!]

(A. P. Sumarokov, *Dramaticheskie sochineniia*, ed. Iu. V. Stennik [Leningrad: Iskusstvo, 1990], 154.) On the notion of "evil profit" see below.

27. Lomonosov, *Polnoe sobranie*, 7:188.

28. Adam Smith, *The Theory of Moral Sentiments*, ed. D. D. Raphael and A. L. Macfie (Indianapolis: Liberty Fund, 1984), 309. For an eloquent expression of this idea in verse, see Edward Young's *Love of Fame the Universal Passion* (1726–1728).

29. Sumarokov, PSVS 10:152.

30. For a modern restatement of this case, see Albert O. Hirschman, *The Passions and the Interests: Political Arguments for Capitalism Before Its Triumph* (Princeton: Princeton University Press, 1997).

31. See, for example, John D. Bishop, "Adam Smith's Invisible Hand Argument," *Journal of Business Ethics* 14, no. 3 (March 1995): 165–80, esp. 68. Cf. this point in Radishchev: "Virtues are either individual or social. Individual virtue grows out of gentleness, kindness, and compassion, and its root is always good. The impetus toward social virtue frequently arises from vanity and ambition [*tshcheslaviia i liubochestiia*]." (A. N. Radishchev, *Puteshestvie iz Peterburga v Moskvu: Vol'nost'*, ed. V. A. Zapadov [St. Petersburg: Nauka, 1992], 53).

32. E. R. Dashkova, *O smysle slova*, 129–30.

33. See her short translation from this work published in 1774 entitled "Society Must Serve the Well-Being of its Members" (*O smysle slova*, 93–94), in which the case is also made for enlightened self-interest (*samoliubie*) as the basis for social and individual good. D'Holbach's work came out anonymously, so as Smagina suggests, it is not possible to say for sure whether Dashkova knew the author's identity (*O smysle slova*, 377). In any

case, the bogeyman of atheism did not become a serious threat until a later period. On the compatibility of natural and supernatural views at the time, see for example Andrew Kahn, "Epicureanism in the Russian Enlightenment: Dmitrii Anchikov and Atomic Theory," in *Epicurus in the Enlightenment*, ed. Neven Leddy and Avi S. Lifschitz (Oxford: Voltaire Foundation, 2009), 119–36, in which he argues that despite his adoption of materialism, Anchikov was not an atheist.

34. For a recapitulation of this Orthodox anthropological notion see Vladimir Lossky, *In the Image and Likeness of God* (Crestwood, NY: St. Vladimir's Seminary Press, 1974), esp. chap. 6.

35. The notion derives from Philippians 2:6–8. Although as a theological concept it may derive from Protestant theology, it has become an accepted term in Russian Orthodoxy, popularized by such works as G. P. Fedotov's *A Treasury of Russian Spirituality* (New York: Sheed & Ward, 1948) and his *The Russian Religious Mind* (Cambridge: Harvard University Press, 1946). For a revisionist reading, see Jostein Børtnes, "Russkii kenotizm: K pereotsenke odnogo poniatiia," in *Evangel'skii tekst v russkoi literatury XVIII–XX vekov: Tsitata, reministsentsiia, motiv, siuzhet, zhanr*, ed. Vladimir N. Zakharov (Petrozavodsk: Izdatel'stvo Petrozavodskogo Universiteta, 1994), 1:61–65.

36. A case in point is Metropolitan Gavriil Petrov, who in his public career as a grandee of Catharine the Great's court "consistently promoted the integration of Christian teaching with the ideology of the Enlightenment" while "in his private life . . . was an ascetic who supported monasticism" and advocated "a return to patristic ascetic traditions." (Viktor M. Zhivov, "Gavriil Petrov (Petr Petrovich Shaposhnikov)," in *Early Modern Russian Writers, Late Seventeenth and Eighteenth Centuries*, Dictionary of Literary Biography 150, ed. Marcus C. Levitt [Detroit: Gale Research, 1995], 274).

37. This contrasts with its translation as "Orthodoxy," meaning "correct doctrine."

38. "Slava" may also occasionally suggest bad reputation or rumor (e.g., *durnaia slava, besslavie*), but these meanings probably derive from translations of "fame."

39. Grigorii D'iachenko, comp., *Polnyi tserkovno-slavianskii slovar'* (Moscow: Izdatel'skii otdel Moskovskogo Patriarkhata, 1993), 613; Maks Vasmer, *Etimologicheskii slovar' russkogo iazyka*, 4 vols. (Moscow: Progress, 1986–1987), 3:664 and 3:680; Vladimir Ivanovich Dal', *Tolkovyi slovar' zhivago velikoruskago iazyka*, 4 vols. (1880–1882; repr., Moscow: Russkii iazyk, 1978–1980), 4:221–23 and 4:227–28. Detractors of Russia often linked "Slav" and "slave," which may also be connected; see for example the etymology given in J. A. Simpson and E. S. C. Weiner, comp., *Oxford English Dictionary*, 2nd ed. (Oxford: Clarendon Press, 1989), online at <http://www.oed.com>. On the image of Slavs as slaves, see Marshall Poe, *A People Born to Slavery: Russia in Early Modern European Ethnography, 1476–1748*, Studies of the Harriman Institute (Ithaca: Cornell University Press, 2000).

40. E. R. Dashkova, *The Memoirs of Princess Dashkova*, ed. Kyril Fitzlyon (Durham: Duke University Press, 1995), 263–64. Unfortunately, there still is no fully authoritative version of Dashkova's memoir, which exists in two basic variants. On the history of the problem, see A. Woronzoff-Dashkoff's "Afterword" in Dashkova, *Memoirs*, 284–89, and his "Additions and Notes in Princess Dashkova's *Mon histoire*," *Study Group on Eighteenth-Century Russia Newsletter* 19 (1991): 15–21. See also the recent composite French text: *Mon histoire: Mémoires d'une femme de lettres russe à l'époque des Lumières*, ed. Alexandre Woronzoff-Dashkoff, Catherine LeGouis, and Catherine Woronzoff-Dashkoff (Paris: L'Harmattan, 1999).

41. Cf. "The past afforded me a certain consolation. The disinterestedness and

firmness of my character gave me a peace of mind which in itself may not have been an adequate substitute for all else, but at least it supplied me with pride and courage to sustain me in my adversity." Dashkova, *Memoirs*, 252. The influence of Stoicism in eighteenth-century Russia remains to be studied.

42. Ibid., 96.

43. On the problem of Dashkova's use of masks, see A. Woronzoff-Dashkoff, "Disguise and Gender in Princess Dashkova's *Memoirs*," *Canadian Slavonic Papers* 33, no. 1 (1991): 61–74, and Levitt, *Early Modern Russian Letters*, 394–96.

44. Derzhavin does concede his hot-blooded temperament, but as has been noted, he often seems secretly proud of his readiness to fight. A characteristic example is when he is called to be a second at a duel, which is halted by reconciliation, but he ends up almost fighting a duel himself with the other second over whether or not it is shameful *not* to duel! (Derzhavin held that it wasn't [Derzhavin, *Sochineniia*, 541]).

45. Ibid., 572, 442, 443, 574.

46. See G. A. Gukovskii, "Russkaia literaturno-kriticheskaia mysl' v 1730–1750 gody," *XVIII vek* 5 (1962), 98–128; and Levitt, *Early Modern Russian Letters*, chap. 4.

47. Here and below I have changed Fitzlyon's "Pavel I" to "Paul I." The quote is from Dashkova, *Memoirs*, 251.

48. Dashkova herself makes the comparison that "my life could serve a subject for a heartrending novel" (E. R. Dashkova, *Zapiski; Pis'ma sester M. i K. Vil'mot iz Rossii*, ed. S. S. Dmitriev, comp. G. A. Veselaia [Moscow: Izd-vo Moskovskogo universiteta, 1987], 35), and the memoir is punctuated with theatrical terms (tragedy, farce, comedy, the stage, etc.). This sort of reference is common in autobiographical writing, but my suggestion is that Dashkova shared the special self-image and discourse about virtue and self-display that were reflected in other Russian classicist literary works, especially tragedy.

49. Dashkova, *Memoirs*, 242.

50. Understandably, the harsh demands of virtue took a big toll on Dashkova and on those around her; but that is another story. Our focus here is on the cultural values of the epoch to which Dashkova gave voice.

51. Derzhavin, *Sochineniia*, 568.

52. In Slavonic, a "*liubochestivyi*" person is one who "loves to give honor according to merit," and the verb *liubochestvovati(sia)* means "to render honors, to raise up, to glorify, to be glorified" (D'iachenko, *Polnyi tserkovno-slavianskii slovar'*, 293). *Liubochestie* in Slavonic may also have the negative meaning of vainglory, but clearly Sumarokov does not mean this. The notion of honor (*chest'*) has complex roots and associations, and may, for example, be connected with political (aristiocratic, monarchial) systems, as in Montesquieu, as well as with other ancient social and religious values. On the latter, see most recently, Kerry Sabbag, "Fame Tropes in Old East Slavic Hagiography," *Slavic and East European Journal* 52, no. 4 (Winter 2008): 545–60, and the works cited there. See also the works cited above in chapter 4, note 39.

A Church Slavonic dictionary defines the word "honor" (*chest'*) as signifying "everything exalted in itself, as opposed to that which is low and base. In relationship to people honor is the expression of the highest worthiness. The highest degree of worthiness is manifested in making oneself like the divine essence [*v upodoblenii sushchestvu Bozhiiu*]. God, Who is the truth, possesses the highest degree of honor, and therefore what is true is also honorable. . . . Falsehood is dishonorable [*bezchestno*], i.e., it is a direct negation of any worthiness" (D'iachenko, *Polnyi tserkovno-slavianskii slovar'*, pribavlenie, 1118–19).

53. Lomonosov, *Polnoe sobranie*, 8:815–16. See the discussion of *"umnoe zrenie"* in chapter 2.

54. Lomonosov, *Polnoe sobranie*, 7:189.

55. Cf. Sumarokov's desolate protest to Catherine the Great for her failure to support him during his clash with Moscow Governor-General P. S. Saltykov: "I have nothing from my dramas except for naked honor; so why try and take that away from me as well?" (G. P. Makogonenko, ed., *Pis'ma russkikh pisatelei XVIII veka* [Leningrad: Nauka, 1980], 139.) "Naked honor" was all the remuneration he expected, but he considered it his right. See my discussion of this issue in connection with the system of patronage in *Early Modern Russian Letters*, chap. 10.

56. See Griffiths, "To Live Forever"; and Anna Lisa Crone, *The Daring of Deržhavin: The Moral and Aesthetic Independence of the Poet in Russia* (Bloomington, IN: Slavica, 2001).

57. The conflict between secular and religious heroism came up in the later nineteenth century around the raising of a monument to Pushkin, which as it were brought Horace's "Exegi monumentum" (in Pushkin's version—"Ia pamiatnik sebe vozdvig nerukotvornyi") to realization. See Marcus Levitt, *Russian Literary Politics and the Pushkin Celebration of 1880*, Studies of the Harriman Institute (Ithaca: Cornell University Press, 1989), 23–26 on the poem and 82–83 on ecclesiastical opposition to the monument.

58. On the Roman notion of civic virtue, see E. A. Judge, "Contemptu famae, contemni virtutes: On the Morality of Self-Advertisement Among the Romans" and "The Literature of Roman Political Self-Advertisement," in *The First Christians in the Roman World: Augustan and New Testament Essays*, ed. James R. Harrison (Tübingen: Mohr Siebeck, 2008), 59–65 and 66–71.

59. In *Classical Culture and the Idea of Rome in Eighteenth-Century England* (New York: Cambridge University Press, 1997), Philip J. Ayres shows this idea's profound influence on the English aristocracy and analyzes it as a response to the Revolution of 1688.

60. See the reference to "shame" and "guilt cultures" in chapter 4, note 39.

61. *The Works of John Adams . . . with a Life of the Author . . . by His Grandson Charles Francis Adams* (Boston: Little, Brown, 1851), 6:243, cited by Lovejoy, *Reflections*, 202–3. Cf. Radishchev's questioning of Roman practices connected to the love of honors in the *Journey*, where it is associated with servility (Radishchev, *Puteshestvie*, 54).

62. On the changing view of Rome in eighteenth-century Russia, see Andrew Kahn, "Readings of Imperial Rome from Lomonosov to Pushkin," *Slavic Review* 52, no. 4 (Winter 1993): 745–68.

63. Montesquieu, *Spirit of the Laws*, book 3, chaps. 6–7.

64. Lomonosov, *Polnoe sobranie*, 6:171. In the eighteenth century, *samoderzhavie* (commonly translated as "autocracy") did not usually have the negative connotation of "despotism." Note that in the following passage Sumarokov uses "autocracy," "monarch," and "tsarist power" as equivalents. Karamzin also used the terms *"samoderzhavie"* and "monarchy" interchangeably. See Richard Pipes, "The Background and Growth of Karamzin's Political Ideas Down to 1810," in *Karamzin's Memoir on Ancient and Modern Russia: A Translation and Analysis*, ed. Richard Pipes (Ann Arbor: University of Michigan Press, 2005), 61–62. See also Isabel de Madariaga's discussion of the term in her review of A. I. Filiushkin, *Tituly russkikh gosudarei* (Moscow: Al'ians-Arkheo, 2006) in *Kritika: Explorations in Russian and Eurasian History* 8, no. 3 (2007): 651–60.

65. DS = Sumarokov, *Dramaticheskie sochineniia*. Joachim Klein (*Puti kul'turnogo importa: Trudy po russkoi literature XVIII veka* [Moscow: Iazyki slavianskoi kul'tury,

2005], 377–90) analyzes Sumarokov's play as a response to A. A. Rzhevskii's *Polozhnii Smerdii* (*The False Smerdius*) (1769), in which a cabal of nobles reclaims the throne from a pretender. He claims that the two plays represent a debate over the authors' allegedly differing political positions. However, it may also be argued that they depict two different political cultures, Persian and Russian, and that what is appropriate for an "oriental despotism" might not be so for Russia as a polity founded on monarchist principles.

66. Cf. Matthew 6. On the change from Roman to Christian value systems in reference to self-advertisement, see Judge, "Contemptu famae."

67. See V. F. Khodasevich, *Derzhavin: A. Biography*, trans. Angela Brintlinger, Publications of the Wisconsin Center for Pushkin Studies (Madison: University of Wisconsin Press, 2007), 207 and 228–30.

68. Dashkova, *Memoirs*, 243.

69. Ibid., 88.

70. Characteristically, in *Mon histoire*, other characters often give voice to Dashkova's claims, e.g., Catherine asks the returning Bestuzhev: "Would you have thought that I would owe the throne to the young daughter of Count Roman Vorontsov?!" (Dashkova, *Memoirs*, 91)—i.e., that Dashkova was the mastermind behind Catherine's rise to power (something which historians still debate). Similarly, she bests Diderot in debate; Diderot is forced to admit that "You have upset ideas I have cherished and withheld for twenty years" (125), the Queen of England declares her a model mother (151), and so on. Derzhavin is also expansive in reporting others' high opinions of him.

71. For a useful brief survey of orders, see Iu. M. Lotman, *Besedy o russkoi kul'ture: Byt i traditsii russkogo dvorianstva, XVIII–nachalo XIX veka* (St. Petersburg: Iskusstvo-SPB, 1994), 34–37.

72. Count Roman Vorontsov was a supporter of Peter III, under whom he served as a senator, and his daughter Elizaveta Romanovna—Dashkova's sister—was Peter's mistress. For the story of their relations, see Woronzoff-Dashkoff, *Dashkova*.

73. Dashkova, *Memoirs*, 86.

74. In his comments on the exchange, Vladimir N. Alekseev notes that as head of the order of St. Catherine, Catherine the Great's decoration must have been especially valuable, and presumes that after she gave it away, she must have had an even more valuable one made for herself since she remained the order's chief. "Nagrady kniagini E. R. Dashkovoi," unpublished paper presented at the tenth *Dashkovskie chteniia*, Moscow, March 26, 2004, page 4.

75. Dashkova, *Memoirs*, 100.

76. The chapter containing the episode with the order of St. Catherine ends with a strange comic inversion. First, when Dashkova sees Grigorii Orlov, whom she had realized was Catherine's lover, wearing the Order of St. Alexander at mass, she goes up to her uncle and Count Razumovskii (with whom the empress had presumably conferred on this mark of distinction), and calls them "a couple of fools." Then she describes an episode a few days later when Ivan Betskoi—who had also been awarded the St. Alexander order—threatened to take it off in front of the empress because, it seems, he felt that he had not been given the credit for raising her to the throne! Catherine appeased him by appointing him caretaker of the royal jewels for the coronation, and she and Dashkova had a good laugh over this "tiring madman" (ibid., 88–89). These incidents suggest a carnivalized inversion of Dashkova's problem, with Orlov a moral inversion—as a man out for personal, material gain, and Betskoi a comic image of her serious (tragic) self-image.

77. Justification of his actions in the Pugachev uprising, which had been officially questioned, may have been Derzhavin's initial motive for writing the memoir, insofar as his actions had come under official suspicion; see Khodasevich, *Derzhavin*, chap. 3, esp. 70–74. Derzhavin's first autobiographical writing was apparently a notebook-journal that he kept during the revolt, and which is included in the *Zapiski*. Derzhavin's adventures probably served as a source for Pushkin's "The Captain's Daughter," and the poet himself was possibly a model for the hero Petr Grinev. See David Bethea and Angela Brintlinger, "Derjavine et Khodassevitsch," in *Derjavine: un poète russe dans l'Europe des Lumières*, ed. Anita Davidenkoff (Paris: Institut d'études slaves, 1994), 167–78.

78. In the case of Catherine the Great, Derzhavin's *Zapiski* perhaps makes a better comparison with her very defensive and pedantic (and anonymously published) *Antidote, ou Examen de mauvais livre superbement imprimé intitulé "Voyage en Sibérie"* (1770), than with her properly autobiographical writings. On the memoirs, see Greenleaf, "Performing Autobiography," and Hilde Hoogenboom's introduction to *The Memoirs of Catherine the Great*, trans. Hilde Hoogenboom and Mark Cruse (New York: Modern Library, 2005), ix–lxx.

79. Derzhavin, *Sochineniia*, 6:522–23.

80. Ibid., 665.

81. Ibid., 665–66.

82. Mikhail Bulgakov, *The Master and Margarita*, trans. Diana Lewis Burgin and Katherine Tiernan O'Connor (New York: Vintage Books, 1996), 241.

83. Derzhavin, *Sochineniia*, 701.

84. It is notable in passing that snuffboxes for two odes are listed in the same breath as one for a report ("*tarif*" [it is not clear what Derzhavin means]), suggesting the equivalence of writing poetry to his work as a statesman. I am not convinced that this is necessarily a devaluation of poetry, as some charge, as it seems an acknowledgement of the major role that poetry played in his advancement. For example, during one of their numerous conflicts, one of Catherine's secretaries, A. V. Krapovitskii, reported to Derzhavin that Catherine was taking his side because "she is unable to blame the author of 'Felitsa'!" (Ibid., 6:607).

## 6: The Seen, the Unseen, and the Obvious

1. On the issue of historicism, see the discussion in chapter 4 and the works cited in notes 22 and 23 of that chapter; on the term "Enlightenment Orthodoxy," see Olga Tsapina, "Pravoslavnoe Prosveshchenie—oksiumoron ili istoricheskaia real'nost'?" in *Evropeiskoe Prosveshchenie i tsivilizatsiia Rossii*, ed. S. Ia. Karp and S. A. Mezin (Moscow: Nauka, 2004), 301–13; and the works cited in chapter 1, note 21.

2. A. P. Sumarokov, *Izbrannye proizvedeniia*, ed. P. N. Berkov (Leningrad: Sovetskii pisatel', 1957), 428–29; also in A. P. Sumarokov, *Dramaticheskie sochineniia*, ed. Iu. V. Stennik (Leningrad: Iskusstvo, 1990), 249–50.

3. There is a distinctly "Protestant" aspect to the theological argument here, as there is in much of eighteenth-century Enlightenment Orthodox thinking. It is notable in this context that the modern full canonical Slavonic translation of the Bible, the so-called Elizabethan Bible, begun under Peter, was published at mid-century (its second edition of 1756 is still the basic text in use), and that the idea of translating the Bible into the vulgar tongue, which for complex political and cultural reasons was not completed for another hundred years, was also raised around this time.

4. See P. N. Berkov, "Kniga v poezii Simeona Polotskogo," *Trudy Otdela drevnerusskoi literatury* 24 (1969): 260–66; A. M. Panchenko, "Slovo i znanie v estetike Simeona Polotskogo," *Trudy Otdela drevnerusskoi literatury* 25 (1970): 232–42, his *Russkaia stikhotvornaia kul'tura XVII veka* (Leningrad: Nauka, 1973), 178; and L. I. Sazonova, *Literaturnaia kul'tura Rossii: Rannee novoe vremia* (Moscow: Iazyki slavianskikh kul'tur, 2006). These poems may be found in Simeon Polotskii, *Vertograd mnogocvetnyj*, ed. Anthony Hippisley and Lydia I. Sazonova, 3 vols. (Köln: Böhlau, 1996–2001). Afanasii Kholmogorskii's *Shestodnev* (ca. 1666) offers another example of this view of the visible world as "full of symbols," and A. I. Esiukov also connects the work's "motifs of ecstasy over the intelligent arrangement of the natural, vegetable, and animal world" to the later eighteenth-century "Enlightenment-rationalist" view of the type analyzed in this chapter (A. I. Esiukov, *Chelovek i mir v pravoslavnoi prosvetitel'skoi mysli Rossii vtoroi poloviny XVIII veka: Istoriko-filosofskie ocherki* [Arkhangel'sk: Pomorskii gos. universitet, 1998], chap. 2, esp. 33).

5. The vanity of earthly concerns is a common theme in Polotskii, for example, in his various poems on the senses and in the cycles on "Slava" and "Chelovek" (A. M. Panchenko, ed., *Russkaia sillabicheskaia poèziia XVII–XVII vv.* [Leningrad: Sovetskii pisatel', 1970], 152–53 and 163–64).

6. *Tvoreniia M. Kheraskova*, 14 vols. (Moscow, 1796–1803), 7:389.

7. F. Göpfert and M. Fainshtein, eds., *Predstatel'nitsy muz: Russkie poetessy XVIII veka* (Welmshorst: F. K. Göpfert, 1998), 152, canto 5, lines 267–72. See my discussion of this passage and the problem of sight in the poem in Marcus Levitt, *Early Modern Russian Letters: Texts and Contexts* (Boston: Academic Studies Press, 2009), chap. 18.

8. Metropolitan Platon (Levshin), "Slovo na den' vozshestviia na prestol eiia imperatorskogo velichestva," in *Pouchitel'nyia slova i drugie sochineniia* (Moscow: Gippius, 1782), 10:277. My thanks to Olga Tsapina for this reference.

9. As Grand Prince Pavel Petrovich (the future Paul I), for whom Platon served as tutor in 1763–1765, explained the essence of Platon's theology: "You assert it as a rule to always demonstrate the conformity [*soglasovanie*] of the rules and facts [*bytii*] contained in Holy Writ with natural reason, and to affirm them by means of the conclusions of healthy human reasoning." Platon (Levshin), *Raznye sochineniia*, 2nd ed. (Moscow, 1780), 7:274. Characteristically, Platon began his widely known *Catechesis* (*Pravoslavnoe uchenie*) with "Natural Knowledge of God" (*Bogopoznanie estestvennoe*), i.e., the conclusions of reason. The following two parts concern "About the Gospel Faith" and "About God's Law." For a discussion of Platon's "Enlightenment-rationalist" Orthodox theology, see Esiukov, *Chelovek i mir*, chap. 6.

10. On physicotheology, with special reference to Germany, see Wolfgang Philipp, *Das Werden der Aufklärung in theologiegeschichtlicher Sicht*, Forschungen zur systematischen Theologie und Religionsphilosophie 3 (Göttingen: Vandenhoeck & Ruprecht, 1957); and Thomas P. Saine, *The Problem of Being Modern, or, The German Pursuit of Enlightenment from Leibniz to the French Revolution* (Detroit: Wayne State University Press, 1997).

11. Saine, *The Problem of Being Modern*, 20–21.

12. Diderot and Hume were the main critics of this philosophical tradition, Diderot in the "Lettre sur les aveugles," for which he was imprisoned in 1749, and Hume in his *Dialogues Concerning Natural Religion* (1776).

13. A main proponent of this view is Philipp, *Das Werden der Aufklärung*.

14. Saine, *The Problem of Being Modern*, 37. Saine's interpretation seems particularly true for Russia, where rationalism did not gain a strong following until the

next century. Lomonosov's "Pis'mo o pol'ze stekla" ("Letter on the Utility of Glass") offers a good example of this validation of traditional values through science. A physicotheological discussion of God's greatness seen in the universe is here linked to sending "His beloved son" to earth for man's salvation (*Polnoe sobranie sochinenii*, 11 vols. [Moscow: Akademiia Nauk SSSR, 1950–1983], 8:319–22).

15. That is, more as a set of generally accepted beliefs than as a formal system, although one believed to rest on firm traditional theological supports. For my purposes, "physico-" and "natural theology" are equivalent; see for example Grigorii Kozitskii's contrast between natural theology and mythology at the start of his article "O pol'ze mifologii," *Trudoliubivaia pchela* (February 1759), 26, which precisely follows "physicotheological" formulas. For a discussion of natural religion from the point of view of the history of religion, see Peter Byrne, *Natural Religion and the Nature of Religion: The Legacy of Deism* (London: Routledge, 1989). On physicotheology in Russia, see chapters 14 and 15 in my *Early Modern Russian Letters*, parts of which are incorporated into the present argument.

16. It was published by I. Z. Serman in V. K. Trediakovskii, *Izbrannye proizvedeniia*, ed. L. I. Timofeev, notes by Ia. M. Strochkov (Leningrad: Sovetskii pisatel', 1963), 196–322, notes on 507–21. The preface was published for the first time in Vasilij Kirillovič Trediakovskij, *Psalter 1753*, ed. and commentary Alexander Levitsky (Paderborn: Ferdinand Schöningh, 1989), 455–70. The story of its failure to be published is complicated. After getting Synodal permission to publish *Feoptiia* at the Academy of Sciences typography in St. Petersburg, Trediakovskii grew frustrated at delays that may have been politically and personally motivated. He then gave the manuscript to the Synod typography in Moscow, where he asked that it be set in church rather than civil type. Despite both the Synod's second approbation and imperial approval, synodal editors objected to the work on various doctrinal matters (including its alleged heliocentrism) and effectively blocked publication. Typesetters at the Moscow typography and members of the Moscow Synodal office (*kontora*) also raised a series of objections, but these seem to have been primarily motivated by a power struggle with the Petersburg leadership.

See the documents and analysis concerning *Feoptiia* and Trediakovskii's Psalter in Trediakovskij, *Psalter 1753*, 471–517 and A. Shishkin, "Sud'ba 'Psaltyri' Trediakovskogo," also in Trediakovskij, *Psalter 1753*, 519–35. See also I. Z. Serman, "Neizdannaia filosofskaia poema V. Trediakovskogo," *Russkaia literatura* 4, no. 1 (1961): 160–68.

17. Trediakovskij, *Psalter 1753*, 467–68.

18. Albert Chérel, *Fénelon au 18e siècle en France: Son prestige, son influence* (1917; repr., Geneva: Slatkine Reprints, 1970), 258. For a thorough analysis of the text of *Feoptiia* and its sources, as well as its poetic and metrical form, see Wilhelm Breitschuh, *Die Feoptija V. K. Trediakovskijs: Ein Physikotheologisches Lehrgedicht im Russland des 18. Jahrhunderts* (Munich: Verlag Otto Sanger, 1979).

19. A. D. Kantemir, *Sochineniia, pis'ma i izbrannye perevody*, ed. P. A. Efremov, notes by V. Ia. Stoiunin, 2 vols. (St. Petersburg: I. I. Glazunov, 1867–1868).

20. See Ernest Tuveson, "Space, Deity, and the 'Natural Sublime,'" *Modern Language Quarterly* 12 (1951): 28–38. Newton's notion of nature as God's body— the "sensorium of God"—was reflected in *An Essay on Man*: "All are but parts of one stupendous whole, / Whose body nature is, and God the soul" (*Poetry and Prose of Alexander Pope*, ed. Aubrey Williams [Boston: Houghton Mifflin, 1969], 129, epistle 1, lines 267–68). On this change of perspective and its effect on English poetry, see Marjorie

Hope Nicolson, *Newton Demands the Muse: Newton's Opticks and the Eighteenth Century Poets* (Princeton: Princeton University Press, 1966).

21. It could be argued that from a Russian Orthodox perspective God's presence in nature was perceived as more immanent than in the West (cf. our discussion in chapter 3). Nevertheless, the pre-eighteenth-century baroque view as expressed by Simeon Polotskii saw that presence as hidden and allegorical and reflected a distinctly premodern view of the natural world. As Anthony Hippisley has shown in his work on the sources for *Vertograd mnogotsvetnyi*, Polotskii's principle sources were Latin and Catholic, so it may be problematic to take Polotskii as representative of Russian views; more work needs to be done on this question. For a history of Russian views of natural science before the eighteenth century and the influence of Western ideas, see B. E. Raikov, *Ocherki po istorii geliotsentricheskogo mirovozzreniia v Rossii: Iz proshlogo russkogo estestvoznaniia* (Moscow: Akademiia nauk SSSR, 1947), chaps. 1–6.

22. "IP" and page numbers refer to V. K. Trediakovskii, *Izbrannye proizvedeniia*.

23. See Henry George Liddell, Robert Scott, Henry Stuart Jones, and Roderick McKenzie, *A Greek-English Lexicon* (Oxford: Clarendon, 1976), 791. The coincidence between the Greek for "god/goddess" (θεός/θεά) and "sight" (θέα) is intriguing. Andrea Nightingale notes that in the case of *theoria* (theory), "Ever since antiquity, people have debated whether the word . . . derives from *theos* (god) or *thea* ('sight,' 'spectacle')," and cites recent discussions. See her *Spectacles of Truth in Classical Greek Philosophy: Theoria in Its Cultural Context* (Cambridge: Cambridge University Press, 2004), 45.

24. *Slovar' russkogo iazyka XVIII veka*, ed. S. G. Barkhudarov and E. E. Birzhakova (Leningrad–St. Petersburg: Nauka, 1984–), 1:80.

25. Gottsched's German translation kept Leibniz's French title word Theodicée. See Gottfried Wilhelm von Leibniz, *Herrn Gottfried Wilhelms Freyherrn von Leibniz Theodicée: Das ist, Versuch von der güte Gottes, Freyheit des Menschen und vom Ursprunge des Bösen*, trans. Johann Christoph Gottsched (1744; repr., Berlin: Akademie Verlag, 1996). Cf. also Christian Huygens's *Kosmotheoros* ("observer of the cosmos") (1698), translated into Russian as *Mirozrenie* in 1717.

26. James Herbert Davis, *Fénelon* (Boston: Twayne Publishers, 1979), 133. The argument concerning theodicy, to quote Pope's famous formulation of Leibniz's argument in *An Essay on Man*, is also an argument about vision, in particular, what we cannot see:

> All Nature is but Art, unknown to thee;
> All Chance, Direction, which thou canst not see;
> All Discord, Harmony not understood;
> All partial Evil, universal Good.
> And, spite of Pride, in erring Reason's spite,
> One truth is clear, "Whatever is, is right."

(*Poetry and Prose of Alexander Pope*, 130, epistle 1, lines 289–94.) If a basic feature of sight is to take in the whole with "one simple glance" (see below), this argument about theodicy depends on the things left unseen. Serman ("Neizdannaia filosofskaia poema," 163–64) stresses that *Feoptiia* echoes the philosophical optimism of the Leibniz-Pope-Shaftesbury tradition.

27. On Wolff's widespread influence in Russia, see Marc Raeff, "The Enlightenment in Russia and Russian Thought in the Enlightenment," in *The Eighteenth Century in Russia*, ed. J. G. Garrard (Oxford: Clarendon Press, 1973), 25–47; T. V. Artemieva and M. I. Mikshin, eds. *Khristian Vol'f i russkoe vol'fianstvo, Filosofskii vek: Al'manakh*

3 (St. Petersburg, 1998); and V. A. Zhukov, ed., *Khristian Vol'f i filosofiia v Rossii* (St. Petersburg: Russkii khristianskii gumanitarnyi institut, 2001).

28. René Descartes, *Meditations on First Philosophy*, trans. and intro. Laurence J. Lafleur (New York: Macmillan, 1951); see Lafleur's comments on xii–xiv. Husain Sarkar has recently restated this problem: "In order to prove that God exists, Descartes needs to justify the rules of logic; but in order to establish the rules of logic, Descartes needs to establish that God exists. Descartes' system is riddled with this circular argument" (*Descartes' Cogito: Saved from the Great Shipwreck* [New York: Cambridge University Press, 2003], 137). See also Bernard Williams, *Descartes: The Project of Pure Enquiry* (London: Routledge, 2005), chapter 7.

29. Stafford H. St. Cyres, *François de Fénelon* (Port Washington, NY: Kennikat Press, 1970), 254–55.

30. François de Salignac de La Mothe-Fénelon, *A Demonstration of the Existence and Attributes of God, Drawn from the Knowledge Of Nature, from Proofs Purely Intellectual, and from the Idea of the Infinite Himself*, 2nd ed. (London: W. Taylor, 1720), 1; the punctuation, orthography, and capitalization have been modernized. In Kantemir's version: "I cannot open my eyes without amazement at the wisdom and art visible in nature; the slightest glance is sufficient [samyi poslednii vid dovol'no] for the all-powerful creator to show his hand" (Kantemir, *Sochineniia*, 2:25).

31. In his phenomenological study of the senses, the philosopher Hans Jonas discusses the "one glance" and the unique power of sight to grasp "persistent existence from the transitory event of sense-affection, which sight at any moment offers in the presentation of the visual field." Hans Jonas, "The Nobility of Sight: A Study in the Phenomenology of the Senses," in *The Phenomenon of Life: Toward a Philosophical Biology* (Evanston: Northwestern University Press, 2001), 137.

32. The architecture of the heavens and its structure—like that of an inverted chalice—seem to indicate vestiges of a premodern cosmology. For example, in the sixth-century *Christian Topography* by Cosmas Indikopleusta (Koz'ma Indikoplov), which was very popular in sixteenth- and seventeenth-century Russia, the heavenly firmament (*svod*) was described as in the shape of a chalice (*chasha*). See Raikov, *Ocherki po istoriia*, 14–17.

33. Wesley Trimpi, *Muses of One Mind: The Literary Analysis of Experience and Its Continuity* (Princeton: Princeton University Press, 1983), chap. 7, esp. 130–33. In the rhetorical tradition, the epistemological issues related to various ways of acting on the audience, as Trimpi puts it, through styles oriented on "intelligibility" (reason) or on "psychagogia" (emotional persuasion).

Aristotle's ideas were adapted in the Christian context and applied to the miraculous by Augustine and Aquinas, among others. See also Peter G. Platt, "Theories of Wonder from Aristotle to the Renaissance," in *Reason Diminished: Shakespeare and the Marvelous* (Lincoln: University of Nebraska Press, 1997); and Debora K. Shuger, *Sacred Rhetoric: The Christian Grand Style in the English Renaissance* (Princeton: Princeton University Press, 1988). For a stimulating discussion of Longinus's place in eighteenth- and early nineteenth-century Russian literature, see Harsha Ram, *The Imperial Sublime: A Russian Poetics of Empire*, Publications of the Wisconsin Center for Pushkin Studies (Madison: University of Wisconsin Press, 2003).

34. *Aristotle: The Poetics; "Longinus": On the Sublime; Demetrius: On Style*, trans. W. Hamilton Fyfe (Cambridge: Harvard University Press, 1946), 125.

35. Vladimir Lossky, *The Mystical Theology of the Eastern Church* (Crestwood, NY: St. Vladimir's Seminary Press, 2002), 222–23, 208–9.

36. The distinction between Aristotelian and sublime wonder also correlates to baroque versus classicist varieties of visual experience. Notably, as part of his criticism of Lomonosov's odic poetics, Sumarokov translated the second chapter of Boileau's translation of Longinus's treatise, which criticizes inflated style and defends the role of reason in art. For the term "sublime" Sumarokov substituted "*iskusstvo vazhnosti slova*" (art of the serious word), perhaps implying a rejection of the concept. (A. P. Sumarokov, "Iz traktata Longinova, O vazhnosti slova s perevoda Boalova," *Trudoliubivaia pchela* [April 1759], 21–24). Curiously, Ram notes that Nikolai Chernyshevskii, with his mid-nineteenth-century "reality-based" (rationalist) attack on idealist aesthetics, denied the very "ontological possibility of the sublime" (*The Imperial Sublime*, 18).

37. Trimpi, *Muses of One Mind*, 32.

38. The image of "nature inscribed in the eyes" as mirrors also recalls the genre of the "speculum mundi," a medieval title for hexaemerons. See the discussion below.

39. Grigorii Palama [Gregory Palamas], *Triady v zashchitu sviashchenno-bezmolvstvuiushchikh*, trans. and ed. V. Veniaminov (Moscow: Kanon+, 2003), 82.

40. There are also elements of traditional "cataphatic" theology in *Feoptiia*, for instance the listing of God's divine names that describe His "self-revealing energies" (as opposed to His incomprehensible essence). A classic statement of the problem of naming God is Pseudo-Dionysius ("the Areopagite" or "Pseudo-Areopagite"), "The Divine Names" (*Pseudo-Dionysius: The Complete Works*, trans. Colm Luibhéid and Paul Rorem [New York: Paulist Press, 1987], 133–41), which was fully assimilated into the Eastern Orthodox tradition. See Lossky, *Mystical Theology*, 33, 39–40, 72, and 80; on the "Areopagitic" works, see 23f. *Feoptiia*'s introduction starts out with a listing of 28 divine names, reminiscent of similar lists in John Damascene and other Orthodox theologians. The Eastern Orthodox connections in Trediakovskii's work deserve further investigation.

41. Edward Young, *Night Thoughts*, ed. Stephen Cornford (New York: Cambridge University Press, 1989), Night VII, lines 1231–37.

42. J. H. S. Formey, 1747, quoted in Chérel, *Fénelon*, 264.

43. G. P. Makogonenko and I. Z. Serman, eds., *Poety XVIII veka*, 2 vols. (Leningrad: Sovetskii pisatel', 1972), 1:82.

44. Cf. Psalm 13 (14 in the Western Psalter), *Trediakovskij, Psalter 1753*, 457.

45. M. V. Lomonosov, *Polnoe sobranie sochinenii*, 11 vols. (Moscow: Akademiia Nauk SSSR, 1950–1983), 7:319.

46. See Paul MacKendrick, with the collaboration of Karen Lee Singh, *The Philosophical Books of Cicero* (New York: St. Martin's Press, 1989), chap. 20.

47. Saine, *The Problem of Being Modern*, 37. On Epicurus in eighteenth-century Russia, see Andrew Kahn, "Epicureanism in the Russian Enlightenment: Dmitrii Anchikov and Atomic Theory," in *Epicurus in the Enlightenment*, ed. Neven Leddy and Avi S. Lifschitz (Oxford: Voltaire Foundation, 2009), 119–36.

48. See Valentin Boss, *Newton and Russia: The Early Influence, 1698–1796* (Cambridge: Harvard University Press, 1972).

49. Lomonosov, *Polnoe sobranie*, 7:320–21.

50. To cite just one well-known example, John Ray's *The Wisdom of God Manifested in the Works of the Creation: In Two Parts: viz. The Heavenly Bodies, Elements, Meteors, Fossils, Vegetables, Animals, (Beasts, Birds, Fishes, and Insects) More Particularly in the Body of the Earth, its Figure, Motion, and Consistency, and in the Admirable Structure of the Bodies of Man, and other Animals, as also in their Generation . . .* [1691] (New York: Garland, 1979).

312 Notes to Pages 169–75

51. Marcus Tullius Cicero, *The Nature of the Gods*, trans. P. G. Walsh (New York: Clarendon Press, 1997), 81.

52. See Trimpi, cited in note 33.

53. Lossky, *Mystical Theology*, 209, cited above in chapter 3. It seems likely that Aristotle's tale as related by Cicero was the direct or indirect source of Symeon's comparison.

54. Ibid.

55. Sumarokov, *Stikhotvoreniia dukhovnyia* (St. Petersburg: Akademiia Nauk, 1774), 11.

56. L. F. Lutsevich, *Psaltyr' v russkoi poezii* (St. Petersburg: Dmitrii Bulanin, 2002), 346.

57. Lomonosov, *Polnoe sobranie*, 4:371.

58. For example, the criticism of St. Augustine in the "Pis'mo o pol'ze stekla" ("Letter on the Utility of Glass") (1752), *Polnoe sobranie*, 8:518.

59. An influential example is William Derham's *Physicotheology: Or, A Demonstration of the Being and Attributes of God from His Works of Creation* (1713; repr., New York: Arno Press, 1977), which was translated into Russian as *Estestvennaia bogosloviia, ili Dokazatel'stvo bytiia i svoistv Bozhiikh, pocherpnutoe iz del tvoreniia*, trans. Mikhail Zavialov (Moscow: I. Lopukhin, 1784).

60. The six-part structure is also true of many other physicotheological works, including Derham's *Physicotheology*, Iermonakh Apollos (Baibakov)'s *Evgeont, ili sozertsanie v nature bozhiikh vidimykh del* (Moscow, 1782), and Edward Young's famous physicotheological poem *The Complaint: or, Night-Thoughts on Life, Death, and Immortality* (1742–1745), which was very popular in Russia. This work was "translated" into Russian several times both in prose and in eccentric paraphrases. See P. R. Zaborov, "'Nochnye razmyshleniia' Iunga v rannikh russkikh perevodakh," in *Russkaia literatura XVIII veka: Epokha klassitsizma*, ed. P. N. Berkov and I. Z. Serman (Moscow: Nauka, 1964), 269–79. Aleksandr Andreev's "translation" from French (!), entitled *Dukh ili nravstvennye mysli slavnogo Iunga, izvlechennye iz Noshchnykh ego razmyshlenii* (St. Petersburg: Gos. Med. Kollegii, 1798), appended thirteen poems, including Lomonosov's two "Meditations."

On the hexaemeron tradition in Russia, see the commentaries to *Shestodnev Ioanna ekzarkha Bolgarskogo*, G. S. Barankova and V. V. Mil'kov, eds. (St. Petersburg: Aleteiia, 2001). See also G. S. Barankova, ed., *Drevnerusskaia kosmologiia* (St. Petersburg: Aleteiia, 2004), esp. 158–170.

61. Lomonosov, *Polnoe sobranie*, 4:375.

62. This latter opinion was held by the author of the anonymous translation from German "Razmyshlenie o bozhiem velichestve, po koliku onoe prilezhnym razsmotreniem i ispytaniem estestva otkryvaetsia," *Ezhemesiachnye sochineniia k pol'ze i uveseleniiu sluzhashchie* (November 1756), 407–38. It is possible that this was the reason the publication was criticized by church authorities. See *Polnoe sobranie postanovlenii i rasporiazhenii po vedomstvu Pravoslavnogo ispovedaniia Rossiiskoi imperii* (St. Petersburg, 1912), vol. 4, no. 1532 (December 20, 1756), 272–73. However, this work's markedly rationalist perspective was not typical of most physicotheological works that appeared in Russia.

63. Levitt, *Early Modern Russian Letters*, chap. 15. The first to draw attention to the "Meditations" as physicotheological works was Walter Schamschula, "Zu den Quellen von Lomonosovs 'kosmologicher' Lyrik," *Zeitschrift für Slavische Philologie* 34,

no. 2 (1969): 225–53; see also Kirill Ospovat,"Nekotorye konteksty 'Utrennogo . . . ' i 'Vechernego razmyslenija o bozhiem velichestve'," *Study Group on Eighteenth-Century Russia Newsletter* 32 (2004): 39–56; and Erik Egeberg, "'Slava Bozhiia ot prirody'— ustami russkikh poetov XVIII veka (Lomonosov, Sumarokov, Derzhavin)," in *Life and Text: Essays in Honour of Geir Kjetsaa on the Occasion of his 60th Birthday*, ed Erik Egeberg, Audun J. Mørch, and Ole Michael Selberg (Oslo: [Universitetet i Oslo, Slavisk-baltisk avdeling], 1997), 111–19. In his unpublished article "Osnovanie liubomudriia," Sumarokov gave what could be taken as a prose paraphrase of the physicotheological argument of the "Morning Meditation" (A. P. Sumarokov, *Polnoe sobranie vsekh sochinenii v stikhakh i proze*, ed. N. I. Novikov, 10 vols. [Moscow: Universitetskaia tipografiia, 1781–1782], 6:287–88).

64. *brenno nashe oko*—a phrase from the "Morning Meditation." The complete line is quoted below.

65. As Lomonosov noted in his "Iz"iasneniia" to the "Slovo o iavleniiakh, ot elektricheskoi sily proiskhodiashchikh," "My ode on the northern lights . . . expresses my long-held opinion that the northern lights might be produced for the movement of ether [*efir*]" (Lomonosov, *Polnoe sobranie*, 2:123). A. A. Morozov suggests that the notion of "frozen steam" refers to the theory of Christian Wolff. See M. V. Lomonosov, *Izbrannye proizvedeniia*, ed. A. A. Morozov and M. P. Lepekhin, 3rd ed. (Leningrad: Sovetskii pisatel', 1986), 510. See also Ospovat, "Nekotorye konteksty," 39–40.

66. References in the text are to Lomonosov, *Polnoe sobranie*. The translation of this passage and some of the following lines from the "Meditations" are from Harold B. Segel, ed. and trans., *The Literature of Eighteenth-Century Russia: An Anthology* (New York:, Dutton, 1967), 1:205–8.

67. Zhiva Benchich uses these terms to describe the poems' central tension in "Barokko i klassitsizm v *Razmyshleniiakh o bozhiem velichestve* Lomonosova," *Russica Romana* 3 (1996): 27–50.

68. See note 65.

69. Majesty is the most outstanding feature of physical reality, combining as it does both power and wisdom. According to physicotheologists, these three traits, together with a fourth—goodness—are the principal attributes of God-the-Creator. (See, for example, "Razmyshlenie o bozhiem velichestve. . . ," from *Ezhemesiachnye sochineniia*, 409.) Notably, in Kokorev's anthology, which went through many editions, the poem mistakenly ends not with a question mark but with an exclamation point, which gives the positive implication of the line added emphasis (A. V. Kokorev, *Khrestomatiia po russkoi literature XVIII veka*, 4th ed. [Moscow: Prosveshchenie, 1965], 140).

70. From the time of their publication in Lomonosov's *Sochineniia* of 1751, the "Meditations" were published together and under the rubric of "spiritual odes." In eighteenth-century publications the "Morning Meditation" preceded the "Evening," but in many later editions the order was reversed. On the basis of metrical analysis, V. M. Zhirmundskii concluded that the "Evening Meditation" was written first ("Ody Lomonosova 'Vechernee' i 'Utrennee razmyshlenie o Bozhiem velichestve': K voprosu o datirovke," in *Russkaia literatura vosemnadtsatogo veka i ee mezhdunarodnye sviazi: Pamiati Pavla Naumovicha Berkova* [Leningrad: Nauka, 1975], 27–30). It is clear to all readers of these poems, starting with the titles, that they are closely connected, and one may suggest that they intentionally comprise a cycle. L. V. Pumpianskii asserted that together with the "Oda, vybrannaia iz Iova, glavy 38, 39, 40 i 41," and several stanzas from the "Oda na pribytie . . . Elizavety Petrovny iz Moskvy v Sanktpeterburg 1742

goda," they form a certain unity ("Ocherki po literature pervoi poloviny XVIII veka," *XVIII vek* 1 [1935], 108). Notably, the "Job" theme often came up in physicotheological literature, which includes many "paraphrases of particular chapters of Job" both in verse and prose. As in Lomonosov's paraphrase, the central problem is the justification of divine justice.

71. See, for example, the discussion of this issue in Marcus Levitt, "Was Sumarokov a Lockean Sensualist? On Locke's Reception in Eighteenth-Century Russia," in *Early Modern Russian Letters*, chap. 8. See also Radishchev's consideration of this problem, cited in chapter 8 below.

72. In this regard it seems significant that in the *Rhetoric*, right after the section that includes the "Evening Meditation" (presented as an example of logical expansion [*rasprostranenie*], § 270), there follows the "conditional syllogism" in which the arguments proving God's existence from *The Nature of the Gods* are presented (Lomonosov, *Polnoe sobranie*, 7:315–19).

73. The following final lines of the poem also emphasize the parallel between divine and human. Man is characterized in terms of creation, and is himself a creator, i.e., a microcosm or image of God (cf. "Vsegda *tvoriti* nauchi," "*Tvorets!*," "tvoiu *tvar*'").

74. Cf. Vladimir Lossky's discussion of revelatory darkness in "Darkness and Light in the Knowledge of God," in *In the Image and Likeness of God* (Crestwood, NY: St. Vladimir's Seminary Press, 1974), chap. 2.

75. Breitschuh, *Die Feoptija*, 127; Serman in IP 515.

76. Breitschuh, *Die Feoptija*, lists echoes of the Psalms and other biblical texts on 478–81. Notably, Trediakovskii planned to publish *Feoptiia* and his Psalter simultaneously.

77. It seems possible that this or a similar canonical text served as a source for Fénelon, and it is not beyond conjecture that Cicero in turn was a direct or indirect source for John of Damascus.

78. Ioann Damaskin, *Istochnik znaniia: Tvoreniia prepodobnago Ioanna Damaskina*, trans. and ed. D. E. Afinogenov, A. A. Bronzov, et al. (Moscow: Indrik, 2002), 160 (book 1, chap. 3, entitled "The Proof of God's Existence").

79. See note 70.

80. Lomonosov, *Polnoe sobranie*, 7:324.

81. Naming the divine force has been, of course, a fundamental problem of monotheism since its beginning (see Exodus 3). Hence also the general problem of eighteenth-century religious terminology, and the often slippery distinctions between "natural religion," "deism," "theism," etc. See also the discussion in chapter 8 on Radishchev.

82. As Wolfgang Phillip puts it, "The 'proof' for a physicotheologian is in reality an irrational act of confession" (*Das Werden der Aufklärung*, 102).

83. Lomonosov, *Polnoe sobranie*, 7:324–26.

84. *Trediakovskij, Psalter 1753*, 457. Trediakovskii also cites Psalm 13 (14) in his discussion of the atheist ideas against which he wrote his poem, 463.

85. These works are mostly founded on a double negative—the rejection of evil (i.e., the vanity of worldly pursuits)—but as discussed in chapter 4, this adds up to a positive. In what terms this positive value—the "wisdom" the author of Ecclesiastes seeks—should be understood, whether Stoic, Epicurean, Christian, or other, is a subject of interpretation. Ecclesiastes embodies a paradoxical "unity of profound and consistent pessimism with peace of mind and fear of God" (Thorleif Boman, *Hebrew Thought Compared with Greek* [London: SCM Press, 1960], 200).

86. On the possible Stoic influence on Ecclesiastes, see Dominic Rudman, *Determinism in the Book of Ecclesiastes* (Sheffield, England: Sheffield Academic Press, 2001), chaps. 1 and 9. On the interpretive problem, see Doug Ingram, *Ambiguity in Ecclesiastes* (New York: T. & T. Clark International, 2006).

87. On the master metaphor, see for example G. V. Sinilo, "Ekklesiast kak metatekst epokhi barokko," *Barokko i klassitsizm v istorii mirovoi kul'tury: Materialy Mezhdunarodnoi nauchnoi konferentsii*, Seriia "Symposium" 17 (St. Petersburg: Sankt-Peterburgskoe filosofskoe obshchestvo, 2001), 32–38. Online at: <http://anthropology.ru/ru/texts/sinilo/baroque_08.html>. According to Iu. Z. Zvezdina, for Dimitrii Rostovskii (Tuptalo)'s sermons, "The most general basis for composing comparisons [*upodobleniia*] and reading secret 'hieroglyphs' in nature were the words from 1 Corinthians (13:10, 12): 'When perfection comes. . . . Now we see but a poor reflection as in a mirror; then we shall see face to face.' The entire system of Christian emblems of the sixteenth to seventeenth centuries was based on this [text]." Iu. Z. Zvezdina, "Predmet i obraz v propovedi svt. Dimitriia Rostovskogo," Gosudarstyvennyi zapovednik "Rostovskii kreml'," online at <http://www.rostmuseum.ru/publication/historyCulture/2000/zvezdina01.html>.

These poems provided support for A. A. Morozov's argument against the very existence of "Russian classicism" ("Sud'by russkogo klassitsizma," *Russkaia literatura* 1 [1974]: 19–20). They formed part of a larger body of verse that offered a conscious alternative to the triumphal ode, and often incorporated themes and formal elements from Horatian and Anacreontic poetry. G. N. Pospelov describes this verse as "philosophical-elegaic," "developed on the basis of rejecting the utopian ideals of progressive noble statism [*gosudarstvennosti*]" and more amenable to the smaller, more personal scale of lyric poetry than to "epic or dramatic realization" (that is, to triumphal odes and tragedies). (*Problemy literaturnogo stilia* [Moscow: MGU, 1970], 188–89).

88. Among the poems in this category we could include: Sumarokov, "Chasy" ("Na suetu cheloveka") (1759); "Oda k M. M. Kheraskovu" ("Oda na suetu mira") (1763); "Iz Sirakha. Glava 3" (1758); "Iz glavy 5" (1763); "O strashnom sude" (1768); "[Oda] O dobrodeteli" ("Vse v pustom lish' tol'ko tsvete, / Chto ni vidim, sueta") (1769); "O liublenii dobrodeteli" (1769); "O strashnom sude" (1769); "Poslednii zhizni chas" and "Chas smerti" (1759); "Plachu i rydaiu" (1760); "Zriashche mia bezglasna" (1769). A. A. Rzhevskii, "Stans" ("Napolnen vek nash suetoiu") (1760); "Rondo" ("Ne luchshe l' umeret', ty chasto rassuzhdaesh'") (1761); "Oda 1" ("Dolgo l' prel'shchat'sia") (1761); "Stansy 1" ("Tot, kto goniaetsia za svetskoi suetoiu"); "Stansy 2" ("O, sueta suet! O, smertnyi, slabyi, strastnyi!") (1761); "Sonet" ("Nadezhdoi, suetoi, snom smertnyi nagrazhden") (1761). V. I. Maikov, "O Strashnom sude" (1763); "Oda na suetu mira, pisannaia Aleksandru Petrovichu Sumarokovu" (1775). M. M. Kheraskov, "Stans" ("Vse na svete sem prekhodit"); "Pocherpnutyia mysli iz Ekkleziasta" (1765; 2nd version 1779); "O suetnykh zhelaniiakh"; "Suety mira"; "Sueta"; "Suestnost'"; "Nichtozhnost'"; "Vremia"; "Tshcheta." On Derzhavin see below.

The above list is not meant to be complete; one could also include many Psalm paraphrases and moralizing poetry as well as translations. See also the list of poems on related themes in Andrew Kahn, "'Blazhenstvo ne v luchakh porfiry': Histoire et Fonction de la Tranquilité (*Spokojstvie*) dans la pensées et de la poésie russes du XVIIIe siècle, de Kantemir au sentimentalisme," *Révue des etudes slaves* 74, no. 4 (2003): 686–88. For Kheraskov, the *vanitas* theme was a significant part of his writing, the religious themes of which await investigation. See E. D. Kukshina's comments in "Poeziia M. M. Kheraskova. Poiski smysla zhizni," *XVIII vek* 22 (2002): 96–110; on themes from Ecclesiastes in his poetry, see the same article, 100f. See also Alexander Levitsky,"Masonic Elements in Russian Eighteenth-Century Religious Poetry: Preliminary Questions and Observations with Regard to the Theoretical Stance and Practices of Sumarokov and Kheraskov," in *Russia and the World of the Eighteenth Century*, ed. Roger P. Bartlett, Anthony Glenn Cross, and Karen Rasmussen (Columbus, OH: Slavica Publishers, 1988), 423n9; in my opinion, Levitsky overstresses the differences between Kheraskov and Sumarokov.

89. It is likely that interest in themes from Ecclesiastes was encouraged by or associated with Masonic ideas. Levitsky notes "the close connection of masonic philosophic beliefs with certain tenets of Christianity, or rather, the exploitation by Masons of canonic books of Christian worship for their own purposes [in poetry and poetic paraphrases]." He includes Ecclesiastes in their number, noting that "it is often difficult to decide just where the canonic Orthodox version of such texts end and masonic interpretation begins" ("Masonic Elements," 419).

90. As G. A. Gukovskii has shown (*Rannie raboty po istorii russkoi poezii XVIII veka* [Moscow: Iazyki russkoi kul'tury, 2001]), the period in which many of these were written—the early 1760s—was a time of widespread experimentation with genres, verse forms, and themes.

91. Makogonenko and Serman, eds., *Poety XVIII veka*, 1:207–8.

92. Virtually all of the scholarly attention to this work has been to issues of metrics and style rather than content. See, for example, K. B. Jensen and U. Møller, "Paraphrase and Style: A Stylistic Analysis of Trediakovskij's, Lomonosov's and Sumarokov's Paraphrases of the 143rd Psalm," *Scando-Slavica* 16 (1970): 57–63; A. B. Shishkin, "Poeticheskoe sostiazanie Trediakovskogo, Lomonosova i Sumarokova," *XVIII vek* 14 (1983): 232–46.

93. Cf. Ecclesiastes 4:1: "Again I looked and saw all the oppression that was taking place under the sun: I saw the tears of the oppressed—and they have no comforter; power was on the side of their oppressors—and they have no comforter." Kheraskov's reworking of Voltaire, analyzed below, leaves this passage out.

On Derzhavin's problems with his paraphrase of Psalm 81, which he entitled "Vlastiteliam i sudiiam," see his account in his *Zapiski* in G. R. Derzhavin, *Sochineniia*, ed. Ia. Grot (1871; repr., Cambridge: Oriental Research Partners, 1973), 6:695–96.

94. *Tvoreniia M. Kheraskova*, 7:232–33. The situation described in this poem recalls Bazarov's meeting with Arkadii on the haystack in chapter 21 of Turgenev's *Fathers and Sons*, when Bazarov reveals his misgivings about the pointlessness of existence. Kheraskov's poem, however, ends on a positive note. This was generally the case with European poetry on the theme, according to Barbara J. Arnason, "The Shadow of Despair: The Tradition and the Exception in Seventeenth- and Eighteenth-Century Interpretation of Ecclesiastes (and Juvenal's Satire X)," (master's thesis, Simon Fraser University, 1985), 9; online at <http://ir.lib.sfu.ca/handle/1892/7702>. According to Arnason, Juvenal's satire provided "the same conclusion that Christian interpretation claimed that the Prophet ["Kohelet," author of Ecclesiastes] arrived at" (9).

95. A. Sumarokov, *Izbrannye proizvedeniia*, ed. N. Berkov (Leningrad: Sovetskii pisatel', 1957), 89–90.

96. The dedication to M. D. Chulkov's mock novel *Prigozhaia povarikha* (The Comely Cook) burlesques the humorless moralizing of Sumarokov's and similar poems on the vanity theme, turning it into a petition for the material benefits of authorship. See S. Iu. Baranov, ed., *Povesti razumnye i zamyslovatye: Populiarnaia bytovaia proza XVIII veka* (Moscow: Sovremennik, 1989), 288. See Alexander Levitsky, "Mikhail Chulkov's *The Comely Cook*: The Symmetry of a Hoax," *Russian Literature Triquarterly* 21, part

2 (1988): 97–116. The Ecclesiastes paradigm as an exercise in truth-seeking may thus devolve into the comic as well as the tragic.

97. On the latter, see Kahn, "'Blazhenstvo.'" Many of the poems that Kahn groups under the "tranquility" theme (686–88) also belong to what we are calling the Ecclesiastes paradigm (although Kahn does not mention Ecclesiastes in his analysis).

98. On Voltaire's "pessimistic trend of the fifties," see, for example, William F. Bottiglia, "Candide's Garden," in *Voltaire: A Collection of Critical Essays* (Englewood Cliffs, NJ: Prentice-Hall, 1968), 101.

99. Arnold Ages, "Voltaire, The Marchioness of Deffand and Ecclesiastes," *Romance Notes* 8 (1966): 53–54. Eric S. Christianson, "Voltaire's Précis of Ecclesiastes: A Case Study in the Bible's Afterlife," *Journal for the Study of the Old Testament* 29, no. 4 (2005): 474. See also N. V. Zababurova, "Vol'ter i Ekklesiast," in *Drugoi XVIII vek: Materialy tret'ei nauchnoi konferentsii po problemam literatury i kul'tury (18–20 apr. 2002 g.)*, ed. N. T. Pakhsar'ian (Moscow: Ekon-Inform, 2002), 30–39.

100. In order to demonstrate the *Précis*'s fidelity to the biblical text, in the original publication Voltaire included translated phrases from the biblical text on pages facing his poem, which most later editions put in footnotes or left out.

101. We may note here that in mid-eighteenth-century Russia it was possible to see Voltaire as a solidly Christian writer, as did Sumarokov; see Levitt, *Early Modern Russian Letters*, 106.

102. See Michela Venditti, "Istolkovanie motivov iz Ekkleziasta v XVIII veke: Vol'ter v perevodakh Kheraskova i Karamzina," *XVIII vek* 24 (2008), 130–57, which focuses primarily on issues of translation.

103. *The Works of Voltaire: A Contemporary Version; A Critique and Biography*, vol. 13, *A Philosophical Dictionary*, ed. Tobias Smollett, trans. William F. Fleming (Akron, OH : Werner, 1905), 244 (entry on "Solomon").

104. Voltaire, *Oeuvres completes*, 70 vols. ([Kehl:] De l'imprimerie de la société litéraire-typographique, 1784–1789), 12:269. Translation by Terry McWilliams, in Christianson, "Voltaire's Précis of Ecclesiastes," 481.

105. Kheraskov's version includes the admonition to love your wife, teach wisdom to your children, and other precepts (e.g., stanza 34) missing in Ecclesiastes (and in Voltaire's *Précis*).

106. Venditti, "Istolkovanie motivov," includes a critical edition of Kheraskov's text (148–57).

107. N. M. Karamzin, *Polnoe sobranie stikhotvorenii*, ed. Iu. M. Lotman (Leningrad: Sovetskii pisatel', 1966), 204–5. Lotman notes that Karamzin began all of his collections of poetry with this poem (394).

108. Cf. the closing lines of Karamzin's programmatic "Poeziia," which offer an ecstatic promise of ultimate "face to face" (i.e., total) vision. Karamzin, *Polnoe sobranie*, 63. Our analysis of Karamzin's poem suggests that the optimistic, ocularcentric position is also characteristic of Russian sentimentalism, which for the purposes of the argument of this book has been subsumed under "classicism." While as we will see in the next chapter the sentimentalist turn inwards could at times reject external vision, in my opinion it ultimately validated the parity between inner and outer reality and the ideal of the "selfless self."

109. Ibid, 202–3.

110. Ibid., 395. (The editor—Iu. M. Lotman—suggests unconvincingly that this note was due to pressure from censorship.)

111. Makogonenko and Serman, eds., *Poety XVIII veka*, 1:208.

112. Kahn, "Blazhenstvo," 675. However, there seems no basis for any connection to the spiritual calm (hesychia) of mystical Orthodoxy; Stoic tranquility is marked by dispassionate disregard of the senses.

113. Sumarokov, *Izbrannye proizvedeniia*, 84–85.

114. The departure from classicist and Enlightenment thematics led Walter J. Gleason to mistakenly conclude that the play is a condemnation of Eumenius's position and a warning to Russian noblemen who neglect their duties (*Moral Idealists, Bureaucracy, and Catherine the Great* [New Brunswick, NJ: Rutgers University Press, 1981], 36–38). On conformity with Sumarkov's dramatic model, see "Sumarokov's Drama 'The Hermit': On the Generic and Intellectual Sources of Russian Classicism," in Levitt, *Early Modern Russian Letters*, chap. 6.

115. Liddell and Scott, *A Greek-English Lexicon*, 721–22.

116. Sumarokov, *Polnoe sobranie*, 4:283–84; the play has been republished in Sumarokov, *Dramaticheskie sochineniia*, 434–50.

117. This was the case with Kheraskov's *Venetsiasnaia Monakhina* (*The Venetian Nun*). On this play, see Michael Green, "Italian Scandal as Russian Tragedy: Kheraskov's *Venetsiasnaia Monakhina*," in *Russia and the World of the Eighteenth Century*, 388–99.

118. Curiously, Derzhavin's irony, which in the poetry encompasses the poet himself, does not extend to the autobiographical self in the *Zapiski*, which as we saw in chapter 5 is virtually bereft of humor and self-directed criticism.

119. Derzhavin's poetry is extremely rich in visual imagery and deserves separate study. On this subject, see E. Ia. Dan'ko, "Izobrazitel'noe iskusstvo v poezii Derzhavina," *XVIII vek* 2 (1940): 166–247; Helmut Kölle, *Farbe, Licht und Klang in der malenden Poesie Deržavins*, Forum Slavicum 10 (Munich: W. Fink, 1966); and the forthcoming monograph by Tatiana Smoliarova, *Zrimaia lirika: Derzhavin* (Moscow: Novoe literaturnoe obozrenie, 2011).

120. Anna Lisa Crone, *The Daring of Derzhavin: The Moral and Aesthetic Independence of the Poet in Russia* (Bloomington, IN: Slavica, 2001). As Crone notes, this same conflict, manifested in analogous stylistic terms, occurs in Radishchev's *Journey*.

121. What we are calling "chance" is often rendered in Russian as *schastie* (счастие, щастие), which may also mean "happiness" and "luck" or "fortune," and hence has richer associations than the English.

## 7: The Icon That Started a Riot

1. Christian Metz introduced the term "scopic regime" to contrast film and theater in *The Imaginary Signifier: Psychoanalysis and the Cinema* (1975; repr., Bloomington: Indiana University Press, 1981) and it has been used not only to contrast visual experiences of other media, but also to define broader cultural, philosophical, and political conceptions of seeing. See Martin Jay, "Scopic Regime," in *The International Encyclopedia of Communication*, ed. Wolfgang Donsbach, 12 vols. (Malden, MA: Blackwell, 2008); and Jay's own use of the term in the latter sense in *Downcast Eyes: The Denigration of Vision in Twentieth-Century French Thought* (Berkeley: University of California Press, 1993). Here he refers to the "scopic regime of the Enlightenment," of "ancien regime France," and of the modern era, which he defines in terms of "Cartesian perspectivalism" (69–70, 103, and passim).

2. *Voltaire and Catherine the Great: Selected Correspondence*, ed. and trans. Antony Lentin (Cambridge: Oriental Research Partners, 1974), 121–22, based on Voltaire, *Correspondence*, ed. Theodore Besterman, 135 vols. (Geneva: Institut et musée Voltaire, 1953–1977), no. 16361. On Catherine's control of press information about the plague, see John Alexander, *Catherine the Great: Life and Legend* (New York: Oxford University Press, 1989), 156–61.

3. In the previous year she had published a vigorous (anonymous) denunciation of Abbé Chappe d'Auteroche's *Voyage en Sibérie* (1768) entitled *Antidote, ou Examen de mauvais livre superbement imprimé intitulé "Voyage en Sibérie"* (1770). See the analysis in Marcus Levitt, *Early Modern Russian Letters: Texts and Contexts* (Boston: Academic Studies Press, 2009), chap. 17. The Plague Riot also took place amid the period of the "satirical journals," another of Catherine's early attempts to expand the public sphere and use it to her advantage. On this see the discussion in Marcus Levitt, "Catherine the Great," in *Russian Women Writers*, ed. Christine Tomei, 2 vols. (New York: Garland, 1999), 1:3–10.

4. Cf. the account quoted by Bolotov: "[I]dleness, greed and accursed superstition resorted to another fabrication. The do-nothings had to concoct a miracle and start a rumor throughout Moscow that all hope was not lost, and that there was still a way to escape the plague through veneration of a certain icon." Andrei Bolotov, *Zhizn' i prikliucheniia Andreia Bolotova, opisannye samim im dlia svoikh potomkov*, 3 vols. (Moscow: Terra, 1993), 3:19.

5. *The Memoirs of Catherine the Great*, ed. Dominique Maroger, trans. Moura Budberg (London: Hamish Hamilton, 1955), 365. This is part of an extended contrast between Petersburg and Moscow, to the former's great favor.

6. A striking example of this is Antoine-Jean Gros's painting *Napoleon at the Pest House in Jaffa* (1804). On its ideological and propagandistic aims, see Thomas Crow, *Emulation: Making Artists for Revolutionary France* (New Haven: Yale University Press, 1995), 243–44; and Albert Boime, *Social History of Modern Art*, vol. 2, *Art in an Age of Bonapartism, 1800–1815* (Chicago: University of Chicago Press, 1990), 86.

The Enlightenment discursive tradition of associating superstitious religious practices with disease and infection (so dramatic in the Plague Riot) survived into the Soviet era as an anti-religious propaganda drive in 1924 that blamed the practice of kissing icons for a rural outbreak of syphilis! Daniel Peris, *Storming the Heavens: The Soviet League of the Militant Godless* (Ithaca: Cornell University Press, 1998), 85; thanks to Shirley Glade for pointing this out to me. On the other side of the coin, Archbishop Filaret, writing in the mid-nineteenth century, described the plague of 1771 not as the result of religious fanaticism, but as God's punishment for Russia's having fallen to prey to the evils of atheistic Enlightenment ("the French plague"), clearly a very anachronistic point of view. See, for example, A. M. Lidov, ed., *Chudotvornaia ikona v Vizantii i drevnei Rusi* (Moscow: Martis, 1996).

7. Lentin (*Voltaire and Catherine the Great*, 52) notes that inoculation was "at that time a controversial proceeding, indeed forbidden in France as interference with the will of Providence." On this episode, see Richard Hingston Fox, *Dr. John Fothergill and His Friends: Chapters in Eighteenth Century Life* (London: Macmillan, 1919), 88–92; W. J. Bishop, "Thomas Dimsdale and the Innoculation of Catherine the Great of Russia," *Annals of Medical History*, n.s., 4 (1932): 321–38; P. H. Clendinning, "Dr. Thomas Dimsdale and Smallpox Inoculation in Russia," *Journal of the History of Medicine and Allied Sciences* 28 (1973): 109–25; and Donald R. Hopkins, *The Greatest Killer: Smallpox in History*

(Chicago: University of Chicago Press, 2002), 65–69. The Russian court *balletmeistr* Gasparo Angiolini celebrated the event with an allegorical ballet entitled "Prejudice Defeated" ("Pobezhdennyi predrassudok"). See Iakob Shtelin [Jakob von Staehlin], *Muzyka i balet v Rossii XVIII veka*, trans. B. I. Zagurskii (Leningrad: Triton, 1935), 164–68.

8. See, for example, Lidov, *Chudotvornaia ikona*.

9. Paul Bushkovitch, *Religion and Society in Russia: The Sixteenth and Seventeenth Centuries* (New York: Oxford University Press, 1992), chaps. 4 and 5, passim.

10. See, for example, Peter Harrison, "Newtonian Science, Miracles, and the Laws of Nature," *Journal of the History of Ideas* 56, no. 4 (October 1995): 531–53.

11. L. A. Uspenskii, *Bogoslovie ikony pravoslavnoi tserkvi* (Moscow: Izd-vo Zapadno-evropeiskogo ekzarkhata, Moskovskii patriarkhat, 1996), 355, citing P. P. Pekarskii, "Materialy dlia istorii ikonopisaniia v Rossii," *Izvestiia Imperatorskogo Arkheograficheskogo obshchestva* 5, no. 5 (1865), 4, 22, 23.

Uspenskii objects to the state regulation of icons and also offers a sharply negative "Slavophile" perspective criticizing modern, eighteenth-century "distortions" of traditional aesthetic canons. For a revisionist view of eighteenth-century icons, stressing the aesthetic value and the coexistence (and occasional cross-fertilization) of ancient, late seventeenth-century, and "painterly" (*zhivopisnoe*) icon styles, see N. I. Komashko, *Russkaia ikona XVIII veka: Stolichnaia ikona, provintsial'naia ikona, narodnaia ikona* (Moscow: Agei Tomesh, 2006).

12. For example, in 1713–1715, an attempt was made to document a complete set of miracle-working images of the Virgin (up to 120 images), a project that was in part meant to counter the influence of D. E. Tveritinov and his followers, who, influenced by Protestant and rationalist ideas, rejected the possibility of miracle-working icons. (See I. A. Kochetov, "Svod chudtvornykh ikon Bogomateri na ikonakh i graviurakh XVIII–XIX vekov," in Lidov, *Chudotvornaia ikona*, 404–20 and 550). The Bogoliubskaia Mother of God that played such a dramatic role in the Plague Riot was among these images (410). On Tveritinov's view of icons, see James Cracraft, *The Church Reform of Peter the Great* (Stanford: Stanford University Press, 1971), 132–33.

13. Alexander V. Muller, trans. and ed., *The Spiritual Regulation of Peter the Great* (Seattle: University of Washington Press, 1972), 15, 20, 29, 107. The Russian text is in *Polnoe sobranie zakonov Rossiiskoi Imperii*, 133 vols. (St. Petersburg: Tipografiia II Otdeleniia Sobstvennoi Ego Imperatorskago Velichestva Kantseliarii, 1830–1916), 6:3718, hereafter PSZ, followed by volume and page. On persecution of "false miracles," see also O. Iu. Tarasov, *Icon and Devotion: Sacred Spaces in Imperial Russia*, trans. R. R. Milner-Gulland (London: Reaktion Books, 2002), 103.

14. By "state regulation" I mean the Synod acting in concert with state legal and regulatory authorities.

15. PSZ, 12:243.

16. PSZ, 12:361.

17. PSZ, 12:243.

18. That is, there is no indication that the regulation of icons was concerned with the style of painting per se (e.g., using old Russian, seventeenth-century, or modern European painterly techniques), but simply with their decency or presentability (*pristoinost'*). Nikolay Andreyev has argued that in the seventeenth century neither aesthetic value, nor beauty of any sort was of any consideration, but only that an icon be in consonance with Orthodox doctrine. See "Nikon and Avvakum on Icon Painting," *Revue des études slaves* 38 (1961): 37–38.

19. See, for example, PSZ, 12:243.

20. PSZ, 15:335.

21. See Michel Foucault, *Discipline and Punish: The Birth of the Prison* (New York: Pantheon Books, 1977).

22. PSZ, 18:341–42.

23. A. P. Vinogradov, *Istoriia kafedral'nogo Uspenskogo sobora v gubernskom gorode Vladimire*, 3rd ed. (Vladimir: Tipo-litografiia Gubernskogo Pravleniia, 1905), 61–63. A plaque with verses marking her visit was affixed to the baldachin. I find no corroborating evidence for Oleg Tarasov's assertion that "Catherine II commanded that she should be represented in the image of St. Catherine on the iconostasis" that she had financed (*Ikona i blagochestie ocherki ikonnogo dela v imperatorskoi Rossii* [Moscow: Progress-Kul'tura, 1995], 107, 313; Tarasov, *Icon and Devotion*, 225). Tarasov may be extrapolating from L. A. Uspenskii (*Bogoslovie ikony*, 363–64), who asserts that "it was precisely according to her instructions that Andrei Rublev's iconostasis was thrown out and replaced by a Baroque one with herself in the image of St. Catherine." (Vinogradov more justly observes that Catherine's recommendation to preserve the remnants of the past had not been followed, and notes that a great number of ancient icon covers and other gold and silver decorative objects were melted down to be reused. *Istoriia*, 65.) Tarasov also asserts that "low-level" (poor quality) variants of icons of St. Catherine "with individual features of the empress's face quickly became wide-spread from the end of the eighteenth century" (*Icon and Devotion*, 225). On Catherine's use of her connection with St. Catherine, see Gary Marker, *Imperial Saint: The Cult of St. Catherine and the Dawn of Female Rule in Russia* (DeKalb: Northern Illinois University Press, 2007), 221–25.

24. Vinogradov, *Istoriia*, 63–65. The repairs were supervised by Pavel's successor, Bishop Ieronim, who approved the replacement of the frescoes; the newly renovated cathedral reopened in May 1774. More than a hundred years later, from 1887 to 1891, the cathedral and its art works were renovated and partially restored with the help of the Moscow Archaeological Society.

V. Dobrokhotov notes that there was a belief that the verses on the wall under the baldachin and above the tombs of Princes Andrei and Georgii were written by Catherine and passed on by her to Bishop Pavel. I reproduce them here:

Хотя кто прав, живет хоть свято,
Но если злобствует сердца,
У них как в законе принято,
Того губити до конца,
Пример тому моя кончина,
Ей зависть с злобою есть причина,
Я прав—тиранен как злодей,
От бижних, сродных мне людей.

[Even if one is right and lives like a saint, / If hearts bear malice / They make it a rule / To destroy that one completely. / My demise is an example; / Envy and malice caused it, / I was treated like a tyrant and evildoer / By people close and kin to me.]

These lines ostensibly refer to Andrei Bogoliubskii's assassination by his courtiers, although their possible relevance as a statement of Catherine's defensiveness is intriguing. V. Dobrokhotov, *Pamiatniki drevnosti vo Vladimire Kliazemskom sobory, Kafedral'nyi Uspenskii i byvshii pridvornym V. K. Vsevoloda-Dmitrievskii* (Moscow: Universitetskaia tipografiia, 1849), 46; also cited in Vinogradov, *Istoriia*, prilozhenie, 17.

25. Vinogradov, *Istoriia*, 74; Dobrokhotov, *Pamiatniki drevnosti*, 21. For criticism of Catherine, see L. A. Uspenskii, cited in note 11, and G. I. Vzdornov, who faults her for the fact that (as Soviet art historians determined) restoration of the frescoes in the Uspenskii Sobor in the Kremlin were done in oil paint, despite the fact that (as Vzdornov himself notes) the empress had written to Moscow Archbishop Amvrosii asking that water colors be used and that "all of the painting be done with the same art [*iskusstvo*] as the ancient [type], with no difference" (A. G. Levshin quoted in Vzdornov, *Istoriia otkrytiia i izucheniia russkoi srednevekovoi zhivopisi: XIX vek* [Moscow: Iskusstvo, 1986], 17).

26. This change did not come about until the later nineteenth century. In the regulations we examined there is no reference at all to stylistic traditions, Byzantine, Russian, baroque, West European, or other.

27. In L. M. Evseeva's words, icons are "illustrations from the gospel reading or saint's life that were read out loud and made visible to all" ("Vizantiiskie ikony proskynesis v bogosluzhebnom obikhode," in *Vostochnokhristianskii khram: Liturgiia i iskusstvo*, ed. A. M. Lidov [St. Petersburg: Dmitrii Bulanin, 1994], 70).

28. On the twelfth-century Bogoliubskaia Mother of God, see N. P. Kondakov, *Ikonografiia Bogomateri*, 2 vols. (St. Petersburg: Akademiia nauk, 1914–1915), 2:299–301 (figures 166, 167); I. A. Sterligova, "Bogoliubskaia ikona Bogomateri v XII–XIII vv.," in *Drevnerusskoe iskusstvo: Vizantiia, Rus', Zapadnaia Evropa—iskusstvo i kul'tura*, ed. L. I. Lifshits and V. N. Lazarev (St. Petersburg: Dmitrii Bulanin, 2002), 187–204; and A. S. Preobrazhenskii, "Bogoliubskaia ikona Bozhiei Materi" in *Pravoslavnaia Entsiklopediia*, 23 vols. (Moscow: Tserkovno-nauchnyi tsentr "Pravoslavnaia entsiklopediia," 2000–), 5:459–63, which contains an extensive bibliography.

29. Among the extensive secondary works on the Vladimir Mother of God, see M. Alpatoff and V. Lasareff, "Ein byzantinisches Tafelwerk aus der Komnenenepoche," *Jahrbuch der preussischen Kunstsammlungen* 46, no. 2 (Berlin, 1925): 140–55 (in Russian as "Vizantiiskaia ikona komninovskoi epokhi," in *Vizantiiskoe i drevnerusskoe iskusstvo: Stat'i i materialy*, ed. V. N. Lazarev [Moscow: Nauka, 1978], 9–29); A. I. Anisimov, *Vladimirskaia ikona Bozhiei Materi* (Prague: Seminarium Kondakovianum, 1928), in English as *Our Lady of Vladimir*, trans. T. N. Rodzianko (Prague: Seminarium Kondakovianum, 1928); Konrad Onasch, "Die ikone der Gottesmutter von Vladimir in der Staalichen Tret'jakov Galerie zu Moskau," *Ostkirchlike Studien* 5 (1956): 56–64; V. Lazarev, *Storia della pittura bizantina* (Torino: G. Einaudi, 1967), 204, 257; E. K. Guseva, N. V. Rozanova, and G. V. Sidorenko, eds., *Bogomater' Vladimirskaia: Sbornik materialov; Katalog vystavki* (Moscow: Avangard, 1995).

30. See V. O. Kliuchevskii, ed., *Skazanie o chudesakh Vladimirskoi ikony Bozh'ei Materi*, Monuments of Early Russian Literature 7 (Oakland: Berkeley Slavic Specialties, 1993). Notably, the story of the Bogoliubskaia Mother of God is absent, and was only added to much later versions of the *Skazanie*. The Vladimir Mother of God was transferred to Moscow in 1395, when it was said to have saved the city from Tamerlane. It is now located in the Tret'iakov Gallery in Moscow.

31. See: Onasch, "Die ikone," and W. Vodoff, "Un 'parti théocratique' dans la Russie du XIIe siècle?" *Cahiers de civilization medieval, Xe–XIIe siècles* 17 (1974): 193–215.

32. Fragments of the life are quoted in V. Dobrokhotov, *Drevnii Bogoliubov gorod i monastyr's ego okrestnostiami* (Moscow: Universitetskaia tipografiia, 1852); the section concerning the miracle of the Bogoliubskaia Mother of God (6–7 and prilozhenie 4, 105–10) coincide with the "Chronicle" account discussed below, which was most likely its source.

33. E. E. Golubinskii, *Istoriia kanonizatsii sviatykh' v russkoi tserkvi* (Moscow: Universitetskaia tipografiia, 1903), 59, 134. The historian A. E. Presniakov speculated that Bogoliubskii's canonization may have been a compensation for the transfer of Alexander Nevskii's relics from the Cathedral of the Assumption in Vladimir to St. Petersburg (Bogoliubskii was also interred in this cathedral, which he had built). See Nikolai Nikolaevich Voronin, *Andrei Bogoliubskii* (Moscow: Vodolei, 2007), 307n8. The transfer of Alexander Nevskii's relics took place in 1723–1724, so if this was in fact compensation, it was quite belated.

34. Golubinskii, *Istoriia kanonizatsii*, 134.

35. "Letopis' Bogoliubova Monastyria c 1158 po 1770 god sostavlennaia po monastyrskim aktam i zapisiam nastoiatelem onoi obiteli igumenom Aristarkhom v 1767–1769 godakh," *Chteniia v Imperatorskom obshchestve istorii i drevnostei rossiiskikh pri Moskovskom universitete* 1 (1878): 1–24.

36. "Letopis'," 1–3. The narrative is clearly anachronistic. It is extremely doubtful, for example, that the celebration of the Bogoliubskaia Mother of God began before the fourteenth century, and scholars' suggestions that it was celebrated in the fifteenth and sixteenth centuries are hypothetical. See the section "Pochitanie" in Preobrazhenskii, "Bogoliubskaia ikona."

37. This is evidently a folk etymology; Prince Andrei had actually taken the name Bogoliubskii earlier from a place name.

38. E. S. Ovchinnikova, "Moskovskii variant 'Bogomateri Bogoliubskoi,'" in *Drevnerusskoe iskusstvo: Zarubezhnye sviazi*, ed. G. V. Popov (Moscow: Nauka, 1975), 343–47. It might be more accurate to say that elements of the narrative developed based on the visual imagery of the icon.

39. For an online catalogue of the main Russian Bogoliubskaia Mother of God icons, see the "Muzei Bogomateri" ("Virgin Museum"), <http://virginmuseum.narod.ru/nazvaik/b/bogoljub.html>. For a selection of images of the Bogoliubskaia Mother of God, see the "Entsiklopediia Pravoslavnoi Ikony" ("Encyclopedia of the Orthodox Icon") at <http://www.obraz.org/>.

40. Paraklesis (Russian: *Moleben*) is also the name of an Orthodox service of intercession. Preobrazhenskii ("Bogoliubskaia ikona") outlines the two basic recensions (*izvody*) of the Bogoliubskaia Mother of God icon: the first, based on the ancient Bogoliubskii icon, has three variants: a) a precise copy of the twelfth-century icon; b) those with Andrei Bogoliubskii falling at Mary's feet, and sometimes including a representation of a monastery; and c) those with a representation of the Bogoliubskii Monastery at Mary's feet. The second recension—the kind to which the Moscow icon belongs—is described in the following section.

41. On the Moscow Bogoliubskaia Mother of God, see Ovchinnikova, "Moskovskii variant," 343–47; A. S. Preobrazhenskii, "Bogoliubskaia Moskovskaia ikona Bozhiei Materi," in *Pravoslavnaia Entsiklopediia*, 5:463–64, available online at <http://www.sedmitza.ru/>. For a typical (historically anachronistic) retelling of the Bogoliubskaia Mother of God narrative, reflected in a multitude of popular accounts, see T. M. Bogoliubskii, "Bogoliubskaia ikona Bozhiei Materi: Ocherk," *Zhurnal Moskovskoi Patriarkhii* 10 (1945): 48–50.

42. N. V. Dmitrieva, *O Tebe raduetsia: Skazaniia o sviatykh chudotvornykh ikonakh Bogomateri* (Moscow: Vstrecha, 2002), 18.

43. Preobrazhenskii, "Bogoliubskaia ikona."

44. Dobrokhotov states that Peter had the church built, and that according to tradition he sent the monastery a clock for the bell tower (*Drevnii Bogoliubov gorod*, 65–66).

45. This is also true of many discussions of Russian icons currently available on the Internet, which share many traits of the oral tradition, in particular, its unreliable, ahistorical, anecdotal quality.

46. M. M. Krasilin, "Ikonograficheskii arkhetip i narodnoe pochitanie chudotvornykh obrazov," in Lidov, *Chudotvornaia ikona*, 392. Krasilin emphasizes the difficulty of establishing the factual history of these icons given the lack of hard data concerning their creation, repainting, replacements, and relocations, as well as believers' attitudes towards them as objects of faith rather than historical artifacts.

47. See variants of the texts in N. P. Kondakov, *Ikonografiia bogomateri*, 2:300–301 (figures 166, 167), and in Ovchinnikova, "Moskovskii variant," 347. In a later seventeenth-century Moscow Bogoliubskaia Mother of God, Jesus is joined by the figure of Divine Wisdom; see I. Kizlasova's commentary in L. I. Lifshits and A. M. Lukashov, *Sofiia Premudrost' Bozhiia: Vystavka russkoi ikonopisi XIII–XIX vekov iz sobranii muzeev Rossii* (Moscow: Radunitsa, 2000), 336–37, fig. no. 124.

48. The gilded silver cover (*riza*) for the twelfth-century Bogoliubskaia Mother of God donated by citizens of Vladimir in 1820 included an image of the ancient Bogoliubskii Monastery (Dobrokhotov, *Drevnii Bogoliubov gorod*, 105–6), suggesting the reverse influence of the later Moscow Bogoliubskaia Mother of God type on the twelfth-century icon.

See O. A. Poliakova, "Arkhitekturnye fony na ikonakh russkikh sviatykh," *Iskusstvo khristianskogo mira: sbornik statei* 2 (1996), 74–85; on two Bogoliubskaia Mother of God icons, see 77–78. Poliakova notes the "special means of vision and the incorporation of the surrounding world" into icons with depictions of recognizable architectural monuments (74).

49. Wendy Salmond, *Russian Icons at Hillwood* (Washington, DC: Hillwood Museum and Gardens, 1998), 56–58 and fig. 28.

50. Ovchinnikova, "Moskovskii variant," 347; see also N. A. Maiasova, I. Nikolaev, and K. Kushnarev, *Pamiatnik s Solovetskikh ostrovov: Ikona "Bogomater' bogoliubskaia s zhitiiami Zosimy i Savvatiia," 1545 g. / Icon from Solovetskiye Islands: Icon "The Virgin Bogolyubskaia with Scenes from the Lives of SS Zosima and Savvati," 1545* (Leningrad: Avrora, 1970).

51. Lifshits and Lukashev, *Sofiia Premudrost' Bozhiia*, 336–37, fig. no. 124.

52. Mariia Makhan'ko, "'Bogomater' Bogoliubskaia': Ob ispol'zovanii drevnikh ikonograficheskikh izvodov v ikonopisi XVI veka," *Iskusstvoznanie* 2 (1998): 250.

53. Ovchinnikova, "Moskovskii variant," 346–47.

54. Mary icons to which churches and chapels are dedicated in Moscow and the Moscow area currently include: the Mother of God "of the Sign" (*Znamenie*) (four churches); the Vladimir Mother of God (two churches); the Mother of God "Unexpected Joy" (*Nechaiannaia radost'*); the Vatopedskaia Mother of God; the Iverskaia Mother of God (two churches); the Mother of God "Quick to Harken" (*Skoroposlushnitsa*); the Mother of God "Consolation of the Afflicted" (*Vsekh skorbiashchikh radost'*) (two churches); the Vlakhernskaia Mother of God; the Kazan Mother of God (two churches); the Mother of God "Life-Giving Source" (*Zhivonosnyi istochnik*); and the Mother of God "Healer" (*Tselitel'nitsa*).

55. See the listing on the Russian Orthodox Cathedral of St. John the Baptist, Washington, DC, online at <http://www.stjohndc.org>, under "Icons of the Mother of God."

56. According to Oleg Tarasov, "the first miracle to proceed from an icon was the healing from leprosy of Abgar, king of Edessa, to whom Christ himself sent his Image Not Made by Hands" (*Icon and Devotion*, 85). The "Image Not Made by Hands" icon, a.k.a. "Veronika's Veil," is one of the most famous "meta-icons" that testify to their miraculous

origins. Indeed a popular folk etymology of the name "Veronika" is "true image" or icon (*vera* plus *icon*).

57. On Kazan, see I. L. Buseva-Davydova, "Bogomater' Sedmizernaia: K voprosu o slozhenii ikonografskogo tipa," in Lidov, *Chudotvornaia ikona*, 363–84, esp. 363; on Tikhvin, see Krasilin, "Ikonograficheskii arkhetip," 394.

58. Poliakova, "Arkhitekturnye fony," 77.

59. Icon in the State Historical Museum (GIM). See picture, p. 214.

60. L. M. Evseeva, "Vizantiiskie ikony," 65–76, esp. 65 and 68. See also L. M. Evseeva and M. M. Shvedova, "Afonskie spiski 'Bogomateri Portaitissy' i problema podobiia v ikonopisi," in Lidov, *Vostochnokhristianskii khram*, 336.

61. Charles de Mertens, *An Account of the Plague Which Raged at Moscow, in 1771* (London: F. and C. Rivington, 1799), 22–23. This is a translation of *Traité de la peste, contenant l'histoire de celle qui a régné à Moscou en 1771* (Vienna, 1784), which in turn was a translation of Mertens's *Observationes medicae de febribus putridis, de peste, nonnullisque aliis morbis* (Vienna, 1778). The mob, mistrusting modern medicine, fought with doctors and among other acts broke into and ravaged Dr. Mertens's house (23).

62. On *proskinesis*, see A. P. Kazdan, ed., *The Oxford Dictionary of Byzantium*, 3 vols. (New York: Oxford University Press, 1991), 3:1738–39.

63. Dmitrieva, *O Tebe raduetsia*, 19. Icon processions are again common practice in post-Soviet Russia.

64. The quoted phrases are from André Grabar, *Les revêtements en or et en argent des icônes byzantines du moyen âge* (Venice: Institut hellénique d'études byzantines et post-byzantines, 1975), 4–6.

65. Ibid., 6.

66. I. A. Sterligova, "O liturgicheskom smysle dragotsennogo ubora russkoi ikony," in Lidov, *Vostochnokhristianskii khram*, 220–26; this quote is from 223.

67. Some critics of icon covers have argued that they reduce icons to "luxury objects" (E. Trubetskoi) and signal their decline as an art form (N. P. Sychev), although one recent scholar sharply rejects these views (V. V. Igoshev, "Simvolika okladov ikon XV–XVII vv.," in *Iskusstvo khristianskogo mira: Sbornik statei* 3 [1999], 111–22).

68. A. D. Koshelev, ed., *Polnoe sobranie russkikh letopisei*, 43 vols. (Moscow: Rukopisnye pamiatniki Drevnei Rusi, 1997–), 2:78 (2009).

69. N. I. Komashko, "'Vsekh skorbiashchikh radost',' ikona Bozhiei Materi," in *Pravoslavnaia entsiklopediia*, 9:707–17.

70. Dmitrieva, *O Tebe raduetsia*, 87; G. V. Ibneeva, "Ekaterina II i pravoslavnoe dukhovenstvo v puteshestvii po Volge 1767 goda," <http://kds.eparhia.ru/bibliot/ konferencia/cerkovnaiaistoria/ibneeva/>, which cites M. Rybushkin, *Kratkaia istoriia goroda Kazani* (Kazan': Tip. L. Shevitsa, 1848), 99.

71. My thanks to Wendy Salmond for this suggestion. The very notion of stylistic choice may be thought at first to be alien in regard to icons, yet as Komashko argues, this was a conscious and palpable issue in the eighteenth century (*Russkaia ikona XVIII veka*, 6–29). Tarasov (*Ikona i blagochestie*, 334–36) discusses "enlightenment" and "romantic" visual trends in icon landscape painting, another indication that no fundamental conflict was perceived at the time between "Russian" and "Western" styles.

72. Stephen Gero, "Byzantine Iconoclasm and the Failure of a Medieval Reformation," in *The Image and the Word: Confrontations in Judaism, Christianity and Islam*, ed. Joseph Gutmann (Missoula, MT: Scholars Press, 1977), 54.

73. See Bushkovitch, cited in note 9.

74. According to one version, Jesus was about to send a hail of stones onto the city as punishment for their lack of attention to the icon, but Mary interceded and convinced him to send only a three-month plague (Bolotov, *Zhizn' i prikliucheniia*, 3:20). For the story of the icon's miraculous salvation of Vladimir (which includes a skeptical Protestant German doctor who becomes convinced of the miracle), see Dobrokhotov, *Drevnii Bogoliubov gorod*, 107. In memory of the miracle, the local church instituted a yearly procession of the icon from the monastery to the city (to the Vladimir Assumption Cathedral) on May 21, and back to the monastery on June 17 (108f). This tradition has been revived in post-Soviet Russia.

75. John T. Alexander, *Bubonic Plague in Early Modern Russia: Public Health and Urban Disaster* (Baltimore: Johns Hopkins University Press, 1980), 93–94. A detailed account of these events by an unnamed eyewitness is presented in A. T. Bolotov, *Zhizn' i prikliucheniia*, 3:18–37.

76. [Hugo Grotius], *Razsuzhdenie protiv ateistov i neutralistov*, trans. Amvrosii (Zertis-Kamenskii) (1765; 2nd ed. Moscow: Universitetskaia tipografiia im. Novikova, 1781).

77. A. Zertsalov, ed., "O miatezhakh v gorode Moskve i v sele Kolomenskom v 1648, 1662 i 1771 g.," *Chteniia v Imperatorskom Obshchestve istorii i drevnostei rossiiskikh pri Moskovskom universitete* 3 (1890): 372, quoted in Alexander, *Bubonic Plague*, 189.

78. Alexander, *Bubonic Plague*, 257–58.

79. Furthermore, Amvrosii had supervised the unpopular levy of clergymen's sons in 1769 for the Russo-Turkish War (ibid., 188). Alexander, passim, presents a thorough recounting of the authorities' measures and their mediocre results.

80. S. R. Dolgova, ed.,"Zapiski ochevidtsa [F. V. Karzhavin] o chumnom bunte v Moskve v 1771 godu," *Sovetskie arkhivy* 6 (1976): 66–70; the cited passage is on 68.

81. Apparently a reference to people of the Chudov Monastery, but a grimly ironic unintentional pun (considering the struggle over a miracle-working [*chudotvornaia*] icon).

82. See Nikolay Andreyev, "Nikon and Avvakum on Icon Painting," *Revue des études slaves* 38 (1961): 37–44, esp. 40–41. According to Andreyev, "it was not the aesthetic content which motivated his loathing of Western art"; rather, it was "because he feared the infiltration of Western religious ideas and also considered the church was [alone] competent to regulate ecclesiastical art forms" (41).

83. Levitt, *Early Modern Russian Letters*, chap. 13.

84. Alexander, *Bubonic Plague*, 227–28 and 300.

85. "The Bogolyubskaya Icon in Kozlov, 18 June/1 July," The Russian Orthodox Cathedral of St. John the Baptist (website), Washington, DC, <http://www.stjohndc.org/Russian/theotokos/9806b.htm>.

86. These miracle tales are still current today, judging by the extremely large popular literature (books and websites) in Russian on miracle-working icons. A search for "Chudotvornaia ikona Bozhiei materi" (Miracle-Working Icon of the Mother of God) on Yandex yielded 443,000 hits, on Nigma, 489,000 (March 5, 2009). Google yielded 47,000 hits, about 4,000 of which refer to Russia.

87. See Preobrazhenskii, "Bogoliubskaia ikona," which also describes the variant types of the later Bogoliubskaia Mother of God icons; see also L. E. Beliankin, *Istoricheskoe issledovanie o prazdnovanii v chest' ikony Presv. Bogoroditsy, imenuemyia Bogoliubskiia, chto u Varvarskikh vorot v Moskve* (Moscow, 1871).

## 8: The Dialectic of Vision in Radishchev's *Journey*

1. For a useful introduction to Radishchev, see Igor Nemirovsky, "Aleksandr Nikolaevich Radishchev," in *Early Modern Russian Writers, Late Seventeenth and Eighteenth Centuries*, Dictionary of Literary Biography 150, ed. Marcus C. Levitt (Detroit: Gale Research, 1995), 323–33.

2. Cf. Thomas Newlin, *The Voice in the Garden: Andrei Bolotov and the Anxieties of Russian Pastoral, 1738–1833* (Evanston: Northwestern University Press, 2001), in which the main anxiety is serfdom. But as Newlin puts it in "Moving Pictures: The Optics of Serfdom on the Russian Estate," in *Picturing Russia: Explorations in Visual Culture*, ed. Valerie A Kivelson and Joan Neuberger (New Haven: Yale University Press, 2008), 71–75, "the history of visual representation of serfdom, both as a social and as an economic system, is by and large one of absence and omission; what is most significant is what we do not see, what is hidden, glossed over, left out entirely" (73). Newlin refers to "the complex sense of anxiety and paranoia" of "the post-Pugachev era" (74) and at the same time to the period's "almost overbearing sense of optic optimism" (73).

3. Paul Dukes, ed., *Russia Under Catherine the Great*, vol. 2, *Catherine the Great's Instruction (Nakaz) to the Legislative Commission, 1767* (Newtonville, MA: Oriental Research Partners, 1977). Cf. K. A. Papmehl, *Freedom of Expression in Eighteenth Century Russia* (The Hague: Nijhoff, 1971).

4. I have left out the opening and closing lines addressed to A. M. Kutuzov.

5. Page citations refer to, first: Aleksandr Nikolaevich Radishchev, *Puteshestvie iz Peterburga v Moskvu: Vol'nost'*, ed. V. A. Zapadov (St. Petersburg: Nauka, 1992); and then Aleksandr Radishchev, *A Journey from St. Petersburg to Moscow*, ed. R. P. Thaler, trans. Leo Weiner (Cambridge, MA: Harvard University Press, 1958), from which the translations have been taken with minor modifications. This quote: 6; 40.

6. Ibid., 66; 142–43.

7. In the "Eulogy on Lomonosov," Radishchev makes clear his admiration for Lomonosov's odic vision as an ideal which he shares, even though he fears that Lomonosov has "followed the common custom" of flattery: "If, without offending truth and posterity, it were possible to do so, I would forgive you because you thereby revealed your soul's gratitude for favors received. But the maker of odes who cannot follow in your footsteps will envy you, he will envy you your superb picture of national peace and quiet—that mighty protector of cities and villages and comforter of kingdoms and of kings [NB: Radishchev is again paraphrasing the odes]; he will envy you the countless beauties of your diction, even if someone manages to attain the uninterrupted harmony of your verses, which no one so far has" (Radishchev, *Puteshestvie/Journey*, 121; 233). This recalls Lomonosov's prediction of the envy of later poets, discussed in chapter 2.

8. Elsewhere in the same section ("Khotilov") Radishchev says two-thirds. Thaler clarifies that "according to the census of 1783, about 94.5 percent of the Russian people were peasants. Of these, about 55 percent were manorial serfs, 39 percent crown serfs, and 6 percent free peasants" (Radishchev, *A Journey*, 267–68).

9. Radishchev, *Puteshestvie/Journey*, 66; 143.

10. Ibid., 66–67; 143.

11. Ibid., 93; 156.

12. Ibid., 75; 157.

13. Cf. Ecclesiastes 4:1: "So I returned, and considered all the oppressions that are done under the sun: and behold the tears of such as were oppressed, and they had no comforter; and on the side of their oppressors there was power; but they had no comforter" (King James Version).

14. V. V. Kapnist, *Izbrannye proizvedeniia* (Leningrad: Sovetskii Pisatel', 1973), 60–61.

15. The reference to "slavery" was itself a challenge to Catherine, as she had hotly rejected this term as applied to serfdom by European critics of Russia like Rousseau, Diderot, and Chappe d'Auteroche.

16. Radishchev, *Puteshestvie/Journey*, 24; 70.

17. A. N. Radishchev, *Polnoe sobranie sochinenii*, 3 vols. (Moscow: AN SSSR, 1938–1952), 2:300–308; Radishchev, *A Journey*, 239–49.

18. E. R. Dashkova, *The Memoirs of Princess Dashkova*, trans. and ed. Kyril Fitzlyon (Durham: Duke University Press, 1995), 125. On Dashkova's views on serfdom, see also Michelle Lamarche Marrese, "Liberty Postponed: Princess Dashkova and the Defense of Serfdom," in *The Princess and the Patriot: Ekaterina Dashkova, Benjamin Franklin, and the Age of Enlightenment*, ed. Sue Ann Prince (Philadelphia: American Philosophical Society, 2005), 23–38.

19. Dashkova connected the serfs' lack of freedom to that of the nobility, suggesting that she adhered to the program of the so-called "Panin party" that had advocated limited monarchy; see Dashkova, *Memoirs*, 60. See also David L. Ransel, *The Politics of Catherinian Russia: The Panin Party* (New Haven: Yale University Press, 1975), esp. 113.

M. M. Safonov has described Dashkova's own problem in terms of purposeful blindness: "The incompatibility of despotic rule [*samovlast'ia*] and Enlightenment gave birth to distressing discord in those people [like Dashkova] who continued to believe in enlightened ideas. . . . To the degree that this became more and more obvious, such people found themselves more and more often facing a difficult choice. They had either to close their eyes to that which had become obvious, in order not to see how much their abstract ideal differed from actuality, and adapt themselves to circumstances, or take the decisive step of breaking with enlightenment illusions." Dashkova was able to do neither ("Ekaterina Malaia i ee 'Zapiski,'" in *Ekaterina Romanovna Dashkova: Issledovaniia i materialy*, ed. A. I. Vorontsov-Dashkov, Studiorum Slavicorum Monumenta 8 [St. Petersburg: Dmitrii Bulanin, 1996], 21). Notably, Catherine suspected Dashkova (wrongly) of conspiring with Radishchev to publish the *Journey*, just as she had faulted her for publishing *Vadim Novgorodskii*.

20. This view has been shared by many Soviet-era critics as well as some Western scholars. Of the latter, see, in particular, Tanya Page, "Radishchev's Polemic Against Sentimentalism in the Cause of Eighteenth-Century Utilitarianism," in *Russian Literature in the Age of Catherine the Great*, ed. A. G. Cross (Oxford: Willem A. Meeuws, 1976), 141–72; and "Helvetianism as Allegory in the 'Dream' and the 'Peasant Rebellion' in Radishchev's 'Journey from Petersburg to Moscow,'" in *Russia and the West in the Eighteenth Century*, ed. A. G. Cross (Newtonville, MA: Oriental Research Partners, 1983), 135–43.

21. See *Slovar' sovremennogo russkogo literaturnogo iazyka*, 17 vols. (Moscow: Akademiia Nauk SSSR, 1950–1965), vol. 16, columns 1186–87 ("Uiazvliat'") and 17, columns 2048–49 ("Iazva, Iazvit'"). In the Russian version of the New Testament, Jesus's wounds on the cross are also "iazvy" (John 20:26; cf. Galatians 6:17); my thanks to Irena Reyfman for this reference. On allusions to the Bible in the *Journey*, see E. D. Kukushkina, "Bibleiskie motivy u A. N. Radishcheva," *Russkaia literatura* 1 (2000): 119–23.

22. *"Rogovoi rastvor"* apparently refers to a substance made from animals' horns that was used for medicinal or other purposes.

23. Radishchev, *Puteshestvie/Journey*, 79; 164.

24. For Radishchev, as for Sumarokov, the desire for profit is something that can deprive one of sight, but may also at times, as is the case with *samoliubie* (self-love), have positive effects. (Unlike Sumarokov, who denigrated capitalist enterprise, Radishchev at one point contrasts the stultifying effects of slave labor to the positive and "powerful stimulus" *koryst'* provides for free commercial activity.)

25. Radishchev, *Puteshestvie/Journey*, 63; 137.

26. Tanya Page sees this as the heart of Radishchev's defense of revolution; see the works cited in note 20.

27. See Radishchev's criticism of the French Revolution's excesses in V. P. Semennikov, *Radishchev: Ocherki i issledovaniia* (Moscow: Gos. izd-vo, 1923), 3–59, cited by Kahn, "Self and Sensibility in Radishchev's Journey from St. Petersburg to Moscow: Dialogism, Relativism, and the Moral Spectator," in *Self and Story in Russian History*, ed. Laura Engelstein and Stephanie Sandler (Ithaca: Cornell University Press, 2000), 280; a version of this article appeared in *Oxford Slavonic Papers* 30 (1997): 40–66.

28. Radishchev, *Puteshestvie/Journey*, 64; 139–40.

29. "Adamant" in both Russian and English is "a legendary stone of impenetrable hardness, formerly sometimes identified with the diamond" (*Dictionary.com Unabridged* [v 1.1], Random House, <http://dictionary1.classic.reference.com/browse/adamant>). "Almaz" in Russian also means "uncut diamond," which of course is not transparent. The quotation comes from Radishchev, *Puteshestvie/Journey*, 36; 90–91.

30. Cf. also the many examples of Cupid's arrows that "sting" in eighteenth-century love poetry. E. D. Kukushkina connects the oppositions of "dream/awakening" and "loss/ regaining of vision" to the poetics and imagery of the Bible ("Bibleiskie motivy," 121).

31. Radishchev, *Puteshestvie/Journey*, 61; 134.

32. Ibid., 64; 139.

33. Radishchev conceives of the divine force not only as omnipresent, but also (and unlike Deism) as an active force in the world and in some way functioning on a personal level. More on this below.

Kahn connects the mystical side of the *Journey* to Freemasonry but also sees traces of parody here ("Self and Sensibility," 291–93). On the debated and probably irresolvable issue of Radishchev's relationship to Freemasonry, see N. D. Kochetkova, "Radishchev i masony," *Russkaia literatura* 1 (2000): 103–7.

34. See note 5.

35. Cf. Andreas Schönle's comment that in Radishchev's book "discourse belongs to no one, except to the truth," and that "the text makes narrator, auxiliary narrator, and author collapse into one" (*Authenticity and Fiction in the Russian Literary Journey, 1790–1840*, Russian Research Center Studies 92 [Cambridge: Harvard University Press, 2000], 35–36). Andrew Kahn comments that "Radishchev's narrator seems to be at times almost without a self" ("Self and Sensibility," 280–304). Schönle finds Radishchev's search for authenticity unfulfilled, insofar as Radishchev "wants us to see humankind both as emanation from and deflection of nature" (*Authenticy and Fiction*, 22). On the other hand, Kahn, who argues against a politicized, monological view of Radishchev, defines the writer's basic position as relativism (Bakhtin's "polyphony"), seen within the context of the sentimental novel and the theory of sensibility. In this connection, Kahn suggests in passing that Adam Smith's notion of the "moral spectator" is amenable to a reading in

terms of Lacan's mirror stage ("Self and Sensibility," 296n58).

36. Cf. Kahn who sees in the paean to a national literature at the end of the *Journey* "the promise of a permanent dialogue and an unfixed self" ("Self and Sensibility," 304).

37. Catherine the Great—and many Soviet commentators after her—interpreted this line to mean that Radishchev "puts his hopes in a peasant rebellion" (Radishchev, *A Journey*, 248). However, this is not an expression of hope but a warning. Quotation from Radishchev, *Puteshestvie/Journey*, 94; 191.

38. Radishchev, *Puteshestvie/Journey*, 17; 57.

39. Ibid., 43–44; 104.

40. He confesses to having infected his innocent wife and children. Note that there is no evidence that this was true of Radishchev himself. See Thaler's introduction to Radishchev, *A Journey*, 28–29.

41. Radishchev, *Puteshestvie/Journey*, 56; 125.

42. For a recent discussion of the Khotilov "project for the future," see K. Iu. Lappo-Danilevskii, "Plan postepennogo osvobozhdeniia krest'ian v 'Puteshestivii iz Peterburga v Moskvu' A. N. Radishcheva," *XVIII vek* 25 (2008), 206–32. Lappo-Danilevskii sees its ideas based on those of A. R. Vorontsov.

43. Radishchev, *Puteshestvie/Journey*, 113; 220.

44. Ibid., 114; 221.

45. Ibid., 102; 201.

46. Ibid., 110; 214–15.

47. Ibid., 121; 234. 48. Radishchev, *Puteshestvie/Journey*, 35–36; 89–90.

49. As Thorleif Bowman writes, "for the Hebrew, the most important of his senses for the experience of truth was his hearing (as well as various kinds of feeling), but for the Greek it had to be his sight" (*Hebrew Thought Compared with Greek* [London: SCM Press, 1960], 206; cf. 200–204 and passim). See also Eric Auerbach's famous contrast between Homer and Genesis in "Odysseus' Scar," in *Mimesis: The Representation of Reality in Western Literature* (Princeton: Princeton University Press, 1953), chap. 1.

50. Radishchev, *Puteshestvie/Journey*, 36; 90–91.

51. Ibid., 36; 89–91. It is hard to agree with Kahn's suggestion that the verses from Addison's "Cato" that follow the words cited and that end the chapter throw an ironic light on the chapter's depiction of revelation ("Self and Sensibility," 293–94). The very same passage ("Cato's dying words" from act 5, scene 1 of Addison's tragedy) is cited as a legacy of honorable suicide that the narrator of "Krestitsy" leaves to his sons (Radishchev, *Puteshestvie/Journey*, 55; 123), and many scholars hold that Cato's action was a model for Radishchev's own suicide. See, for example, Iu. M. Lotman, "The Poetics of Everyday Behavior in Russian Eighteenth-Century Culture," in Iu. M. Lotman and B. A. Uspenskii, *The Semiotics of Russian Culture*, trans. Ann Shukman (Ann Arbor: Dept. of Slavic Languages and Literatures, University of Michigan, 1984), 248–50.

52. Bowman argues that the device of constant repetition of the "vanity of vanities" theme in Ecclesiastes exemplifies the Biblical model of aural perception (*Hebrew Thought*, 203).

53. Radishchev, *Puteshestvie/Journey*, 121; 233.

54. Cf. The second stanza of Lomonosov's poem: "Песчинка как в морских волнах, / Как мала искра в вечном льде, / Как в сильном вихре тонкой прах, / В свирепом как перо огне, / Так я, в сей бездне углублен, / Теряюсь, мысльми утомлен!" (M. V. Lomonosov, *Polnoe sobranie sochinenii*, 11 vols. [Moscow: Akademiia Nauk SSSR, 1950–1983], 8:120–21). Radishchev echoes the italicized words.

55. Radishchev, *Puteshestvie/Journey*, 54; 122–23. The "mirror of truth" was both a metaphor and an actual object that was "in the form of a [large] three-sided prism . . . designed to stand on the desk of every government official during legal proceedings" in Imperial Russia (Julia Bekman Chadaga, "Mirror Writing: The Literary Traces of the Zertsalo," *Russian Review* 61, no. 1 [January 2002]: 74). On representations of the "all-seeing eye" (also known as "the eye of Providence"), which is common to various mystic traditions (alchemy, Kabbalah, astrology) as well as to Christianity (including Russian Orthodox) and Freemasonry, see Albert M. Potts, "The Eye of Providence," *Documenta Ophthalmologica* 34, no. 1 (February 1973): 327–34, also in his *The World's Eye* (Lexington: University Press of Kentucky, 1982), chap. 8. Potts traces the image to ancient Greece, but also notes many possible biblical references (333); notably, he cites Ecclesiastes 34:16 ("For the eyes of God are upon those that love him") as "the keynote." <http://www.springerlink.com/content/102872/?p=f9655a47106348d38f4f4f0 2037b8130&pi=0>

56. Radishchev, *Puteshestvie/Journey*, 54–55; 122–23.

57. Ibid., 27; 76.

58. G. I. Sennikov considers this episode the culminating point of the entire *Journey* and the best example of the genre of "satirical dream" ("O satiricheskikh 'snakh' v russkoi literature XVIII veka," in *Problemy izucheniia russkoi literatury XVIII veka*, vol. 1, *Ot klassitsizma k romantizmu*, ed. V. A. Zapadov [Leningrad: Leningradskii gos. ped. institut, 1974], 72–73).

59. Radishchev, *Puteshestvie/Journey*, 27; 66.

60. On the argument over satire, see, for example, Lurana O'Malley, *The Dramatic Works of Catherine the Great: Theatre and Politics in Eighteenth-Century Russia* (Aldershot, England: Ashgate, 2006), 6, 108, and via the index.

61. Dreams for Radishchev are responses both to material and physiological stimuli: "the humors stirred up by my thoughts [that] streamed to my head and, stimulating the tender substance of my brain, aroused a variety of images" expressed in the dream (Radishchev, *Puteshestvie/Journey*, 22; 66). As in this case, dreams also serve as privileged sources of divine truth.

62. Ibid., 22; 66–67.

63. Ibid., 22–23; 68.

64. Ibid., 23; 69.

65. See the commentary by V. A. Zapadov, *Puteshestvie*, 647–51.

66. The Russian more explicitly echoes the dedication's description of man's problem as "not looking straight [*vziraet nepriamo*] at the objects around him," which is also echoed elsewhere in the text. The metaphor of the eye doctor is also used to explain Lomonosov's passion for (visual) enlightenment: "Like a blind man who has not seen the light since he left his mother's womb and who suddenly perceives the glory of the light of day when his vision is restored by the skillful hand of the oculist [*glazovrachevatelia*]: with a quick glance he surveys all the beauties of nature and admires its variety and simplicity. . . . He feels its splendor more vividly than those who have always been accustomed to see; he is delighted and goes into ecstasies." (Radishchev, *Puteshestvie/Journey*, 226; 116–17).

67. Ibid., 26; 73.

68. Ibid., 27; 74–75.

69. Ibid., 25; 72.

70. Ibid., 28; 76.

71. The *Belisarius* subtext was suggested by D. M. Sharypkin, "Radishchev i roman Marmontelia 'Velizarii,'" *XVIII vek* 12 (1977): 166–82, although he does not draw attention to this specific passage. Sharypkin disagrees with Koplan's suggestion that the probable source of the dream is several works by Louis-Sebastian Mercier, including some used in I. A. Krylov's satirical journal *Pochta dukhov* (B. Koplan, "Filosoficheskie pis'ma 'Pochty dukhov' [1789]," in *A. N. Radishchev: Materialy i issledovaniia*, ed. A. S. Orlov [1936; repr., Düsseldorf: Brucken-Verlag, 1972], 355–99; see esp. 384–92).

72. The twelve translators were: I. P. Elagin, Z. G. Chernyshev, S. M. Kuzmin, G. G. Orlov, D. V. Volkov, A. V. Naryshkin, A. I. Bibikov, S. P. Meshcherskii, V. G. Orlov, G. V. Kozitskii, and Catherine herself. See I. P. Kondakov, ed., *Svodnyi katalog russkoi knigi grazhdanskoi pechati XVIII veka, 1725–1800*, 5 vols. (Moscow: Izd. Gos. biblioteki SSSR imeni V. I. Lenina, 1962–1967), vol. 2, no. 4060, 218–19; and *Sochineniia Imperatritsy Ekateriny II: Na osnovanii podlinnykh rukopisei*, ed. A. N. Pypin, 12 vols. (1901–1907; repr., Hildesheim: Georg Olms, 1998), 5:17. (Note: the *Svodnyi katalog* list leaves out Meshcherskii.) The novel came out in three editions, of 1768, 1773, and 1785; it was also translated separately by P. P. Kurbatov (1769, 1786, 1791, and 1796).

73. Sharypkin refers to the translation as a reiteration of the *Instruction* "dressed up in imaginative artistic form" ("Radishchev i roman," 168).

74. See Sharypkin, "Radishchev i roman," 177–81; of course, Radishchev probably would not have known this fact. The chapter is reproduced in *Sochineniia Imperatritsy Ekateriny II*, 5:3–29. The correspondence concerning the translation (between Marmontel, Catherine, Voltaire, and others), also reproduced in this edition, is filled with high-flown Enlightenment rhetoric of heroism, philosophy, and glory.

75. Jean François Marmontel, *Belisarius* (New York: Garland, 1975) (facsimile of the London, 1767, edition), 237.

76. In 1796 the new Emperor Paul I put an end to Radishchev's Siberian exile and in 1801 Alexander I awarded him full rehabilitation, appointing him to his own commission to draft a new law code. He committed suicide on September 11, 1802, after being given a "friendly rebuke" by another member of the commission for his overly radical ideas (Nemirovsky, "Aleksandr Nikolaevich Radishchev," 331).

77. There have been some who have denied that "Spasskaia polest'" was addressed to Catherine, e.g., G. A. Gukovskii, who found the idea "absurd" because it would have been "stupid, insane" for Radishchev to have directed "such bold things" to her; the message, he held, was intended instead for progressive Russian intellectuals (G. A. Gukovskii, *Ocherki po istorii russkoi literatury XVIII veka; dvorianskaia fronda v literature 1750-kh–1760-kh godov* [Moscow: Akademiia nauk, 1936], 150).

78. See Douglas Smith, "Banned Books: Alexander Radishchev's *Journey from St. Petersburg to Moscow* and the Limits of Freedom of Speech in the Reign of Catherine the Great," unpublished paper presented at Columbia University, Seminar on the History of Free Speech in the Eighteenth Century, November 2007. My thanks to Dr. Smith for sharing his work and allowing me to cite it. The argument in this section is indebted to his analysis, which examines Radishchev's selective quoting of his sources, especially Herder.

79. In the latter case, he argues that pornographic literature, which he notes does not yet exist in Russia, is not itself at fault but is due to the existence of prostitution (note that the older, original meaning of "pornography" is "writing about prostitutes"). On the problem of defining pornography as regards Russia, see *Eros i pornografiia v russkoi kul'ture / Eros and Pornography in Russian Culture*, ed. M. Levitt and A. Toporkov (Moscow: Ladomir, 1999).

80. Radishchev, *Puteshestvie/Journey*, 167–68; 80–81.

81. Ibid., 168; 81.

82. Ibid., 171–72; 83.

83. Ibid., 168–69; 81. The "idol with feet of clay" from Daniel 2 became a powerful image for the struggle with authority in nineteenth-century literary discourse, often played out in terms of erecting and demolishing monuments. See Marcus Levitt, *Russian Literary Politics and the Pushkin Celebration of 1880*, Studies of the Harriman Institute (Ithaca: Cornell University Press, 1989), esp. 25–26.

84. Radishchev, *Puteshestvie/Journey*, 169; 81.

85. Ibid., 169; 82.

86. Ibid., 171; 83.

87. Jürgen Habermas's definition of the "public sphere" is as "a category of bourgeois society" in which commercial interests play a leading role in securing political rights (see *The Structural Transformation of the Public Sphere: An Inquiry into a Category of Bourgeois Society* [Cambridge: MIT Press, 1989]). Scholars continue to debate its applicability to Russia. See, for example, David I. Burrow, "Russian Social Networks, Public Opinion, and Intelligentsia Identity in the First Half of the Nineteenth Century" (PhD diss., University of Wisconsin Madison, 2005).

88. Smith, "Banned Books."

89. In Pushkin's witty "Journey from Moscow to St. Petersburg," which reversed Radishchev's trajectory, he suggested that the attack on Lomonosov was the author's main purpose. Pushkin also criticized Radishchev's desire to get rid of censorship. Ironically, Pushkin was unable to publish this work, which only came out posthumously—and with censors' cuts—in 1841. (A. S. Pushkin, *Polnoe sobranie sochinenii*, ed. B. V. Tomashevskii, 10 vols. [Moscow: Nauka, 1977–1979], 7:184–209 and 492–93; see esp. 190–91.)

90. Radishchev, *Puteshestvie/Journey*, 237; 123.

91. Ibid., 224; 115.

92. The use of developmental metaphors (e.g., infancy, childishness, immaturity, premature senility) to describe problems of Russian culture is very widespread in Russian sources as well as in European "Russica," e.g, Rousseau's description of Russians' premature aging from *The Social Contract*, cited in chapters 4 and 9.

93. Radishchev, *Puteshestvie/Journey*, 165; 79.

94. In one of his more sober moments, Radishchev acknowledged that "there has never been and perhaps will never be until the end of the world the example of a tsar who voluntarily yields any of his power while sitting on the throne" (A. N. Radishchev, "Pis'mo k drugu, zhitel'shvuiushchemu v Tobol'ske, po dolgu zvaniia svoego" [1790], *Polnoe sobranie sochinenii* [Moscow: Akademiia nauk, 1938], 1:151).

95. While the *Journey* did pass the censor (who later admitted that he had not read the book but merely judged it by the title!), Radishchev confessed that he had illegally added some material after it had been approved.

96. Indeed, Radishchev has often been described as the first Russian "intelligent" and progenitor of the Russian intelligentsia, e.g., Allen McConnell, "The Origin of the Russian Intelligentsia," *Slavic and East European Journal* 8, no. 1 (Spring, 1964): 1–16.

97. Furthermore, despite—or perhaps because of?—the fact that "No book in Russia or Europe was so long and so thoroughly suppressed" as *The Journey*, Radishchev's image as a martyr was kept alive in the later tradition (Ia. L. Barskov,

*Materialy k izucheniiu 'Puteshestviia iz Peterburga v Moskvu' A. N. Radishcheva* [Moscow: Academia, 1935], 334).

## Conclusion

1. Alexander Griboedov, *Woe from Wit* (1824), act 3, scene 32, lines 394–95.

2. Bruno Latour, "Visualization and Cognition: Thinking with Eyes and Hands," *Knowledge and Society* 6 (1986), 10.

3. William Shakespeare, *The Tempest*, act 4, scene 1.

4. Martin Malia, *Russia Under Western Eyes: From the Bronze Horseman to the Lenin Mausoleum* (Cambridge: The Belknap Press of Harvard University Press, 1999), 74 and 75.

5. See, for example, Priscilla R. Roosevelt, *Life on the Russian Country Estate: A Social and Cultural History* (New Haven: Yale University Press, 1995).

6. The number of actual books and issues is of course many times larger. See I. P. Kondakov, ed., *Svodnyi katalog russkoi knigi grazhdanskoi pechati XVIII veka, 1725–1800*, 5 vols. (Moscow: Izd. Gos. biblioteki SSSR imeni V. I. Lenina, 1962–1967). See also Gary Marker, *Publishing, Printing, and the Origins of Intellectual Life in Russia, 1700–1800* (Princeton: Princeton University Press, 1985).

7. On the language, see Victor Zhivov, *Language and Culture in Eighteenth-Century Russia* (Boston: Academic Studies Press, 2009). On the cultural significance of the Academy dictionary, see Myriam Lefloch, "'Master of many tongues': The Russian Academy Dictionary (1789–1794) as a Socio-historical Document" (PhD diss., University of Southern California, 2002).

8. Gary Marker, "Nikolai Ivanovich Novikov," in *Early Modern Russian Writers, Late Seventeeth and Eighteenth Centuries*, Dictionary of Literary Biography 150, ed. Marcus C. Levitt (Detroit: Gale Research, 1995), 252.

9. See Pierre Bourdieu, *The Rules of Art: Genesis and Structure of the Literary Field*, trans. Susan Emanuel (Stanford: Stanford University Press, 1996), part 1. Bourdieu's analysis considers the status of art primarily in the later nineteenth-century capitalist context, but his terms seem especially useful in describing the non-commercial, pre-capitalist literary market in which symbolic values (glory, approbation) were paramount.

10. This story has been told many times. See especially Nicholas V. Riasanovsky, *A Parting of Ways: Government and the Educated Public in Russia, 1801–1855* (Oxford: Clarendon Press, 1976). Not all historians share a bleak view of the Nicholaevan period, which was also a time of reform, especially in the sphere of education. We may speak here again of the profound gap between "objective" historical conditions and the cultural-psychological perception on the part of Russian intellectuals.

11. The question of Russia's failure to develop a cohesive sense of nationhood or national identity remains an issue, and has arisen with new urgency after the collapse of the USSR. See Geoffrey A. Hosking, "Can Russia Become a Nation-State?" *Nations and Nationalism* 4, no. 4 (1998): 449–62; this is also a central issue in his *Russia: People and Empire, 1552–1917* (Cambridge: Harvard University Press, 1997).

12. Lauren G. Leighton, ed., *Russian Romantic Criticism: An Anthology* (New York: Greenwood Press, 1987), 58–59. This edition is valuable not only for the primary texts but for Leighton's extensive commentaries.

13. See P. N. Berkov, "Problemy izucheniia russkogo klassitsizma," in *Russkaia literatura XVIII veka: Epokha klassitsizma*, ed. P. N. Berkov and I. Z. Serman (Moscow: Nauka, 1964), 5–29; and his *Vvedenie v izuchenie istorii russkoi literatury XVIII veka*, part 1, *Ocherk literaturnoi istoriografii XVIII veka* (Leningrad: Leningradskii universitet, 1964).

14. E.g., Leighton, *Russian Romantic Criticism*, 13, 69, 165, 174; see also the notes to these essays, for which Leighton traces some of the sources for these opinions.

15. Marshall Poe, *A People Born to Slavery: Russia in Early Modern European Ethnography, 1476–1748*, Studies of the Harriman Institute (Ithaca: Cornell University Press, 2000). See also his *Foreign Descriptions of Muscovy: An Analytic Bibliography of Primary and Secondary Sources* (Columbus, OH: Slavica, 1995).

16. Jean-Jacques Rousseau, *The Social Contract and Discourses*, trans. and intro. G. D. H. Cole, rev. ed. by J. H. Brumfitt and John C. Hall (New York: Dutton, 1979), 198–99.

17. See Marcus Levitt, *Early Modern Russian Writers: Texts and Contexts* (Boston: Academic Studies Press, 2009), chaps. 17 and 19.

18. On Russia's changing image in Western Europe (for the worse) during the early nineteenth century, see Riasanovsky, *A Parting of Ways*.

19. Ilaria Marchesi, "In Memory of Simonides: Poetry and Mnemotechnics chez Nasidienus," *Transactions of the American Philological Association* 135, no. 2 (2005): 400–401n18; see also Ellen Oliensis, *Horace and the Rhetoric of Authority* (New York: Cambridge University Press, 1998), 73. The line "O imitatores, servum pecus" refers to imitators of Horace himself, but also became associated with his criticism of trying to emulate the Greeks (e.g., in Ode 2 of Book 4, Satire 10, Book 1, lines 34–35), as did the character Servilius Balatro ("servile buffoon") who appears in Satire 8 of Book 2. Cf. the discussion of imitation and originality in Epistle 3, Book 2 (the "Ars Poetica"), line 133f.

20. See the texts in Izora Scott, *Controversies Over the Imitation of Cicero in the Renaissance: With Translations of Letters between Pietro Bembo and Gianfrancesco Pico, On Imitation; and a Translation of Desiderius Erasmus, the Ciceronian (Ciceronianus)* (1910; repr., Davis, CA: Hermagoras Press, 1991).

21. Laura Willett, *Poetry & Language in 16th-Century France: Du Bellay, Ronsard, Sébillet*, Renaissance and Reformation Texts in Translation 11 (Toronto: Centre for Reformation and Renaissance Studies, 2004), 17; cf. on the problem of imitation Terence Cave, *The Cornucopian Text: Problems of Writing in the French Renaissance* (Oxford: Clarendon Press, 1979), 35–77. Similar debates occurred in Italy, England, and Germany.

22. "An Elegy on the Death of Dr. Donne, Dean of St. Paul's," in *The Poems and Masque of Thomas Carew . . .* , ed. Joseph Woodfall Ebsworth (London: Reeves and Turner, 1893), 111.

23. Abbé (Jean-Baptiste) Dubos, *Réflexions critiques sur la poésie et sur la peinture* (Paris, P.-J. Mariette, 1733), 431. Note the typically classicist slant on originality and the genius of the language achieved by following (correct) models.

24. See Zhivov, *Language and Culture*, 335, 359, 362. On Boileau in Russia, see A. M. Peskov, *Bualo v russkoi literature XVIII–pervoi treti XIX veka* (Moscow: Moskovskii universitet, 1989). The need for a scapegoat (a negative image to be overcome) was also at work in the harsh criticism of Trediakovskii that Irina Reyfman has described in mythological terms in *Vasilii Trediakovsky: The Fool of the "New" Russian Literature* (Stanford: Stanford University Press, 1990).

25. Wolfgang Gesemann, "Herder's Russia," *Journal of the History of Ideas* 26, no. 3 (July–September 1965): 424–34.

26. Leighton, *Russian Romantic Criticism*, 112.

27. Ibid., 113.

28. Ibid., 113.

29. *The Philosophical Works of Peter Chaadaev*, ed. Raymond T. McNally and Richard Tempest (Dordrecht: Kluwer Academic Publishers, 1991), 25.

30. Ibid., 21.

31. Boris Groys, "Poisk russkoi natsional'noi identichnosti," *Voprosy filosofii* 9 (1992): 52–60; citation refers to the translation from Boris Groys, "Russia and the West: The Quest for Russian National Identity," *Studies in Soviet Thought* 43 (1992): 186–87. See also Boris Grois [Groys], "Rossiia kak podsoznanie Zapada," in *Iskusstvo utopii: Gesamtkunstwerk Stalin; stat'i* (Moscow: Khudozhestvennyi zhurnal, 2003), 150–67.

32. Groys, "Russia and the West," 188.

33. Ibid.

34. Ibid., 197.

35. Ibid., 189.

36. Ibid., 191.

37. Ibid.

38. Groys writes: "If, by the way, the Enlightenment in the West started as a liberation movement against the ancien régime, the Russian absolutist government legitimized its power over the uneducated Russian masses by its superior access to enlightened knowledge. In Russia, the Enlightenment was from the beginning associated with repression and mechanisms of power, and the liberation with the 'Otherness' of Russian life" (Groys, "Russia and the West," 190).

39. Among the attempts at a "synthesis" of "Russia and the West" was the canonization of Pushkin, who Apollon Grigor'ev had argued represented a resolution to Chaadaev's crisis that had led to the Slavophile-Westernizer controversy. On Pushkin in Russian culture, see the anthology V. M. Markovich and G. E. Potapova, eds., *A .S. Pushkin, pro et contra: lichnost' i tvorchestvo Aleksandra Pushkina v otsenke russkikh myslitelei i issledovatelei* (St. Petersburg: Russkii Khristianskii gumanitarnyi institut, 2000), and on the special circumstances surrounding his elevation to "national poet," see Marcus Levitt, *Russian Literary Politics and the Pushkin Celebration of 1880*, Studies of the Harriman Institute (Ithaca: Cornell University Press, 1989).

40. "Façade" has been a favorite metaphor for Russian historians of Catherine and later rulers. Thus A. A. Kizevetter characterized Catherine's reforms: "The façade of the state edifice was renovated and repainted but everything that this façade concealed was only weakly affected by the changes." He also cited V. O. Kliuchevskii's visual metaphor of the empress's reign as a "picture painted in broad and coarse strokes and hence aimed at a distant viewer" (i.e., to deceive), so that historians must examine it more closely (Kizevetter, *Istoricheskie ocherki* [1912; The Hague: Europe Printing, 1967], 238). Cf. also A. B. Kamenskii, ed., *Ekaterina II: fasad i zadvorki imperii* (Moscow: Fond Sergeia Dubova, 2007); D. Richard Little, *Liberalization in the USSR: Façade or Reality?* (Lexington, MA: D. C. Heath, 1968); Paul R. Gregory, *Behind the Façade of Stalin's Command Economy: Evidence from the Soviet State and Party Archives* (Stanford: Hoover Institution Press, Stanford University, 2001).

41. Albert Lortholary, *Le Mirage russe en France au XVIIIᵉ siecle* (Paris: Boivin, 1951). For discussions of Lortholary's thesis, see Sergej Karp and Larry Wolff, eds., *Le*

*mirage russe au XVIIIe siècle* (Ferney-Voltaire: Centre international d'étude du XVIIIe siècle, 2001).

42. Zhivov, *Language and Culture*, 351.

43. Gaspard Monge, "A Memoir Relative to the Optical Phenomenon known by the name of Mirage," in *Memoirs Relative to Egypt: Written in That Country During the Campaigns of General Bonaparte in the Years 1798 and 1799 by the Learned and Scientific Men Who Accompanied the French Expedition* (London: R. Phillips, 1800), 77. The original French version, of which this is a translation, appeared in multiple editions and languages.

44. Alexander von Humboldt, *Personal Narrative of Travels to the Equinoctial Regions of the New Continent during the Years 1799–1804*, trans. Helen Maria Williams (London, 1818), 4:328–29, cited from The Humboldt Digital Library: <http://www.avhumboldt.net>, which tallies 22 occurrences of the word "mirage."

45. From definition 2 in the Oxford English Dictionary (<http://oed.com>), which includes historical examples of its use. The German term is *Luftspiegelung*; Italian *miraggio*. For French usage of "mirage," see the ARTFL database (Project for American and French Research on the Treasury of the French Language), <http://www.lib.uchicago.edu/efts/ARTFL/databases/TLF07/>. Early nineteenth-century French authors who used the term include Pierre Beranger, George Sand, Alfred de Musset, Lamartine, Quinet, Paul Leroux, Balzac, Hugo, and Eugenie Sue.

In Russian the term (*mirazh*) is included in the *Slovar' tserkovno-slavianskogo i russkogo iazyka, sostavlennyi Vtorym otdeleniem Imp. Akademii nauk*, 4 vols. (St. Petersburg: Akademiia Nauk, 1847), 2:308, defined as *"marevo"* (meaning "haze" or "mirage"; cf. "marevo," 2:87). In V. I. Dal''s *Tolkovyi slovar' zhivogo velikorusskogo iazyka*, 4 vols. (St. Petersburg, 1863–1866), *mirazh* is listed under *mara*; in the second edition of 1881 it has its own entry. The word does not seem to have been used by Gogol', who often describes illusions and deceptions, but is common in Dostoevsky's early works of the late 1840s (e.g., *White Nights*).

46. See: V. N. Toporov, *Peterburgskii tekst russkoi literatury: Izbrannye trudy* (St. Petersburg: Iskusstvo-SPB, 2003); and V. M. Markovich, ed., *Mezhdunarodnaia nauchnaia konferentsiia Peterburgskaia tema i "Peterburgskii tekst" v russkoi literature XVIII–XX vekov . . . : Sbornik statei* (St. Petersburg: S.-Peterburgskii universitet, 2002).

47. Hans J. Rindisbacher, *The Smell of Books: A Cultural-Historical Study of Olfactory Perception in Literature* (Ann Arbor: University of Michigan Press, 1992); Maksim Klymentiev, "The Dark Side of 'The Nose': The Paradigms of Olfactory Perception in Gogol's 'The Nose,'" *Canadian Slavonic Papers* 51, nos. 2–3 (June–September 2009): 217–36.

48. G. Z. Kaganov, *Images of Space: St. Petersburg in the Visual and Verbal Arts*, trans. Sidney Monas (Stanford: Stanford University Press, 1997), 104.

49. What Vladimir Odoevskii wrote in *Russkie nochi* (1844) clearly refers to Russia: "At the beginning of the nineteenth century, Schelling was what Christopher Columbus was in the fifteenth: he disclosed to man an unknown part of his world, about which only some legendary tales had existed—man's *own soul*!" (*Russian Nights*, trans. Olga Koshansky-Olienikov and Ralph E. Matlaw [Evanston: Northwestern University Press, 1997], 43).

50. A sampling of titles: Max Hoschiller, *Le mirage du soviétisme* (Paris: Payot, 1921); Jacob H. Rubin and Victor Rubin, *Moscow Mirage* (London: G. Bles, 1935); Roy Linney Deal, *Lenin's Master Plan: Miracle or Mirage? Miracle for Fourteen*

*Million Communist Party Members, Mirage for a Hundred Forty Million Adult Non-Party Russians* (New York: Vantage Press, 1972); Richard Ericson, *The Mirage of Soviet Economic Reform* (Washington, DC: National Council for Soviet and East European Research, 1991); Jonathan Steele, *Eternal Russia: Yeltsin, Gorbachev, and the Mirage of Democracy* (Cambridge: Harvard University Press, 1994); Valerii Cherkashin and Nataliia Cherkashina, *Mirazhi imperii* (Moscow: Muzei Metropoliten Cherkashina, 2002); Al'fred Mirek, *Krasnyi mirazh: Krakh moguchei Rossii* (Ekaterinburg: Informatsionno-izdatel'skii otdel Ekaterinburgskoi eparkhii, 2004); Al'fred Mirek, *Krasnyi mirazh: palachi Velikoi Rossii* (Mozhaisk: Mozhaisk-Terra, 2006); K. E. Tsiolkovskii, *Mirazhi budushchego obshchestvennogo ustroistva* (Moscow: Samoobrazovanie, 2006); Aleksandr Bushkov, *Mirazh velikoi imperii* (Moskva: Olma-Media Grupp, 2007). There are also a great number of Russian novels, poems, stories, and memoirs with "mirage" or "mirages" in the title.

51. E.g., in Lortholary, *Le mirage russe.*

52. See especially Sheila Fitzpatrick, *Stalin's Peasants: Resistance and Survival in the Russian Village After Collectivization* (New York: Oxford University Press, 1994), 16–18 and 262–85, which describes "Potemkinism" as a "Stalinist discourse." The phrase "Potemkin Village" also continues to be applied to later periods and issues, e.g., Mikhail Tsypkin, *Gorbachev's "Glasnost": Another Potemkin Village?* (Washington, DC: Heritage Foundation, 1987); Christian Kalkar, *The Potemkin Village: The Quasi-Market Economy and Russia's Transitional Crisis* (Copenhagen: København, 2002); Jessica Allina-Pisano, *The Post-Soviet Potemkin Village: Politics and Property Rights in the Black Earth* (Cambridge: Cambridge University Press, 2008).

53. John T. Alexander, *Catherine the Great: Life and Legend* (New York: Oxford University Press, 1989), 256. See also G. V. Ibneeva, "Puteshestvie Ekateriny II po Volge v 1767 g.," in *Evropeiskaia identichnost' i rossiiskaia mental'nost'*, ed. T. V. Artem'eva and M. I. Mikeshin (St. Petersburg: Sankt-Peterburgskii tsentr istorii idei, 2001): 85–103, and her *Puteshestviia Ekateriny II: opyt "osvoeniia" imperskogo prostranstva* (Kazan': Kazanskii gos. universitet, 2006).

54. George Soloveytchick, *Potemkin: Soldier, Statesman, Lover and Consort of Catherine of Russia* (New York: W. W. Norton, 1947), 3 and 182. See also A. M. Panchenko, "'Potemkinskie derevni' kak kul'turnyi mif," in *Iz istorii russkoĭ kul'tury*, vol. 4, *XVIII–nachalo XIX veka*, ed. A. D. Koshelev (Moscow: Iazyki russkoi kul'tury, 1996), 685–700. Helbig's book was published anonymously, first in 1797–1799 in the journal *Minerva*, and then translated into French (1808), English (1811 and 1813), and other languages. The English title is: *Memoirs of Prince Potemkin . . . Comprehending Numerous Original Anecdotes of the Russian Court; Translated from the German*, 2nd ed. (London: Colburn, 1813); on Potemkin's deceptions, see 116–20.

55. Soloveychik, *Potemkin*, 182.

56. Panchenko, "'Potemkinskie derevni,'" 688.

57. On Soviet manipulations of the media, see for example: Leon Trotsky, *The Stalin School of Falsification* (New York: Pathfinder Press, 2004); Anatoliy Golitsyn, *New Lies for Old: The Communist Strategy of Deception and Disinformation* (New York: Dodd, Mead, 1984); David King, *The Commissar Vanishes: The Falsification of Photographs and Art in Stalin's Russia* (New York: H. Holt, 1999); and Fitzpatrick, *Stalin's Peasants*, chap. 10 ("Potemkinism"). See also Solzhenitsyn's "The Buddha's Smile," chap. 59 of *The First Circle*, as well as his remarkable expose of Stalinist propaganda in *The Gulag Archipelago*.

58. Abram Tertz [Andrei Siniavskii], *The Trial Begins and On Socialist Realism* (New York: Vintage, 1960), 95. (Derzhavin is a prime example for Tertz.) On a more rarefied level, Socialist Realism as a doctrine may be said to embody an idealist, albeit covert utopian subtext similar to classicism, insofar as it presents "the truthful, historically concrete representation of reality in its [ideal!] revolutionary development" (*Pervyi Vsesoiuznyi s"ezd sovetskikh pisatelei 1934: Stenograficheskii otchet* [1934; repr., Moscow: Sovetskii pisatel', 1990], 712). See the example I give apropos of the view of nature in E. S. Urusova's *Polion* (1774) in Levitt, *Early Modern Russian Writers*, 372.

59. Boris Groys, *The Total Art of Stalinism: Avant-Garde, Aesthetic Dictatorship, and Beyond*, trans. Charles Rougle (Princeton: Princeton University Press, 1992). For a dissenting view, see, for example, Laura Engelstein, "Paradigms, Pathologies, and Other Clues to Russian Spiritual Culture: Some Post-Soviet Thoughts," *Slavic Review* 57, no. 4 (Winter 1998): 873–74.

60. Vladislav Todorov, *Red Square, Black Square: Organon for Revolutionary Imagination* (Albany, NY: State University of New York Press, 1995), 163.

61. Ibid., 160, 161, and 164.

62. J. Arch Getty, "State Violence in the Stalinist Period," in *Times of Trouble: Violence in Russian Literature and Culture*, ed. Marcus C. Levitt and Tatyana Novikov (Madison: University of Wisconsin Press, 2007), 186–87.

63. Groys, "Russia and the West," 197.

# INDEX

Abbé Dubos (Jean-Baptiste Dubos), 258–59
Abgar, king of Edessa, 324n56
Abraham (Biblical patriarch), 239
absolutism, absolute power, 122, 194, 223, 246, 280n32, 336n38
Academy of Fine Arts, 139, 254
Academy of Sciences, 126, 127, 254, 297n71
Adams, John, 140–41
Addison, Joseph, *Cato (The Dying Cato)*, 118, 293n33, 330n33
adulthood, adult consciousness, 234, 251, 257
Aesop, Aesopian mode, 128, 292n22
aesthetics, as sensual perception, 75
Aetna, 59
Africa, 198
Ageeva, O. G., 277nn7–9
aggression (in odes), 36, 50–60
Akhmat, Khan, 202
Alekseev, Vladimir N., 299n12, 305n74
Alekseeva, N. Iu., 274n36, 281n1, 282n22, 283n29
Aleksei ("Man of God"), Saint, 208
Aleksei Mikhailovich, 82
Alexander I, 261, 332n76
Alexander Nevskii, Saint, 82
Alexander Nevsky Monastery Seminary, 217
Algarroti, Francesco, on the "window on Europe," 22, 279n28
All-Seeing Eye, 35, 56, 110, 240–41, 331n55
Amazons, 267
America, 254, 265
Amvrosii (Zertis-Kamensky), Archbishop, 195, 196, 197, 198, 216–20, 322n25, 326n76, 326n79

Anacreon, Anacreontic poetry, 290n15, 315n87
Anchikov, Dmitrii, 302n33
Andreyev, Nikolay, 322n18, 326n82
Angiolini, Gasparo, 320n7
Anna (Empress), 28, 49–50, 52, 55, 56–57
Anna Leopol'dovna (regent), 57, 283n34
anticpated self, 25, 39, 51, 61, 64–65, 79, 251, 268
Apollo, 28, 35, 37, 49
Apollos (Baibakov), Iermonakh, *Evgeont, or the Contemplation of Visible Divine Matters in Nature (Evgeont, ili sozertsanie v nature bozhikh vidiymkh del)*, 312n60
apophatic theology. *See* Eastern Orthodoxy
approbation, approbativeness, 128, 130, 132–33, 137–39, 142, 225, 248, 257, 267, 298n2, 334n9. *See also* Lovejoy, Arthur
Aquinas, Thomas, Saint, 167, 310n33
argument from design, 158, 165–83 passim
Aristarkh, Hegumen: "Chronicle of the Bogoliubov Monastery from 1158 to 1770" ("Letopis' Bogoliubova Monastyria c 1158 po 1770 god"), 203–4, 206, 207, 221, 322n32
Aristotle, Aristotelianism, 18, 22, 24, 98, 160, 163, 166–70 passim, 273n16, 256, 289n48, 310n33, 311n36, 312n53
    wonder: *see* Aristotelian versus sublime wonder
art, the arts, 6, 7, 12, 14, 22, 26, 30–31, 81, 83, 84, 100, 113–14, 124, 137, 142, 150, 161, 197, 218, 220, 225, 254, 260, 275n40, 299n9, 309n26, 310n30, 325n67